Protecting the Brand
Volume I

Protecting the Brand
Volume I

Counterfeiting and Grey Markets

Peter Hlavnicka and Anthony M. Keats

Leader in applied, concise business books

Protecting the Brand, Volume I: Counterfeiting and Grey Markets

Copyright © Business Expert Press, LLC, 2022.

Cover design by Charlene Kronstedt

Interior design by Exeter Premedia Services Private Ltd., Chennai, India

First published in 2021 by
Business Expert Press, LLC
222 East 46th Street, New York, NY 10017
www.businessexpertpress.com

ISBN-13: 978-1-63742-151-2 (paperback)
ISBN-13: 978-1-63742-152-9 (e-book)

Business Expert Press Business Law and Corporate Risk
Management Collection

Collection ISSN: 2333-6722 (print)
Collection ISSN: 2333-6730 (electronic)

First edition: 2021

10 9 8 7 6 5 4 3 2 1

Description

***Protecting the Brand, Volume I: Counterfeiting and Grey Markets
is a handbook for law practitioners as well as business executives.***
It is a unique perspective of best practices in addressing issues around
counterfeiting and grey markets—from a legal as well as a business point
of view. The authors explore the threats posed by counterfeiting and grey
markets to a variety of industries and illuminate what problems these
may cause. Before setting forth the range of legal strategies for remedying
incidents of counterfeiting and grey markets, the authors outline
preventive measures businesses can take to combat the threats, and
showcase some of the emerging technologies that can serve as enablers of
Brand Protection's 3 IPR's (3 I's = Intelligence, Investigation, Innovation;
3 P's = Protection, Perseverance, Perpetuation; 3 R's = Remedy, Recovery,
Rehabilitation).

Keywords

intellectual property; trademarks; brand protection; counterfeiting; grey
market; parallel import; best practices; case law; prevention; commercial
secrets; cybersquatting; remedies; procedures; enforcement; law practitioners; business leadership; Lanham Act; global brand; technology;
online; websites; copyrights

Contents

Testimonials

"The authors, clearly experts in their field, have provided a very useful guide for counsel, business executives and IP professionals faced with counterfeiting and grey-market challenges. I highly recommend this book."—**Brian Monks, VP & Chief Security Officer at UL LLC**

"If you are involved in Brand Protection, you need this book!
It is packed with practical information, including ways to leverage new technologies to support your work. And, it cuts through the clutter around a myriad of services that may assist you, helping you find the right fit for your organization."—**Jacqueline A. Leimer, former Vice President and Associate General Counsel, Global Intellectual Property, Kraft Foods; former President, International Trademark Association**

"Tony Keats is one of the top anticounterfeiting lawyers in the world. This book is an invaluable resource on anticounterfeiting and one of the only such guides available to practitioners as well as academics."—**Barbara Kolsun, Director of the FAME Program and Professor of Practice, Cardozo Law School**

"A must-read book for any leader or start-up entrepreneur navigating in an age of IP warfare. Peter Hlavnicka is a global expert in IP, Brand Protection and Anti-Counterfeiting and clearly explains his craft from concept to theory to practical execution for any novice or advanced reader."—**Leesa Soulodre, General Partner R3i Ventures Pte. Ltd. and Singapore Management University Adjunct Faculty Member**

Preface

There are many good books discussing brand protection, the grey market, and counterfeit goods. These books generally take a narrow approach to individual subjects and are typically intended for strictly legal or strictly business practitioners.

This book provides a unique combination of legal and business best practices related to intellectual property protection and in more detail with respect to two specific threats—grey marketing and counterfeiting. The primary emphasis is on providing advice to U.S. companies about how to navigate the complex domestic as well as global intellectual property terrain. This book also serves as a single source of reference for both law practitioners (educating them about the nonlegal remedies available to their clients) and any person or team tasked with intellectual property rights enforcement and compliance. Specifically, this book focuses on leveraging trademark enforcement while also commenting on copyright and patent enforcement, establishing a framework for successful brand protection in the future.

Acknowledgments

We would like to express our gratitude, thanks, and acknowledge all those who contributed to the writing of this book.

Important contributions were made by a number of our colleagues who assisted in all the ways, large and small, necessary to produce a work of this scope. We would like to thank the attorneys, legal assistants, and researchers at Keats Gatien LLP, including Konrad Gatien, Matthew Graham, Darrell Orme Mann, and Brett Voets. We would also like to acknowledge all of our colleagues at Fitbit (acquired by Google), Dolby Laboratories, UL LLC., R3i Ventures, and many others who share the same passion for protecting intellectual property rights, as well as to Ryan Drimalla for his contribution to the topic of Cybersquatting and to our peers at the International Anticounterfeiting Coalition, International Trademark Association, and Union des Fabricants.

Many thanks to Business Expert Press for the opportunity to publish this book and to our editors, Scott Isenberg and John Wood, for their guidance.

Our deepest gratitude goes to our families, friends, and clients for their continued support in all our endeavors.

CHAPTER 1

Introduction of Intellectual Property

Intellectual Property (IP) is an integral and invaluable building block of many industries. It is an intangible key asset and a primary method for securing business' return-on-investment (ROI) from innovation and reputation. Besides protecting a company's innovations from competitors (including counterfeiters), IP assets are also an important source of cash-flow through licensing arrangements or sales. For start-ups, in particular, IP is also a significant asset by which to attract investors.

In addition, IP is a significant ingredient in a company's ethos or "brand." Brands are the means by which goods and service providers develop relationships with consumers. Brands are often described as having strong or weak equity. This equity has been defined by such factors as consumer loyalty, consumer awareness, association with quality, societal relevance, consumer engagement, and leadership among peers. Counterfeiting and grey markets dilute the equity of the brand by interfering and often destroying the factors noted above.

What Are IP Assets?

Patents, trademarks, copyrights, designs, trade secrets, including confidential and proprietary (business critical) information such as product specifications, new product release plans, marketing, pricing, client and customer confidential information.

The survival of many companies depends on robust and diverse measures to protect it. Companies proactively investing in securing their IP from the beginning will benefit enormously in the long run.

What Are the Most Common Threats to IP and How to Address Them?

1. **IP and confidential information divulgence**. The costs of recovering lost or leaked IP is much higher than the cost usually needed to protect it. Protection is often achieved by implementing cybersecurity or other technological measures or some simpler protection methods such as:

   (a) Restricting critical information to the leadership team only;

   (b) Safely storing confidential documents in a highly secure online repository providing detailed tracking of the site's access and use; and

   (c) Assigning permissions-based roles for data access.

   Protection may also be enhanced by requiring extremely rigorous nondisclosure and confidentiality agreements to deter employees and third parties from divulging sensitive data.

2. **Patents** are an important part of the overall IP protection strategy. However, they should not be the sole protective method employed (The number of patents being invalidated is increasing with estimates suggesting that over half of U.S. patents granted are struck down[1]).

3. **Free-riding**. Whether IP is leaked via employee, obtained illicitly or incidentally, any opportunistic free rider can exploit it for their own gain.

Business growth and preventing potential revenue losses in the future from leaked, stolen, or copied IP depends on defining a clear and early IP strategy, which should include:

- Identifying IP assets to protect;
- Registering the core IP as soon as possible;
- Prioritize IP protection needs by locale (operating markets);
- Adapt to the local IP protection competencies and practices;

---

[1] www.economist.com/leaders/2004/11/11/monopolies-of-the-mind (accessed April 19, 2021).

- Deploy technology to "fight technology" (cybersecurity, analytics);
- Identify and catalog your trade secrets;
- Online protection; and
- Budget accordingly.

Good IP protection strategy should include the 4 components as shown in Figure 1.1.

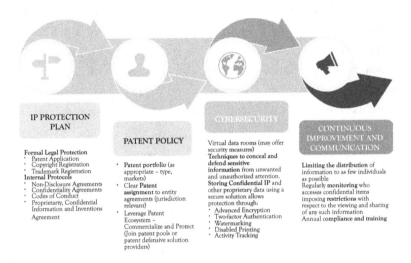

IP PROTECTION PLAN

Formal Legal Protection
· Patent Application
· Copyright Registration
· Trademark Registration
Internal Protocols
· Non-Disclosure Agreements
· Confidentiality Agreements
· Codes of Conduct
· Proprietary, Confidential Information and Inventions Agreement

PATENT POLICY

· Patent portfolio (as appropriate - type, markets)
· Clear **Patent assignment** to entity agreements (jurisdiction relevant)
· Leverage Patent Ecosystem - Commercialize and Protect (Join patent pools or patent defensive solution providers)

CYBERSECURITY

Virtual data rooms (may offer security measures)
Techniques to conceal and defend sensitive information from unwanted and unauthorized attention.
Storing Confidential IP and other proprietary data using a secure solution allows protection through:
· Advanced Encryption
· Two-factor Authentication
· Watermarking
· Disabled Printing
· Activity Tracking

CONTINUOUS IMPROVEMENT AND COMMUNICATION

Limiting the **distribution** of information to as few individuals as possible
Regularly **monitoring** who accesses confidential items imposing **restrictions** with respect to the viewing and sharing of any such information
Annual **compliance and training**

Figure 1.1 IP protection strategy components

Where and When to Protect IP?

Owing to a "first-to-file system" in most countries, local formal legal protection/registrations are usually necessary to protect IP. Therefore, ideally the IP protection strategy has to be in place at least 12 months (in order to obtain necessary registrations) before entering local markets. Late-obtained IP registrations will limit the options of preventive measures and risk and associated costs will be higher.

It is absolutely essential to understand that IP rights are territorial. And as result IP rights are often enforceable only upon valid domestic registration. (Exceptions include the European Union where multicountry patent filing is available, or Myanmar where IP filing is not yet available.)

While much of this book provides detailed guidance on protection of a brand, your business and legal strategies must include the family of IP assets.

Trademarks

Trademarks consist of recognizable words, phrases, designs, sounds, colors, even scents with the specific and primary purpose to identify the origin of goods or services, allowing the consumers to distinguish one producer from another. Trademark registrations are obtained for a specific class of goods and/or services offered by its owner. Trademarks are registered in individual countries or regional territories (e.g. European Union). Trademarks are the vehicle by which consumers can visually and audibly identify a brand and the source of the product or service bearing the trademark. We also refer to these brand names and logos as "source identifiers."

Copyrights

Copyrights provide legal protection to authors or creators of original literary, musical, artistic, choreographic, and architectural works. The body of law also includes "moral rights," which are personal and cannot be waived, licensed, or transferred and "economic rights," which give you the exclusive right to exploit the work for economic gain, including the right to reproduce, distribute, perform, and use other means to exploit the work. Copyright protects only the tangible expression of an idea (a "work"), not the idea itself.

Design

A design generally refers to a product or article's external appearance as a result of features added in an industrial process such as shape, configuration, pattern, or ornament.

Patent

A patent provides an exclusive right granted over an invention and prevents an invention from being used, commercially exploited, distributed, or sold without the consent of the patent owner. Patent structures may vary but there are three common types of patents:

- Utility (use of a machine, process, system and method)
  - USPTO—Nonprovisional, Provisional
  - WIPO—Utility Model, Utility Patent
- Design (how it looks)
- Plant (organic plants)

What is the difference between utility patent and utility model patent and nonprovisional and provisional patent? Why does it matter? Some of the basic differences are shown in Table 1.1.

Trade Secret

Generally, in order for an information to be classified as a trade secret it must:

- Be nonpublic (it must not be known by the general public or by competitors);
- Have actual/potential commercial value (it must give the owner a competitive advantage or be capable of generating economic benefit; and
- Have its confidentiality reasonably protected by the owner.

When a trade secret is leaked or disclosed, it is often very difficult to recover. Damage is already done even if a legal action is successful. Documenting trade secret protection measures is important for supporting legal claims including trade secret policy, confidentiality, nondisclosure, and noncompete agreements.

In some cases, a choice between protection by patent registration or maintenance of a trade secret is required. Patents require public disclosure. Information such as supplier and customer lists, research, financial data are not patentable and are best protected as trade secrets. Novel inventions are generally protected as patents in most cases. When it comes to chemical formulations, pharmaceuticals, and manufacturing processes, it is not as obvious as these can be protected as patents or trade secrets.

Table 1.1 WIPO and USPTO utility patent differences

	WIPO		USPTO	
	Utility Model (small/petty patent)	**Utility Patent**	**Non-Provisional Utility Patent**	**Provisional Utility Patent**
Faster (6–12 months)	Slower (3–5 years)	Fast	Slower (22–30 months) prioritized examination utility patents can cut the time down to 6–12 months
Not Examined (Novelty assessment) Formality Exam	Examined	Not Reviewed	Reviewed and Granted
Harder to Invalidate - Lower Inventiveness, Substantiative Feature and Progress	Easier to Invalidate (High Inventiveness, Notable Substantial Progress)	Establishes the Filling Date	
Minor inventions not requiring full patentability	Methods and Products	Within 12 months of disclosing the invention to the public regardless of whether it was published, demonstrated, sold or otherwise	Within 12 months of disclosing the invention to the public regardless of whether it was published, demonstrated, sold or otherwise
Lower Costs	Higher Costs	"patent pending" designation	
Shorter Life Span (i.e. 10 years)	Longer Life Span (i.e., 20 years)	12 months	20 years
Suitable for Structural Products and Easy to Replicate (short life cycle and shorter commercial availability)	Suitable for Long Development Products commercially available for long time (pharma, biotech)	Early Competitive Advantage	
12 Month window to apply for Utility Patent		12 Months to apply for Non-Provisional	
ONLY VALID IN COUNTRY FILED	MULTI-COUNTRY (EU)	Should the patent be ultimately granted, it will enjoy a patent term starting from the date of filing the Provisional Patent Application	Should the patent be granted, it will enjoy a patent term starting from the date of filing the Provisional Patent Application (if applied)

Table 1.2 Patent vs. Trade Secret Basic Comparison

	Patents	**Trade Secret**
Example	Edison's light Bulb	Coca-Cola secret formula
Scope	New, Useful innovations	Any secret Information of economic value to the business
Duration	< 20 years	Indefinitely (until disclosed/leaked)
Rights	Patent holder's right to prevent others from making, selling, using the invention	Owners rights against misappropriation
Discovery	Published and easily discoverable, though direct copying and re-engineering is prohibited during the patent lifetime	Not published (unless leaked/disclosed) and does not prevent anyone from independent discovery or reverse engineering of the information or technology
Enforcement	Enforced against infringements (with or without patent knowledge)	Difficult to enforce especially when the secret if leaked/disclosed in public
Territory	Territorial (only protected in countries where granted)	No restrictions
Cost	Cost to draft, file, maintain	Cost of maintaining the secret (overhead)
Management	Fees to renew and update	Active to maintain the secrecy

A basic comparison between trade secret and patent is shown in Table 1.2.

In some situations, however, a single patent or trade secret may not be sufficient to protect the technology or product portfolio, and as a result a mix of patents and trade secrets may be needed to protect various aspects of the invention(s).

All of these legally supported IP assets play a role in the growth and protection of a BRAND. Now, let's talk about the brand in a bit more detail ...

CHAPTER 2

What Is a Brand and Why Protect It?

Brand Protection—What Is It and Why Is It So Important?

"The American Marketing Association (AMA) defines a brand as a 'name, term, sign, symbol or design, or a combination of them intended to identify the goods and services of one seller or group of sellers and to differentiate them from those of other sellers.'"

"Your brand resides within the hearts and minds of customers, clients, and prospects. It is the sum total of their experiences and perceptions, some of which you can influence, and some that you cannot."[1]

A successful brand "infuses emotion into the product"[2] or service, which includes a bundle of special characteristics that consumers "expect to receive ... on every occasion."[3] Purchasers of Coca-Cola expect the

---

[1] L. Lake. 2021. "What Is Branding and How Important Is It to Your Marketing Strategy?" *About.com Marketing*. Available at http://marketing.about.com/cs/brandmktg/a/whatisbranding.htm (accessed February 22, 2021).

[2] Goldstein. August 2000. "Protecting Against the Gray Market in the New Economy." *22 Loyola U.L.A. Int. & Comp. L. Rev.* 507, pp. 530–531.

[3] 15 U.S.C. § 1127 (the Lanham Act defines a "trademark" as "any word, name of symbol, or device" used "to identify and distinguish" a "unique product" and/or the "source of the goods").

First Circuit: Societe Des Produits Nestle, S.A. v. Casa Helvetia, 982 F.2d 633, 636 (1st Cir. 1992) ("Every product is composed of a bundle of special characteristics. The consumer who purchases what he believes is the same product expects to receive those special characteristics on every occasion").

Federal Circuit: Bourdeau Brothers, Inc. v. International Trade Commission, 444 F.3d 1317, 1320 (Fed. Cir. 2006) ("the public associates a trademark with goods having certain characteristics").

bottle or the can to have a certain look and the product to taste a certain way. Similarly, when purchasing an appliance, a consumer choosing Whirlpool has certain expectations of the product based on the reputation of the brand. A well-established brand thus reduces consumer search costs, because purchasers know what they are getting based on prior experience or knowledge, or both, of the brand from the owner's marketing efforts.[4]

In exchange for "lower search costs and the assurance of consistent quality," consumers will pay a premium or choose a specific brand rather than a competing product.[5] To get consumers to develop a preference for a particular brand, however, requires companies to spend millions, and sometimes billions, of dollars on advertising, quality control, and service distribution networks.[6] "The larger the price premium that a firm can charge, the greater the value of the brand name."[7]

Companies' investments in their brands represent a significant part of their overall value. Approximately 67 percent of Kellogg's market capitalization stems from the value of its brands.[8] Brand valuation reports track the valuations of the top global brands annually.[9] These valuations and the substantial investments that owners make in their brands require

---

[4] S.M. Auvil. Spring 1995. "Gray Market Goods Produced by Foreign Affiliates of the U.S. Trademark Owner: Should the Lanham Act Provide a Remedy?" *Akron L. Rev.* 28, p. 437.

[5] *Id.* See also, "The Value of a Brand Name." Available at http://pages.stern.nyu.edu/~adamodar/New_Home_Page/lectures/brand.html (accessed February 22, 2021). ("One of the benefits of having a well-known and respected brand name is that firms can charge higher prices for the same products, leading to higher profit margins and hence to higher price-sales ratios and firm value").

[6] Dan-Foam A/S v. Brand Named Beds, LLC, 500 F. Supp.2d 296, 299 (S.D.N.Y. 2007) (the trademark owner "spent in excess of $250 million in connection with [its] advertisement and promotion of products bearing the TEMPUR-PEDIC® trademark in order to establish this trademark in the minds of consumers as a source of high-quality bedding products").

[7] "The Value of a Brand Name." Available at http://pages.stern.nyu.edu/~adamodar/New_Home_Page/lectures/brand.html (accessed February 22, 2021).

[8] *Id.*

[9] See https://brandirectory.com/rankings/global/ (accessed February 22, 2021).

companies to spend significant resources to stop counterfeiters and grey marketers.[10] Counterfeiters and grey marketers[11] seek to profit from companies' investments in their brands without incurring the associated costs. The result is dilution of and damage to the value of the brand.[12]

Besides the well-known fact that counterfeits may cause serious harm to consumers relying on the quality and safety associated with known brands, counterfeit and grey market goods also inflict enormous damage on brand owners.[13] Damages include lost goodwill and sales, and societal costs. When consumers who purchase grey or counterfeit goods fail to receive the expected bundle of special characteristics from the branded

---

[10] CMO Council. 2009. "Marketer's Fight Against Fakes." 12, p. 23. Available at www.cmocouncil.org/thought-leadership/reports/protection-from-brand-infection (accessed February 22, 2021). The complete report is available for purchase.

[11] For further discussion, see § 1.03 and § 1.04 *infra*.

Compare, Bordeau Brothers, Inc. v. International Trade Commission, 444 F.3d 1317, 1322 (Fed. Cir. 2006) (federal courts define a "grey market good" as "a foreign-manufactured good, bearing a valid United States trademark that is imported without the consent of the United States trademark holder"), *with* Yamaha Corp. v. United States, 961 F.2d 245, 248 (D.C. Cir. 1992) (counterfeit goods have the trademark or similar mark but are not authorized to use the mark).

In contrast, the Alliance for Gray Market and Counterfeit Abatement (AGMA), a trade association of major technology companies, including CISCO, IBM, and Microsoft, defines grey market goods as "the unauthorized sale of new, branded products diverted from authorized distribution channels or imported into a country for sale without the consent or knowledge of the manufacturer" and counterfeits as goods that are an "unauthorized copy of the product" and/or goods that "are marked with a 'counterfeit mark' made to appear like the genuine trademark of the good." https://agmaglobal.org/ (accessed February 22, 2021). Grey market goods do not violate the federal law if they are identical to their U.S. cousins, but are illegal if they are materially different from the domestic goods. See American Circuit Breakers Corp. v. Oregon Breakers, Inc., 406 F.3d 577, 585–586 (9th Cir. 2005) (grey market circuit breaker that was identical to U.S. circuit breaker in all material aspects other than color, which was not material, was a genuine good and did not violate the Lanham Act).

[12] S.M. Auvil. Spring 1995. "Gray Market Goods Produced by Foreign Affiliates of the U.S. Trademark Owner: Should the Lanham Act Provide a Remedy?" *Akron L. Rev.* 29, pp. 437–448.

[13] See Ch. 2 *infra*.

product, they blame the brand, resulting in loss of goodwill and brand erosion.[14] Likewise, because "exclusivity" is an important part of the brand for many high-end consumer products, grey market sales outside of authorized, high-end retailers diminish the brand in consumers' minds.[15] Counterfeit and grey market goods also harm the brand owner's distributor relations,[16] sales force morale, and customer service efforts.[17] In addition, grey markets cause companies to incorrectly forecast and track sales, profits, and customer demand.[18] Moreover, counterfeit and grey goods can result in the manufacturer/brand owner paying millions of dollars in unauthorized warranty service on these goods that do not come with warranty and receive service without the consumer paying the associated warranty costs.[19] The consequences of warranty and service abuse, besides loss of revenue and increased grey market activity, include decline in

---

[14] Bourdeau Brothers, Inc. v. International Trade Commission, 444 F.3d 1317, 1320 (Fed. Cir. 2006).

[15] E. Dugan. 2001. "United States of America, Home of the Cheap and the Gray: Comparison of Recent Court Decisions Affecting the U.S. and European Gray Markets." *Wash. Int'l L. Rev.* 33, p. 397.

[16] United States v. Braunstein, 281 F.3d 982, 985 (9th Cir. 2002) (grey goods sold "at much cheaper price[s] ... hurt the sales of [authorized] distributors ... and cause[] ... resentment ...."). See also, S.T. Cavusgil. Winter 1988. "How Multinationals Can Counter Gray Market Imports." *Columbia J. World Bus.* pp. 75–85.

[17] M.B. Myers. 1999. "Incidents of Gray Market Activity Among U.S. Importers: Occurrences, Characteristics, and Consequences." *Journal of International Business Studies* 30, p. 105.

[18] P. Lansing, and J. Garriella. Fall 1993. "Clarifying Gray Market Gray Areas." *Am. Bus. L. J.* 31, pp. 313–316.

[19] For further discussion, see Ch. 2 *infra*. See also: Hyundai Construction Equipment U.S.A., Inc. v. Chris Johnson Equipment, Inc., 2008 WL 4210785 at **1–2 (N.D. Ill. September 10, 2008) (grey market construction equipment sold in the United States without warranty and at step discount compared to machines sold by authorized distributor that all came with standard, comprehensive warranty); "AGMA, Price WaterhouseCoopers Expose Multi-Billion Dollar Threat to Technology Industry: Warranty and Service Abuse; New Study Defines Problem and Presents Methods to Effectively Manage Growing Threat." October 20, 2009. Available at https://agmaglobal.org/uploads/whitePapers/Final%20PwC%20 Service%20Blues%20(10-26-09).pdf (accessed February 22, 2021).

customer confidence and company reputation, preventable service costs, and increased research and development costs.[20]

Where there are only "subtle" differences, if any, in the physical appearance of the genuine and fake goods, consumers often do not know that they are purchasing nongenuine goods.[21] Consumers may also wind up with unsafe products,[22] not meant for use or consumption.[23] Extreme examples of this are counterfeits that pose great risk to consumers, including death.[24] For example, in 2007 in Hamilton, Ontario, Canada, a registered pharmacist knowingly dispensed counterfeit doses of Norvasc® to heart patients—pills filled only with talc. The local coroner investigated five patient deaths—all caused by heart attack or stroke—that may have been brought about by the substitution of the counterfeit drug.[25]

Brand value is not constant and is highly susceptible to fluctuation. For instance, the consequence of dangerous products to the value of a brand could be enormous. Toyota was once the world's most profitable

---

[20] M. Hlavnicka. March 28, 2010. "Waging War Against Service Abuse." *ITChannelPlanet.*

[21] Societe Des Produits Nestle, S.A. v. Casa Helvetia, 982 F.2d 633, 641 (1st Cir. 1992) ("subtle differences" that are "not blatant enough to make it obvious to the average consumer that the origin of the product differs from his or her expectations[]" are likely to confuse and/or disappoint the average consumer). See also, "Counterfeit Software Can Cost Businesses in Many Ways." Available at https://news.microsoft.com/2009/03/23/counterfeit-software-can-cost-businesses-in-many-ways/#:~:text=Beyond%20raising%20obvious%20concerns%20about,prolonged%20downtime%20and%20identity%20theft. (accessed February 22, 2021) states that 37 percent of its midsized customers unknowingly purchased counterfeit products.

[22] S. Hargreaves. September 27, 2012. "Counterfeit Goods Becoming More Dangerous." *CNN Money.* Available at http://money.cnn.com/2012/09/27/news/economy/counterfeit-goods/index.html (accessed February 22, 2021).

[23] For further discussion, see Ch. 2 *infra.*

[24] UHC. 2002. *Prevention of Counterfeit Drugs: Working Together for Safer Drugs.* Counterfeit Action Sheet.

[25] "Hamilton Pharmacist Charged with Handing Out Counterfeit Drugs." *CBC News*; September 10, 2005 11:30 AM ET. Available at www.cbc.ca/news/canada/hamilton-pharmacist-charged-with-handing-out-counterfeit-drugs-1.568647 (accessed February 22, 2021).

carmaker; extensive automobile recalls because of pedal problems, however, resulted in at least a $2 billion plus loss in 2010 through 2011 from the cost of repairs and anticipated sales loss from the negative publicity and a significant loss in market share.[26]

"An inability to compete with grey markets can wreak havoc on firms and industries."[27] The grey market has had a significant impact on the cell phone industry.[28] Nokia lowered its historical mobile phone market share, based on grey market mobile phone vendors in emerging markets (particularly in Asia).[29] Grey market mobile phone sales in China were estimated to be 145 million units in 2009, which constituted approximately 19 percent of all mobile phones sold in emerging markets (China, India, and Brazil) that year.[30] In Malaysia, grey market cell phones account for as many as 70 percent of total cell phone sales.[31]

In addition to loss of good will, companies suffer substantial lost sales from counterfeit and grey market products. The value of counterfeit goods

---

[26] C.R. Kim. 2010. "Scenarios: Impact of Recall Saga on Toyota's 2010/11 Earnings." Available at www.reuters.com/article/idUKTRE61M25P20100223 (accessed February 22, 2021).

[27] K.D. Antia, M. Bergen, and S. Dutta. October 15, 2004. "Competing with Gray Markets." *MIT Sloan Management Rev.* Available at http://sloanreview.mit.edu/article/competing-with-gray-markets/ (accessed February 22, 2021).

[28] O. Kharif. November 11, 2009. "Booming Gray Market Threatens Cell-Phone Industry." *Bloomberg Businessweek.* Available at www.bloomberg.com/news/articles/2009-11-11/booming-gray-market-threatens-cell-phone-industry (accessed February 22, 2021).

[29] "Unlicensed Mobile Phone Vendors Could Hurt Nokia's Emerging Markets Business." March 23, 2010. Available at www.trefis.com/articles/13452/unlicensed-mobile-phone-vendors-could-hurt-nokias-emerging-markets-business/2010-03-23 (accessed February 22, 2021).

[30] Wang. 2009. "Cell Phone Industry's Dirty Little Secret: China's 145 Million Unit Gray Market." *iSuppli.com.* Available at www.isuppli.com/china-electronics-supply-chain/news/pages/cell-phone-industrys-dirty-little-secret-chinas-145-million-unit-gray-market.aspx (accessed February 22, 2021); "Talk is Cheap; Counterfeit Handsets Proliferate in China." *The Economist,* November 21, 2009.

[31] K.D. Antia, M.E. Bergen, and S. Dutta. 2004. "Competing with Gray Markets." *MIT Sloan Management Review* 46, no. 1, p. 63.

has increased more than 10,000 percent in the past two decades.[32] According to the Global Brand Counterfeiting Report 2018, the volume of international trade in counterfeit goods reached $1.2 trillion in 2017[33] and was expected to rise to $1.82 trillion in 2020.[34] From 2000 through 2019, seizures of infringing goods by U.S. Customs and Border Protection (CBP) and U.S. Immigration and Customs Enforcement (ICE) increased from 3,244 to 27,599, while the domestic Manufacturer Suggested Retail Price (MSRP) value of seized merchandise increased from $0.045 billion to $1.4 billion.[35] Counterfeit goods represent an estimated 5 percent to 7 percent of annual world trade.[36] The losses to specific industries are significant:

1. Apparel and footwear pirated goods—$12 billion;
2. Counterfeit music recordings—$4.6 billion;
3. Counterfeit motion pictures—$3.5 billion;
4. Counterfeit drugs and pharmaceuticals—$32 billion;
5. Software piracy—$12 billion; and
6. Counterfeit automobile parts—$16 billion.[37]

Another study found that as much as 43 percent of all software installed worldwide in 2013 was pirated, with a commercial value of $62.7

---

[32] See www.ibanet.org/Article/NewDetail.aspx?ArticleUid=02FB8505-E9C4-4F23-B271-C5BF64A8326D (accessed February 22, 2021).

[33] "Counterfeit Luxury Goods." Available at www.worldtrademarkreview.com/anti-counterfeiting/counterfeit-luxury-goods#:~:text=According%20to%20the%20Global%20Brand,expected%20to%20keep%20on%20growing (accessed February 22, 2021).

[34] "Global Brand Counterfeiting Report 2018–2020." ResearchAndMarkets.com. May 15, 2018. Available at www.researchandmarkets.com/research/hzjb9c/global_brand?w=4 (accessed February 22, 2021).

[35] "Fiscal Year 2019 Seizure Statistics." September 2020. Available at www.cbp.gov/document/report/fy-2019-ipr-seizure-statistics (accessed February 22, 2021).

[36] "Counterfeiting Intelligence Bureau." Available at www.iccwbo.org/products-and-services/fighting-commercial-crime/counterfeiting-intelligence-bureau/ (accessed July 16, 2016).

[37] "Counterfeiting and Piracy Endangers Global Economic Recovery, say Global Congress Leaders." December 2009. Available at www.wipo.int/pressroom/en/articles/2009/article_0054.html (accessed February 22, 2021).

billion.[38] It is estimated that the IT industry loses $5 billion in profits a year to counterfeiting.[39]

Like counterfeit goods, grey market products cause brand owners to lose sales. In the *Kirtsaeng v. John Wiley & Sons* (Parallel Importation Case), "[] the [court] … notes that libraries have pointed to the 200 million foreign made works in its collections"; that used bookstores have purchased books made abroad and that it cannot always easily predict whether the copy was made domestically or abroad; that "automobiles, microwaves, calculators, mobile phones, tablets, and personal computers" contain copyrightable software that would prevent the resale of even a car without permission of the rightsholder of every copyrighted piece; that retailers noted that over $2.3 trillion worth of foreign produced goods were imported in the United States in 2011 that may contain copyrighted packaging and $220 billion of which constituted traditional copyrighted work; and that museums' ability to display foreign made art would be impeded. Thus, "reliance upon the 'first sale' doctrine is deeply embedded in the practices of those, such as book sellers, libraries, museums, and retailers, who have long relied upon its protection," notes the significant impacts, pointed out by several amici, that would occur if the Court were to reject international exhaustion principles.[40] This, however, is not a new problem. "In 1984 IBM was the victim of grey marketers who accounted for as much as 10 percent of the company's personal computer sales."[41]

With the increase in counterfeit and grey goods, it is not surprising that the number of seizures by the U.S. Department of Homeland

---

[38] "The Compliance Gap, BSA Global Software Survey." June 2014. Available at http://globalstudy.bsa.org/2013/ (accessed February 22, 2021).

[39] KPMG. 2021. "Managing the Risks of Counterfeiting in the Information Technology Industry." Available at https://agmaglobal.org/uploads/whitePapers/KPMG-AGMA_ManagingRiskWhitePaper_V5.pdf (accessed February 22, 2021).

[40] "Analysis of Kirtsaeng v. John Wiley & Sons (Parallel Importation Case); Supreme Court Applies International Exhaustion." 2013. Available at www.keionline.org/22159 (accessed February 22, 2021).

[41] Reference for Business. "Grey Market." Available at www.referenceforbusiness.com/encyclopedia/Gov-Inc/Gray-Market.html (accessed February 22, 2021).

Security in 2019 was valued at more than $1.4 billion,[42] with watches and jewelry, wearing apparel and accessories, footwear and consumer electronics as the top commodities.[43]

In addition to the loss of sales and goodwill, counterfeit and grey goods impose social costs.[44] For example, substandard counterfeit and grey goods have infiltrated IT systems for controlling air traffic, financial and telecommunication networks, and military weaponry and intelligence gathering.[45] Terrorist groups, including those involved in the 1993 New York City World Trade Center bombing, have been linked to counterfeit goods.[46] Counterfeit goods cause the loss of jobs in the United States; in 2006, the U.S. Federal Trade Commission estimated that the auto industry could hire 250,000 additional American workers if the sale of counterfeit parts were eliminated.[47] Because counterfeiters do not

---

[42] Fiscal Year 2019 Seizure Statistics. September 2020. Available at www.cbp.gov/document/report/fy-2019-ipr-seizure-statistics (accessed February 22, 2021).

[43] *Id.*

[44] FBI. May 06, 2010. "Departments of Justice and Homeland Security Announce 30 Convictions, More Than $143 Million in Seizures from Initiative Targeting Traffickers in Counterfeit Network Hardware." Available at www.fbi.gov/news/pressrel/press-releases/departments-of-justice-and-homeland-security-announce-30-convictions-more-than-143-million-in-seizures-from-initiative-targeting-traffickers-in-counterfeit-network-hardware (accessed February 22, 2021). (According to the then-Assistant Secretary of Immigration and Customs Enforcement, "counterfeit and substandard hardware … could affect the health and safety of others in a hospital setting or the security of our troops on the battlefield … They pose a triple threat to our nation by stealing from our economy, threatening U.S. jobs and potentially putting the safety of our citizens at risk").

[45] J. Hlavnicka. March 01, 2010. "Debunking Common Myths About Counterfeits: Falsely Branded Goods Waste Money, Cheat Buyers and Vendors, Cause Network Failures, and Risk Security. Preinfected Components, Anyone?" *Bloomberg Businessweek*. Available at www.bloomberg.com/bw/stories/2010-03-01/debunking-common-myths-about-counterfeitsbusinessweek-business-news-stock-market-and-financial-advice (accessed February 22, 2021).

[46] S. Horwitz. June 08, 2004. "Cigarette Smuggling Linked to Terrorism." *Washington Post*, at A1. Available at www.washingtonpost.com/wp-dyn/articles/A23384-2004Jun7.html (accessed February 22, 2021).

[47] Global Intellectual Property Center. 2021. "Counterfeiting and Piracy: Threats to Consumers and Jobs." Available at www.ncsl.org/Portals/1/documents/standcomm/sclaborecon/CaliaFactSheet.pdf (accessed February 22, 2021).

generally pay taxes, counterfeit goods cost the U.S. government billions of dollars in tax revenue.[48]

The need for improved brand protection was highlighted in a report by the Chief Marketing Officer (CMO) Council, whose members spend billions of dollars annually on aggregated marketing.[49] According to the CMO Council:

- "Marketers are decidedly behind the curve on the issue of brand protection and are struggling to understand, monitor and measure the impact of brand corruption and product knockoffs on consumer trust and confidence." But they've awakened to the threat trademark trespassing has on bottom line business, and the real cost of lost brand value, integrity, and consumer trust. Spending on brand protection solutions, tools, programs, and campaigns [is] poised to trend upward as marketers launch greater protective measures to fend off attack and preserve the value of their brand.
- "Marketers have a great deal of work ahead in grasping the extent of the problem, measuring its impact and instituting measures to fend off attack and clean up widespread brand pollution."[50]

This book will assist internal and external counsel and corporate brand protection and marketing divisions in protecting their clients' brands by:

---

[48] WTR. May 18, 2017. "Estimating the Global Economic and Social Impacts of Counterfeiting and Piracy." Available at www.worldtrademarkreview.com/anti-counterfeiting/estimating-global-economic-and-social-impacts-counterfeiting-and-piracy (accessed February 22, 2021).

[49] CMO Council. 2009. "Protection From Brand Infection. Marketer's Fight Against Fakes, Frauds and Infringements." Available at www.cmocouncil.org/thought-leadership/reports/protection-from-brand-infection (accessed February 22, 2021).

[50] Id.

1. Analyzing how grey market and counterfeit goods and cybersquatting can destroy the substantial investments their clients have in their brands;

2. Providing proactive internal procedures that can help protect brands from grey and counterfeit goods; and

3. Reviewing applicable legal recourses available to fight grey market and counterfeit goods and cybersquatting.

The Effects of the Internet and Globalization on Brand Protection

The Internet and the globalization of commerce have served as catalysts for the expansion of counterfeit trade. The Internet allowed grey and counterfeit sellers to emerge from sometimes nefarious and out-of-the-way places and consumers can now purchase grey and counterfeit goods from the safety and comfort of their own homes.[51] Moreover, the Internet decreases access barriers and search costs for consumers looking to purchase grey and counterfeit goods and makes finding grey and counterfeit sellers as easy as a few keyboard strokes.[52] Current technology has made the time and cost of setting up online stores negligible. Infringers can set up copycat websites and begin to offer fake products within an hour. The Internet also reduces the cost of advertising and selling for grey and counterfeit sellers and auction sites often hide sellers' identities.[53] Likewise, globalization has caused the segmenting of global markets into smaller "customer groups [that] are charged a range of prices," which creates arbitrage opportunities for grey marketers.[54]

eBay "revolutionized the online sale of goods … "[55] and, along with other auction sites such as Alibaba, AliExpress, and MercadoLibre,

---

[51] A.G. Galstian. 1999. "Protecting Against the Gray Market in the New Economy." *Loy. L.A. Int. & Comp. L. Rev.* 22, pp. 507–512.

[52] *Id.*; S. Ghosh. Fall 1999. "Gray Markets in Cyberspace." *J. Intell. Prop. L.*7, no. 3, p. 6.

[53] For further discussion, see Ch. 12 *infra*.

[54] K.D. Antia, M. Bergen, and S. Dutta. Fall 2004. "Competing with Gray Markets." *MIT Sloan Management Rev*iew 46, pp. 1–4.

[55] Tiffany v. e-Bay, Inc., 600 F.3d 93, 96 (2d Cir. 2010).

presents probably the best demonstration of the convergence of the Internet and globalization of the grey and counterfeit markets. Since its inception, eBay's auction and listing services have facilitated "hundreds of millions" in sales among persons who, absent being connected by eBay, would not have been able to transact business.[56] Despite the fact that eBay has taken steps to limit sales of counterfeit software and has implemented stringent antifraud measures,[57] however, an estimated 90 percent of the software sold on eBay is counterfeit or improperly copied.[58]

Over the years, most major brand owners have developed strategies to combat online threats. There are several avenues that owners can take to protect their brands from abuse at the hands of counterfeit and grey sellers on the Internet, including protection of the brand's domain names,[59] such as registering the key top-level domains (TLDs) defensively to prevent their use for malicious purposes. Of course, defensive registrations of TLDs can be costly, so some brand owners choose more reactive approach and choose to act only when there is an actual threat. Domain names are managed by the Internet Corporation for Assigned Names and Numbers (ICANN), which adopted a set of rules known as the Uniform Dispute Resolution Policy (UDRP) to assist legitimate brand owners in protecting their brands. The UDRP provides for relatively inexpensive, rapid and fair methods, whereby persons with trademark rights may force the transfer of ownership of a registered domain name from a person without any legitimate interest in the name who registered and uses the domain name in bad faith.[60] Likewise, the Anti-Cybersquatting Consumer Protection Act (ACPA) provides slower, more expensive but more expansive relief

---

[56] *Id.*

[57] Ebay Against Counterfeits. Available at http://pages.ebay.com/againstcounterfeits/ (accessed February 22, 2021).

[58] Gross Computerworld. March 20, 2008. "Software Group Files Lawsuits Against eBay Sellers." Available at http://www.computerworld.com/s/article/9070362/ (accessed February 22, 2021).

[59] See Ch. 4 *infra.*

[60] ICANN. 2021. "Uniform Domain-Name Dispute-Resolution Policy." Available at www.icann.org/en/udrp/udrp.htm (accessed February 22, 2021).

to the brand owner.[61] So, it is important for brand owners to register the domain names associated with their trademarks.

Comparatively recent changes to the domain name world and the launch of 600 publicly available generic TLDs may force brand owners to rethink and devise new strategies. For example, luxury brands need a strategy to deal with TLDs such as .cheap, .discount, and .bargain in order to protect their brand value and reputation, web traffic, and revenues.[62]

The Grey Market

What Is the Grey Market?

Grey market goods, also referred to as "parallel imports," include genuine products with legitimate, authorized trademarks that are intended for sale and use in specific markets/countries, but which are imported and sold in other markets/countries without the consent of the trademark owner or authorized distributor of like domestic goods.[63] Grey markets typically arise under three ownership arrangements. Using an example of a U.S.-based trademark owner: (1) a domestic company, not related to the foreign trademark owner, purchases the exclusive rights to the foreign trademark in the United States; (2) a domestic company, which is controlled by the foreign trademark owner (i.e., a subsidiary), has the exclusive right to the foreign trademark in the United States; or (3) a domestic owner of a U.S. trademark gives a foreign company the right to use the mark outside of the United States.[64] In each of these three situations, goods with legitimate trademarks that are similar to the domestic goods, but not intended to be sold or used in the United States, wind up being

---

[61] 15 U.S.C. § 1125(d).

[62] Fuller, Trademarks & Brands Online. July 25, 2014. "Brand Protection: Turning Buyers into Allies." Available at http://www.trademarksandbrandson-line.com/article/brand-protection-turning-buyers-into-allies (accessed February 22, 2021).

[63] Bourdeau Brothers. Fed. Cir. 2006. "Inc. v. International Trade Commission." 444 F.3d, pp. 1317–1322.

[64] K-Mart Corp. v. Cartier, Inc., 486 U.S. 281, 286–287, 108 S.Ct. 1811, 100 L.Ed.2d 313 (1988).

sold in the United States in direct competition with the U.S. trademark holder.[65]

Unlike counterfeit (black market) goods, which contain unauthorized copies of marks,[66] grey goods may be lawfully sold in the United States if they are "identical" to their U.S. cousins.[67] Grey goods that are "materially different," however, violate federal and state law, and cannot be sold in the United States.

Trademark owners facing grey markets define grey goods more broadly to include "the unauthorized sale of new, branded products diverted from authorized distribution channels (or even more broadly, authorized supply chain,)" without the permission or knowledge of the trademark owner.[68] This broad definition appears to have been adopted by several federal courts in dealing with products obtained through improper means and without the knowledge or consent of the trademark holder and sold outside the holder's authorized distribution network. In a Sixth Circuit case, the defendant, an authorized Hewlett-Packard (HP) distributor, submitted false "volume discount" requests to acquire thousands of laptop computers from HP, for sale to a large customer in the United States.[69] The defendant, however, actually sold the laptops to an unauthorized retailer in Saudi Arabia. The district court referred to these improperly obtained

---

[65] *Id.*

[66] In contrast to grey goods, which have legitimate, authorized marks, counterfeit goods contain unauthorized marks. See Yamaha Corp. v. United States, 961 F.2d 245, 248 (D.C. Cir. 1992). See also, The Alliance for Grey Market and Counterfeit Abatement (AGMA). Available at https://agmaglobal.org/AGMA-University/Glossary-of-terms (accessed February 22, 2021) (counterfeit goods are "unauthorized copies of merchandise "and/or goods that "are marked with a 'counterfeit mark' made to appear like the genuine trademark of the good").

[67] American Circuit Breakers Corp. v. Oregon Breakers, Inc., 406 F.3d 577, 585–586 (9th Cir. 2005) (grey market circuit breaker that was identical to U.S. circuit breaker in all material aspects other than color, which was not material, was a "genuine" good and did not violate the Lanham Act).

[68] AGMA. https://agmaglobal.org/AGMA-University/Glossary-of-terms (accessed February 22, 2021).

[69] Hewlett-Packard Co. v. Capital City Micro, Inc., 2006 WL 149034 at **1–2 (W.D. Tenn. January 19, 2006).

but otherwise identical goods as "grey market" products. Similarly, the Ninth Circuit referred to Apple computers purchased from Apple's Latin American authorized distributor, but sold in the United States at cut-rate prices by the defendant, as grey market Apple computers.[70]

Secondary Markets Distinguished From Grey Market

The grey market should not be confused with the legitimate aftermarket, more often called the secondary market. Secondary markets originate from sale of used, genuine goods purchased by customers for their own use but sold to other users, brokers, dealers, or back to the manufacturers. Many manufacturers offer their own branded remarketing programs with warranty protection and support. As long as the unauthorized secondary market seller is not affiliated with the trademark holder and is selling used or refurbished goods, trading in the secondary market does not violate trademark laws.[71]

Trading in secondhand (used, refurbished) equipment is a legitimate business as long as: (1) the potential buyers are aware that they are buying secondhand goods and receive the goods they expected and paid for; (2) the sellers do not blend the secondary market goods with counterfeits or grey market goods; and (3) the goods do not infringe IP rights (by having been refurbished or refitted with counterfeit parts, or being sold in packaging that infringes trademarks or copyrights or other IP).

In some industries, independent secondary market vendors (ISMVs) create more robust and faster supply chains by joining associations made up specifically of the ISMV trading of secondary market products, creating marketplaces and auctions where the associated members can trade-in their goods. Many ISMVs have stringent rules regarding business ethics and strictly prohibit counterfeiting and grey market activity. These rules and restrictions are required to sustain ISMV members' relationships with manufacturers, since the members may have direct agreements

---

[70] United States v. Braunstein, 281 F.3d 982 (9th Cir. 2002).

[71] See: Dow Jones & Co. v. International Securities Exchange, *Inc.* 2006. 451 F.3d 295, 308 (2d Cir. 2006); Polymer Technology Corp. v. Mimran, 975 F.2d 58, 61–62 (2d Cir. 1992).

with manufacturers regarding resale of obsolete, discontinued, or excess inventories.

For years, these genuine goods that remained unsold (excess and aged inventory) or were returned were sold off directly by the manufacturers into the open market, or disposed of, with little attention or control, and in many cases fueled grey markets or even black markets (when these goods were then intentionally misrepresented or modified by the sellers to deceive consumers into buying these "new" products). Manufacturers now realize that they can significantly increase their revenue from sales of these goods by focusing more attention on infusing greater control over when, how, and to whom they sell these goods.[72]

Ignore Grey Goods at Your Own Peril

"The grey market is a fact of life."[73] Trademark owners who choose to ignore the grey market are exposed to potential serious damage to the goodwill they have built up with customers, to consumer confidence, and to their distribution and service networks. Because grey marketers usually sell their wares for less than the genuine domestic goods, they are able to undercut and take sales from the trademark owner's authorized distribution network.[74] Estimates of grey goods vary by industry, but the value is substantial. Although somewhat outdated, the 2003 KPMG report estimated the grey market for IT products alone to be $40 billion a year

---

[72] D. Dobromir. February 10, 2020. "Obsolete Inventory and How to Deal With It." Available at https://magnimetrics.com/obsolete-inventory-and-how-to-deal-with-it/ (accessed February 22, 2021).

[73] United States v. Braunstein, N. 8 supra, 281 F.3d at 991.

[74] *Second Circuit:* Osawa & Co. v. B&H Photo, 589 F. Supp. 1163, pp. 1166–1167 (S.D.N.Y. 1984).

Seventh Circuit: Hyundai Construction Equipment U.S.A., Inc. v. Chris Johnson Equipment, Inc., No. 06 C 3238, 2008 WL 4210785 at *1 (N.D. Ill. September 10, 2008).

Ninth Circuit: United States v. Braunstein, 281 F.3d 982, 984–985 (9th Cir. 2002).

in sales, with $5 billion in lost profits annually for U.S. manufacturers.[75] Likewise, IT warranty abuse, which includes improper service on and returns of grey goods that do not come with warranty and should not be returned, costs manufactures more than $10 billion annually.[76]

The grey market poses a very serious threat to a trademark holder's investment in its brands. Grey marketers seek to profit from investments in trademarks without incurring any of the associated costs, while also diluting and damaging the value of the brand.[77] When consumers of grey goods fail to receive the expected bundle of characteristics from the product, they blame the trademark owner, resulting in decline in customer loyalty and erosion of the owner's goodwill.[78] This threat is particularly acute in the IT industry and for high-priced goods (i.e., vehicles and high-end watches) because grey goods are not subject to the trademark holder's internal distribution channel or strict quality control measures, and so there is a likelihood that the goods will be mishandled or damaged before reaching the customer.[79]

---

[75] AGMA. https://agmaglobal.org/uploads/whitePapers/KPMG-AGMA_ManagingRiskWhitePaper_V5.pdf (accessed February 22, 2021).

[76] "AGMA, PricewaterhouseCoopers Expose Multi-Billion Dollar Threat to Technology Industry: Warranty and Service Abuse, New Study Defines Problem and Presents Methods to Effectively Manage Growing Threat." October 20, 2009. *Marketwire*. Available at https://agmaglobal.org/uploads/whitePapers/Final%20PwC%20Service%20Blues%20(10-26-09).pdf (accessed February 22, 2021).

[77] See S.M. Auvil. Spring 1995. "Gray Market Goods Produced by Foreign Affiliates of the U.S. Trademark Owner: Should the Lanham Act Provide a Remedy?" *Akron L. Rev.* 29, pp. 437–438.

[78] "Bourdeau Brothers, Inc. v". *International Trade Commission*, 444 F.3d 1317, 1321 (Fed. Cir. 2006) (when the public fails to receive the expected bundle of characteristics from the branded product, the goodwill of the trademark holder is eroded).

[79] AGMA. "Gray Markets: An Evolving Concern, Unauthorized Sales Continue to Raise Costs and Damage Brand Reputation." KPMG (2016) https://agmaglobal.org/uploads/whitePapers/2-25-16%20Gray%20Market%20Survey-2015%20KPMG%20AGMA.pdf (accessed February 22, 2021).

Grey market goods also harm the trademark owner's relations with its distributors,[80] sales force morale, and customer service efforts,[81] and can create a shadow inventory that will result in the trademark holder being unable to anticipate or accurately forecast demand and being left with excess, unwanted, and outdated inventory,[82] which very well might end up in the grey market.[83]

How, Why, and When Do Products Enter the Grey Market?

As in all markets, profit-seeking drives the grey market.[84] Grey marketers search for opportunities to purchase branded products at a discount. If the price of the products and cost of transportation and sale are less than the price of the genuine, domestic goods, the grey marketer can sell the grey goods for less than the domestic distributor does but still make a profit.[85] This price discrepancy can emerge where the trademark holder sells

---

[80] United States v. Braunstein, 281 F.3d 982, 985 (9th Cir. 2002) (grey goods sold "at much cheaper price[s] ... hurt the sales of [authorized] distributors ... and cause[] ... resentment ... ."). See also, S.T. Cavusgil, and T. Sikora. Winter 1988. "How Multinationals Can Counter Gray Market Imports." *Columbia J. World Bus,* pp. 75–85.

[81] M.B. Meyers. 1999. "Incidents of Gray Market Activity Among U.S. Importers: Occurrences, Characteristics, and Consequences." *30 J. Int. Bus. Studies.* 105.

[82] AGMA. "Gray Markets: An Evolving Concern, Unauthorized Sales Continue to Raise Costs and Damage Brand Reputation." KPMG (2016). https://agmaglobal.org/uploads/whitePapers/2-25-16%20Gray%20Market%20Survey-2015%20KPMG%20AGMA.pdf (accessed February 22, 2021).

[83] "United States v. Braunstein." 281 F.3d 982, pp. 984–985 (9th Cir. 2002).

[84] P. Lansing, and J. Gabriella. Fall 1993. "Clarifying Gray Market Gray Areas." *Am. Bus. L.J.* 31, pp. 313–315.

[85] *Second Circuit:* Osawa & Co. v. B&H Photo, F. Supp 589, 1163, 1166–1167 (S.D.N.Y 1984).

Seventh Circuit: Hyundai Construction Equipment U.S.A., Inc. v. Chris Johnson Equipment, Inc., 2008 WL 4210785 at *1 (N.D. Ill. September 10, 2008).

See: S.M. Auvil. Spring 1995. "Gray Market Goods Produced by Foreign Affiliates of the U.S. Trademark Owner: Should the Lanham Act Provide a Remedy?" *Arkon L. Rev.* 29, pp. 437–438. ("if the price difference exceeds transportation costs, the grey market may profitably sell the goods domestically" for less than "the domestic price"); G. Assmus, and C. Wiese. Spring 1995. "How to Address the Gray Market Threat Using Price Coordination." *Sloan Management Rev.,* pp. 31–41. ("If sufficient price differentials exist between the two export markets,

its products internationally, to both developing and developed countries, particularly countries such as the United States, that practice free trade and with consumers who have large disposable incomes and appetites for luxury and high-tech goods.[86] There are several reasons why prices for similar or same goods vary by country, including currency fluctuations, sunk costs[87] and overhead costs, manufacturers' pricing schemes, varying government regulations, and consumer preferences.[88]

Currency Differential

A strong dollar means that in the United States a grey market importer can purchase its goods abroad for less money. "In the early 1980s for example, the strong dollar allowed U.S. purchasers to purchase goods abroad at significant discounts and import these goods into the United States."[89] As a result, grey market importers in the United States were able to purchase grey goods, which are already generally cheaper, at an even greater discount, which causes increased importation of grey goods into the United States.[90] The U.S. grey market in luxury automobiles,

---

then product sales will occur through unauthorized channels from the low priced market to the high priced market"); R.E. Weigand. Fall 1989. "The Gray Market Comes to Japan." *Columbia J. World Bus.* pp. 18–24.

[86] United States v. Braunstein, 281 F.3d 982, 985 (9th Cir. 2002). See also, P. Lansing, and J. Garriella. September 1993. "Clarifying Gray Market Gray Areas." *Am. Bus. L.J.* 31, pp. 313–315.

[87] Sunk costs are costs that have been incurred and cannot be reversed, for example, spending on advertising or researching a product idea. See http://www.economist.com/economics-a-to-z/s#node-21529345 (accessed February 22, 2021).

[88] A.G. Goldstein. August 2000. "Protecting Against the Gray Market in the New Economy." *Loy. L.A. Int. & Comp. L. Rev.* 22, pp. 507–508.

[89] C. Oppenheim, G.E. Weston, P.B. Maggs and R.E. Schecter. 1992. *Unfair Trade Practices and Consumer Protection*, 4th ed. p. 12.

[90] N.T. Gallini, and A. Hollis. March 1999. "A Contractual Approach to the Gray Market." *Int. Rev. L. & Econ.* 19, p. 1. ("the incentive to engage in the grey market is more pronounced when exchange rates change rapidly but nominal prices in different markets are not sufficiently responsive. Prices may not respond to exchange rate fluctuations because of informational problems or adjustment costs. Grey markets seem to flourish at times of currency appreciation"). Available at https://ideas.repec.org/p/tor/tecipa/gallini-96-01.html (accessed February 22, 2021).

for instance, grew 2,000 percent between 1981 and 1986 on the tail of considerable dollar appreciation.[91]

Varying Cost Structures

United States and European distributors often have significantly higher cost structures than foreign counterparts in developing countries or domestic grey market sellers, including:

1. Substantial sunk costs to build a solid, recognizable brand that captures the public's goodwill, that is advertising and marketing outlays;
2. Quality control processes to ensure consistent, high-quality products;
3. Funding and maintaining reliable distribution and service networks, including warranty programs; and
4. Maintaining sufficient product and parts inventory levels to meet customer demand.[92]

Trademark owners will often first invest substantial costs in developed markets to build up the brand. By the time like goods are sold to developing counties, the brand is often internationally recognized and the initial sunk costs invested in the United States or European market are not needed to build the brand overseas.[93] As a result, distributors in

---

[91] L.S. Lowe, and K. McCrohan. 1993. "Gray Markets in the United States." *J. Consumer Marketing.* 5, no. 1, pp. 45–51.

[92] Osawa & Co. v. B&H Photo, 589 F. Supp. 1163, 1166–1167 (S.D.N.Y. 1984). See: S. Ghosh. 1994. "An Economic Analysis of the Common Control Exception to Gray Market Exclusion." *U. Pa. J. Int. Bus. L.* 15. *373*; S. Samiee. 1992. "Book Note." *J. Int. Bus. Studies.* p. 186. (Reviewing S.E. Lipner. 1990. *The Legal and Economic Aspects of Gray Market Goods*). Available at http://www.jstor.org/pss/154892 (accessed February 22, 2021).

[93] E. Dugan. 2001. "United States of America, Home of the Cheap and the Gray: Comparison of Recent Court Decisions Affecting the U.S. and European Gray Markets." *Geo. Wash. Int. L. Rev.* 33, pp. 397–410.

new, developing or emerging markets can sell like goods for lower prices because they do not have the same sunk costs and overhead costs.[94]

One district court case presents a good example of the high cost structure faced by the trademark holder, which the grey marketer does not incur but benefits from (e.g., a free rider).[95] The trademark holder in this case manufactured and sold "premium foam-based mattresses ... under the TEMPUR-PEDIC® trademark."[96] In the three years preceding this case, to establish the TEMPUR-PEDIC mark as a source of high-quality bedding products, the plaintiff spent more than "$250 million in connection with [] advertisement and promotion" of its mark.[97] As part of its marketing strategy, the trademark holder also offered a comprehensive 20-year warranty to "original purchasers."[98] Because it had no quality control expenditures, the grey marketer was able to undersell the authorized distributors.

Price Discrimination

Additionally, lower prices in foreign markets can be the result of an intentional business decision.[99] For example, as part of a market penetration strategy, manufacturers will often sell like goods in emerging markets at substantially lower prices to gain market share.[100] Likewise, a brand that is only sold in upscale retail outlets in developed markets might be sold at deeply discounted prices by local mom and pop merchants in developing countries.[101]

---

[94] *Id.*

[95] Dan-Foam A/S v. Brand Named Beds, LLC, 500 F. Supp.2d, pp. 296–299 (S.D.N.Y. 2007). For more detailed discussion of this case, see § 2.03 *infra.*

[96] *Id.,* 500 F. Supp.2d at 298.

[97] *Id.,* 500 F. Supp.2d at 299.

[98] *Id.*

[99] L.J. Oswald. 2006–2007. "Statutory and Judicial Approaches to Gray Market Goods: The 'Material Differences' Standard." *Ky. L.J.* 95, pp. 107–109.

[100] L.M. Friedman. Spring 1998. "Business and Legal Strategies for Combating Grey-Market Imports." *Int. Law.* 32, pp. 27–28.

[101] *Id.*

Manufacturers sometimes will price discriminately because consumers in developing countries cannot pay the same prices as those in the United States and Europe.[102] Charging developing markets less than more developed markets allows companies to enter markets that they would not be able to access and gain additional market share.[103] In one case, the manufacturer of brailers (typewriters for the blind) sold its brailers in South Africa at less than half the price they sold them for in the United States.[104]

Differences in Government Regulations

Goods sold overseas also sell for less than like domestic U.S. and European goods because developing countries do not have as stringent safety and environmental regulations.[105] For example, a Seventh Circuit case involved heavy construction equipment destined for China. The construction company did not comply with Environmental Protection Agency (EPA) and Occupational Safety and Health Administration (OSHA) regulations because the machines were not to be used in the United States.[106] Without the consent of the exclusive U.S. distributor, however, the defendant/grey marketer imported and sold these noncompliant machines in the United States for much less than the cost of comparable machines in the United States, in part because these unsafe machines were not EPA and OSHA compliant.[107]

---

[102] S.M. Auvil. 1995. "Gray Market Goods Produced by Foreign Affiliates of the U.S. Trademark Owner: Should the Lanham Act Provide a Remedy?" *Akron L. Rev.* 29, pp. 437–438.

[103] L.Z. Asher. 2001. Note: "Confronting Disease in a Global Arena." *Cardozo J. Int. & Comp. L.* 9, pp. 135–141.

[104] Perkins School for the Blind v. Maxi-Aids, Inc., 274 F. Supp.2d 319, 322 (E.D.N.Y. 2003).

[105] S. Ghosh. 1994. "An Economic Analysis of the Common Control Exception to Gray Market Exclusion." *U. Pa. J. Int. Bus. L.* 15, p. 373.

[106] Hyundai Construction Equipment U.S.A., Inc. v. Chris Johnson Equipment, Inc., 2008 WL 4210785 at *1 (N.D. Ill. September 10, 2008).

[107] "Hyundai Construction Equipment U.S.A., Inc. v. Chris Johnson Equipment." Inc., 2008 WL 2325353 (N.D. Ill. March 24, 2008).

Consumer Preferences

Prices also differ from country to country because manufacturers often modify branded goods to the preferences of local consumers.[108] Where these local preferences result in changes to the product or packaging, the prices of the branded products in the countries can be different. In a case heard by the First Circuit, the plaintiff manufactured two very different types of chocolates sold under the "Perugina" brand—one for Europe and the United States and the other for South America.[109] The European/U.S. chocolate: (a) is manufactured in Italy and shipped in "refrigerated containers"; and (b) upon arrival in the receiving country, the manufacturer verifies temperature, randomly tests the shipment for quality, and refrigerates the chocolates until sale.[110] The South American chocolate, in contrast, is manufactured in Venezuela and is not shipped or stored in refrigeration units or tested before sale.[111] Likewise, the European/U.S. chocolate is richer (higher butter fat content) than the South American chocolate and uses higher quality ingredients.[112] The European/U.S. chocolates are sold in gold or silver boxes with a "glossy finish"; whereas the South American chocolates come in red, blue, or yellow boxes without a shiny finish.[113] Given the above differences, it is not surprising that the European/U.S. chocolates sell for 50 percent more than the South American chocolates.[114]

---

[108] "Societe Des Produits Nestle, S.A. v. Casa Helvetia." 982 F.2d 633, 642 (1st Cir. 1992).

[109] *Id.,* 982 F.2d at 642–643.

[110] *Id.*

[111] *Id.*

[112] *Id.*

[113] "Societe Des Produits Nestle, S.A. v. Casa Helvetia." 982 F.2d 633, 643 (1st Cir. 1992).

[114] *Id.*

Dumping

Grey markets also develop when foreign distributors "dump" overstock, obsolete, or soon-to-be-obsolete products into the market at a substantial discount.

"In the current aggressive economic and highly competitive environment businesses are under pressure to increase revenue in the short term and protect brand integrity in the long term. This is a difficult balance to achieve, particularly in a rapidly changing business ecosystem with conflicting deliverables. Some companies may not enforce contracts written to prevent grey market activity in order to reduce unit costs through increased production levels."[115]

"This allows large customers to sell excess inventory to low volume unauthorized dealers for more than their cost, thus reducing their costs and unloading the extra inventory at a small profit."[116]

A Ninth Circuit holding demonstrates how "dumping" goods into the grey market takes place.[117] The grey marketer purchased "excess or obsolete Apple computers at greatly reduced prices" from the "Apple Latin America Company" ("Apple Latin America"), a "subdivision" of Apple."[118] The purchaser, which was not an authorized Apple distributor, then sold these computers in the United States, in direct competition with Apple's authorized distributors, "at prices substantially below Apple's listed wholesale prices for such products.[119] An internal report by Apple determined that Apple Latin America's sales to the grey marketer were the result of Apple: (1) putting Apple Latin America "under tremendous pressure to sell large numbers of product" and to increase "sales volume rather than profit margins"; (2) paying Apple Latin America's employees solely on commission; (3) failing to monitor Apple Latin America's operations and not making it accountable for dumping; and (4) not implementing any processes or procedures to monitor sales to ensure that

---

[115] F.V. Cespedes, E.R. Corey, and V.K. Rangan. July–August 1988. "Gray Markets: Causes and Cures." *Harvard Business Review*, pp. 75–82.

[116] *Id.*

[117] United States v. Braunstein, 281 F.3d 982, 992 (9th Cir. 2002).

[118] *Id.*, 281 F.3d at 984.

[119] *Id.*

products sold by Apple Latin America were not being resold in the United States in "direct competition with Apple's United States distributors."[120] An internal report also showed that Apple ignored the following evidence that should have alerted it to a serious grey market problem:

"(1) registration and warranty cards for the computers sold by [Defendant] to United States distributors that were returned to Apple; (2) tracking records documenting the return of those registration and warranty cards; (3) serial number lists for all computer sales to [Defendant]; (4) damage claims submitted by United States dealers who bought from [Defendant]; and (5) warranty claims and requests for technical services from [Defendant's] United States buyers."[121]

The Apple case demonstrates some common internal weaknesses that allow grey markets to develop and grow:

1. A corporate culture that tolerates a grey market;
2. Use of unauthorized resale channels to increase short-term profits or cut short-term losses by dumping excess inventory;
3. Failure to have in place distribution agreements with subsidiaries that limit and restrict sales to certain geographic areas;
4. Lack of communication and enforcement with distribution partners;
5. Poor product data management (e.g., serial numbers tracking) and point-of-sale (POS) and end-user data collection and analysis;
6. Lack of sales trend and history tracking (e.g., Sales In Sales Out (SISO));
7. Ineffective process controls and due diligence in authenticating end-user information;
8. Poor inventory management and demand forecasting; and
9. Lack of a disposal/recycling program for obsolete products.[122]

---

[120] *Id.*, 281 F.3d at 985–986.

[121] *Id.*, 281 F.3d at 987–988.

[122] PricewaterhouseCoopers. 2009. "Service blues, Effectively Managing the Multi-Billion Dollar Threat from Product Warranty and Support Abuse." Available at https://agmaglobal.org/uploads/whitePapers/Final%20PwC%20Service%20 Blues%20(10-26-09).pdf (accessed February 22, 2021).

Fraud

In addition, grey marketers often obtain products at substantial discounts by fraudulent and other unscrupulous means and then sell these products for less than the price of identical goods sold by authorized dealers. To obtain fraudulent discounts, grey market suppliers employ several techniques, including: (1) overordering on valid accounts with preferential discounts; (2) falsifying large customer accounts to obtain volume discounts; and (3) submitting false (unqualified) returns or requesting nonexistent warranty work.[123] In each of these situations, the authorized purchasers that fraudulently obtain the discounted products can afford to resell these goods on the grey market for below-market prices at profit.

Volume discount fraud was perpetrated by an authorized Hewlett-Packard (HP) reseller that falsified documents to obtain 1,500 laptops under HP's "'Big Deal' program[,] which allows authorized resellers to provide competitive pricing to qualified, large volume end-users."[124] To obtain this volume discount, the defendant/authorized reseller falsified documents to create a fictitious end-user. Instead of selling the laptops to the approved end-user, however, the reseller sold the computers at a substantial discount on the grey market to unauthorized purchasers.

Another common fraud is a false application for academic or educational discounts. In 2007, authorized Microsoft distributors formed

---

[123] United States v. Braunstein, 281 F.3d 982, 987–988 (9th Cir. 2002); Federal Bureau of Investigation, San Francisco Division. November 17, 2009. "Pennsylvania Man Pleads Guilty to Warranty Fraud." Available at https://archives.fbi.gov/archives/sanfrancisco/press-releases/2009/sf111709.htm (accessed February 22, 2021). (defendant fraudulently registered serial numbers that were not assigned to devices, then reported problems with these non-existent devices, causing the manufacturer to ship him replacements pursuant to its warranty program); S. Gaudin. March 15, 2007. "Another Week, Another Scam on Cisco Systems." *Network Computing*. Available at www.networkcomputing.com/networking/another-week-another-scam-cisco-systems (accessed February 22, 2021). (defendants "conspired to submit fraudulent service contract claims to Cisco to receive replacement computer networking parts that they were not entitled to" and then "sold these so-called replacement parts to customers…").

[124] "Hewlett-Packard Co. v. Capital City Micro." Inc., 2006 WL 149034 at *2 (M.D. Tenn. January 19, 2006).

nominee corporations that purchased existing corporations holding Microsoft licensing agreements to participate in Microsoft's Authorized Education Reseller (AER) program, which provides Microsoft software at steeply discounted prices for resale to academic institutions. Using these nominee entities, the defendants purchased more than $29 million worth of AER software from Microsoft and sold this software to nonacademic entities, in violation of their agreement with Microsoft, netting more than $5 million in profits.[125]

Another grey market scheme to fraudulently obtain lower priced goods occurs, when an authorized foreign distributor receives a price discount by falsely representing that it will sell the goods in a specific developing country but sells the product in a developed market at a profit and below market price in that county.[126]

Materially Different Standard

To prevail in a legal action against a grey marketer, the U.S. trademark holder is usually required to prove that the grey goods are "materially different" from their domestic counterparts. In the often-cited grey market case *Societe Des Produits Nestle, S.A. v. Casa Helvetia*, the First Circuit Court

---

[125] DOJ. October 25, 2007. "Four Defendants Sentenced in Scheme to Defraud Microsoft Corporation." Available at http://www.justice.gov/archive/criminal /cybercrime/press-releases/2007/aliSent.htm (accessed February 22, 2021) (Defendants "were convicted of 30 counts of conspiracy, mail fraud, wire fraud, and money laundering." *** "[F]rom January 1997 through January 2001, the defendants formed several nominee corporations and purchased existing corporations holding Microsoft licensing agreements for the purpose of participating in Microsoft's Authorized Education Reseller (AER) program, a program that provides Microsoft software at steeply discounted prices for resale to academic institutions only." Using these nominee entities, defendants "purchased more than $29 million worth of AER software from Microsoft and sold this software to nonacademic entities, in violation of the Microsoft agreement, for a profit of more than $5 million").

[126] Johnson & Johnson Products, Inc. v. Dal International Trading Co., 798 F.2d 100, 101–102 (3d Cir. 1986) (defendant purchased "80,000 dozen" toothbrushes from manufacturer based on representation that they would be sold in Poland, when defendant intended to and did sell them in the United States).

of Appeals held that a single material difference creates a *presumption* that the grey goods have a "potential to mislead or confuse consumers about the nature or quality of the product."[127] Actual confusion is not required. "[A]ny difference ... that consumers would likely consider to be relevant when purchasing a product" constitutes a material difference.[128] Material differences are not limited to "physical differences" and include "subtle differences" that are "not blatant enough to make it obvious to the average consumer that the origin of the product differs from his or her expectations," and thus are likely to confuse or disappoint the average consumer.[129]

Even though the threshold of materiality is low, "a plaintiff in a grey market trademark infringement case must establish that *all or substantially all* of its sales are accompanied by the asserted material difference in order to show that its goods are materially different."[130] "To permit recovery by a trademark owner when less than 'substantially all' of its goods bear the material difference ... would allow the owner itself to contribute to the confusion by consumers that it accuses grey market importers of creating."[131] Although a trademark owner has the right to determine the set of characteristics that is associated with its trademark, the owner cannot authorize the sale of trademarked goods with a set of characteristics and at the same time claim that these characteristics should not be associated with the trademark.[132]

---

[127] "Societe Des Produits Nestle, S.A. v. Casa Helvetia." 982 F.2d 633, 640 (1st Cir. 1992). (Emphasis added.)

[128] *Id.*, 982 F.2d at 641.

[129] *Id.*, 982 F.2d at 642.

[130] "SKF U.S.A., Inc. v. International Trade Commission." 423 F.3d 1307, 1315 (Fed. Cir. 2005). (Emphasis added.)

[131] *Id.*

[132] *Id. SKF USA, Inc.* illustrates the dangers that trademark owners who fail to maintain consistent distribution and quality control practices face in trying to stop grey goods. The plaintiff in *SKF USA, Inc.* claimed that the grey goods were materially different from domestic goods because the domestic goods came with postsale technical support, while grey goods did not. In affirming the ITC, the Federal Circuit held that because 12.6% of plaintiff's products were sold directly to entities that did not provide postsale technical support, the plaintiff failed to meet the materially different test requirement that all or substantially all of the domestic goods are different from the grey goods, 423 F.3d at 1317–1318.

Differences Found to Be Material

U.S. distributors facing a grey market threat should look to differences that could affect the distributor's ability to control the quality of the goods, impugn its goodwill, negatively affect its relationship with authorized U.S. dealers, or potentially lead to consumer confusion. As detailed below, courts have found the following differences material:

(a) Altered or obliterated serial numbers;
(b) Non-English language instructions, manuals, or labels;
(c) A significantly reduced price from that of the U.S. exclusive distributor or lack of the standard, comprehensive U.S. warranty; and
(d) Physical differences, including packaging or product composition or both.

Altered or Obliterated Serial Numbers

A good example of altered serial numbers constituting a material difference is found where the grey marketer sold grey goods with the "batch codes" removed and replaced with numbers that did not correspond to any actual products— grey or domestic.[133] Holding this to be a material difference, one district court found that "obliterated" "manufacturer's codes":

1. "Degrade[] the appearance of the product," creating an appearance that "the product had in some way been tampered with," resulting in a likelihood of confusion;[134] and
2. "Deprive Plaintiffs of their exclusive right to control the quality of their products."[135] "[B]atch codes are vital to Plaintiffs' quality control effort in that those codes are the only means for the Plaintiffs to identify and recall defective or outdated products."[136] It did not

---

[133] "Davidoff & CIE SA v. PLD International Corp." 2000 WL 1901542 (S.D. Fla. September 25, 2000).

[134] Id., 2000 WL 1901542 at **2–4.

[135] Id., 2000 WL 1901542 at **13–14.

[136] Id., 2000 WL 1901542 at *12.

matter that the manufacturer "never recalled any of its products ... it is the right to control the quality—as well as the actual quality—that is afforded ... protection[]."[137]

In another sale of grey goods with "obliterated batch codes," which were the "only effective way [for plaintiff] to identify specific products for quality control purposes in the event that recall of products is necessary,"[138] the court held that the obliterated batch codes constituted a material difference because they were "vital" to the plaintiff's quality control efforts.[139] The fact that plaintiff never had a product recall was irrelevant, because "it is the right to control quality—as well as the actual quality—that is afforded one of the most important protections under the Lanham Act."[140] The court also noted that the "crudity" of the "obliteration of the batch codes" left "noticeable scars" that made the grey goods "physically inferior" to the domestic product and could tarnish the domestic distributor's goodwill because consumers will likely attribute [the obliteration] to the plaintiff.[141]

A First Circuit district court found the U.S. distributor of "high quality and highly priced" pens sought to enjoin importation of pens with "altered" serial numbers without the standard manufacturer's warranty.[142] Citing a material difference, the court held that "serial numbers are a vital part of [plaintiff's] quality control efforts" and their removal prevented the manufacturer from being able to recall, track, or identify lost or stolen pens. It did not matter that plaintiff did not identify any actual quality control problems because it is the ability of plaintiff to maintain quality control, not actual quality, that is protected.[143]

---

[137] *Id.*, 2000 WL 1901542 at **12–13.

[138] John Paul Mitchell System v. Pete-N-Larry's, Inc., 862 F. Supp. 1020 (W.D.N.Y. 1994).

[139] *Id.*, 862 F. Supp. at 1026.

[140] *Id.*

[141] *Id.*

[142] Montblanc-Simplo GMBH v. Staples, Inc., 172 F. Supp.2d 231, 238 (D. Mass. 2001).

[143] *Id.* See also, Beltronics USA, Inc. v. Midwest Inventory Distribution, LLC, 562 F.3d 1067, 1070 (10th Cir. 2009) (affirming the district court's finding that

Foreign Language Decals and Manuals

Grey goods with foreign language decals and manuals also violate the Lanham Act. In a 2006 case, John Deere sought to prevent the sale in the United States of "harvesters" that Deere "manufactured solely for sale in Europe."[144] The Federal Circuit held that each of the following constituted a "material difference":

- The "North American harvesters" have "warning labels and safety decals" with "pictures and English writing," while the "European forage harvesters carry only pictures";
- "[t]he operator's manuals of the European version forage harvesters are in the language of the target country, while the American forage harvesters are in English"; and
- "the warranty services provided by Deere differ for the North American and European version[s]."[145]

Similarly, another grey marketer sold "Kubota" tractors in the United States that were manufactured in and intended for sale and use in Japan.[146] "Kubota-US," a subsidiary of "Kubota-Japan," the Japanese manufacturer of the tractors, was the "exclusive" distributor of Kubota tractors in the United States.[147] The court found that Kubota–Japan manufactured tractors for specific use in the United States and that:

- the United States machines "bear English-language controls and warnings, and have English-language dealers and users manuals";

---

sale of radar detectors without manufacture's original serial number constituted a material difference).

[144] Bourdeau Brothers, Inc. v. International Trade Commission, 444 F.3d 1317, 1320 (Fed. Cir. 2006).

[145] Id., 444 F.3d at 1324–1325.

[146] "Gamut Trading Co. v. International Trade Commission." 200 F.3d 775, 776–777 (Fed. Cir. 1999).

[147] Id., 200 F.3d at 776.

- Kubota-U.S. "imported" the United States machines "and sold [them] through a nationwide dealership network which provides full maintenance and repair service and maintains an inventory of parts"; and
- "Kubota-US conducts training classes for its dealership employees, instructing them on service and maintenance procedures."[148]

The grey market importer contended that the aforementioned did not constitute material differences because the importer's customers knew that they were purchasing "Japanese" tractors and the "Japanese labels" were "readily apparent."[149] Rejecting this contention, the International Trade Commission found that the lack of English "instructional and warning labels, operator manuals, and service manuals[]" were material, particularly because they "are necessary to the safe and effective operation" of the machine.[150]

---

[148] *Id.*, 200 F.3d at 777.

[149] *Id.*, 200 F.3d at 780.

[150] *Id.*

See also:

Second Circuit: Original Appalachian Artworks v. Granada Electronics, 816 F.2d 68, 73 (2d Cir. 1987) (material difference between Cabbage Patch dolls and defendant's dolls intended for sale in Spain with Spanish language "adoption papers"); Fender Musical Instruments Corp. v. Unlimited Music Center Inc., 35 U.S.P.Q.2d 1053, 1056 (D. Conn. 1995) (guitars with owner's manuals in Japanese); Helene Curtis v. National Wholesale Liquidators, Inc., 890 F. Supp. 152, 155 (E.D.N.Y. 1995) (labels in French and English instead of only English as standard in the United States); Osawa & Co. v. B&H Photo, 589 F. Supp. 1163, 1169 (S.D.N.Y. 1984) ("instruction manuals written in foreign languages [] cause[] understandable consumer dissatisfaction").

Seventh Circuit: PepsiCo, Inc. v. Nostalgia Corp., 18 U.S.P.Q.2d 1404, 1405–1406 (N.D. Ill. December 20, 1990) (Pepsi bottled in Mexico with Spanish language labels).

Lack of Standard Domestic Warranty at a Substantially
Reduced Price

Likewise, the sale of grey goods as "new," without the manufacturer's standard warranty or at a significant discount to the price offered by the U.S.
distributor, constitutes a material difference. A grey marketer purchased
grey goods overseas at a substantial discount to U.S. prices and resold
them in the United States at a substantial discount to retail prices and
without the manufacturer's standard warranty.[151] The court held that,
even if physically identical to the domestic goods, the grey goods were
materially different because the discounted sale without the standard U.S.
warranty or with an "inferior" warranty would likely "cause confusion as
to both the quality and source."[152]

Another grey marketer sold cameras "at prices far below the prices
of authorized [U.S.] dealers" and without the manufacturer's standard
warranty.[153] Finding these to be material differences, the court noted
that the U.S. distributor "had devoted extensive expenditures, activities
and energies to the successful development of goodwill for the [brand],"
including: (1) "advertising and … other public relations expenses"; and (2)
only selling the product through authorized dealers, which are required to
receive continuing training from the distributor and keep a full inventory
of product and parts on hand to meet customer needs.[154] The court also
found that "[c]ustomer confusion" can result from "wide price disparities
between legitimate and grey imports" because "consumers will wonder
why the same equipment can be purchased so much more cheaply" overseas and "will no doubt assume the explanation is that the plaintiff is
gouging, which will engender hostility to the mark."[155] Such price dispar-
ity can result in "disaffection among authorized dealers," which in turn
"creates a substantial risk of loss of enthusiasm or bad-mouthing (where it

---

[151] Perkins School for the Blind v. Maxi-Aids, Inc., 274 F. Supp.2d 319, 322
(E.D.N.Y. 2003).

[152] Id., 274 F. Supp.2d at 324.

[153] Osawa & Co. v. B&H Photo, 589 F. Supp. 1163, 1166 (S.D.N.Y. 1984).

[154] Id., 589 F. Supp. at 1165.

[155] Id., 589 F. Supp. at 1166.

matters most since buyers are likely to look to dealers for advice on brands and equipment)."[156]

Product Composition or Physical Differences or Both

In addition, even minor differences in the composition of the product or physical appearances can constitute material differences. The District of Columbia Circuit found that minor differences in ingredients and packaging between U.S. and UK versions of bath soap constituted a material difference,[157] while a Third Circuit district court held that a UK version of "TIC TAC" breath mints was materially different from the U.S. version because each UK mint had an extra one-half calorie and the mints came in slightly different packaging.[158] However, the Ninth Circuit held that the fact that grey market circuit breakers, which were, in "an ironic twist," "grey" in color, as compared to the "black" domestic

---

[156] Many other federal courts have also found that sale of a grey market good without the standard U.S. warranty is a material difference.

See:

Second Circuit: Movado Group, Inc. v. Matagorda Ventures, Inc., 2000 WL 1855120 at *4 (S.D.N.Y. December 19, 2000) ("the sale of its watches without the factory warranty makes Defendant's watches distinctly different"); Fender Musical Instruments Corp. v. Unlimited Music Center, 1995 WL 241990 at *4 (D. Conn. February 16, 1995) (product sold without usual service guaranty); J. Atkins Holdings Ltd. v. English Discounts, Inc., 729 F. Supp. 945, 953 (S.D.N.Y. 1990) (gray goods "covered by a qualitatively different warranty from those distributed in U.S. through authorized channels").

Federal Circuit: Bourdeau Brothers Inc. v. International Trade Commission, 444 F.3d 1317, 1325, n.3 (Fed. Cir. 2006) (material difference where "the warranty services provided by Deere differ for the North American and European version[s]" of tractors); Gamut Trading Co. v. International Trade Commission, 200 F.3d 775, 777 (Fed. Cir. 1999) (finding material difference because Japanese tractors were not covered under United States warranty that provides for full coverage by specially trained "nationwide dealership network").

[157] "Lever Brothers Co. v. United States." 877 F.2d 101, 103 (D.C. Cir. 1989).

[158] Ferrero U.S.A., Inc. v. Ozak Trading, Inc., 753 F. Supp. 1240, pp. 1243–1244 (D.N.J. 1991).

circuit breakers, was not a "material difference" under the Lanham Act.[159] The defendant, a U.S. company, purchased the grey market circuit breakers, which were manufactured in Canada by the authorized Canadian trademark holder that produced black circuit breakers for the exclusive U.S. trademark holder and grey circuit breaks for the Canadian market. After the U.S. defendant purchased the grey circuit breakers from a third party and began selling them in the United States, the U.S. trademark owner sued. Affirming the district court's dismissal, the Ninth Circuit held that the grey circuit breakers were not "materially different" from the black (domestic) circuit breakers because other than the color, which did not affect performance, they were identical.[160] Because the U.S. consumers who purchased the grey circuit breakers got "exactly the same circuit breaker, both in specification and quality, as they would purchase from [the plaintiff/U.S. trademark owners],"[161] there is not, as a matter of law, "legal confusion."[162] There was no allegation that grey circuit breakers "undermine[d] the [plaintiff's] goodwill."[163]

Example Involving Several Material Factors

An example of grey goods litigation that involved several of the previously mentioned material differences comes from a U.S. District Court in Illinois. The defendant (grey marketer) purchased at least 29 Hyundai heavy construction machines in Korea from Korean dealers who purchased the 29 machines directly from the manufacturer (Hyundai-Korea), the parent company of the plaintiff (Hyundai-U.S.A.).[164] The grey marketer was able to purchase all 29 units at well below the cost for which Hyundai–U.S.A. sold like domestic machines to its dealers. As a result, the grey seller sold

---

[159] "American Circuit Breakers Corp. v. Oregon Breakers." *Inc.*, 406 F.3d 577, pp. 585–586 (9th Cir. 2005).

[160] *Id.*, 406 F.3d at 585.

[161] *Id.*

[162] *Id.*, 406 F.3d at 586.

[163] *Id.*

[164] "Hyundai Construction Equipment U.S.A., Inc. v. Chris Johnson Equipment." *Inc.*, 2008 WL 4210785 at *1 (N.D. Ill. September 10, 2008).

the grey machines at well below the cost of those sold by authorized Hyundai–U.S.A. dealers.

Hyundai–Korea, however, intended for these 29 machines to be sold and used in Korea and in China, not in the United States. These 29 units did not have the standard "bumper-to-bumper" warranty that all U.S. machines came with and that was a cornerstone of Hyundai–U.S.A.'s quality control and marketing strategy. Furthermore, in an attempt to hide the source of the 29 machines, the serial numbers for all of the machines had been crudely altered. In addition, many of the 29 grey market units: (1) had non-English language safety, operational, and maintenance labels and manuals, unlike domestic Hyundai–U.S.A. machines; (2) contained non-EPA compliant engines; and (3) included model numbers for machines not sold in the United States.[165]

The grey marketer did not take issue with the prior differences, which the court held were all material. Instead, the defendant contended that there was no "actual consumer confusion" because its buyers were "sophisticated" and "knew" the 29 grey machines "were intended for sale in foreign markets," "differed from" domestic machines sold by Hyundai–U.S.A., did not come with the standard Hyundai–U.S.A. warranty, and that the grey marketer was not "an authorized Hyundai dealer."[166] The purchasers, according to the grey marketer, only cared about the low price. The court held that this did not matter because "actual confusion" is not a requirement under the Lanham Act and because this knowledge "would not protect subsequent customers."[167]

The defendant also contended that Hyundai–U.S.A. did not have standing because it did not own the trademark and its agreement with Hyundai–Korea was not exclusive. Rejecting this contention, the court held that "the primary purpose of the Lanham Act is to protect consumers"[168] and the goodwill of U.S. distributors. Therefore, Hyundai–U.S.A.

---

[165] *Id.*, 2008 WL 4210785 at **7–8.

[166] *Id.*, 2008 WL 4210785 at **3–4.

[167] *Id.*, 2008 WL 4210785 at *8.

[168] *Id.*, 2008 WL 4210785 at *4.

had standing because: (1) it "spends large amounts of money in advertising and promoting Hyundai products from which [the grey marketer] benefited";[169] and (2) lost sales to lower priced and materially different grey machines "could lead to ... the loss of goodwill."[170] The court went on to enjoin, permanently, the grey marketer from importing or selling any Hyundai heavy construction equipment with less than 100 hours of operational time and awarded Hyundai–U.S.A almost $1 million (the grey marketer's profits on the 29 grey market machines) in damages and its costs.

What Is the Black Market?

In contrast to grey goods, which bear an authorized trademark but are improperly diverted, black market goods do not bear an authorized trademark and are per se illegal (generally referred to as "counterfeits"), even if identical to the genuine goods or may even be genuine goods that have been acquired illegally (e.g., through theft).[171] The Alliance for Gray Market and Counterfeit Abatement (AGMA), a trade association of major technology companies including Cisco, IBM, and Microsoft, defines counterfeiting as: "is a deliberate intent to deceive buyers by copying and distributing goods bearing trademarks (and/or copyrights and/or patents) without authorization from IP rights holders."[172] "Counterfeiting has become the crime of the 21st century,"[173] is valued in the billions of dollars, and causes numerous problems for both trademark holders and society.[174]

---

[169] *Id.*, 2008 WL 4210785 at *5.

[170] "Hyundai Construction Equipment U.S.A., Inc. v. Chris Johnson Equipment." *Inc.*, 2008 WL 4210785 at *5 (N.D. Ill. September 10, 2008).

[171] "Yamaha Corp. v. United States." F.2d 961, 245–248 (D.C. Cir. 1992).

[172] AGMA. https://agmaglobal.org/AGMA-University/Glossary-of-terms (accessed February 22, 2021).

[173] International Standards Organization, "Crackdown on Counterfeiting." Available at www.iso.org/iso/news.htm?refid=Ref1809 (accessed February 22, 2021).

[174] See Ch. 2 *infra*.

Counterfeiting takes many forms, including:

1. Unauthorized production of branded goods;
2. Relabeling or repackaging, or both, products to falsely appear to be branded products that they are not, when the original products are used, obsolete, or quality-rejected goods, or lower quality versions of the same product; and
3. Combining parts, components, compounds, and subsystems from many sources that are fraudulently labeled as branded goods.

This last category is referred to as "Frankenstein engineering" and often combines genuine components with fake and genuine but substandard parts.[175]

A study by the Anti-Counterfeiting Group (ACG) found that in 2007, 5 percent of the UK population purchased counterfeit luxury goods.[176] "The most popular 'luxury' fakes are: clothing, shoes, watches, leather goods, and jewelry."[177] Thirty-one percent of the buyers bought fakes thinking that they were genuine goods and only 17 percent of respondents reported being confident about being able to differentiate "[b]etween a genuine and a fake product."[178] The study also revealed the rising social acceptance of counterfeits, in that 64 percent of the respondents, up from 45 percent in 2006, told their family and friends that the item was a fake.[179]

Many buyers seeking counterfeits are likely misguided by common misconceptions about counterfeiting, which should be considered nothing more than urban legends.

Myth #1: Corporate greed causes counterfeiting, which provides a social benefit by allowing consumers to purchase branded goods they cannot otherwise afford.

---

[175] P. Korzeniowski. September 06, 2007. "The Trouble With Used Networking Gear." *Information Week*. Available at http://www.drdobbs.com/the-trouble-with-used-networking-gear/201804362 (accessed February 22, 2021).

[176] "Counterfeiting Luxury: Exposing the Myths." Available at www.wipo.int/ip-outreach/en/tools/research/details.jsp?id=583 (accessed February 22, 2021).

[177] *Id.*

[178] *Id.*

[179] *Id.*

Counterfeit goods cause a host of potential problems for trademark holders and society generally, including: customer confusion, threat of personal injury, dissatisfied partners, increased cost of the legitimate products, and revenue for criminal organizations, including terrorists.[180]

Myth #2: Counterfeits are the same or better than the genuine goods but cost much less.

Counterfeit products cause property and personal injury because they are not subject to the trademark holder's quality control standards and processes. For example, IT counterfeit products frequently do not meet the quality standards of genuine equipment and have significantly higher failure rates than genuine equipment.[181] Because these substandard goods are inserted into larger networks or systems, the failure of one counterfeit piece of hardware can have serious consequences.[182]

Myth #3: All counterfeits come from China.

Although "15% to 20% of all well-known brands in China[183] are counterfeit and [brand owners] estimate their losses to be in the tens of

---

[180] See Ch. 2 *infra*. See also, P. Hlavnicka. March 01, 2010. "Debunking Common Myths About Counterfeits." *Bloomberg Businessweek*. Available at http://www.bloomberg.com/bw/stories/2010-03-01/debunking-common-myths-about-counterfeitsbusinessweek-business-news-stock-market-and-financial-advice (accessed February 22, 2021).

[181] See Ch. 2 *infra*. See also, T. Espiner. May 2008. "Cisco Partners Sell Fake Routers to US Military." *ZDNet*, Aavailable at http://www.zdnet.com/cisco-part-ners-sell-fake-routers-to-us-military-1339288994/ (accessed February 22, 2021).

[182] U.S. Chamber of Commerce, Global Intellectual Property Center. March 10, 2010. "Debunking Common Myths About Counterfeits." Available at http://www.theglobalipcenter.com/debunking-common-myths-about-counterfeits/ (accessed February 22, 2021). According to then-U.S. Customs and Border Protection Assistant Commissioner, "entire bank branches went offline for days in 2004 after the failure of fake wide-area-network interface cards installed in routers. In the same year a government agency conducted a network upgrade to its North American weather communication system using counterfeit network hardware. The network hardware and the entire communication system failed upon installation." *Id.*

[183] F. Boumphrey. July 27, 2007. "Fake Brands Recognising a Real Trend, Euromonitor Global Market Research Blog." Available at http://blog.euromoni-

billions of dollars per year,"[184] the counterfeit problem knows no boundaries, national or jurisdictional, and presents significant problems globally, including in the United States.[185]

Myth #4: Developing countries have few or no rules against counterfeiting, so it is a waste of time trying to enforce them.

Developing countries do have laws on their books against counterfeiting.[186]

---

tor.com/2007/07/fake-brands-recognising-a-real-trend.html (accessed February 22, 2021).

China is often the first country that comes to mind in terms of major producers of counterfeit parts. There are certain factors that played a significant role in "establishing" China as world largest counterfeit hotspot. China's style of capitalism differs from the Western worlds, with China's emphasis on both privately owned and state-owned enterprises. At no other time in history has a country the size of China progressed so far in so little time. This is perhaps the main reason why the concept of protecting intellectual property was not well established. China's communist ideology placed emphasis on common or group ownership, which basically restrained China's socioeconomic system and severely neglected legal system. Regardless of the reasons, the lack of regard for the intellectual property of others is at the root of the counterfeit and grey market issues today, especially as more and more manufacturing is being done in China. The fact that it was only in March 2007 that the National People's Congress enacted a law giving individuals the same legal protection for their property as the state helps put things in perspective. This law was 13 years in the making and it will take several more years for it to really establish protection of private property rights in China. Given that it has taken this long just to ensure the basic property rights of China's citizenry, the lack of protection for intellectual property as a whole is really not surprising.

[184] D.C.K. Chow. April 20, 2004. "Secretary for the China Anti-counterfeiting Coalition. Counterfeiting in China and Its Effect on U.S. Manufacturing." Available at www.hsgac.senate.gov/download/testimony-chow-042004 (accessed February 22, 2021).

[185] DOJ. March 12, 2010. "Father and Son Plead Guilty to Selling Counterfeit Software Worth $1 Million." Available at http://www.justice.gov/opa/pr/2010/March/10-crm-257.html (accessed February 22, 2021). Although China is responsible for the exportation of 80 percent of the counterfeit goods seized at U.S. borders, Taiwan, Hong Kong, Russia, India, Pakistan, and Uruguay have also been reported as major producers and exporters of counterfeit goods.

[186] See Ch. 14 *infra*.

Myth #5: We take precautions, so it cannot happen to us.

Even when a company is serious about protecting its IP and takes preventive measures, it needs to constantly enforce the measures, internally and externally. Strict rules of business engagement—business ethics and employee training, screening, and tools (as simple as computer privacy filters and robust password controlled and "need-to-know" only access to all sensitive information), a clear travel policy, and corporate security audits—can help reduce the prospect of sensitive information getting into the wrong hands.[187]

Having procedures and policies in place on paper, however, is not enough. To protect brands from counterfeit and grey market goods, companies must practice what they preach. Not practicing or implementing internal rules and regulations is almost as bad as not having any.

---

[187] See Ch. 4 *infra*.

CHAPTER 3

Problems Caused by Counterfeit and Grey Market Goods

Degradation of Brand and Loss of Good Will

Counterfeit product is the making or selling of unauthorized copies of merchandise. The counterfeit goods are marked with a "counterfeit mark" which is made to appear like the genuine trademark of the good. A counterfeit mark is a false mark that is used in connection with the trafficking in goods or services that is identical with or indistinguishable from a genuine mark. In the case of high technology, counterfeit products can comprise individual components, whole parts, finished product, packaging, documentation, software, and even the cartons and boxes that finished goods are shipped in. The Alliance for Grey Market and Counterfeit Abatement (AGMA) provides the following definitions of counterfeits and the grey market:

"Counterfeit goods are non-genuine goods that infringe on the intellectual property of rights holders. Counterfeiting is a deliberate intent to deceive buyers by copying and distributing goods bearing trademarks without authorization from trademark owners.

Counterfeiting is a deliberate effort to deceive buyers by copying and distributing goods bearing trademarks (and/or copyrights and/or patents) without authorization from IP rights holders."[1] "Grey Marketing is unauthorized transacting in genuine branded goods resulting from diversion from authorized channels into the hands of third parties, including the open market. Also known as parallel importing, grey marketing is the sale

---

[1] See https://agmaglobal.org/AGMA-University/Glossary-of-terms (accessed February 23, 2021).

of genuine branded products that have been diverted from authorized distribution channels or that have been imported into another country without the consent and knowledge of the brand owner."[2]

Counterfeit and grey market goods can cause serious problems for brand owners, including loss of goodwill, loss of sales, and injury to consumers. When consumers fail to receive the expected bundle of characteristics from a branded product, they blame the brand owner, resulting in loss of goodwill and brand erosion.[3] This chapter examines how counterfeit and grey market goods: (1) harm the brand owner's authorized distributor relations;[4] (2) hurt sales force morale and customer service efforts;[5] (3) cause companies to inaccurately forecast and track sales, profits, and consumers' demand;[6] (4) result in warranty and service abuse;[7] and (5) impose social costs.

---

[2] *Id.*

[3] "Bourdeau Brothers, Inc. v. International Trade Commission." 444 F.3d 1317, 1321–1323 (Fed. Cir. 2006) (when the public fails to receive the expected bundle of characteristics from the branded product, the goodwill of the trademark holder is eroded); Dugan, "United States of America, Home of the Cheap and the Gray: Comparison of Recent Court Decisions Affecting the U.S. and European Gray Markets," 33 Geo. Wash. Int. L. Rev. 397 (2001).

[4] United States v. Braunstein, 281 F.3d 982, 985 (9th Cir. 2002) (grey goods were sold "within the United States at a much cheaper price than the other United States distributors were offering, which hurt the sales of those distributors and caused confusion and resentment in the market"). See also, Cavusgil and Sikora, "How Multinationals Can Counter Gray Market Imports," Columbia J. World Bus., pp. 75–85 (Winter 1988).

[5] M.B. Myers. 1999. "Incidents of Gray Market Activity Among U.S. Exporters: Occurrences, Characteristics, and Consequences," *Journal of International Business Studies* 30, no. 1, pp. 105–126.

[6] P. Lansing, and G. Garriella. Fall 1993. "Clarifying Gray Market Areas." *Am. Bus. L.J.* 31, pp. 313–316.

[7] Hyundai Construction Equipment U.S.A., Inc. v. Chris Johnson Equipment, Inc., 2008 WL 4210785 at **1–2 (N.D. Ill. September 10, 2008) (grey market construction equipment was sold in the United States without warranty and at a steep discount compared with machines sold by authorized distributor, which all came with standard, comprehensive warranty). See also, Alliance for Grey Market and Counterfeit Abatement, "Service Blues: Effectively managing the multi-billion dollar threat from product warranty and service abuse," available at https://agmaglobal.org/uploads/whitePapers/Final%20PwC%20Service%20 Blues%20(10-26-09).pdf (accessed February 23, 2021).

Customer Confusion and Dissatisfaction

A brand constitutes a "bundle of special characteristics" that consumers "expect … to receive … on every occasion."[8] When consumers' expectations are not met, they blame the manufacturer.[9] Counterfeit goods "by their very nature cause confusion"[10] and threaten brand owners.

Well-established brands reduce consumer search time and costs because purchasers are already aware of what to expect when selecting the product, based on prior experience or as a result of the owner's marketing efforts.[11] Based on this knowledge, consumers choose a specific brand over competing products and may pay a premium for the product.[12] The biggest cause of consumer confusion and dissatisfaction comes when a

---

[8] *First Circuit:* Societe Des Produits Nestle, S.A. v. Casa Helvetia, 982 F.2d 633, 636 (1st Cir. 1992) ("Every product is composed of a bundle of special characteristics. The consumer who purchases what he believes is the same product expects to receive those special characteristics on every occasion.").

Federal Circuit: Bourdeau Brothers, Inc. v. International Trade Commission, 444 F.3d 1317, 1320 (Fed. Cir. 2006) ("the public associates a trademark with goods having certain characteristics").

See 15 U.S.C. § 1127 (the Lanham Act defines a "trademark" as "any word, name of symbol, or device" used "to identify and distinguish" a "unique product" and/or the "source of the goods").

[9] "Bourdeau Brothers, Inc. v. International Trade Commission." 444 F.3d 1317–1321 (Fed. Cir. 2006) (when the public fails to receive the expected bundle of characteristics from the branded product, the goodwill of the trademark holder is eroded).

[10] Proctor & Gamble Co. v. Xetal, Inc., 2008 WL 361140 at *7 (E.D.N.Y. February 08, 2009).

[11] S.M. Auvil. Spring 1995. "Gray Market Goods Produced By Foreign Affiliates of the U.S. Trademark Owner: Should the Lanham Act Provide a Remedy?" *Akron L. Rev.* 28, pp. 437–447.

[12] S.M. Auvil. Spring 1995. "Gray Market Goods Produced By Foreign Affiliates of the U.S. Trademark Owner: Should the Lanham Act Provide a Remedy?" *Akron L. Rev.* 28, pp. 437–448; "The Value of a Brand Name." Available at http://pages.stern.nyu.edu/~adamodar/New_Home_Page/lectures/brand.html (accessed February 23, 2021). ("One of the benefits of having a well-known and respected brand name is that firms can charge higher prices for the same products, leading to higher profit margins and hence to higher price-sales ratios and firm value").

consumer receives a nongenuine product, and it fails to conform to the consumer's expectations. This is particularly true when the nongenuine product appears to be exactly the same as the legitimately distributed genuine product. "Subtle" differences between illegitimate and genuine goods can result in consumers not knowing that they are purchasing counterfeit goods until after making the purchase.[13]

High-end genuine products usually come with additional quality control efforts and provide an example of the subtle, yet important, differences consumers notice only after purchase. TEMPUR-PEDIC®, for example, has a reputation for providing consumers with high-quality mattresses at a high price point.[14] To ensure the expected quality, the manufacturer ships the mattresses in boxes designed to keep the mattresses flat and firm at all times. The company has also instituted strict guidelines for authorized and specially trained delivery persons.[15] In contrast, unauthorized sellers of TEMPUR-PEDIC®-branded mattresses are able to sell the products at a discount, in part because they do not follow the quality control requirements. Yet, consumers are unaware of the lack of these quality control procedures. They expect that they are getting a TEMPUR-PEDIC® mattress for what appears to be a good price. When consumers experience problems with the mattresses after purchase, they fault the brand owner and not the unauthorized seller.[16]

---

[13] See Societe Des Produits Nestle, S.A. v. Casa Helvetia, 982 F.2d 633, 641 (1st Cir. 1992) ("subtle differences" that are "not blatant enough to make it obvious to the average consumer that the origin of the product differs from his or her expectations" are likely to confuse or disappoint the average consumer). See also, "The Surprising Risks of Counterfeit Software in Business." http://download.microsoft.com/documents/rus/antipiracy/Surprising_Risks_of_Counterfeit_in_Business_Final.pdf (accessed February 23, 2021) (Microsoft survey found that: (a) 37 percent of its midsized customers unknowingly purchased counterfeit products; (b) 48 percent of the survey participants were not able to tell the difference between genuine and counterfeit software; and (c) only 41 percent know how to check if a product is pirated or counterfeit).
[14] Dan-Foam A/S v. Brand Named Beds, 500 F. Supp.2d 296, 324 (S.D.N.Y. 2007).
[15] Id., 500 F. Supp.2d at 301.
[16] Id., 500 F. Supp.2d at 322–332.

Consumers also experience confusion and disappointment when they unknowingly purchase a grey market product intended for sale in another country and designed to the tastes and language of that country.[17] Consumers buying a trademarked product in the United States rightfully assume it is identical to the domestic product with which they are familiar.[18] For example, Nestle sells two very different types of chocolate under the PERUGINA® brand—one for Europe and the United States, and the other for South America.[19] The European and U.S. chocolate is richer, higher in butter fat content, and uses higher quality ingredients that require refrigeration until sale.[20] As a result, the European and U.S. PERUGINA® chocolate sells for 50 percent more than the South American PERUGINA® chocolate.[21] But U.S. consumers who purchase the chocolate meant for sale in South America do not know of the differences when looking at the packaging and, upon purchase and consumption, blame the brand owner when the product does not conform to their expectations.[22]

Similarly, companies often sell the same product around the world, yet affix labels and include product labels and manuals printed in the language of the country in which the product is intended to be sold.

---

[17] See Societe Des Produits Nestle, S.A. v. Casa Helvetia, 982 F.2d 633, 636 (1st Cir. 1992) (brands "often tailor" products "to specific national conditions," resulting in a product that "differs from nation to nation").

[18] "Hyundai Construction Equipment U.S.A., Inc. v. Chris Johnson Equipment." Inc., 2008 WL 4210785 at *2 (N.D. Ill. September 10, 2008).

[19] See Societe Des Produits Nestle, S.A. v. Casa Helvetia, N. 17 supra, 982 F.2d at 642.

[20] *Id.*

[21] *Id.*

[22] "Societe Des Produits Nestle, S.A. v. Casa Helvetia." 982 F.2d 633–642 (1st Cir. 1992). The following resulted in a presumption of consumer confusion:

Third Circuit: Ferrero U.S.A., Inc. v. Ozak Trading, Inc., 753 F. Supp. 12401243 (D.N.J. 1991) (the U.K. version of "TIC TAC" breath mints containing an extra one-half calorie and packaged slightly differently).

District of Columbia Circuit: Lever Brothers Co. v. United States, 981 F.2d 1330, 1331 (D.C. Cir. 1993) (differences in ingredients and packaging between U.S. and UK versions of Lever brand bath soap, including smell, lathering ability and packaging logo script).

Consumers who purchase products with foreign language instructions or decals may become dissatisfied because they cannot read the instructions and properly use the product. Moreover, these labels and instructions in a foreign language do not include all information required by domestic laws and regulations, causing the product's failure to comply with domestic regulations, such as environmental, health, and safety laws.[23]

Another source of consumer dissatisfaction and confusion arises in the case of product warranty. Manufacturers often sell the same product at a discount in countries outside the United States without the service warranty that comes with domestic sales. However, domestic consumers expect that all products sold by an authorized distributor will come with the same comprehensive warranty.[24] As a result, the sale of identical grey market products without the domestic product's standard warranty can cause serious consumer confusion and dissatisfaction.[25] Some manufacturers refuse to service

---

[23] See:

Second Circuit: Original Appalachian Artworks, Inc. v. Granada Electronics, Inc., 816 F.2d 68, 73 (2d Cir. 1987) (defendant's Cabbage Patch Dolls with Spanish-language birth certificates, adoption papers, and instructions were materially different from dolls with English-language papers).

Seventh Circuit: Hyundai Construction Equipment U.S.A., Inc. v. Chris Johnson Equipment, Inc., 2008 WL 4210785 at *1 (N.D. Ill. Sept. 10, 2008) (heavy construction equipment destined for China that did not comply with OSHA regulations because operation labels and manuals were in Korean).

Federal Circuit: Bourdeau Brothers, Inc. v. International Trade Commission, 444 F.3d 1317, 1324 (Fed. Cir. 2006) (American forage harvesters have "warning labels and safety decals" with "pictures and English writing," while the "European forage harvesters carry only pictures"; and "[t]he operator's manuals of the European version forage harvesters are in the language of the target country, while the American forage harvesters are in English"); Gamut Trading Co. v. International Trade Commission, 200 F.3d 775 (Fed. Cir. 1999) (grey market tractors had Japanese warning labels and user manuals).

[24] See "Hyundai Construction Equipment U.S.A., Inc. v. Chris Johnson Equipment, Inc." 2008 WL 4210785 at *2 (N.D. Ill. Sept. 10, 2008) (a "consumer who is buying a trademarked product in the United States is certainly entitled to assume that it is identical to the domestic product").

[25] *Second Circuit*: Perkins School for the Blind v. Maxi-Aids, Inc., 274 F. Supp.2d 319 (E.D.N.Y. 2003) (the grey marketer purchased grey goods overseas at a substantial discount to U.S. prices and resold them in the United States at a

grey or counterfeit goods even if the customer will pay for such service.[26] Consumers who believe from experience that the manufacturer's domestic goods come with a warranty become disappointed when the manufacturer or distributor denies their warranty claims for the grey goods.[27]

In some cases, manufacturers will provide warranty service for the unauthorized, cheaper product.[28] This tactic may backfire, however, if the

---

substantial discount to retail prices and without the manufacturer's standard warranty. The court held that, even if physically identical to the domestic goods, the grey brailers were materially different because the discounted sale without the standard U.S. warranty or with an "inferior" warranty would likely "cause confusion as to both the quality and source."); Movado Group, Inc. v. Matagorda Ventures, Inc., 2000 WL 1855120 at *4 (S.D.N.Y. December 19, 2000) ("the sale of its watches without the factory warranty makes Defendant's watches distinctly different"); Fender Musical Instruments Corp. v. Unlimited Music Center, 1995 WL 241990 at *4 (D. Conn. February 16, 1995) (product sold without usual service guaranty); J. Atkins Holdings Ltd. v. English Discounts, Inc., 729 F. Supp. 945, 952 (S.D.N.Y. 1990) (grey goods "covered under qualitatively different warranty from those distributed in U.S. through authorized channels"); Osawa & Co. v. B&H Photo, 589 F. Supp. 1163 (S.D.N.Y. 1984) (the grey marketer sold cameras "at prices far below the prices of authorized [U.S.] dealers" and without the manufacturer's standard warranty).

Federal Circuit: Bourdeau Brothers, Inc. v. International Trade Commission, 444 F.3d 1317, 1325 n.3 (Fed. Cir. 2006) (material difference where "the warranty services provided by Deere differ for the North American and European version[s]" of tractors); Gamut Trading Co. v. International Trade Commission, 200 F.3d 775, 777 (Fed. Cir. 1999) (material difference because Japanese tractors were not covered under United States warranty that provides for full coverage by specially trained "nationwide dealership network").

[26] The reasoning behind not servicing unauthorized products, even if the customer will pay, is that brand owners do not want to encourage the proliferation of such goods. Some brand owners, however, will service grey goods to preserve customer goodwill.

[27] *Eleventh Circuit:* Tuckish v. Pomano Motor Co., 357 F. Supp.2d 1313, 1315 (S.D. Fla. 2004) (grey market Chrysler not covered under manufacturer's warranty).

State Courts:

Iowa: Roberts v. Moore, 445 N.W.2d 384, 385 (Iowa App. 1989) (grey market Mercedes not serviced under warranty).

[28] Osawa & Co. v. B&H Photo, 589 F. Supp. 11631169 (S.D.N.Y. 1984) ("[c]onsumer confusion" can result from "wide price disparities between legitimate

consumer assumes that the price difference was a result of intentional price gouging by the manufacturer.[29]

Grey market products also cause consumer confusion and dissatisfaction when unauthorized sellers deface unique product identifiers, such as serial numbers, in an effort to impede brand owners' ability to track the source of the goods. With repackaged goods particularly, consumers will not notice the difference until after purchase and may attribute the product degradation to the brand owner, not to the unauthorized seller.[30]

Finally, because "exclusivity" remains important for many high-end consumer products, grey market and counterfeit sales outside of authorized, exclusive retailers diminish the brand in consumers' minds.[31] For example, certain high-end hair care products are only sold at salons because the proper use of the products requires consultation with hairstylists. Consumers who purchase the products without proper instruction may use them incorrectly and become frustrated and dissatisfied with their effectiveness.[32] Similarly, high-quality cameras, pens, mattresses, and

---

and grey imports" because "consumers will wonder why the same equipment can be purchased so much more cheaply" overseas and "will no doubt assume the explanation is that the plaintiff is gouging, which will engender hostility to the mark").

[29] *Id.*

[30] *Second Circuit:* John Paul Mitchell System v. Pete-N-Larry's, Inc., 862 F. Supp. 1020, 1026–1027 (W.D.N.Y. 1994) (the "crudity" of the "obliteration of the batch codes" left "noticeable scars" that made the grey goods "physically inferior" to the domestic product and could tarnish the domestic distributor's goodwill because consumers "will likely attribute [the obliteration] to the plaintiff").

Seventh Circuit: Hyundai Construction Equipment U.S.A., Inc. v. Chris Johnson Equipment, Inc., 2008 WL 4210785 at *2 (N.D. Ill. September. 10, 2008) (serial numbers on heavy construction machines altered to hide source of goods).

[31] Dugan, E. 2001. "United States of America, Home of the Cheap and the Gray: Comparison of Recent Court Decisions Affecting the U.S. and European Gray Markets." *Geo. Wash. Int. L. Rev,* 33 p. 397.

[32] See: *First Circuit:* Montblanc-Simplo GMBH v. Staples, Inc., 172 F. Supp.2d 231, 232–234 (D. Mass. 2001) ("high quality and highly priced" pens authorized for sale only in a "limited number of select upscale retailers and jewelers").

watches are often sold only at exclusive, authorized dealers who possess a required level of training and product knowledge.[33]

Dangers Caused by Grey and Counterfeit Goods

Consumers who purchase grey and counterfeit goods may receive unsafe products, not meant for use or consumption. In the automobile industry, counterfeit parts include brake linings made of compressed grass or sawdust; vehicle hoods without crumple zones; and windshields without shatterproof glass.[34] As many as 36,000 fatalities and 1.5 million accidents on U.S. roads have been attributed to defective automotive parts.[35] The European Office of Intellectual Property (EUIPO) estimated that €2.2 billion is lost every year by the legitimate parts industry to counterfeit tire sales and €180 million each year due to counterfeit battery sales. Yet this represents only one part of the problem, there are other automotive parts that are frequently counterfeited in huge volumes:

Second Circuit: John Paul Mitchell System v. Pete-N-Larry's, Inc. 862 F. Supp. 1020, 1022 (W.D.N.Y. 1994) (hair care product trademark holder authorized its products for sale only in "professional hair salons" so that purchasers would "have the opportunity to consult with or receive the recommendation and advice of trained professional hairstylists"); Osawa & Co. v. B&H Photo, 589 F. Supp. 1163, 1166–1168 (S.D.N.Y. 1984) (to ensure customer satisfaction, authorized U.S. distributor of high-end camera required to "maintain vast inventory" of product and parts and to have sufficient trained staff to field questions and service products).

Seventh Circuit: Matrix Essentials, Inc. v. Karol, 1992 WL 142292 at *2 (N.D. Ill. June 17, 1992).

[33] See Montblanc-Simplo GMBH v. Staples, Inc., 172 F. Supp.2d 231, 232–234 (D. Mass. 2001) ("high quality and highly priced" pens authorized for sale only in a "limited number of select upscale retailers and jewelers").

[34] Automotive Aftermarket Suppliers Association. December 2012. "IPR Protection for Everyone: Information and Resources for Automotive Aftermarket Suppliers." Available at https://docplayer.net/14486074-Ipr-protection-for-everyone-information-and-resources-for-automotive-aftermarket-suppliers.html (accessed February 23, 2021).

[35] www.safety-security-crazy.com/real-or-fake.html (accessed February 23, 2021).

.[36] Furthermore, 2 percent of airline parts installed each year are counterfeit[37] and may have caused 174 crashes from 1973 to 1996.[38]

In the heavy construction machine industry, grey market machines have been found not to comply with EPA and OSHA requirements, particularly when the machines come with important safety information in foreign languages.[39] Such machines cause customer confusion even if the seller warns the direct purchaser that the goods are not in regulatory compliance because such warnings do not protect subsequent purchasers.[40]

Likewise, counterfeit drugs, which include fake, diluted, and expired drugs, pose a threat to the pharmaceutical industry.[41] The World Health Organization (WHO) has reported that an estimated 1 in 10 medical products circulating in low- and middle-income countries is either

---

[36] www.worldtrademarkreview.com/anti-counterfeiting/counterfeit-automotive-parts-increasingly-putting-consumer-safety-risk (accessed February 23, 2021).

[37] www.safety-security-crazy.com/real-or-fake.html (accessed February 23, 2021).

[38] *Id.*

[39] "*Seventh Circuit:* Hyundai Construction Equipment U.S.A." Inc. v. Chris Johnson Equipment, Inc., 2008 WL 4210785 at *2 (N.D. Ill. September. 10, 2008) (grey market construction equipment sold in the United States by defendant "had safety, operation, and maintenance instructions and safety decals in Korean rather than in English," as standard in U.S., and "has non-EPA compliant engines").

Federal Circuit: Bourdeau Brothers, Inc. v. International Trade Commission, 444 F.3d 1317, 1324 (Fed. Cir. 2006) (American forage harvesters have "warning labels and safety decals" with "pictures and English writing," while the "European forage harvesters carry only pictures"; and "[t]he operator's manuals of the European version forage harvesters are in the language of the target country, while the American forage harvesters are in English"); Gamut Trading Co. v. International Trade Commission, 200 F.3d 775 (Fed. Cir. 1999) (grey market tractors had Japanese warning labels and user manuals).

[40] *First Circuit:* Montblanc-Simplo GMBH v. Staples, Inc., 172 F. Supp.2d 231, 243 (D. Mass. 2001).

Seventh Circuit: Hyundai Construction Equipment U.S.A., Inc. v. Chris Johnson Equipment, Inc., 2008 WL 4210785 at *3 (N.D. Ill. Sept. 10, 2008).

[41] R. Bate. July 19, 2008. "Stopping Killer Counterfeits." *The Washington Post*, p. A15. Available at www.washingtonpost.com/wp-dyn/content/article/2008/07/18/AR2008071802446.html (accessed February 23, 2021).

substandard or falsified.[42] Since 2013, WHO has received 1,500 reports of cases of substandard or falsified products. Of these, antimalarials and antibiotics are the most commonly reported. Most of the reports (42 percent) come from the WHO African Region, 21 percent from the WHO Region of the Americas, and 21 percent from the WHO European Region.[43] In 2016, international trade in counterfeit pharmaceuticals reached USD 4.4 billion.[44] Because counterfeit drugs do not function as intended, they pose great risk, and may even cause death.[45] Counterfeit baby formula has caused children in the United States to become ill.[46] Similarly, an increase in drug prescriptions for "off-label" uses has resulted in a surge in grey market pharmaceuticals.[47]

Counterfeit perfumes and cologne also present a serious health concern for consumers.[48] Unsuspecting consumers often do not realize they have purchased a counterfeit product until they apply the fragrance.[49]

---

[42] www.who.int/news/item/28-11-2017-1-in-10-medical-products-in-developing-countries-is-substandard-or-falsified (accessed February 23, 2021).

[43] *Id.*

[44] See www.oecd.org/gov/trade-in-counterfeit-pharmaceutical-products-a7c7e054-en.htm (March 23, 2020) (accessed February 23, 2021).

[45] D.G. McNeil, Jr. February. 20, 2007 "In the World of Life-Saving Drugs, a Growing Epidemic of Deadly Fakes," *The New York Times, F1* (). Available at www.nytimes.com/2007/02/20/science/20coun.html (accessed February 23, 2021).

[46] United States v. Hanafy, 302 F.3d 485 (5th Cir. 2002). See also, M. Burros. September 06, 1995. "Eating Well, FDA Targets Baby Formula." *The New York Times, A1* (). Available at www.nytimes.com/1995/09/06/garden/eating-well-fda-target-baby-formula.html (accessed February 23, 2021).

[47] "Marketing Off-Label Uses: Shady Practices Within a Gray Market." *Psychiatric Times 26*, no. 8, pp. 22–24. August 08, 2009. Available at www.psychiatrictimes.com/view/marketing-label-uses-shady-practices-within-gray-market (accessed February 23, 2021).

[48] Medical Daily. February 07, 2014. "Fake Perfumes Containing Urine Could Lead To Adverse Health Side Effects, How To Spot Counterfeit Fragrances." Available at www.medicaldaily.com/fake-perfumes-containing-urine-could-lead-adverse-health-side-effects-how-spot-counterfeit-268902 (accessed February 23, 2021) (UK source).

[49] *Id.*

Upon application, the consumer realizes that the product does not smell like the fragrance he or she expected because counterfeit fragrances contain cheaper ingredients that break down quickly, resulting in an alcohol smell.[50] Some consumers also experience severe allergic reactions when counterfeit fragrances contain urine and dangerous chemicals that should not be put on the skin.[51]

Counterfeit batteries, which all portable electronic products now contain, also pose serious safety risks for consumers. For example, Canon issued a warning for counterfeit batteries, noting that they "are not equipped with protective devices that meet the quality standards set out by Canon."[52] When these counterfeit lithium-ion batteries were used or charged, they could cause "malfunction, abnormal heat generation, leakage, ignition, rupture and other such incidents."[53]

Bundling With Legitimate Products

Bundling occurs when counterfeit parts are commingled with grey market goods.[54] For instance, a computer that is sold legitimately by a

---

[50] *Id.*

[51] *Id.*

[52] "Updated Safety Notice: Counterfeit Lithium-Ion Battery Packs." August 01, 2019. Available at https://canoncanada.custhelp.com/app/answers/answer_view/a_id/4090/~/updated-safety-notice%3A-counterfeit-lithium-ion-battery-packs (accessed February 23, 2021).

[53] *Id.*

[54] It is important to understand the distinction between counterfeit products and grey market goods. "Counterfeit products are produced by unauthorized suppliers–these parts may appear identical to legitimate products in terms of packaging, branding and trademarks, but they have been produced without the original manufacturer's authorization and may disregard adherence to safety and quality standards. Grey market products [are] produced by authorized manufacturers but are . . . distributed in an unauthorized channel in violation of the original manufacturer's distribution agreement." MEMA Brand Protection Council, "Special "Report: Understanding the Flow of Counterfeit and Gray Market Goods through the U.S. Automotive and Commercial Vehicle Parts Marketplace." January 06, 2009. Available at www.aftermarketsuppliers.org/Doc-Vault/Archive/Special-Report-Flow-of-Counterfeit-Goods.pdf (accessed February 23, 2021).

brand-name store could include various counterfeit parts, including fake motherboards, software, and batteries.[55] Brand owners and enforcement agencies have struggled to curb the rise of bundled goods because counterfeit products can enter the grey market distribution cycle at any point. One common entry point occurs when a broker selling counterfeit goods claims they are legitimate goods and sells them to another unsuspecting broker, distributor, or reseller.[56] Once this transaction occurs, counterfeit products are commingled with genuine products on the grey market and it becomes extremely difficult to distinguish the two products.[57]

The commingling of counterfeits with grey market goods poses serious consequences for both manufacturers and consumers.[58] First, manufacturers who directly compete with counterfeiters suffer a direct loss in sales.[59] As a result of the reduction in revenue, the integrity of the "supply

---

[55] S.L. Elgan. February 29, 2008. "How Fake is Your PC." *InternetNews*. Available at www.internetnews.com/commentary/article.php/3731436/How-Fake-is-Your-PC.htm (accessed February 23, 2021).

[56] "Counterfeit Goods Fraud: An Account of its Financial Management." June 04, 2019. *SpringerLink*. Available at https://link.springer.com/article/10.1007/s10610-019-09414-6 (accessed February 23, 2021).

[57] *Id.* When "gray market goods flow in and alongside a brand owner's intended chain of distribution without detection, the integration of counterfeit goods is inevitable. It is estimated that 5-7 percent of all world trade ($250 billion) is in counterfeit goods." Sugden, *Gray Markets*, 7 (2009).

[58] Governments are also affected by bundled goods. For example, they lose out on unpaid taxes and suffer large costs in enforcing IP rights. Organisation for Economic Co-operation and Development (OECD), "The Economic Impact of Counterfeiting," p. 4 (1998).

[59] Organisation for Economic Co-operation and Development ("OECD"), "The Economic Impact of Counterfeiting," p. 22 (1998). Counterfeiters can afford to sell their goods at lower prices because they do not incur all of the costs that a manufacturer incurs. "The price of an authentic product produced by a legitimate original equipment manufacturer (OEM) reflects the cost of research and development, brand development, manufacturing, marketing, and sales. By paying only the cost of manufacturing and sales, the counterfeiter is able to sell the counterfeit product below the price of the authentic one and make a significant profit."; KPMG, "Managing the Risks of Counterfeiting in the Information Technology Industry" 3. Available at https://agmaglobal.org/uploads/whitePapers/KPMG-AGMA_ManagingRiskWhitePaper_V5.pdf (accessed February 23, 2021).

and demand" business model is compromised.[60] For instance, when a shadow inventory of bundled goods on the secondary market satisfies consumer demands, manufacturers are unable to accurately forecast the future demand for particular products.[61] Moreover, consumer loyalty and resulting demand for the genuine product may decrease because consumers are unsure if they are purchasing quality, authentic goods instead of inferior counterfeits.[62] Second, when consumers purchase bundled goods, there is a risk that the consumer is purchasing substandard products, including "products that may have been altered in some way, or used products represented as new."[63] Not only do consumers run the risk of purchasing inferior products, but they may also be exposed to health and safety dangers.[64] In the case of laptop computers, counterfeit batteries have been known to explode or catch fire.[65] Third, in certain instances, the inclusion of counterfeit parts may void the manufacturer's warranty, "disappointing consumers and hurting the manufacturer's reputation."[66]

---

[60] KPMG. "Managing the Risks of Counterfeiting in the Information Technology Industry." 3. Available at https://agmaglobal.org/uploads/whitePapers/KPMG-AGMA_ManagingRiskWhitePaper_V5.pdf (accessed February 23, 2021).

[61] A.B.A. Section of Bus. L., "Combating Gray Market Goods" 10 (December 09, 2009).

[62] Mahmut Sonmez, Deli Yang and Gerald Fryxell. June 2013. "Interactive Role of Consumer Discrimination and Branding against Counterfeiting: A Study of Multinational Managers' Perception of Global Brands in China." *Journal of Business Ethics* 115, no. 1, pp. 195–211 (17 pages), Published By: Springer Available at www.jstor.org/stable/23433914 (accessed February 23, 2021).

[63] "The Dangers of Adulterated, Counterfeit and Substandard Health Products." May 19, 2018. Available at www.hsa.gov.sg/consumer-safety/articles/illegal-health-products (accessed February 23, 2021).

[64] Organisation for Economic Co-operation and Development (OECD). 1998. "The Economic Impact of Counterfeiting." p. 4.

[65] S.L. Elgan, February 29, 2008. "How Fake is Your PC." *InternetNews*. Available at www.internetnews.com/commentary/article.php/3731436/How-Fake-is-Your-PC.htm (accessed February 23, 2021).

[66] See Kia Motors America, Inc. v. Autoworks Distributing, 2009 WL 499543 at *4 (D. Minn. February 26, 2009) (defendant's parts did not fall within the warranty because the warranty was strictly limited to KIA products).

An example taken from the information technology (IT) field highlights the potential consequences of purchasing bundled goods.[67] In Texas, a grey market broker was marketing a computer server system to a major hospital for one-half of the manufacturer's price. Despite the manufacturer's warnings, the hospital decided to purchase the system from the grey market broker. When the hospital received the product, there were many problems with the system, including incorrect cabling, counterfeit system memory, no user manuals, no original software licenses, inadequate memory cards, and replacement hard drives. The system also did not meet the manufacturer's warranty requirements because most of the system and components were not the manufacturer's authentic products. Once the hospital discovered the problems, hospital administrators attempted to contact the grey market broker. Because they could not locate the broker, the administrators were unable to return the system, get refunds, or acquire postsale service. When the hospital contacted the manufacturer, the manufacturer offered to replace the system for the out-of-pocket expenses plus the difference in price in order to have the evidence to prosecute the grey market broker. Rather than become involved in the litigation, the hospital decided to scrap the system and incur the additional expense and purchased a new system.

Channel Partner Dissatisfaction

Authorized distributors and other channel partners[68] who spend substantial resources marketing and servicing branded products lose sales to

---

[67] A.B.A. Section of Bus. L., "Combating Gray Market Goods." 12 (December 09, 2009).

[68] "A channel partner is a person or organization that provides services or sells products on behalf of a software or hardware vendor. Value-added resellers (VARs), managed service providers (MSPs), consultants, systems integrators (SIs), original equipment manufacturers (OEMs) and distributors may all be called channel partners. Many companies ... have formed channel partnership programs to work more closely with the distributors for their products. Channel partnerships provide an opportunity for companies to promote certain products or services. In return, channel partners receive access to product and marketing training, discounts, technical support, lead generation tools and beta versions of releases." Available at http://searchitchannel.techtarget.com/definition/channel-partner (accessed February 23, 2021).

unauthorized distributors who do not incur these costs.[69] When authorized distributors, particularly in high-quality and high-price industries, lose sales to counterfeit and grey market distributors, these distributors often blame the brand owner for: (1) not doing enough to stop counterfeit goods; (2) dumping excess inventory into authorized channels;[70] or (3) gouging prices in certain countries.[71]

Channel partner dissatisfaction arises when manufacturers "dump" or "flush" overstock or obsolete or soon-to-be obsolete products into the market at a substantial discount. Companies may not enforce contracts written to prevent grey market activity and instead allow large distributors to sell excess inventory to low-volume unauthorized dealers for more than their cost as a means of raising revenue.[72] In one case, a grey marketer purchased overstock of obsolete computers from the Latin American division of a company and sold the computers in the United States for much less than the going price.[73] Not surprisingly, the company's authorized distributors in the United States were disenchanted with the company when they lost sales to these lower priced goods. The threat of unauthorized goods to legitimate distributors is enormous. The global value of counterfeit goods is significant;[74] counterfeit goods represent an estimated 7 percent of annual world trade.[75]

---

[69] See § 2.05 *infra*.

[70] United States v. Braunstein, 281 F.3d 982, 992 (9th Cir. 2002).

[71] Osawa & Co. v. B&H Photo, 589 F. Supp. 1163, 1168 (S.D.N.Y. 1984) (lower priced grey good can cause "disaffection among authorized dealers," which in turn "creates a substantial risk of loss of enthusiasm or bad-mouthing (where it matters most since buyers are likely to look to dealers for advice on brands and equipment").

[72] Cespedes, F.V.,Corey, E.R., and Rangan, K. July-August. 1988. "Gray Markets: Causes and Cures." *Harv. Bus. Rev.*, pp. 75–82. See § 1.03[4][f] *supra*.

[73] See United States v. Braunstein, 281 F.3d 982–992 (9th Cir. 2002). For further discussion, see § 1.03[1] *supra*.

[74] International Anti-Counterfeiting Coalition, "About Counterfeiting." Available at www.iacc.org/resources/about/what-is-counterfeiting (accessed February 23, 2021). For more details, see § 1.01 *supra*.

[75] Lagerqvist and Bruck. "Luxury Brands in the Digital World." *Intellectual Assets Management Magazine* 53. Available at www.iam-media.com/Intelligence/IP-Value/2014/Legal-perspectives-Cross-border/Luxury-brands-in-the-digital-world (accessed February 23, 2021).

Furthermore, grey market goods have become increasingly more prevalent in the market and displace significant sales the manufacturer would have received.[76] The IT industry has been hit particularly hard by grey goods.[77] An estimated $58 billion in grey goods were sold worldwide in 2007, an 81 percent increase from 2002.[78] It is estimated that in Brazil, 30 percent of audio and video equipment, 50 percent of handheld computers, and 63 percent of personal computers are sold on the grey or black markets.[79]

Effect on Quality Control

Building and maintaining brand goodwill often requires the brand owner to maintain strict quality control procedures, including keeping tight control on service and distribution networks.[80] Manufacturers in the high-tech and luxury goods industries have strict quality control measures. Grey goods and counterfeit goods, however, are never subject to such rigorous controls; furthermore, it is likely that grey and counterfeit goods will be mishandled or damaged before reaching the customer.[81]

For example, to ensure the quality of its TEMPUR-PEDIC® mattresses and customer satisfaction, the brand owner expends substantial resources,

---

[76] For further discussion, see § 1.03[4][f] *supra*.

[77] See § 1.01 *supra* for more a detailed discussion.

[78] L.S. Lowe, and K.F. McCrohan. November-December 1989. "Minimize the Impact of the Gray Market." The *Journal of Business Strategy*, pp. 47–50 .

[79] Brazil-US Business Council. 2021. "Counterfeiting and Piracy in Brazil: The Economic Impact." Available at https://iccwbo.org/publication/economic-impacts-counterfeiting-piracy-report-prepared-bascap-inta/ (accessed February 23, 2021).

[80] Dan-Foam A/S v. Brand Names Beds, 500 F. Supp.2d 296, 299 (S.D.N.Y. 2007) (the trademark owner "spent in excess of $250 million in connection with the advertisement and promotion of products bearing the TEMPUR PEDIC trademark in order to establish this trademark in the minds of consumers as a source of high-quality bedding products").

[81] Alliance for Gray Market and Counterfeit Abatement, KPMG. 2016. "Gray Markets: An Evolving Concern." https://agmaglobal.org/uploads/whitePapers/2-25-16%20Gray%20Market%20Survey-2015%20KPMG%20AGMA.pdf (accessed February 23, 2021).

including: (1) training retailers on proper use and care of the product; (2) ensuring that retailers pass along the necessary care and use information to their purchasers; and (3) ensuring compliance with required storage and delivery procedures.[82] Proper use, storage, and delivery of these mattresses are critical to maintaining the brand's reputation for high quality, because the mattresses are susceptible to damage if not handled and used properly.[83] To protect the high quality of the TEMPUR-PEDIC® mattresses, the brand owner requires that they be: (1) shipped in a box that was designed specifically to keep the mattress flat and firm; and (2) kept flat at all times.[84] Also, because the TEMPUR-PEDIC® mattresses are made of special material that is susceptible to damage by cold and folding, the manufacturer requires that: (1) in cold weather the mattresses be delivered to customers' homes and then allowed to "soften" before installation; and (2) where delivery requires the mattresses to be folded to fit around a corner, they be folded and unfolded in a certain way to avoid damage.[85]

In one case the defendant/grey marketer, who was not an authorized TEMPUR-PEDIC® distributor, sold TEMPUR-PEDIC® mattresses for reduced prices, in part because it did not follow any of the aforementioned required quality control procedures.[86] For example, to "reduce shipping costs," the defendant shipped the TEMPUR-PEDIC® mattress in boxes smaller than the mattresses themselves by folding the mattresses to fit into the boxes.[87] The defendant also did not use delivery drivers trained by the manufacturer, and these drivers would often leave the mattresses outside in freezing temperatures.[88] Because the grey marketer did not have the quality control expenses incurred by the trademark holder, it could undersell authorized distributors.[89]

---

[82] Dan-Foam A/S v. Brand Names Beds, N. 1 supra, 500 F. Supp.2d at 301.

[83] Id.

[84] Id.

[85] Dan-Foam A/S v. Brand Names Beds, 500 F. Supp.2d 296, 301 (S.D.N.Y. 2007).

[86] Id., 500 F. Supp.2d at 302–303.

[87] Id. at 303.

[88] Id.

[89] First Circuit: Montblanc-Simplo GMBH v. Staples, Inc., 172 F. Supp.2d 231, 232–234 (D. Mass. 2001) ("high quality and highly priced" pens authorized for sale only in a "limited number of select upscale retailers and jewelers").

Grey market goods also negatively affect quality control because many grey goods have defaced or altered serial numbers to hide their source. Product unique identifiers such as serial numbers are vital to manufacturers' quality control processes because they are often the only way a manufacturer can recall or trace defective products.[90]

Similarly, unlike grey market goods, the majority of genuine products sold through authorized channels have a manufacturer's warranty, which provides manufacturers with the ability to control the quality of their

---

Second Circuit: Dan-Foam A/S v. Brand Names Beds, 500 F. Supp.2d 296, 299 (S.D.N.Y. 2007); John Paul Mitchell System v. Pete-N-Larry's, Inc., 862 F. Supp. 1020, 1022 (W.D.N.Y. 1994) (hair care product trademark holder authorized its products for sale only in "professional hair salons" so that purchasers would "have the opportunity to consult with or receive the recommendation and advice of trained professional hairstylists"); Osawa & Co. v. B&H Photo, 589 F. Supp. 1163, 1166–1168 (S.D.N.Y. 1984) (to ensure customer satisfaction, authorized U.S. distributor of high-end camera required to "maintain vast inventory" of product and parts and to have sufficient trained staff to field questions and service products).

Seventh Circuit: Matrix Essentials, Inc. v. Karol, U.S. Dist. LEXIS 8699 (N.D. Ill. June 17, 1992).

[90] *First Circuit:* Montblanc-Simplo GMBH v. Staples, Inc., 172 F. Supp.2d 231 (D. Mass. 2001) ("serial numbers are a vital part of [plaintiff's] quality control efforts" and their removal prevented the manufacturer from being able to recall, track or identify lost or stolen pens. It did not matter that plaintiff did not identify any actual quality control problems because it is the ability of plaintiff to maintain quality control, not actual quality, that is important).

Second Circuit: John Paul Mitchell System v. Pete-N-Larry's, Inc. 862 F. Supp. 1020, 1026–1027 (W.D.N.Y. 1994) (the "crudity" of the "obliteration of the batch codes" left "noticeable scars" that made the grey goods "physically inferior" to the domestic product and could tarnish the domestic distributor's goodwill because consumers "will likely attribute [the obliteration] to the plaintiff").

Seventh Circuit: Hyundai Construction Equipment U.S.A., Inc. v. Chris Johnson Equipment, Inc., 2008 WL 4210785 at *2 (N.D. Ill. September. 10, 2008) (serial numbers on heavy construction machines altered to hide source of goods).

Eleventh Circuit: Davidoff & CIESA v. PLD International Corp., 2000 WL 1901542 at *4 (S.D. Fla. September. 25, 2000) ("obliterated" "manufacturer's codes" "degrade[d] the appearance of the product," resulting in "a likelihood of confusion").

products because goods brought in for warranty service provide manufacturers with notice of potential defects and allow for correction in future runs or recalls before the defective products are sold.[91]

Service and Warranty Abuse

Product warranty and service abuse relate to the use of services or warranties to which the consumer or recipient is not entitled.[92] Warranties entail postsale support that the consumer receives from the manufacturer, including replacement parts and software and technical support.[93] In most cases of such abuse, business partners, such as third-party service organizations and resellers/distributors, use their positions fraudulently

---

[91] *Second Circuit:* Movado Group, Inc. v. Matagorda Ventures, Inc., 2000 WL 1855120 at *4 (S.D.N.Y. December 19, 2000) ("the sale of its watches without the factory warranty makes Defendant's watches distinctly different"); J. Atkins Holdings Ltd. v. English Discounts, Inc., 729 F. Supp. 945, 952 (S.D.N.Y. 1990) (grey goods "covered under qualitatively different warranty from those distributed in U.S. through authorized channels"); Osawa & Co. v. B&H Photo, 589 F. Supp. 1163 (S.D.N.Y. 1984) (the grey marketer sold cameras "at prices far below the prices of authorized [U.S.] dealers" and without the manufacturer's standard warranty); Fender Musical Instruments Corp. v. Unlimited Music Center, 1995 WL 241990 at *4 (D. Conn. February. 16, 1995) (product sold without usual service guaranty).

Federal Circuit: Bourdeau Brothers, Inc. v. International Trade Commission, 444 F.3d 1317, 1325 n.3 (Fed. Cir. 2006) (material difference where "the warranty services provided by Deere differ for the North American and European version[s]" of tractors); Gamut Trading Co. v. International Trade Commission, 200 F.3d 775, 777 (Fed. Cir. 1999) (material difference because Japanese tractors were not covered under United States warranty that provides for full coverage by specially trained "nationwide dealership network").

[92] PricewaterhouseCoopers. 2009. "Service blues: Effectively Managing the Multi-Billion Dollar Threat from Product Warranty and Support Abuse." 5. Available at https://agmaglobal.org/uploads/whitePapers/Final%20PwC%20Service%20Blues%20(10-26-09).pdf (accessed February 23, 2021).

[93] *Id.*

to obtain services or warranties.[94] Because they have access to service contract numbers and product serial numbers, they are in a better position to exploit weaknesses in the company's process of servicing claims.[95]

During a study conducted by the Alliance for Grey Market and Counterfeit Abatement (AGMA), five major forms of service abuses were identified.[96] The primary form of fraud is *undercoverage*. This occurs "when a customer buys a certain number of devices, but only a fraction of that many service contracts."[97] The customer then uses the service contracts to cover all of the devices, even though it did not purchase warranties for all of the products.[98] Undercoverage can affect a company's profitability in two ways. First, the manufacturers experience a drop in revenue because customers are purchasing fewer service contracts. Second, companies incur higher costs by "providing non-entitled services, including cost of customer support responding to invalid claims."[99] Moreover, customers

---

[94] Campbell. October 23, 2009. "Report: Warranty, Services Abuse Cost Vendors Billions Each Year." *CRN*. Available at www.crn.com/news/channel-programs/220900395/report-warranty-services-abuse-costs-vendors-billions-each-year.htm (accessed February 23, 2021).

[95] PricewaterhouseCoopers, N. 1 *supra*, at 9. Entitlement abusers may also include organized crime, career criminals, and unethical end-users. *Id.*

[96] *Id.* at 4. There are other sources of warranty and service abuses. First, "buy one, sell several" refers to a scheme where service companies buy a small number of service contracts, and resell those service contracts to a large number of customers. Second, "simple service abuse" occurs when a customer submits a service request for a replacement part to un-entitled products. Oftentimes, the company will fulfill the request because it has insufficient information to refute the claim. Third, in a "fraudulent service claim" scheme, a third-party service provider uses valid serial numbers and customer information to submit claims for services that are not actually provided. *Id.* at 11–12.

[97] Campbell, N. 3 *supra*.

[98] *Id.* "An offshoot of that is buying 'express' service for some equipment and using those overnight, or sometimes even shorter, response time guarantees for products that have a standard service contract." *Id.*

[99] PricewaterhouseCoopers. 2009. "Service blues: Effectively managing the multi-billion dollar threat from product warranty and support abuse." 8. Available at https://agmaglobal.org/uploads/whitePapers/Final%20PwC%20Service%20Blues%20(10-26-09).pdf (accessed February 23, 2021).

with valid service claims are negatively affected because service providers are supporting illegitimate claims and inventory for parts is being depleted.[100]

Overcoverage is the second form of fraud, and it occurs when a customer buys an equal number of service contracts and devices, but files more service inquiries than a manufacturer would normally expect.[101] These customers file excessive requests to acquire newer or updated devices for no charge.[102] Overcoverage causes manufacturers to suffer: (1) costs of replacing products shipped without valid entitlement; (2) skewed failure rate statistics, which affect research and development and quality assurance; and (3) a loss of product when returned products are disposed of because of questionable source or quality.[103]

The third form, *just-in-time coverage*, refers to a scheme where the customer does not purchase a service contract at the time of original purchase, but rather waits until a product breaks down to purchase one.[104] Shortly thereafter, the customer files a claim for service on the product, using the newly acquired coverage.[105] As a result, companies incur higher costs because more customers are filing service claims.[106] Moreover, revenues may be diverted to distributors or third-party servicers when they sell service plans to customers without compensating the company.[107]

Fourth, *nonreturn exploitation* occurs when customers submit requests for replacement goods on warranty or service contracts without

---

[100] *Id.*

[101] Campbell. October 23, 2009. "Report: Warranty, Services Abuse Cost Vendors Billions Each Year." *CRN*. Available at www.crn.com/news/channel-programs/220900395/report-warranty-services-abuse-costs-vendors-billions-each-year.htm (accessed February 23, 2021).

[102] *Id.*

[103] PricewaterhouseCoopers, N. 8 *supra*, at 8.

[104] *Id.* at 11.

[105] PricewaterhouseCoopers. 2009. "Service Blues: Effectively Managing the Multi-Billion Dollar Threat from Product Warranty and Support Abuse." 11. Available at https://agmaglobal.org/uploads/whitePapers/Final%20PwC%20Service%20Blues%20(10-26-09).pdf (accessed February 23, 2021).

[106] *Id.* at 8.

[107] *Id.*

sending back the defective products.[108] Because the defective part is never returned, companies have no idea whether the product was actually defective.[109] The United States Attorneys' Office prosecuted the president of a company for nonreturn exploitation.[110] In that case, the president created fictitious personal and company names, associated those names and particular Cisco parts with Cisco service contracts, and subsequently used the fictitious names to file false claims on defective parts.[111] When Cisco delivered the replacement parts to the president, he then sold them to Cisco equipment resellers for thousands of dollars.[112] According to the complaint, the president carried out the fraud more than 1,300 times, resulting in a loss to Cisco of $15,455,695.[113] As this case demonstrates,

---

[108] *Id.* at 11.

[109] J. Campbell. October 23, 2009. "Report: Warranty, Services Abuse Cost Vendors Billions Each Year." *CRN.* Available at www.crn.com/news/channel-programs/220900395/report-warranty-services-abuse-costs-vendors-billions-each-year.htm (accessed February 23, 2021). In some cases, the customer may return scrap, a different product, or even a counterfeit product.

[110] United States Department of Justice, "Owner and Operator of Massachusetts Computer Parts Company Pleads Guilty to Wire Fraud and Money Laundering in Connection with $15.4 Million Dollar Cisco Networking Equipment Fraud." (April 10, 2009). Available at www.justice.gov/sites/default/files/criminal-ccips/legacy/2012/03/15/dalyPlea.pdf (accessed February 23, 2021). In a similar case, Hewlett-Packard filed suit against four companies and one individual, alleging that the parties fraudulently filed false warranty claims from January 2001 to June 2002 to obtain parts and equipment that were then sold on the grey market. Zarley, "HP Files Suit Accusing Partners of Diverting Warranty Parts to Gray Market," CRN (November 04, 2003). Available at www.crn.com/news/channel-programs/18831000/hp-files-suit-accusing-partners-of-diverting-warranty-parts-to-gray-market.htm (accessed February 23, 2021).

[111] United States Department of Justice. April 10, 2009. "Owner and Operator of Massachusetts Computer Parts Company Pleads Guilty to Wire Fraud and Money Laundering in Connection with $15.4 Million Dollar Cisco Networking Equipment Fraud." Available at www.justice.gov/sites/default/files/criminal-ccips/legacy/2012/03/15/dalyPlea.pdf (accessed February 23, 2021).

[112] *Id.*

[113] *Id.* The president pleaded guilty to both wire fraud and money laundering. *Id.*

nonreturn exploitation can be a major source for grey market goods.[114] Consequently, companies suffer both revenue loss and downward price pressure.[115]

Finally, *software-download-key abuse* refers to a unique type of fraud where customers have access to web-enabled services.[116] In this scheme, a fraudster purchases a software service agreement from a company to gain system access.[117] Once the fraudster has access, he can download additional software without paying an additional license fee.[118] The reseller may also provide (share for profit) system access to unauthorized resellers or other parties who have not obtained valid licenses.[119] As with other forms of abuse, companies suffer lost revenues and licensing fees.[120]

Although there are many different forms of abuse, the negative consequences of each of these abuses are similar. They include lost revenues, increased costs, and greater consumer dissatisfaction.[121] The problem has become so severe that manufacturers in a survey reported that between 3 percent and 5 percent of their revenue is lost to services abuse.[122] That equates to about $9 to $15 billion, *annually*.[123]

---

[114] PricewaterhouseCoopers. 2009. "Service Blues: Effectively Managing the Multi-Billion Dollar Threat from Product Warranty and Support Abuse." 11. Available at https://agmaglobal.org/uploads/whitePapers/Final%20PwC%20Service%20Blues%20(10-26-09).pdf (accessed February 23, 2021).

[115] *Id.*

[116] *Id.* at 12.

[117] *Id.*

[118] *Id.*

[119] *Id.*

[120] PricewaterhouseCoopers. 2009. "Service Blues: Effectively Managing the Multi-Billion Dollar Threat from Product Warranty and Support Abuse." 8. Available at https://agmaglobal.org/uploads/whitePapers/Final%20PwC%20Service%20Blues%20(10-26-09).pdf (accessed February 23, 2021).

[121] *Id.*

[122] S. Campbell. October 23, 2009. "Report: Warranty, Services Abuse Cost Vendors Billions Each Year." *CRN*. Available at www.crn.com/news/channel-programs/220900395/report-warranty-services-abuse-costs-vendors-billions-each-year.htm (accessed February 23, 2021).

[123] *Id.*

Free Rider

Each year, companies spend millions of dollars on advertisements and marketing to develop goodwill, or "the association a consumer makes with a product concerning its reliability, its performance, and its relative value."[124] Goodwill includes establishing a reputation for safety, reliability, and service,[125] maintaining inventory,[126] and shaping the "contours" of the product's reputation.[127] Free riding results when unauthorized distributors use the established goodwill to sell counterfeit or grey market products.[128] Although free riders benefit from the reputation that manufacturers have created to sell their own products, they do not bear the marketing costs.[129]

There are two types of free riding: advertising free riding and point-of-sale service free riding. Advertising free riders reap the benefits of

---

[124] D.G. Mazur. 1990. "The Gray Market After *K Mart*: Shopping for Solutions." *Cardozo Arts & Ent. L.J.* 8, pp. 641–671. (Goodwill "includes a reputation for delivering a certain quality of product and service, brand awareness, pre-sale information and post-sale services (such as warranties), and is created by investment into marketing, customer service, quality control and protection from counterfeits."); N.T. Gallini, and A. Hollis. March 1999. "A Contractual Approach to the Gray Market." *Int. Rev. of Law & Econ.* 19, no. 1, pp. 1–2. See also, Dan Foam A/S v. Brand Named Beds, 500 F. Supp. 2d 296, 299 (S.D.N.Y. 2007) (Dan-Foam and Tempur-Pedic spent more than "$250 million in Connection with their Advertisements and Promotion of Products Bearing the TEMPUR-PEDIC Trademark in Order to Establish this Trademark in the Minds of Consumers as a Source of High-Quality Bedding Products.").

[125] Gamut Trading Co. v. International Trade Commission, 200 F.3d 775, 783 (Fed. Cir. 1999) ("Kubota-US has established a reputation for safety, reliability, and service that consumers associate with the 'Kubota' mark, and . . . the used tractors bearing the 'Kubota' mark undermine the investment that Kubota-US made in consumer goodwill").

[126] Osawa & Co. v. B & H Photo, 589 F. Supp. 1163, 1167 (S.D.N.Y. 1984).

[127] "Societe Des Produits Nestle, S.A. v. Casa Helvetia." 982 F.2d 633, 637 (1st Cir. 1992).

[128] "Societe Des Produits Nestle, S.A. v. Casa Helvetia" 982 F.2d 633, 637 (1st Cir. 1992); Lipner, *The Legal and Economic Aspect of Gray Market Goods*, 9 (1990).

[129] E. Dugan. 2001. "United States of America, Home of the Cheap and the Gray: A Comparison of Recent Court Decisions Affecting the U.S. and European Gray Markets." *Geo. Wash. Int. L. Rev.* 33, pp. 397–411.

consumer recognition and product reputation.[130] Point-of-sale service free riders misappropriate the services that authorized sellers provide to their customers.[131] These services include product instructions, spare parts, repair services, and warranties.[132]

When authorized sellers and brand owners lose sales to grey and counterfeit goods, their incentive to invest in their products decreases. This affects consumers in the long run because authorized sellers no longer have an incentive to provide product information or services and parts, and manufacturers lose their incentive to create new, innovative products.[133]

The fragrance industry faces serious free-riding problems. The cost of marketing perfumes can account for more than 30 percent of the selling price. However, shipping costs are relatively low, accounting for only 10 percent of the price.[134] Because grey marketers free ride on the authorized seller's marketing, they are able to price perfumes above marginal cost but below the price set by the authorized seller.[135]

---

[130] S.E. Lipner. 1990. *The Legal and Economic Aspect of Gray Market Goods*, 9; L.H. Liebeler. 1987. "Trademark Law, Economics and Grey-Market Policy." *Ind. L.J.* 62, 753, pp. 754–755.

[131] Liebeler, N. 7 *supra*, at 755.

[132] Lipner, N. 7 *supra*, at 9. "Another type of free rider in this category sells trademarked goods without taking sufficient safeguards to ensure product integrity by compromising on packing transportation, storage, or inspection costs in order to keep the price of goods lower." *Id.*

[133] Most trademark owners have a network of authorized sellers to whom they sell for resale to the consumers. These authorized sellers are responsible for the promotion, support and service of the product necessary to maintain the trademark's goodwill. See Coalition to Preserve the Integrity of American Trademarks v. United States, 598 F. Supp. 844, 850 (D.D.C. 1984), appeal docketed, No. 84-5890 (D.C. Cir. December 28, 1984).

[134] N.T. Gallini, and A. Hollis. March 1999. "A Contractual Approach to the Gray Market." *International Review of Law & Economics* 19, no. 1, p. 7.

[135] *Id.*

Impact on Economy and Society

In addition to the loss of sales and goodwill, counterfeit and grey goods impose social costs.[136] They "pose a triple threat to our nation by stealing from our economy, threatening U.S. jobs and potentially putting the safety of our citizens at risk."[137]

With respect to public safety,[138] grey and counterfeit products in automobiles and pharmaceuticals pose a serious risk to the public. In addition, substandard counterfeit and grey goods have infiltrated computer systems for air traffic control, banking, and the military, which puts these areas at risk for systemic failure.[139]

Just as serious a threat to public safety is the fact that each year, hundreds of billions of dollars from criminal enterprises are laundered through the sale of counterfeit and grey goods. "Evidence suggests that criminal networks use similar routes and modus operandi to move counterfeit goods as they do to smuggle drugs, firearms and people ... . Counterfeiting is a hugely profitable business, with criminals relying on the continued high demand for cheap goods coupled with low production costs. One widely used figure from the OECD places the value of counterfeiting in Europe of $250 billion per year. This figure, however, includes neither domestically produced and consumed counterfeit products nor the significant volume of pirated digital products being distributed via the Internet which would

---

[136] See "Departments of Justice and Homeland Security Announce 30 Convictions, More Than $143 Million in Seizures from Initiative Targeting Traffickers in Counterfeit Network Hardware" (May 06, 2010). Available at www.fbi.gov/news/pressrel/press-releases/departments-of-justice-and-homeland-security-announce-30-convictions-more-than-143-million-in-seizures-from-initiative-targeting-traffickers-in-counterfeit-network-hardware (accessed February 23, 2021) (according to the third Assistant Secretary of Homeland Security for ICE, "counterfeit and substandard hardware ... could affect the health and safety of others in a hospital setting or the security of our troops on the battlefield").

[137] Id.

[138] For further discussion, see § 2.01[2] supra.

[139] J. Hlavnicka. March 01, 2010. "Debunking Common Myths About Counterfeits: Falsely Branded Goods Waste Money, Cheat Buyers and Vendors, Cause Network Failures, and Risk Security. Preinfected Components, Anyone?" Business Week.

lead the figure of worldwide counterfeiting to be 'several hundred billion dollars more.'"[140] Terrorist groups, including the 1993 New York City World Trade Center bombers, use counterfeit goods to fund their operations.[141] Seized al-Qaeda training manuals recommend the sale of counterfeit goods for financing terrorist activities.[142] Similarly, the terrorists in the Madrid train bombings, which killed 191 people in 2004, funded their activities with proceeds from the sale of pirated CDs and DVDs.[143]

Unauthorized goods also negatively affect the U.S. economy. Counterfeit goods cause the loss of 750,000 jobs annually in the United States.[144] The U.S. automotive industry could hire 250,000 additional American workers if the sale of counterfeit parts were eliminated.[145] Additionally, because counterfeiters do not pay taxes, counterfeit goods cost the U.S. government an estimated $8.6 billion in tax revenue annually.[146] In New

---

[140] "The Illicit Trafficking of Counterfeit Goods and Transnational Organized Crime." United Nations Office on Drugs and Crime. Available at www.unodc. org/documents/counterfeit/FocusSheet/Counterfeit_focussheet_EN_HIRES. pdf (accessed February 23, 2021).

[141] S. Horwitz. October 01, 2001. "Cigarette Smuggling Linked to Terrorism." *Washington Post*, p. A1 (June 08, 2004); "Terrorist Links to Diversion and Counterfeiting." *Authentication News*, p. 9; Green and Bruce. April 2008. "Riskless Crime?" *Forbes*, pp. 101–102 (August 11, 1997).

[142] Pollinger, "From Balenciaga to Bombs: How Terrorist Groups are Exploiting the Global Counterfeit Goods Trade for Profit and Murder." *Harvard University Course Paper*. Available at https://euipo.europa.eu/ohimportal/documents/11370/71142/Counterfeiting+%26%20terrorism/7c4a4abf-05ee-4269-87eb-c828a5dbe3c6 (accessed February 23, 2021).

[143] A. Malone. May 24, 2010. "Revealed: The True Cost of Buying Cheap Fake Goods." *Daily Mail*. Available at www.dailymail.co.uk/news/article-471679/Revealed-The-true-cost-buying-cheap-fake-goods.html (accessed February 23, 2021).

[144] D. Thomas. January 09, 2009. "The Fight Against Fakes." *Harper's Bazaar*. Available at www.harpersbazaar.com/culture/features/a359/the-fight-against-fakes-0109/ (accessed February 23, 2021).

[145] "Statement of Senator Carl Levin on Intellectual Property Rights." June 07, 2006. Available at www.uscc.gov/sites/default/files/06_06_7_8_levin_carl.pdf (accessed February 23, 2021).

[146] "New Report Highlights Significant Contributions to the U.S. Economy by Copyright Industries." *Am. Chemical.* July 20, 2009.

York City alone, counterfeit goods deprived the city of $1 billion in sales tax revenues in one year.[147] The loss of this revenue significantly affects the ability to deliver essential services, such as education, public safety, and sanitation.

Grey market trading also hinders disadvantaged persons in third-world countries because many grey goods originally were humanitarian products offered for sale at steep discounts. For example, a manufacturer of typewriters for the blind sold its brailers to South Africa at less than half the price it sold them for in the United States.[148] The trademark holder offered this discounted price "as part of an effort to make these brailers more accessible to individuals in developing countries."[149] Unscrupulous grey marketers, using shell corporations posing as nonprofits, fraudulently obtained the discounted brailers and imported them back into the United States at sale prices well below the price offered by sellers in the United States.[150]

---

[147] City of New York, Office of the Comptroller; W.C. Thompson, Jr. November 2004. "Bootleg Billions: The Impact of The Counterfeit Goods on Trade on New York City."; See also, Y.T. Liu. 2001. "A Right to Vend: New Policy Framework for Fostering Street Based Entrepreneurs in New York City." Available at http://comptroller.nyc.gov/wp-content/uploads/documents/Bootleg-Billions.pdf (accessed February 23, 2021).

[148] "Perkins School for the Blind v. Maxi-Aids, Inc." 274 F. Supp.2d 319, 322 (E.D.N.Y. 2003).

[149] *Id.*

[150] *Id.*

CHAPTER 4

Incidents of Counterfeiting and Grey Marketing in Various Industries

Introduction

Grey market and counterfeit products are truly global threats. They affect small and large businesses in all industries worldwide. Once a business achieves brand recognition on a local or global level, it will become a target for counterfeiters or grey marketers, especially if there is a demand versus supply imbalance to exploit. The purpose of this chapter is to demonstrate the "no boundaries" aspect of grey market and counterfeit goods and to provide a "sample" sizing of these threats as well as ideas about how to successfully "combat" them. If there are executives or practitioners who think that grey market and counterfeit goods do not affect their businesses and clients because their industries are unique or that their business has high barriers of entry, perhaps this will persuade them to reconsider.

Grey Market and Counterfeit Goods

Fashion and Luxury Goods

The counterfeiting of fashion items (in some shape and form) has occurred for a very long time, and, arguably, clothes, shoes, and accessories historically have been (aside from currencies) the most frequently counterfeited items.

Global Brand Protection Report states that losses from the online sale of counterfeits amounted to $32 billion in 2017; however, it is difficult to estimate the actual losses to luxury brands. However, the harmful effects are even more menacing in the luxury industry where originality and scarcity are the main drivers of success. If a luxury good becomes commonplace, it will stop selling, and all the research and development, design, marketing, and advertising resources invested in creating something distinctive will be lost.[1]

The fashion brand Coach, Inc. filed a lawsuit in 2010, claiming that Kmart Corporation had infringed on the Coach Op Art trademark and copyright, and seeking unspecified damages and an order barring Kmart from infringing Coach trademarks.[2] According to Reuters, "Coach alleged that on Jan. 25, 2010 it paid $79.99 for a black-and-white three-piece luggage set, including two suitcases and a satchel, at a Kmart store …" The luggage set was examined by Coach and found to be counterfeit merchandise, reflecting a "confusingly similar" design and overall quality and craftsmanship that does not meet Coach's high quality standards … The average manufacturer's suggested retail price for an authentic Coach suitcase and satchel are approximately $500 and $350, respectively, and not $79.99 …"[3]

In another case,[4] the judge awarded significant damages against recidivist importers and retailers of counterfeit Louis Vuitton merchandise.[5]

According to *The Daily Telegraph*, on March 03, 2011, detectives in Sydney, Australia, confiscated more than 13,000 items branded Chanel, Gucci, Louis Vuitton, Tiffany & Co., Prada, and Jimmy Choo from a retail shop and a house. These goods, estimated to be worth $2 million, were suspected to be counterfeits. In February 2011, police confiscated

---

[1] www.worldtrademarkreview.com/anti-counterfeiting/counterfeit-luxury-goods (accessed March 02, 2021).

[2] Coach Inc. v. Kmart Corp., No. 10-01731 (S.D.N.Y. March 04, 2010).

[3] J. Stempel. March 04, 2010. "Coach Alleges Kmart Product Will Confuse Consumers." *Reuters*. Available at www.reuters.com/article/kmart-coach-lawsuit-idUSN0415997920100304 (last visited March 02, 2021).

[4] Louis Vuitton Malletier S.A. v. 486353 B.C. Ltd. (dba Wynnie Lee), 2008 BCSC 799, 2008 B.C.C. LEXIS 1315 (June 19, 2008).

[5] See § 14.08[3] *infra*.

more than 6,000 watches, pieces of jewelry, handbags, sunglasses, and other fashion items during a raid of market stalls at Sydney's Haymarket.[6]

The Italian fashion house Fendi recorded victory on March 11, 2010, when a federal judge ordered Filene's Basement to stop selling handbags and other goods bearing the Fendi name or trademark without permission.[7] The month before, the same court ordered Burlington Coat Factory Warehouse Corp. to pay Fendi approximately $4.7 million for selling Fendi-branded products without Fendi's permission.[8]

Other luxury goods companies are also trying to thwart alleged counterfeiters whose products they believe will damage their reputation, confuse consumers, and reduce sales. In March 2010, "[a]lone in Manhattan federal court, Burberry Group Plc (BRBY.L) sued TJ Maxx parent TJX Cos (TJX.N), Coach Inc. (COH.N) sued Sears Holdings Corp's (SHLD.O) Kmart unit, and LVMH Moet Hennessy Louis

---

[6] "$2m in Counterfeit Fashion Goods Seized." (March 04, 2011). Available at www.abc.net.au/news/2011-03-04/police-seize-2m-of-counterfeit-goods-in-sydney/1966136 (accessed March 02, 2021).

[7] Fendi Adele S.R.L. v. Filene's Basement, Inc., 2009 U.S. Dist. LEXIS 32615 (S.D.N.Y. March 24, 2009) (judge granted a permanent injunction, stopping sales of handbags and other goods bearing the Fendi name or trademark without permission: "[I]t is undisputed that Filene's used Fendi's famous marks and trade name in commerce after the marks had become famous.").

[8] Fendi Adele S.R.L. v. Burlington Coat Factory Warehouse Corp., Docket No. 06-cv-0085 (S.D.N.Y. 2010) (LBS) (MHD). Fendi Adele S.r.l., Fendi S.r.l. and Fendi North America, Inc. ("Fendi") announced on October 21, 2010, that it had settled its damages claims against Burlington Coat Factory Warehouse Corporation for the unauthorized sales of Fendi-branded goods, in the amount of $10,050,000.00. Burlington's agreement to pay followed a judge's recommendation (from August 2010) that Burlington be ordered to pay Fendi treble damages, attorney's fees, and costs for willful counterfeiting in the amount of $5.6 million, in addition to the $4.7 million judgment entered against Burlington in February 2010. "Fendi, Burlington in $10 mln Counterfeiting Accord." *Reuters*, October 21, 2010. Available at www.reuters.com/article/fendi-burlingtoncoatfactory-settlement/fendi-burlington-in-10-mln-counterfeiting-accord-idUSN2024526220101020 (accessed March 02, 2021).

Vuitton SA (LVMH.PA) sued Hyundai Motor Co (005380.KS) over alleged trademark violations."[9]

On January 24, 2020, following their sensational seizure in mid-November 2019 of six tons of counterfeit goods valued at €5.2 million, Austrian airport customs officers have uncovered yet another audacious case of product piracy. About 869 of the counterfeit goods seized, numbering approximately 2,400 in total, were fake luxury watches. Based on the retail selling price for watches of the luxury brands counterfeited in the consignment, the equivalent original value can be assumed to total €15 million. A Chinese trading company arranged for these counterfeit products, such as the luxury watches, designer shoes, and designer handbags, as well as branded tracksuits, to be processed via a transport company in Hong Kong, which forwarded the goods via Taiwan to Austria. Austria was only to serve as a hub; the ultimate destination of the 1.5 tons of counterfeit goods was Bratislava in Slovakia.[10]

ICT

In January 2012, Microsoft Corp. took legal action against a UK retailer, alleging production of counterfeits and sales of more than 94,000 sets of counterfeit Windows Vista and Windows XP recovery CDs to customers buying Windows-loaded PCs and laptops in the retailer's outlets across the United Kingdom.[11]

---

[9] J. Stempel. March 12, 2010. "Fendi Wins Counterfeits Injunction Against Filene's." *Reuters*. Available at www.reuters.com/article/fendi-filenes-counterfeit/fendi-wins-counterfeits-injunction-against-filenes-idUSN1212599020100312?edition-redirect=uk (accessed March 02, 2021).

[10] Federal Ministry of Austria. January 24, 2020. "Biggest Seizure of Counterfeit Luxury Watches in Austria, with an Equivalent Original Value Totalling EUR 15 million" www.bmf.gv.at/en/press/press-releases/2020/january-2020/Biggest-seizure-of-counterfeit-luxury-watches-in-Austria,-with-an-equivalent-original-value-totalling-EUR-15-million-.html (accessed March 02, 2021).

[11] "Microsoft Takes Legal Action Against U.K. Retailer Comet." January 04, 2012. Available at https://news.microsoft.com/2012/01/04/microsoft-takes-legal-action-against-u-k-retailer-comet/ (accessed March 02, 2021).

In September 2009, two brothers pled guilty to one count of counter-feit trafficking. The brothers sold counterfeit goods branded as Cisco to federal agencies; the U.S. military, including the Marine Corps and the Air Force; the Federal Bureau of Investigation (FBI); the Federal Aviation Administration (FAA); the Department of Energy; and several defense contractors, universities, school districts, and financial institutions.[12] Similarly, in 2008, in the Northern District of Georgia, a man was con-victed of trafficking in counterfeit Cisco-branded computer products, sentenced to 36 months' imprisonment, and ordered to pay $208,440 in restitution.[13]

On February 28, 2008, the Criminal and Cyber Divisions of the FBI, U.S. Immigration and Customs Enforcement, U.S. Customs and Border Protection, and the Royal Canadian Mounted Police (RCMP) jointly announced the results of "Cisco Raider," an international enforcement initiative led by the United States and Canada. The main purpose of "Cisco Raider" was to stop distribution of counterfeit networking equip-ment manufactured in China. At the time, the operation yielded "36 search warrants that identified approximately 3,500 counterfeit network

---

[12] The investigation was commenced by Immigration and Customs Enforce-ment (ICE) in February 2006 after U.S. Customs in an Anchorage FedEx facility inspected a shipment of 1,800 empty Cisco-branded boxes and labels suspected of being part of a common counterfeiting practice of shipping non-branded counterfeit computer goods separately from the branded counterfeit packaging and labeling. Further investigation revealed that in 2006 the defend-ants wired approximately $437,000 to China, where they routinely purchased Cisco-branded products for sale in the United States. "Texas brothers plead guilty to selling counterfeit 'Cisco' computer products *Customers included federal agencies and U.S. Military."* (September 08, 2009). Available at www.justice.gov/archive/usao/txs/1News/Releases/2010%20September/090710%20Edman.htm (accessed March 02, 2021).

[13] "[F]rom late 2003 until early 2007, Richard imported shipments of counter-feit Cisco computer components from China, and separate shipments of counter-feit Cisco-branded labels. He then affixed the fake labels to the fake components and sold the products on eBay, claiming that they were legitimate Cisco items. Richard sold over $1 million worth of counterfeit Cisco products in this manner." U.S. Department of Justice (February 28, 2018). Available at www.justice.gov/archive/opa/pr/2008/February/08_crm_150.html (accessed March 02, 2021).

components with an estimated retail value of over U.S. $3.5 million and has led to a total of ten convictions and U.S. $1.7 million in restitution."[14]

With today's technology, replicating most consumer electronics goods is not very difficult. The low prices of these counterfeit goods can be very appealing to retailers, particularly smaller ones that may not have a direct agreement with the vendor itself, and help leverage larger volume price points. "Technological advances have allowed hundreds of small Chinese companies, some with as few as 10 employees, to churn out what are known [in China] as shanzhai, or black market, cellphones, often for as little as $20 apiece."[15]

Counterfeiters do not stop at faking just individual goods; they can go much further. For example, in 2006, it was reported that a fake NEC company was found. According to this report, instead of producing fake devices, counterfeiters created an entire company with "[a]bout 50 products, including home entertainment systems, MP3 players, batteries, microphones and DVD players. In addition to knock-offs of NEC products, this bogus company had developed its own products that are not in the legitimate NEC's range ..."[16]

Counterfeit cell phones are often substandard and even dangerous: "Counterfeit mobile phones have unsafe battery packs that are prone to catching fire ... That is why some mobile phone manufacturers, such as Nokia, put so much time and effort into fighting the knockoff market."[17] Nokia sued two Chinese companies for a knock-off design of its 7260 model. "In May [2006], [Nokia was] awarded $1,360,000 from a Florida court in a counterfeit trafficking case against two other companies."[18]

---

[14] *Id.*

[15] D. Barboza. April 27, 2009. "In China, Knockoff Cellphones Are a Hit." *New York Times.* Available at www.nytimes.com/2009/04/28/technology/28cell.html (accessed March 02, 2021).

[16] P. Clarke. May 04, 2006. "Fake NEC Company Found, Says Report." *EE Times.* Available at www.eetimes.com/fake-nec-company-found-says-report/# (accessed March 02, 2021).

[17] Del Conte. October 27, 2006. "Nokia: Knockoff Cell Phones Could Explode." *PC Magazine.* Available at www.pcmag.com/article2/0,2817,2042934,00.asp (accessed March 02, 2021).

[18] *Id.*

Organisation for Economic Co-operation and Development (OECD) report "Trade in Counterfeit IT Goods" finds that smartphone batteries, chargers, memory cards, magnetic stripe cards, solid-state drives, and music players are also increasingly falling prey to counterfeiters. On average, 6.5 percent of global trade in information and communication technology (ICT) goods is in counterfeit products, according to the analysis of 2013 customs data. That is well above the 2.5 percent of overall traded goods found to be fake in a 2016 report.[19]

Transportation (Automotive and Aviation)

"Counterfeit parts in the automotive industry will soon be worth more than the annual gross domestic product of Canada, Brazil or Italy. According to World Trademark Review, the estimated global economic cost of counterfeiting in the automotive industry could reach $2.3 trillion by 2022. In Europe, it is estimated that €2.2 billion ($2.4 billion) is lost annually to counterfeit tire sales alone, while counterfeit battery sales effectively steal €180 million ($198 million) from other equipment manufacturers (OEMs)."[20]

According to a Motor & Equipment Manufacturers Association (MEMA) Brand Protection Council special report from January 2009:

> [T]he motor vehicle parts industry—those manufacturers who produce the parts and components used to repair everything from passenger cars to over-the-road trucks—have been hit hard by counterfeiting. It is estimated that counterfeiting costs the global motor vehicle parts industry $12 billion a year and $3 billion in the United States alone, according to the Federal Trade

---

[19] OECD. March 28, 2017. "Trade in ICT Counterfeit Goods." www.oecd.org/gov/trade-in-counterfeit-ict-goods-9789264270848-en.htm (accessed March 02, 2021).

[20] "Fighting the Fakes." Spring 2020. *Automotive Logistics.* Available at https://automotivelogistics.h5mag.com/al_fvl_spring_2020/counterfeit_parts (accessed March 02, 2021).

Commission (FTC) and the World Customs Organization in Interpol. The problem grows larger every year ...[21]

The FAA[22] estimates that about 520,000 counterfeit or unapproved parts are currently making it into planes annually, which is about 2 percent of the overall 26 million active parts. While 2 percent may seem like a small number, consider that a typical passenger aircraft contains up to 6 million parts, and consider the extreme tolerances for failure to which each part must adhere.[23] "A printout of an internal FAA database ... showed that from 1973 to 1993, bogus parts played a role in at least 166 U.S.-based aircraft accidents or less serious mishaps."[24]

In January 2009, a court in Beijing issued an injunction and ordered the defendant to pay approximately $3.11 million in compensation to a German bus maker for infringement of its design patents.[25]

Pharmaceuticals

According to a report on counterfeit drugs by Pfizer, profits from counterfeit pharmaceuticals today surpass profits made from heroin and cocaine.[26] A company that specializes in brand protection states that "The

---

[21] MEMA Brand Protection Council. 2009. "Understanding the Flow of Counterfeit and Gray Market Goods though the U.S. Automotive and Commercial Vehicle Parts Marketplace."

[22] See www.faa.gov/ (accessed March 02, 2021).

[23] "An Unnerving Reality", Aerospace Manufacturing and Design, (February 04, 2009) www.aerospacemanufacturinganddesign.com/article/an-unnerving-reality/ (accessed March 02, 2021).

[24] *Id.*

[25] Neoplan Bus GmbH, which held the design patent for its Starliner Coach since September 2004, filed a design patent infringement lawsuit against the defendants in the spring of 2006, claiming RMB 40 million (about U.S. $5.88 million) in damages. The court stated that the "Zhongwei's A9 Bus has Too Much in Common with Neoplan's Starliner for the Resemblance to be Accidental." "China Busmaker Compensates Neoplan for Copying" Available at www.theautochannel.com/news/2009/01/21/377745.html (accessed March 02, 2021).

[26] Finlay. 2021. "Counterfeit Drugs and National Security." *Stimson Center.* Available at www.files.ethz.ch/isn/127562/Counterfeit_Drugs_and_National_Security.pdf (accessed March 02, 2021).

World Health Organization (WHO) estimates that as much as 30 percent of the medicines sold in parts of Asia, Africa, and Latin America are counterfeit. In 2011, 64 percent of antimalarial drugs in Nigeria were found to be counterfeit. Worldwide, an estimated 10 percent of all medicines are counterfeit."[27]

The United Nations Office on Drugs and Crime (UNODC) cited the World Health Organization (WHO) estimates "[t]hat 10 percent of the global medicine supply is counterfeit, rising to 30 percent in the developing world ... as much as 50 to 60 percent of anti-infective medications tested in parts of Asia and Africa have been found to have active ingredients outside of the acceptable limit ..."[28]

According to *Science Daily*, "estimates suggest that global sales of counterfeit medicines are worth more than $75 billion, having doubled in just five years between 2005 and 2010 ..."[29]

In its 1999 "Guidelines for the Development of Measures to Combat Counterfeit Drugs,"[30] WHO provided an overview of the problem and identified key factors that enable drug counterfeiting. Among others, the key causes are the demand exceeding the supply, high prices, weak legislation and drug regulation, and lack of enforcement, absence of drug regulatory authority, transacting through many intermediaries, lack of regulation within free trade zones, and absence of a legal mandate for

---

[27] E.A, Blackstone, J.P. Fuhr, and S. Pociask. June 2014. "The Health and Economic Effects of Counterfeit Drugs." *7 Am. Health & Drug Benefits, No. 4 - Business.* Available at www.ahdbonline.com/issues/2014/june-2014-vol-7-no-4/1756-the-health-and-economic-effects-of-counterfeit-drugs (accessed March 02, 2021).

[28] UNODC. 2010. "The Globalization of Crime: A Transnational Organized Crime Threat Assessment." Available at www.unodc.org/documents/data-and-analysis/tocta/TOCTA_Report_2010_low_res.pdf (accessed March 02, 2021).

[29] ScienceDaily. February 22, 2012. "Fake Drug Sales Are Increasing On the Internet and Turning Up in Legitimate Supply Chains, Review Finds." Available at www.sciencedaily.com/releases/2012/02/120222093503.htm (accessed March 02, 2021).

[30] Department of Essential Drugs and Other Medicines, Guidelines for the Development of Measures to Combat Counterfeit Drugs, Geneva, Switzerland: World Health Organization, 1999. WHO/EDM/QSM/99.1. Available at http://apps.who.int/iris/bitstream/10665/65892/1/WHO_EDM_QSM_99.1.pdf (accessed March 02, 2021).

licensing of manufacture and import of drugs. The director-general of the Nigerian National Agency for Food and Drug Administration and Control (NAFDAC) wrote in a communiqué, "NAFDAC is of the view that a more permanent solution would be for developed countries to consider the need to approve legislation that would apply the same measure of quality standard to medicines consumed locally with those intended for export."[31]

The WHO estimates that "[t]he prevalence of counterfeit medicines ranges from less than 1 percent of sales in developed countries, to over 10 percent in developing countries, depending on the geographical area..." WHO provides analysis that:

"Counterfeiting is greater in those regions where regulatory and legal oversight is weaker, and therefore:

- Most developed countries with effective regulatory systems and market control (e.g. U.S., EU, Australia, Canada, Japan, New Zealand) currently have a very low proportion, i.e., less than 1 percent of market value. However, we must keep in mind that indications point to an increase in the prevalence of counterfeit medicines even in developed countries;
- Many developing countries of Africa, parts of Asia, and parts of Latin America have areas where more than 30 percent of the medicines on sale can be counterfeit. Other developing markets, however, have less than 10 percent; overall, a reasonable estimate is between 10 and 30 percent;
- Many of the former Soviet republics have a proportion of counterfeit medicines which is above 20 percent of market value—this falls into the developing country range;

---

[31] R.B. Taylor, O. Shakoor, R.H. Behrens, M. Everard, A.S. Low, J. Wangboonskul, . . . and J.A. Kolawole. 2001. "Pharmacopoeial Quality of Drugs Supplied by Nigerian Pharmacies." *Lancet Issue* 357, no. 9272, pp. 1933–1936.

- Medicines purchased over the Internet from sites that conceal their actual physical address are counterfeit in over 50 percent of cases ..."[32]

The President and CEO of the Pharmaceutical Research and Manufacturers of America (PhRMA) stated "it has long advocated for increasing jail sentences for counterfeit medicine crimes ..." to at least 20 years from the current "national average of three years."[33] He also commented on the Counterfeit Drug Penalty Enhancement Act passed by the Senate, "which would create national jail sentencing guidelines for criminals in the counterfeit medicine business. This is a step in the right direction..."[34]

In February 2021, Chinese police have arrested more than 80 people who were making counterfeit COVID-19 vaccines, state media said, as China races to inoculate millions before the Lunar New Year holiday. The gang had been putting saline water into vials and selling them as COVID-19 vaccines in an operation that had been running since last September, according to Xinhua News Agency. Police swooped on several locations across Beijing and multiple cities in the eastern provinces of Jiangsu and Shandong, seizing "more than 3,000 fake COVID-19 vaccines on the spot."[35]

During the week of action (March 03–10, 2020), authorities in participating INTERPOL countries inspected more than 326,000 packages of which more than 48,000 were seized by customs and regulatory authorities. Overall, authorities seized around 4.4 million units of illicit pharmaceuticals worldwide. Among them were:

---

[32] Impact. November 15, 2006. "Counterfeit Medicines: An Update on Estimates." Available at www.who.int/medicines/services/counterfeit/impact/TheNewEstimatesCounterfeit.pdf (accessed March 02, 2021).

[33] J.J. Castellani. March 28, 2012. "Counterfeit Medicine Threat Knocking on America's Doors." *The Hill.* Available at http://thehill.com/blogs/congress-blog/homeland-security/218699-john-j-castellani-president-and-ceo-pharmaceutical-research-and-manufacturers-of-america (accessed March 02, 2021).

[34] *Id.*

[35] Xinhua News Agency. February 03, 2021. "Chinese Police Bust Counterfeit Covid-19 Vaccine Ring." www.japantimes.co.jp/news/2021/02/03/asia-pacific/crime-legal-asia-pacific/fake-vaccines-ring/ (accessed March 02, 2021).

- Erectile dysfunction pills
- Anticancer medication
- Hypnotic and sedative agents
- Anabolic steroids
- Analgesics/painkillers
- Nervous system agents
- Dermatological agents
- Vitamins

More than 37,000 unauthorized and counterfeit medical devices were also seized; the vast majority of which were not only surgical masks and self-testing kits (HIV and glucose) but also various surgical instruments.[36]

Personal Hygiene Products and Cosmetics

In the summer of 2007, counterfeit Colgate toothpaste was found on discount-store shelves. The counterfeit toothpaste lacked fluoride, an ingredient found in real Colgate toothpaste, and some of the toothpaste contained diethylene glycol, which is typically used in antifreeze.[37]

Two Chinese brothers were charged with making fake "Gillette" razor blades in 2006. During a raid on the brothers' home, authorities confiscated approximately 30,000 blades. Approximately 120,000 blades with an estimated value of about $336,000 had been shipped to Shanghai.[38]

---

[36] Interpol. March 19, 2020. "Global Operation Sees a Rise in Fake Medical Products Related to COVID-19." www.interpol.int/en/News-and-Events/News/2020/Global-operation-sees-a-rise-in-fake-medical-products-related-to-COVID-19 (accessed March 02, 2021).

[37] Colgate-Palmolive. June 15, 2007. "Update: Counterfeit Toothpaste Falsely Labeled as 'Colgate'." Available at http://investor.colgate.com/ReleaseDetail.cfm?ReleaseID=249237&ReleaseType=Company&ReleaseDate=%7Bts '2007-06-15 00:00:00'%7D&header=&Archive (accessed March 02, 2021).

[38] Reuters. September 19, 2007. "Brothers on the Cutting Edge of Knock-Offs." Available at www.reuters.com/article/idUSPEK3851020070919 (accessed March 02, 2021).

Counterfeit makeup seizures in the United States and abroad are becoming alarmingly common. The Los Angeles Police Department (LAPD) confiscated counterfeit beauty products worth $700,000 in the Santee Alley fashion district in April 2018. And in January 2020, the LAPD seized more than $300,000 in counterfeit makeup products mimicking Kylie Jenner's company Kylie Cosmetics.[39]

In 2020, counterfeit facemasks, substandard hand sanitizers, and unauthorized antiviral medication were all seized under Operation Pangea XIII, which saw police, customs, and health regulatory authorities from 90 countries take part in collective action against the illicit online sale of medicines and medical products.

The operation resulted in 121 arrests worldwide and the seizure of potentially dangerous pharmaceuticals worth more than U.S. $14 million. The seizure of more than 34,000 counterfeit and substandard masks, "corona spray," "coronavirus packages," or "coronavirus medicine" reveals only the tip of the iceberg regarding this new trend in counterfeiting.[40]

In March, April, and May 2020, in many provinces across Turkey, more than 60 tons of counterfeit detergent and disinfectant products were seized, which directly threatened public health.[41]

Cameras

When it comes to fighting counterfeiting, leading producers of digital cameras are no exception. In its 2019 press release, Canon stated:

---

[39] Sayari Analytics, LLC & Sayari Labs, Inc. August 21, 2020. "The Dark Side of Beauty: An Overview of the Counterfeit Cosmetics Industry." *India-Forums.* Available at https://sayari.com/blog/the-dark-side-of-beauty-an-overview-of-the-counterfeit-cosmetics-industry/ (accessed March 02, 2021).

[40] Interpol. March 19, 2020. "Global Operation Sees a Rise in Fake Medical Products Related to COVID-19." www.interpol.int/en/News-and-Events/News/2020/Global-operation-sees-a-rise-in-fake-medical-products-related-to-COVID-19 (accessed March 02, 2021).

[41] Mondaq. May 13, 2020. "Turkey: Combating Counterfeit Hygiene Products, Along With COVID-19." www.mondaq.com/turkey/trademark/946264/combating-counterfeit-hygiene-products-along-with-covid-19 (accessed March 02, 2021).

Counterfeit accessories, such as battery packs, battery chargers and AC adapters, intended for use with Canon camera or video camcorder products, are not equipped with protective devices that meet Canon's designated quality standards. As a result, when they are used with these products, or charged, they can cause abnormal heat generation, leakage, ignition, rupture, and other malfunctions in the products they are used with. In the worst case, not only could these counterfeit accessories damage the cameras and video camcorders in which they are used, but they could also cause fire, burns, blindness, and other serious accidents and injuries. These types of incidents have been reported to, and investigated by, Canon and it has been determined that counterfeit accessories were often the direct cause of the malfunction that resulted in the damage and/or injury.[42]

Cameras are not the only concern. Accessories can often present much more danger to consumers than fake cameras. In its "Did you know that counterfeit accessories could melt and burn? Protect your Canon product from counterfeit accessories," released in 2019,[43] Canon confirmed circulation of counterfeit lithium-ion battery packs and chargers for Canon Digital Cameras and Digital Video Cameras on Internet auction sites. Canon warned that these fake batteries could cause camera malfunction, generate excessive heat, and rupture and leak, potentially causing fire and injuries to the users. In order to ensure the safety of its consumers, Canon provides examples of the counterfeit products, ways to identify the genuine product, and asks consumers not to buy the batteries on auction sites. Figure 4.1, Figure 4.2, and Figure 4.3 show an example of the genuine and the counterfeit battery packs images as released by Canon.

---

[42] "Did you Know that Counterfeit Accessories Could Melt and Burn? Protect your Canon Product from Counterfeit Accessories." January 08, 2019. Available at https://canoncanada.custhelp.com/app/answers/answer_view/a_id/4090/-/updated-safety-notice%3A-counterfeit-lithium-ion-battery-packs (accessed February 23, 2021).

[43] *Id.*

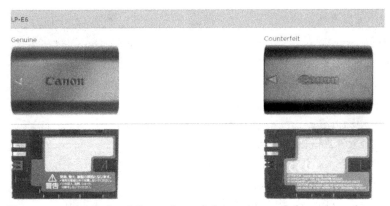

Figure 4.1 Example of Canon branded genuine and the counterfeit batteries (images)

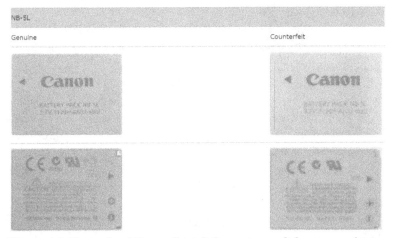

Figure 4.2 Example of Canon branded genuine and the counterfeit battery packs (images)

Figure 4.3 Example of Canon branded genuine and the counterfeit battery chargers (images)

Watches and Textbooks

The examples of grey market watches and textbooks are bundled together for the purpose of this book, not because they are in any way similar, but because they are involved in two of the most influential cases determining the "fate" of grey marketing in the United States. In *Costco Wholesale Corp. v. Omega, S.A.*, the Supreme Court affirmed the Ninth Circuit's ruling that the first sale doctrine is limited to copies "legally made ... in the United States."[44] This brought new hope to rights holders in the United States as a step in the right direction in the fight against grey marketing and was welcomed by rights holders affected by this global threat.[45]

---

[44] See § 8.07[3] *infra*.

[45] Costco Wholesale Corp. v. Omega, S.A., __ U.S. __, 131 S.Ct. 565, 178 L.Ed. 470 (2010). The Supreme Court's stated: "[t]he judgment is affirmed by an equally divided Court." *Id.*

The Costco Wholesale Corp. v. Omega, S.A., (08-1423) case began in 2004 after Omega sold the Omega Seamasters watches to authorized distributors outside the United States, who sold the watches to unnamed buyers who subsequently resold them to a company that sold them to Costco in the United States. Costco then sold the watches for U.S. $1,299, while Omega was selling the same model for $1,999 MSRP. Omega sued Costco, claiming copyright infringement based on the "Omega Globe Design" logo engraved on the back of the case, which is registered with the U.S. copyright office.

Omega appealed to the Ninth Circuit Court of Appeals in San Francisco, which reversed the decision, arguing that the first sale doctrine only applies to goods manufactured in the United States. Omega S.A. v. Costco Wholesale Corp., 541 F.3d 982 (9th Cir. 2008).

Costco appealed to the U.S. Supreme Court, which in October 2010, in a 4–4 decision, affirmed the lower court's (the 9th Circuit) ruling. Omega, S.A. v. Costco Wholesale Corp., 541 F.3d 982 (9th Cir. 2008), *aff'd per curiam* No. 08-1423, 562 U.S. ___ (U.S. December 13, 2010).

While affirming the lower court's decision, "[i]t is not an endorsement of the Ninth Circuit's interpretation of the first sale doctrine, nor does it set a nationwide precedent. ... this recent development explores the implications of the decision, specifically, the impact on the grey market, consumers, and the manufacturing industry in the United States, as well as the implications for the utility of copyright as an import control ... ." Aldridge. Spring 2011. "Costco v. Omega and the First Sales Doctrine." *N.C.J.L. & Tech* 12, pp. 325–344. Available at https://core.ac.uk/download/pdf/151515334.pdf (accessed March 02, 2021).

For further discussion of this case, see § 8.07[3] infra.

Another important case regarding the future of grey markets is *Kirtsaeng v. John Wiley & Sons*,[46] in which the Supreme Court decided to "[t]ake a second crack at reconciling two apparently contradictory provisions in the Copyright Act: one that permits buyers to resell goods without worrying about permission from U.S. copyright holders, and another that controls the importation of copyrighted material into the United States…"[47] Although the district court ruled in favor of John Wiley & Sons and imposed statutory damages, the Supreme Court decided by a 6-to-3 vote that, under the Copyright Act, the first sale doctrine does apply to works first sold abroad, and that importation of those goods for resale into the United States is not an infringement.[48] This decision gives a green light to purchase abroad, import, and resell lower-priced "grey market" copyrighted goods and will likely have noticeable consequences for the international market for copyrighted works and goods.[49]

---

[46] Kirtsaeng v. John Wiley & Sons, __ U.S. __, 132 S.Ct. 1905, 182 L.Ed.2d 770 (2012). Kirtsaeng, a native of Thailand, came to the United States to attend college and decided to make money to pay for his education by buying foreign-made, cheaper editions of college textbooks abroad, and bringing them to the United States for resale. Overall, Kirtsaeng had sold $37,000 worth of Wiley & Sons textbooks when Wiley & Sons sued in federal court in New York.

In John Wiley & Sons, Inc. v. Supap Kirtsaeng, 654 F.3d 210 (2d Cir. 2011), the judge rejected Kirtsaeng's claim relying on the first-sale doctrine (Copyright Act, 17 U.S.C. § 109(a)), concluding that the doctrine does not apply to goods made abroad. http://caselaw.findlaw.com/us-2nd-circuit/1577369.html (accessed March 02, 2021). The Second Circuit upheld a district court decision that the first sale doctrine does not apply to copyrighted works produced outside of the United States.

[47] Reuters. April 17, 2012. "Supreme Court Takes Another Look At Gray Market Resales." Available at www.reuters.com/article/us-frankel-graymarket/supreme-court-takes-another-look-at-gray-market-resales-idUS-BRE83G15H20120417 (accessed March 02, 2021).

[48] Kirtsaeng v. John Wiley & Sons, Inc., __ U.S. __, 133 S.Ct. 1351, 185 L.Ed.2d 392 (2013).

[49] A. Albanese. March 19, 2013. "Supreme Court Upholds First Sale in Landmark Kirtsaeng Ruling." *PW.com*. Available at www.publishersweekly.com/pw/by-topic/digital/copyright/article/56435-supreme-court-upholds-first-sale-in-landmark-kirtsaeng-ruling.html (accessed March 02, 2021). For further discussion of these cases, see § 8.07[3] *infra*.

Toys

The UK Anti-Counterfeiting Group estimates "[t]hat 12 percent of toys for sale in the UK are fakes..."[50] According to Toy Industries of Europe, counterfeit toys with a "retail value of €24,123,549 were seized at the EU's external border in 2010 ... China was the main source (98.76 percent) of counterfeit toys in 2010..."[51]

U.S. Customs and Border Protection officers at the Port of New York/Newark have seized more than $1 million in counterfeit toys ahead of the holidays, authorities announced Monday (December 21, 2020). A total of 141,112 UNO card games; 9,600 LOL Surprise! Under Wraps balls; and 1,980 LOL Surprise! Under Wraps capsule toys were recovered, officials said, and if authentic, they would have a manufacturer's suggested retail price of approximately $1.3 million. [52]

In April 2012, "The RCMP raided four stores across Winnipeg ... , seizing $70,000 worth of counterfeit plushies, T-shirts, and toys..." that carried a variety of brand names, including Nintendo, John Deere, Hello Kitty, NHL, Hasbro, Sesame Street, and Transformers. The Royal Canadian Mounted Police worked with the rights holders to identify stores that sell these counterfeits.[53]

---

[50] M. King. December 07, 2011. "Christmas Shoppers Warned Over Flood of Counterfeit Toys." *Guardian.* Available at www.guardian.co.uk/money/2011/dec/07/christmas-shopping-counterfeit-toys?newsfeed=true (accessed March 02, 2021).

[51] "Counterfeit toys worth almost €25 billion seized at EU borders." July 14, 2011. *Toy Industries of Europe.* Available at www.tietoy.org/news/article/counterfeit-toys-worth-almost (accessed March 02, 2021).

[52] "More than $1M in counterfeit toys seized at Port of New York/Newark." December 22, 2020. *Eyewitness News,* see https://abc7ny.com/counterfeit-toys-port-of-new-yorknewark-customs-and-border-protection-toy-bust/8955581/ (accessed March 02, 2021).

[53] Winnipeg Free Press–Online Edition. April 27, 2012. "RCMP Seize Counterfeit Toys from City Stores." Available at www.winnipegfreepress.com/local/RCMP-seize-counterfeit-toys-from-city-stores-149275025.html (accessed March 02, 2021).

Near the end of 2011, U.S. Customs and Border Protection officers confiscated 13,843 counterfeit toys worth $198,000 at the Otay Mesa San Diego border crossing. Shipments included:

> 5,472 counterfeit Barbie dolls, 24 counterfeit Cinderella dolls, 12 counterfeit Bratz dolls, 4,692 counterfeit Barbie medical playsets, 1,600 counterfeit hand-held Tetris electronic games, 36 counterfeit Lego blocks sets, 20 Chargers Bolt masks, 10 Superman mask/cape combinations, 9 Spiderman mask/cape combinations, 816 toy cell phones with counterfeit Barbie, Mickey Mouse, and Winnie the Pooh images, and 1152 counterfeit Disney's 101 Dalmatians toy dogs.

According to the officials, most of the toys were transshipments to Mexico but some were also destined for the U.S. market.[54]

Cigarettes

In June 2020, three men were arrested in simultaneous raids on at least eight locations for their suspected involvement in the import of 1.5 million packets of counterfeit cigarettes with a street value of over $1.1 million. The cigarettes, plastered with fake trademark labels, were discovered in three containers by Singapore Customs awaiting re-export to other countries.

"The trademark right holder of the cigarettes had lodged a notice with Singapore Customs requesting the cigarettes' seizure as they violate intellectual property rights, leading to the operation."[55]

---

[54] U.S. Customs and Border Protection. December 2010. "CBP Seizes More Than 10,000 Toys in the Months Before Holidays." Available at www.cbp.gov/newsroom/local-media-release/cbp-seizes-more-10000-toys-months-holidays (accessed March 02, 2021).

[55] The Straits Times. June 02, 2020. "1.5 Million Packets of Counterfeit Cigarettes Seized, Three Arrested." www.straitstimes.com/singapore/15-million-packets-of-counterfeit-cigarettes-seized-three-arrested (accessed March 02, 2021).

The Organized Crime and Corruption Reporting Project reports that "Chinese counterfeit cigarette factories now churn out an unprecedented 400 billion cigarettes a year, enough to supply every U.S. smoker with 460 packs a year..."[56]

In July 2011, in Federal Court in Chicago, two tobacco companies filed suit against 12 local wholesale distributors, alleging trademark infringement, unfair competition, and counterfeit trafficking, and seeking to recover substantial damages, costs, and fees.[57]

Candy and Soft Drinks

Copyright law can be used successfully to litigate against grey marketers when a product or its packaging bears a particular design, such as a logo. In such a case, the competitor's actions may constitute copyright infringement.[58]

---

[56] P. Chen. 2021. "China's Marlboro Country: A Massive Underground Industry Makes China the World Leader in Counterfeit Cigarettes." Available at www.reportingproject.net/underground/index.php?option=com_content&view=article&id=9&Itemid=22 (accessed March 02, 2021).

[57] Top Tobacco L.P. v. Midwestern Cash and Carry LLC, Case No. 1:11-cv-04460 (N.D. Ill. September 27, 2012).

[58] In Kraft Canada Inc. v. Euro Excellence Inc., 2004 F.C.J. No. 804, 2004 FC 652 (2006), Kraft sought to prevent its former distributor from distributing unauthorized TOBLERONE® and CÔTE D'OR® chocolate bars Euro imported from Europe and sold in Canada in the original European packaging and additional labels to comply with Canadian regulations. Kraft obtained Canadian rights to the artwork on the chocolate bar wrappers (specifically a mountain, a bear, an elephant, a shield, and scripted wording) and secured copyright registrations in Canada by its two affiliates. Kraft alleged that Euro was distributing the copyrighted artwork on the chocolate wrappers even though the TOBLERONE® and CÔTE D'OR® chocolate bars were genuine.

Pursuant to Section 27(2) of the Canadian Copyright Act, the Federal Court of Canada awarded $300,000 in damages to Kraft for past infringement, costs and interest, and ordered Euro to stop "selling, distributing, exposing or offering for sale copyright packaging design elements." Subsequently, the court held that the defendant Euro could sell the chocolate bars providing Euro covered up the copyrighted artwork on the packaging. (2004 F.C.J. No. 1015, 2004 FC 832, notice of appeal filed on May 12, 2004 (Docket A-258-04)).

The strategy employed by Kraft has a number of benefits: (i) A copyright registration can be obtained quickly and inexpensively; (ii) copyright is the longest

In July 2011, a joint effort by local police and law enforcers resulted in warehouses storing 20 tons of counterfeit drinks being shut down. The goods seized consisted of "4,500 boxes of fake beverages, many of which bore brand names like Coca-Cola, Wahaha and Jinmailang..."[59] In 2012, a similar effort in Nigeria led to the confiscation of fake energy drinks with fake labeling and packaging different from that of the original product.[60]

Pepsico filed trademark infringement and dilution charges against a company for importing and selling grey market drinks manufactured in Mexico bearing the Pepsi® and Manzanita Sol® trademarks and not authorized for sale in the United States. Pepsico alleged that the Mexican drink is materially different from authorized products sold in the United States in many ways, including labeling that is not in accordance with the Food and Drug Administration regulations.[61]

---

lasting of all intellectual property rights: usually copyright will last for the duration of the author's life and 50 years thereafter; (iii) there are no time limits for obtaining a copyright registration; (iv) copyright applies to the act of creation of a work; and (v) in connection with grey market products, the copyright law can be used where patent and trademark law could not be asserted, and require evidence that the grey market products are materially different from the trademarked products authorized for sale in Canada. For further discussion, see § 14.08 *infra*.

[59] Asian One News. July 23, 2011. "20 Tons of Fake Drinks Confiscated in China." *China Daily/Asia News Network*. Available at www.asiaone.com/News/Latest+News/Asia/Story/A1Story20110723-290603.html (accessed March 02, 2021).

[60] "NAFDAC Raids Markets For Fake Energy Drink." March 07, 2012. Available at www.nigeriaa2z.com/2012/03/07/nafdac-raids-markets-for-fake-energy-drink/ (accessed March 02, 2021).

[61] Pepsico, Inc. v. SPE Trading, Inc., CV10-6833 DDP (C.D. Cal. 2010). U.S. trademark owners can prevent the importation of grey goods that are "materially different" from those authorized for sale in the United States, as will be discussed further in Ch. 6 *infra*. In determining what is considered "materially different," 19 C.F.R. § 133.2(e) provides (among others) the following examples of differences between authorized and grey market products: (i) performance and/or operational characteristics; (ii) the specific composition such as chemical formula, product components, structure, and so on; (iii); differences resulting from legal or regulatory requirements, certification, and so on; (iv) other differences that would likely lead to consumer deception or confusion.

Humanitarian Sales to Third-World Countries

Drugs sold to Third-World countries at substantially reduced prices are often diverted and then sold in the grey market in the United States and Europe at prices lower than the market prices:

> [D]rugs sold at reduced cost in the Third World will find their way back to markets in North America and Europe ... through ... grey market[s] ... History offers numerous examples of corrupt officials in developing countries who have sold drugs donated to help those nations, and sent the proceeds to private Swiss bank accounts. The high cost of antiretrovirals ... presents even greater incentive for Westerners to procure them from developing countries ... This would, indeed, cut into pharmaceutical companies' profits, and, by extension, their ability to fund innovation..."[62]

In one case, GlaxoSmithKline, in a humanitarian gesture, sold two HIV drugs in a different colored coating (red) at cost to African markets in order to differentiate them from the more expensive tablets destined for markets elsewhere.[63] In 2005, the company challenged a UK parallel trader for allegedly supplying the red tablets to the National Health Service.[64]

PepsiCo, Inc. v. Pacific Produce, Ltd., 2000 U.S. Dist. LEXIS 12085 (D. Nev. 2000), cites a number of cases where product failure to comply with FDA regulations with respect to the labeling constituted a sufficient material difference.

[62] S. Williams. May 2002. "Innovation vs. Access: Two Epidemics Transform the Pharmaceutical Patent Law Debate into an International Controversy." *J. Young Investigators.* 5, no. 8. Available at www.jyi.org/2002-may/2002/5/23/innovation-vs-access-two-epidemics-transform-the-pharmaceutical-patent-law-debate-into-an-international-controversy (accessed March 02, 2021).

[63] In-PharmaTechnologist.com. May 24, 2005. "GSK to Use Technology to Prevent Parallel Imports." Available at www.in-pharmatechnologist.com/Packaging/GSK-to-use-technology-to-prevent-parallel-imports (accessed March 02, 2021).

[64] R.C. Bird, and P.E. Chaudhry. 2010. "Pharmaceuticals and the European Union: Managing Gray Markets in an Uncertain Legal Environment." *Va. J. Int. L.* 50, no. 3, p. 751. Available at http://opiniojuris.org/2010/04/16/pharmaceu-

A Yale University economist proposed that drug companies surrender their patent rights in poor countries but enforce them in wealthier ones,[65] thereby creating two parallel drug markets. In poor countries, competition among generic drug makers would keep prices low, while in wealthier countries high prices would fund ongoing R&D. Such tiered pricing, however, would likely present a challenge for the drug makers to confine these cheaper drugs within the borders of the poorer countries, and at the same time an opportunity for grey marketers to import drugs from poorer to wealthier countries. "Pfizer has already produced a new tablet formulation of fluconazole, so that the free drug provided to poor countries can be distinguished from the original capsule formulation sold at market rate in developed countries..."[66]

"In some cases, 'charities' have approached donors for humanitarian goods allegedly destined for such clearly benign causes as schools, hospitals, and refugee camps, only to convert donations into [funds and] material for armed terrorist groups. This has been particularly the case in the West Bank and Gaza ... The most obvious way to do this is by dumping the unneeded goods on the grey market, which is always willing to accept below-wholesale products..."[67]

---

ticals-and-the-european-union-managing-gray-markets-in-an-uncertain-legal-environment/ (accessed March 02, 2021).

[65] Highleyman. Summer/Autumn 2001. "The Global Epidemic." *The Body*. Available at http://img.thebody.com/legacyAssets/26/11/patents.pdf (accessed March 02, 2021).

[66] *Id.*

[67] D.E. deKieffer. 2007. "Trade Diversion as a Fund Raising and Money Laundering Technique of Terrorist Organizations." In *Counterfeiting the Financing Of Terrorism*, Ch. 6 eds.

CHAPTER 5

Proactive Internal Procedures to Combat Counterfeiting and the Grey Market

When it is obvious that the goals cannot be reached, don't adjust the goals, adjust the action steps.

—Confucius

Overview

Understandably, the parties that are most concerned about grey marketing and counterfeiting are the rights holders and their authorized channels. To avoid damage to their brand reputation and erosion of their profits, the parties will jointly seek ways to curb the grey market and counterfeit problem, equipping themselves with instruments from the intellectual property rights (IPR) "war chest" currently available to them—unfair competition, trademark and copyright laws, or other prosecutable IPR infringements. The parties may exercise their IPR against the importing, sale, and advertising of grey market and counterfeit goods.[1]

---

[1] In 2002, for example, after four years of battle in courts, Levi Strauss was able to prevent Tesco (UK-based supermarket) from selling grey market Levi's jeans. "Tesco defeated in cheap jeans battle." BBC News (July 31, 2002), available at http://news.bbc.co.uk/1/hi/business/2163561.stm (accessed March 04, 2021); Case T-415/99 Levi Strauss v. Tesco Stores. Tesco Stores Ltd, Tesco plc (C-415/99), available at http://curia.europa.eu/juris/liste.jsf?num=C-414/99&language=en (accessed March 05, 2021).

There are limits to enforcing IPR, such as the first sale doctrine in the United States[2] and the doctrine of the exhaustion of rights in the European Union.[3] There are, however, other ways to counteract grey market activities. Rights holders may refuse to honor the warranties for grey market goods, and they can justify this by arguing that the higher price for the products sold by authorized distributors is due to a higher level and quality of service even though rights holders do not necessarily control authorized distributors' prices (voiding warranty will initially cause some negative publicity and resulting customer loyalty issues).[4] They can

---

[2] In Summit Technology, Inc. v. High-Line Medical Instruments, 922 F. Supp. 299 (C.D. Cal. 1996), the court held that medical laser devices made for sale abroad were not "grey market goods" when they were reimported into the United States because plaintiff distributed systems abroad itself, making the goods "genuine" and not "parallel," thus reducing the likelihood of customers' confusion regarding the source of these goods.

[3] In Sun Microsystems Inc. v. M-Tech Data Ltd., [2009] EWHC 2992 (Pat) (November 25, 2009), the High Court of England and Wales held that Sun Microsystems, Inc. was entitled to summary judgment in respect to parallel import of computer equipment by M-Tech Data Ltd., and rejected M-Tech's defense of exhaustion of rights by Sun Microsystems. However, in Oracle America Inc. (formerly Sun Microsystems Inc.) v. MTech Data Ltd., [2010] EWCA Civ 997, the Court of Appeal (CA) overturned the decision to grant summary judgment and remitted the case to the High Court, ordering "that Oracle makes an application in the Chancery Division for a case management conference (CMC) to be held as soon as practicable," bearing in mind that a reference to the European Court of Justice (ECJ) might be necessary. See www.bailii.org/ew/cases/EWCA/Civ/2010/997.html (accessed March 05, 2021). This is a worrying development as it threatens the clear trademark jurisprudence applied by UK courts in favor of an unclear competition law. (Until this judgment by the CA, the approach of the UK courts (and the ECJ) to parallel imports had been clear and consistent: unless the parallel importer can establish that the goods were sold in the European Economic Area ("EEA") by the trademark owner or with its consent, the parallel importer commits trademark infringement.)

[4] Kia Motors America, Inc. v. Autoworks Distributing, 2009 WL 499543, 90 U.S.P.Q.2d 1598 (D. Minn. 2009), held that Kia's warranties for the cars and the parts it sells (which included a basic warranty, a powertrain warranty, and genuine Kia replacement parts and accessories warranty), were materially different

also leverage existing local laws governing distribution and packaging (e.g., the language on labels, nutritional disclosure, units of measurement, operating instructions, and safety and regulatory certification) to differentiate and curb unauthorized resale.[5] Rights holders may also differentiate products with distinct product numbers (serial numbers) in different parts of the world (even though otherwise the products may be identical), so they can identify unauthorized imports. Some manufacturers use batch codes to enable bulk tracing of their products and identify grey imports. As a result, some dealers and brokers often remove the numbers or relabel the products with fake labels in order to conceal the source of their supplies. In the United States, courts have acknowledged that such decoding or alteration that causes even slight damage to the product is a material alteration, rendering the product infringed.[6] Advertising of grey market goods on Google, eBay, or other auction websites can be successfully countered with enforcement of trademark or copyright laws. This can be successfully addressed by working directly with the auction sites, as many of them will remove listings of such products even in countries

---

from limited replacement parts warranty sold with defendant's grey market cars since defendant's car parts lacked plaintiff's genuine warranty, making Kia's claim sufficient under 43(a) of the Lanham Act.

[5] In Gamut Trading Co. v. International Trade Commission, 200 F.3d 775 (Fed. Cir. 1999), the grey marketer sold Kubota tractors in the United States that were manufactured in and authorized for sale in Japan. The court held that Kubota-Japan specifically manufactured U.S. tractors for use in the United States and that (i) the controls, instructions, and warnings as well as users' manuals were all in English; and (ii) Kubota-US sold the tractors through nationwide dealerships providing full maintenance and repair service. The court rejected the grey market importer's claims that the customers knew they were buying Japanese tractors because the Japanese labels were readily noticeable and therefore there was no material difference, and held that the lack of English control, instructional, warning labels, and service manuals was material, especially since they were essential to the safe operation of the tractors.

[6] See Zino Davidoff SA v. CVS Corp., 571 F.3d 238 (2d Cir. 2009), finding that defendant infringed plaintiff's trademarks by selling plaintiff's products without a unique production code (UPC), which impeded the trademark holder's quality control and subjected the reputation of plaintiff's mark to risk of injury.

where their purchase and use is not against the law.[7] The development of regional codes used for DVDs, and other digital media regional-lockout techniques, are examples of technological solutions designed to restrict the flow of grey market goods.

The first step in protecting IP is to strengthen the rights holders' IPR by:

- Registering trademarks with the U.S. Patent and Trademark Office (generally Title 15, Sections 1051 et seq. of the United States Code) and recording the registrations with U.S. Customs (generally Title 19, Section 133.2 of the Code of Federal Regulations); outside of the United States, registering with the appropriate country's patent and trademark office and Customs authorities (where required).
- Registering copyrightable works with the Copyright Office (generally Title 17, Section 101 of the United States Code; Title 37, Section 202 of the Code of Federal Regulations) and recording the registrations with U.S. Customs (generally Title 19, Section 133.31 of the Code of Federal Regulations).

---

[7] On eBay in particular, registered rights owners of certain marks can use eBay's Verified Rights Owner (VeRO) program—automated Internet-based reporting tool allowing registered rights owners to report to eBay any listed offering potentially infringing on their IP right, so that eBay can remove such reported listings. Tiffany, Inc. v. eBay, Inc., 576 F. Supp.2d 463, 478–479 (S.D.N.Y. 2008) (discussing eBay's efforts to combat counterfeit sales in part through VeRO, which registered rights owners of marks can use as a commercially effective method to initiate takedown of auction listings of infringing items as a means of protecting intellectual property and maintaining brand integrity. The court found that plaintiff's reporting of defendant's sale of plaintiff's clearly marked goods on eBay, and eBay's subsequent removal of these unauthorized goods and suspension of defendant's account, were within both plaintiff's and eBay's rights. ¶¶ 13–14, 17. The court granted plaintiff's motions for summary judgment regarding federal trademark counterfeiting, federal trademark infringement, federal unfair competition, and trademark infringement and unfair competition under California common law and the California Business & Professions Code).

- Cultivating use of IP. A brand owner should use trademarks and trade names consistently and as adjectives. The ® symbol should be used for all registered trademarks and a copyright notice (© 2021 [Company Name]) should be used for all copyrightable works.
- Monitoring supply and distribution channels, anticipating problems, and enforcing policies. Suppliers, wholesalers, distributors, retailers, and customers can all be valuable resources in identifying and responding to infringements in the marketplace. Counterfeit, pirated, and grey market goods can appear anywhere in the distribution channels. Monitoring Internet sale and auction sites, flea markets, closeout and dollar stores, house party programs, and even major retail chains is a good place to start.

Once a brand owner builds "the foundations" by establishing and strengthening its intellectual property rights, the subsequent step is to develop a plan of action including these four critical prerequisites:

- *Knowing (setting) the goals.* Impeding the infringements and related loss is usually the highest priority. Other goals may include identifying the sources of the infringing goods, creating positive media and customer awareness, deterring other infringers, and, of course, financial recovery. Identifying clear goals and priorities at the outset is crucial to efficient and effective enforcement.
- *Selecting ("painting") the targets carefully.* Even if a brand owner dedicates significant and, often, global resources to its brand protection efforts, it cannot possibly be everywhere at all times and address every infringement that occurs. Selecting the right targets should be based on selection criteria that have to be consistent with or complement the set of goals. Some criteria are high impact (volume and dollar) value from the potential recoveries, and the "low hanging fruit"—that is pursuing targets with the already existing resources and framework and that yield positive returns—either cash recoveries, positive publicity, and so on. The targets can be

manufacturers, individual sellers, importers, brokers, distributors, retailers, or other participants in the manufacturing and
distribution chain.

- *Knowing (selecting) the appropriate enforcement option.*
  The enforcement options can be very broad and, again, should
  complement the overall goals. The enforcement actions may
  include Cease and Desist (C&D) letters, website or ecommerce listing takedowns, government or law enforcement
  referrals, Customs seizures, and pursuing civil and criminal
  litigation. Some industry or nonprofit associations might also
  provide enforcement options that are available to brand owners. Seizure orders, injunctions, and damages (including statutory damages) are available against counterfeiters and vary by
  jurisdiction in the United States (see Title 15, Sections 1116
  and 1117 of the United States Code). Injunctions, seizure
  orders and forfeiture, and damages (including statutory damages) are also available under the U.S. Copyright Act (see Title
  17, Sections 502, 503 and 504 of the United States Code).[8]

- *Knowing the constraints.* Brand owners may face budget,
  resource, or time constraints. As a result, they may choose not
  to enforce certain IPR violations in certain jurisdictions or
  markets or where there is minimum risk of consumer confusion. Knowing and evaluating the constraints are essential
  factors in setting goals and selecting an enforcement strategy,
  and in running successful brand protection efforts.

---

[8] "DSC Communications Corp. v. DGI Technologies, Inc., 898 F. Supp. 1183
(N.D. Tex. 1995)." the court held that defendant's copying of firmware embedded in plaintiff's operating system software was not fair use. The court specified
four criteria the plaintiff must satisfy in order to obtain injunctive relief: (1) that
they are substantially likely to succeed on the merits of their claims, (2) that
the court's failure to issue the injunction poses a substantial threat of irreparable
injury, (3) that the threatened injury outweighs any damage that the injunction's
issuance might cause to the opposing party, and (4) that the injunction's issuance
will not undermine the public interest. The court held that since the copied and
modified firmware constituted articles that can be reproduced it was clearly subject to seizure under the Copyright Act, 17 U.S.C. 503(a).

Companies have more control in curbing grey marketing than they do in curbing counterfeiting, theft, or fraud. There is no "one size fit all" approach for every company and every industry, but if a rights holder is serious about protecting its IP, it needs to start with an aggressive corporatewide brand protection policy and communications, and implement processes and technology solutions to minimize its exposure while adopting industry standards and best practices. These should include:

- Defining robust "agreements" between a corporation and its business partners (distributors, resellers, suppliers, join ventures, licensees, etc.). Contracts need to include specific language regarding authorized and unauthorized product transactions and the remedies associated with breach of the contract terms, as well as reinforce the distribution, license, and service agreement value proposition.

- Warranty and maintenance policy, including support, or rather, nonsupport, of unauthorized products.

- Continuously communicating policy and guidelines to customers and channel partners to drive and enforce compliance. Annual Compliance Review—either online acknowledgment (signature) or signed written compliance letter. This could cover multiple policies, including business ethics, software licensing and use, use of e-business tools (software piracy, grey market, counterfeiting, service fraud—attaching the policies to the acknowledgment letter signed by the customer and partners (as appropriate; not all policies have to be acknowledged).

- Connecting and communicating with business partners and the public (end users, analysts, government agencies, consumers, etc.).

- Improving (software licensing) security and other e-business solutions and thwarting unauthorized access.

First, however, companies should make an effort to understand and appreciate what it takes to be successful from a distributor's viewpoint, as implementing and enforcing policies and procedures that would place further strains on relationships and a distributor's competitiveness are doomed to fail.

Rights holders can also minimize the tiers of distributors, or harmonize or synchronize them. If they minimize the number of hand-offs, their products and customers will stay more visible to them and be easier to trace. This reduces the manufacture's dependence on the distributor for end-user fulfillment and satisfaction.

In terms of best practices in brand protection, the answers are different for each rights holder, and in each region. The idea is to focus on the root causes of problems in each of those markets, and the opportunity to regain control and profit. There are many levers to handle, but if handled successfully, this can have a rather significant impact on revenue and growth and direct market improvement.

Just like any strategic initiative or project, the Brand Protection Program, if it is to succeed, needs to have clearly defined objectives, structure, deliverables, timelines, and resources accountable for completion of the individual tasks. The following simplified concepts show some of the elements that a successful brand protection program should incorporate.

Brand Protection Program—Phases			
STAGE 1: Business Alignment	Current Milestone	Next Milestone	Release Date
Intelligence Gathering and Analysis (Sizing)	Complete	Review/Adjust	09/30/__
Establishing IP Protection Policy, Executive Sponsor	Complete	Review/Adjust	01/31/__
Resources Identified and Committed	Release	Complete	02/15/__
Internal Communications, Corporate Training	Release	Complete	03/31/__
Tools and Processes Delivered (Website, Database, as required)	Release	Complete	03/31/__
STAGE 2: Protect the Assets			
Broad External Communications—Policy Education Customs and Law Enforcement Education and Materials	Trial	Release	04/30/__

Warranty, Agreement Language Update (renewals)	Trial	Release	05/30/__
Investigations Initiated, Seizures and Raids Coordination	Trial	Release	05/30/__
Software Licensing Process and Tools	Trial	Release	06/15/__
Serial Number Tracking			
Service Contracts	Development	Trial	06/30/__
Warranty	Development	Trial	06/30/__
Point of Sales (POS)	Development	Trial	07/31/__
Incentive Programs	Development	Trial	07/31/__
STAGE 3: Remediation and Rehabilitation			
Partner, Customer Audits	Hypothesis	Development	08/31/__
Infringements: Findings and Corrections, Renegotiations	Hypothesis	Development	09/31/__
Litigation	Hypothesis	Development	09/31/__
STAGE 4: Recovery, Monitoring, Improvement			
Program Review vs. Sales Trends, Market, Partners' Feedback	Trial	Release	11/30/__
Process, Tools, Communications Evolution	Hypothesis	Development	12/01/__
Product/Authentication Enhancements	Hypothesis	Development	07/30/__

For years, many leading brand owners have been designing and implementing measures to dissuade counterfeiters within their supply chains, including authorized distributors. However, many authorized distributors no longer buy directly from the brand owners but buy from either their authorized outsourced manufacturers (other equipment manufacturers (OEM), as other device manufacturers (ODM), etc.) or stocking distributors, increasing the risk of infiltration of counterfeits into the entire supply chain. As a result, the brand owners and authorized distributors have to implement additional and often new techniques in their daily business routines, techniques that are specifically designed to reduce the exposure to counterfeits.

These techniques include but are not limited to:

(a) *Educating everyone in the supply chain*—employees, suppliers, licensees, and buyers, by developing and deploying anti-counterfeit, antipiracy (unauthorized/unlicensed product) education materials and training programs for internal and external stakeholders, especially multitier channels.

(b) *Securing distribution channels*—using strict contracts and auditing processes to ensure that distribution agreements contain specific language and provisions for auditing and enforcement of terms and conditions of the agreement. Such language should include restrictions on purchasing and sale of the goods, specific remedies for noncompliance, reporting discrepancies, and other provisions.[9]

(c) *Developing and implementing processes to identify risks*—having a robust communications plan targeted at specific audiences, including buyers, distributors, and third-party service providers, provides a simple means by which suspected products, websites, or other infringements can be reported.

(d) *Providing means (tools) to enable information to reach the rights holder*—immediately, when counterfeiting or other unauthorized activity is suspected, buyers and distributors, Customs and law enforcement (and consumers) should know where to go and how to report any such incident to rights holders, allowing them (where possible) to take enforcement action against illegal activities, using civil and criminal remedies where appropriate.

(e) *Reacting swiftly to suspected infringements*—brand owners and authorized distributors should be prepared to act quickly and actively

---

[9] "Faltings v. International Business Machines Corp., 854 F.2d 1316 (4th Cir. 1988)." holding that defendant was justified in terminating contract with plaintiff reseller because plaintiff violated terms of the parties' Retailer Dealer Agreement by selling large amounts of defendant's equipment to unauthorized grey market resellers, while the agreement expressly forbade sale to resellers. The court relied on the agreement provision that the Dealer shall have no right to, and agrees it will not, appoint additional authorized dealers, warranty service centers, or distributors of IBM.

assist Customs and law enforcement and other authorities by providing information and product and operational expertise, training, and "on the job" tools to them.

By implementing these steps, rights holders and their authorized distributors can build best practices that provide valuable benefits to all authorized resellers, brand owners, consumers, and the industry as a whole.

A company committed to a brand protection program needs to budget and allocate resources, and constantly monitor and adjust/reallocate these resources when there is an imminent brand threat, in order to ensure that the brand protection program phases (suggested previously) are executed correctly and on time. Of course, this requires assigning the responsibilities and accountability for key initiatives of the program. Following is an example of a software-related brand protection program:

Brand Protection Program Status		
Key Deliverables	**Summary**	**Leader**
Training Development	Training content and delivery tools Webbased (January ____) Classroom (January ____)	_____ _____
Software Licensing and Distribution Agreement Language	Software license agreement (March ____) Distribution agreement (March ____)	_____ _____
Software Licensing Tools Development	Web-based security tools (April ____) ERM integration (July ____)	_____ _____
Communications and Channel Governance	External communication templates Customs and law enforcement materials (April ____) Customs–ports training schedule (May ____) Internal communications templates, website (April ____) Partner and customer communications (July ____)	_____ _____ _____
Warranty	Global warranty policy—new release (July ____) New warranty document release (August ____)	_____ _____

(Continued)

Brand Protection Program Status		
Key Deliverables	**Summary**	**Leader**
Legal Representation Selection	Proposals and selection process (March ____) Criminal and civil litigation representatives (September ____) Initial litigation (September ____)	_____ _____
Serial Number Tracking	Architect S/N tracking solution (May ____) Implement POS by S/N (Aug. ____) Implement service and warranty S/N-based entitlement (August ____)	_____ _____ _____
Process and Technology Improvements	Examples: Call-home features, auto-reporting, auto-provisioning, remote-monitoring, etc. (August)	_____ _____ _____

Licensing and Distribution Agreements

A study of the importance of channel management in reducing grey market goods by the Alliance for Grey Market and Counterfeit Abatement (AGMA) and KPMG, the audit, tax, and advisory firm,[10] identified the following trends:

- Most companies have contractual provisions addressing unauthorized-channel issues.
- Many companies have not adopted effective means to monitor their channels for adherence to those provisions.
- Companies that have the means to monitor are often reluctant to take strong action to preserve the integrity of their authorized channels and enforce a change in behaviors that are detrimental to the channel as a whole.

---

[10] KPMG Gray Market Study Update. 2008. "Effective Channel Management Is Critical in Combating the Gray Market and Increasing Technology Companies' Bottom Line." Available at https://agmaglobal.org/uploads/whitePapers/KPMG-AGMA%20Effective%20Channel%20Management..pdf (accessed March 05, 2021).

The lack of clear and concise provisions in distribution agreements can prevent businesses from taking any meaningful corrective action against unauthorized transacting in their branded goods.[11] Although better late than never, businesses based on distribution models with existing contractual provisions at least have the choice to take the corrective actions. Following are examples of provisions that should be included in every distribution agreement.

Scope and Grant of Rights

Resale contracts need to include clear and concise language identifying key objectives of the contract and explicitly state what is permitted and what is prohibited under the contract, such as the following example:

---

[11] "Adobe Systems Inc. v. One Stop Micro, Inc., 84 F. Supp.2d 1086 (N.D. Cal. 2000)." holding that defendant, which was authorized educational reseller of plaintiff's educational versions of "Adobe PageMaker," "Adobe Photoshop," "Adobe Premiere," and "Adobe Illustrator," sold these to unauthorized resellers, which violated the licensing agreement between the parties and infringed on plaintiff's copyrights. The agreement specifically stated that defendant agrees to sell the Educational Software Products to certain customers who are Educational End Users. Defendant admitted that it sold modified versions of plaintiff's software to unauthorized end users. The court found that defendant's admitted sale of educational versions of Adobe software to noneducational end users was outside the scope of agreement with Adobe and in violation of its rights as reseller, and found that defendant had also committed copyright infringement as a matter of law under 501(a).

See also, Abercrombie & Fitch v. Fashion Shops of Kentucky, Inc., 363 F. Supp.2d 952 (S.D. Ohio 2005) holding that defendant's sale of certain of plaintiff's goods in the United States was in violation of plaintiff's "Sell-Off Compliance Agreement," which clearly outlined the terms under which defendant could sell such merchandise (merchandise of a lower quality designated to be sold only in foreign countries) and granted preliminary injunction to plaintiff, preventing defendant from selling any of plaintiff's merchandise until inspected by plaintiff. The court noted that this merchandise, which was evidently brought into United States in violation of the Agreement, would be grey goods, as these goods were only authorized under plaintiff's mark for production and sale abroad).

For Authorized Products and subject to the terms herein, Reseller is hereby granted a personal, nontransferable, nonexclusive right to:

(a) Purchase directly from Rights Holder or its authorized Distributors Products for Resale to End Customers within the Territory; and

(b) Transfer Software acquired by Reseller from Rights Holder or through its Distributors to End Customer within the Territory.

Further, a Rights Holder may at its sole discretion authorize Reseller in writing to resell products or services, or both, or transfer Rights Holder software to other authorized Resellers within the territory (who may then resell the products and/or services and transfer the software to end-customer). In order to acquire products or services directly from a Rights Holder, Reseller must be approved by the Rights Holder and agree to additional terms and conditions. Reseller may purchase authorized products for its internal use within the territory. Certain products may not be available for resale and authorization to resell specific products may be based upon the completion of accreditation/training requirements or such other requirements as may be specified by the manufacturer.

Purchasing and Resale Constraints

Following is an example of distribution language addressing a required set of behaviors a rights holder should expect from the contracted reseller or distributor:

Reseller agrees to:

1. Comply with and meet or exceed all applicable industry standards for sales and support of the Products Distributed by Reseller under this Agreement;

2. Distribute the Products and Services to End Customers within the Territory, in accordance with the terms and conditions of this Agreement and support the Products in the Territory in a manner, which will not damage either the quality or the functionality of the Products. The pricing Reseller receives from Rights Holder is contingent on Reseller's agreement to:

(a) Resell Products solely to End Customers (and/or contracted 2d Tier resellers, Sales Agents, Affiliates, etc.);

(b) Only Purchase Products directly from Rights Holder or Rights Holder-authorized Distributors;

(c) Refrain from purchasing or selling products purported to be Rights Holder products. Such activities are strictly prohibited. In the event Rights Holder discovers that Reseller has engaged in such activities, Reseller agrees that Rights Holder may submit an invoice to Reseller in an amount that is equal to [___] percent (%) of the Retail Price for the respective Product. Reseller hereby agrees to and shall make payment for any such invoiced amount in accordance with standard Payment Terms attached hereto. Reseller further agrees that the activities described above shall constitute a material breach of this Agreement, entitling Rights Holder to the remedy set forth above and all other available remedies, including, but not limited to, termination of this Agreement;

(d) Be responsible for addressing all guarantees/warranty issues with its customers and for that portion of any warranty which exceeds, whether in time or scope, that provided for the applicable Product to Reseller by Rights Holder;

(e) Promptly make available to Rights Holder documents that Reseller is required to maintain under this Agreement (e.g., point of sale information or executed Software Licenses when applicable);

(f) Require each affiliate to agree in writing to be bound by all the provisions of this Agreement and further agrees to accept responsibility for and guarantee the performance of its affiliates' obligations; and

(g) Purchase all its requirements of the Product solely from Rights Holder or from Rights Holder-Authorized Distributors in the Territory that are authorized by Rights Holder to sell the Products. The purchase of Products from any other source is strictly prohibited.

To further instill the proper distributors' behavior, rights holders should publish periodic updates or notices about their resale policies and the restrictions as well as the remedies and retributions for noncompliance. The letter could be written in the following format:

Limitation of Resale Authorization   *Date/issue*

[Territory] Distribution Notice

To: [Territory] contracted Resellers, Partners (collectively referred to herein as "Partner") and Distributors authorized by [Rights Holder] to resell [Rights Holder] products.

[Rights Holder's] distribution strategy has included restrictions which authorize Partners to purchase products under a resale agreement and to be sold to end customers only. Purchases by Distributors have been authorized for resale to [Rights Holder]-authorized Partners only. Resale of such products among Partners or to nonauthorized parties has been, and continues to be, prohibited.

The above authorizations are governed under the terms and conditions under which Partners and Distributors have agreed to resell [Rights Holder] products. Exceptions to these authorizations may be granted on a case-by-case basis, where necessary, to address the market. Violations by Distributors or Partners may result in restitution as specified in Partner's agreement or termination of the agreement in its entirety.

[Rights Holder] appreciates each Partner's and Distributor's adherence to the current distribution strategy. It is [Rights Holder's] intent to ensure that the Distributors engaged in wholesale distribution are the best in the industry and committed to delivering superior value to all [Rights Holder]-authorized Partners. [Rights Holder] will ensure its Partners are equipped to provide the highest quality sales and support to their end customers.

Any questions or clarifications regarding this matter should be directed to your Sales Account Representative or Customer Relationship Management.

Officer Name

Title

_____

Signature

Audits

Conducting audits of end-users, distributors, resellers, and suppliers alike became standard practice across all industries. Audits are best performed in a nonadversarial manner, and, therefore, the audit targets should not be selected based only on risk assessment and suspected compliance issues, but rather as periodic business reviews—a standard practice to monitor and enforce compliance with contractual terms and prevent a long-term impact stemming from noncompliance. Audits are also an invaluable tool in compliance enforcement where a company already has discovered noncompliance (prior to an actual audit, such as a desk audit, or internal reviews, or other investigative activities) and is seeking remedies and corrective actions.

The most common areas of discrepancy identified in these audits are:

- Purchases from unauthorized parties;
- Unauthorized domestic sales;
- Sales outside of authorized territories (foreign sales);
- Rebate overpayment;
- Omission of returns in rebate processing;
- Inaccurate point of sale (POS) reporting;
- Excessive marketing development funds (MDF) program payments.

The level of grey market activity identified during the audit is usually a surprise. Commonly, only a small proportion of a company's products are affected by the grey market. The affected products are usually products with the highest profit margin that are not locally specific, and are in high demand. The level of grey market activity can vary widely from region to region, but once it exists, schemes spread quickly and the weaknesses are rapidly exploited. As a result, the financial effect on a rights holder and its partners can be quite large.

Virtually all audits encounter some errors in auditees' reporting, inappropriate product sale or purchase, incorrect incentive claims, or erroneous pricing used. Very few of these problems are detected by the internal controls during company's internal audits. The main reasons are:

- Failure of both the third party (auditee) and the rights holder to devote sufficient resources to manage contractual relationships;
- Systems weaknesses at the third party and the rights holder to support compliance with contractual obligations.

There are clear benefits to a well-established auditing program:

- *Financial Recoveries*—Typically, rights holders that implement channel reviews initially receive recoveries well beyond the cost of the reviews. Subsequent reviews should yield fewer recoveries where the implemented compliance remedies are working.
- *Impact on Sales Teams*—In regions where grey products are competing with authorized products, sales and account management teams may be affected. These individuals lose commissions, while conversely, sales teams in regions where grey products are flowing from may be unfairly benefiting.
- *Revenue and Margin Erosion*—Based on the KPMG/AGMA white paper,[12] approximately $10 billion of margin per annum is lost because of grey marketed products. Performing channel reviews of partners typically reduces grey transactions at those partners previously reviewed and where proper remedies are being implemented.
- *Damage to Authorized Channel and Partners*—Authorized vendors who invest in the vendors' brand and comply with

---

[12] "KMPG/AGMA Survey Projects Global 'Gray Market' of $58 Billion for Information Technology Manufacturers." December 11, 2008, Available at www.agmaglobal.org/press_events/12-11-08%20KPMG%202nd%20release%20for%20WP.pdf (accessed March 05, 2021).

channel agreements may feel disadvantaged by the availability of grey market products. Consequently, these partners often look to the vendor for additional discounts or may buy grey to be competitive with the marketplace.

- *Sarbanes–Oxley (SOX) and Regulatory Requirements*—Many companies are likely subject to SOX, the Foreign Corrupt Practices Act (FCPA), and other regulatory requirements (including a license requirement on technology under U.S. export controls). As such they may want to consider responsibilities of their channel partners, who could be considered an extension of the control environment.

In order to run successful reviews a company needs to:

- Announce externally to the channel that the company is performing reviews of its channel programs;
- Define clear policies and procedures and corrective actions for enforcement of noncompliance with contractual terms and conditions found during the review (including instances when partners refuse to undergo the review);
- Announce internally the objectives, likely outcome, and escalation route for issues;
- Develop an internal policy on how to address internal and external weaknesses identified through completion of the reviews;
- Define consequence management of what to expect throughout the review process:
  - Issues
  - Define a clear escalation process for noncompliance with incentive terms;
  - Partner delays in complying with data requests;
  - Appropriate documentation to support claims that are not made available during the review; and
  - Findings not consistently enforced.
- Impacts
- Incentives incorrectly paid may not be easily recovered;

- Reduced effectiveness of reviews;
- Potential manipulation of data, documents, and inventory to conceal reporting irregularities; and
- Negotiated settlements may mean the partner is not dissuaded from future violations.

For example, here are the common incentive and rebate programs issues that an audit needs to look into:

Program	Description	Potential Compliance Issues
Special Pricing	Special pricing and discounts offered on sale to specific customers or markets.	Products purchased are outside the scope of the sales intent (e.g., not the intended customer or market). Potential unbundling, diversion, or cherry-picking of products "entitled" to special pricing.
Volume Programs	Pricing and discounting for high volume transactions (such as large direct customers/distributors, international corporations, governments, etc.).	Overreported sales and incentives because of inclusion of unauthorized products (grey market, secondary market, trial and demo equipment), sales to nonqualifying customers and markets.
Price Protection	Program offered to key customers/distributors to protect large inventory purchases.	Mixing products purchased inside and outside of the authorized price protection period. Overstating inventories and overpayments to the partners. Potentially including grey market products.
Marketing Activities	Special cooperative activities to incentivize business partners to perform specific activities to boost sales of specific products.	Unauthorized use of marketing (comarketing) funds/incentives. Determining how the funds have been used.
Sales Promotions	Time-limited campaigns to increase sales in specific markets or target segments.	Promotion/rebate claims may include (blend in) products purchased from grey market, noncompliance with the promotion/rebate terms, and double-dipping (claims of same sales under different promotional programs).

Program	Description	Potential Compliance Issues
Trade-In Programs	Programs designed to encourage customers to trade-in competitors' or outdated equipment by offering additional incentives.	Verification of trade-in returned equipment or certificate of destruction. Claims for returned equipment that originated from grey market or counterfeits. Noncompliance with the terms and conditions of the program.
Stock Rotation	Returns of outdated stock, usually requiring placing order for the corresponding product value.	Noncompliance with the terms and conditions of the program. Returns may include unauthorized equipment originated from grey market or other unauthorized sources (counterfeits).
Success Incentives	Based on specific attainment targets such as growth, product adoption, margins during specified periods.	Lack of verification resulting in claims may include sales from/to unauthorized targets (grey market resellers). Attainment levels may be understated, or payments are made without prudent verification (targets not met).

In order to reveal any discrepancies in reporting, sales, inventories, incentives, or discounting, auditors need to review specific data. The most common datasets an audit will test are:

Data	Description	Review
Sales Out or POS	Data reported directly during the review period or obtained for other partner by Auditors during channel review.	Comparing previously reported data with data provided to Auditors; and partner's customer data for completeness of reported data. End-user testing and negative testing.
Inventory Data	Data reported directly during the review period or obtained for other partner by Auditors during channel review.	Comparing previously reported data with data provided to Auditors; investigating instances claims for grey market products (returned, refurbished, etc.).
Vendor Shipments Data and Other's POS	Vendor internal shipment/sales data verification against partner's data provided to Auditors and data reported by other partners.	Comparing vendor's internal data with data provided to Auditors; Investigation of unauthorized sourcing (grey market, counterfeits, secondary market).

(Continued)

Data	Description	Review
Claims and Payments/Credits/ Rebates Paid	Claims received from partners, vendor payment, credit, and rebates issues to partners. Any terms and conditions outside of standard agreement.	Verification of end-user rebates and other programmatic claims against payments and amounts. Identification of dual claims or payments, and claims paid for products sourced from unauthorized channels.

Intent to Audit

Following is an example of an *"Intent to Audit Letter"* that may be used to notify an authorized reseller and/or distributor:

VIA E-MAIL & EXPRESS MAIL
[Date]

[Name]

[Company]

[Address]

[Phone]

[E-mail]

Cc: [Name], [E-mail]

Subject: *Intent to Audit Letter*

Dear [Partner/Customer NAME]:

This is to advise you that, pursuant to Section [#] of the Company Reseller Agreement by and between [Rights Holder] and [Company] effective on [date] ("Agreement"), [Rights Holder] will be undertaking an audit. The audit will be conducted by [Auditing Firm] and [Mr./ Mrs. XYZ] will be in contact with you shortly to discuss the scope and the data requirements.

The audit would be inclusive of, but not limited to, the following procedures:

- *Interview [Company] personnel to understand how [Company] identifies and tracks sales of the products to ensure that all data have been provided to [Rights Holder] as prescribed in the Agreement.*
- *Reconcile total sales per internal system to audited financial statements to ensure that sales were captured and reported correctly.*
- *Reconcile inventory balances to account for products sold by [Company].*
- *Ensure that sales data have been properly captured and reported on all products subject to the Agreement.*
- *Reconcile Point of Sales (POS) and product serial number data captured and reported to [Rights Holder] with [Company's] internal accounting (or other) systems.*
- *Reconcile purchases of products with sales records and inventory turnover.*
- *Confirm sale of all products has been in accordance with terms of the Agreement and/or other applicable [Rights Holder] programs (including, but not limited to, the marketing funds, rebates, volume, and other discounts, sales rewards, other incentive programs) to ensure [Company] received all incentives and rewards it is entitled to for the actual sales.*

To conduct this audit efficiently, it will be essential that [Auditing Firm] receives electronically the following document and records from [Company] by [date], which will help minimize any disturbances in [Company] working schedule.

1. *Detailed product listing [Company] sold under the Agreement within the specified period (from [date to date]).*
2. *Detailed sales register/Invoice associated with the product in 1 (this should agree with quarterly financial statements), showing:*
   a. Invoice number/date
   b. Customer name/number/address (including URL)
   c. Product serial number/other product identified/product description

d. Quantity invoiced/shipped

e. Product unit price/invoiced amount.

This information should be comprehensive and contain all sales data, including sales of products sold by all divisions, and/or subsidiaries, affiliates, sales agents, etc. Please let the [Auditing Firm] know if the data are captured and reported in multiple locations or in a centralized location, as this can greatly affect the scope of the audit.

1. *Summary of financial statements (i.e., quarterly). This is needed to tie total revenue information to the detailed sales registration/invoice listing.*
2. *Daily/Weekly/Monthly/Quarterly ending inventory balances for all products.*
3. *Daily/Weekly/Monthly/Quarterly sales and POS reports reported to [Rights Holder] and supporting sales orders and invoicing.*
4. *Organization charts/processes flow of all divisions/entities/subsidiaries/affiliates/sales agents/others involved in the process of sales, shipping, invoicing, accounting, etc.*
5. *Any additional supporting documentation.*

Please note that additional documentation or materials may be needed or requested, and you will be advised of the same promptly.

We appreciate [Company's] support and effort in facilitating this audit.

Please do not hesitate to contact me at [(___) ___-____] or at xyz@ rightsholder.com, should you have any concerns or questions.

Yours sincerely,

Officer Name

Title

_____

Signature

Cc: [Company] General Counsel or Chief Legal Officer

The *"Intent to Audit Letter"* should be handled as a legal document and should follow the same procedures the rights holder uses for all legal documents and correspondence, for traceability preservation. It is a good practice to send the intent to audit letters by e-mail with return receipt requested as well as by certified mail or delivery with receipt requested.

In the case where the recipient of the notification does not respond by a specified date (as usually determined in the auditors' letter that follows the notification), the rights holder or its attorneys should follow up with a second notification (an example of such a notification is shown as follows):

VIA E-MAIL & EXPRESS MAIL

[Date]

To: [Mr./Mrs. Name]

[Company]

[Address]

[E-mail]

Subject: *Follow-up to the Intent to Audit Letter dated [date]*

Dear [Partner/Customer Name],

This letter is in follow-up to our earlier communication to you regarding our Intent to Audit. Pursuant to your Agreement with [Rights Holder] [insert full name and term of the agreement and Section(s) references to right to audit], you are required to permit [Auditing Firm] appointed by us to perform the audit to verify compliance with terms and conditions of the Agreement. We urge you to contact [Auditing Firm] [Mr./Mrs. NAME] or us promptly to initiate this audit. Assuming your failure to respond to our initial Letter was an oversight, we are kindly sending you this reminder. However, should you fail to contact [Auditing Firm] or us within next 5 business days, we will take necessary steps to enforce the terms and conditions of the Agreement.

Please respond to this e-mail with the name and telephone number of a contact person responsible for this audit at xyz@rightsholder.com by [MM/DD/YYYY, 5 business days].

If you have any questions, please contact me directly.

With best regards,

Officer Name

Title

Signature

Cc: [Partner/Customer name] General Counsel or Chief Legal Officer

The final steps depend heavily on:

- Company's experience in pursuing contract breaches via arbitration or litigation or both; and
- Locale of the noncompliant party, since the enforcement may be more difficult in some countries than in others.

The decision to terminate usually depends on circumstances, and litigation is generally more difficult and costly than arbitration proceedings when the contract is still in full force.

Software License Agreements

In a high-tech industry, software is a continuously growing portion of overall revenues while hardware is becoming commoditized and facing increasing price pressures and decreasing profit margins. With most high-tech products, the key competitive differentiators are functionality, added applications, and performance, which now prevalently reside in products' software. Moreover, most rights holders now outsource manufacturing to OEMs) (also referred to as ODMs), which often produce products for competing brands. Since these OEMs usually control their own supply chains, the hardware components used in many of the competing products are actually identical. OEMs now also provide design services, so the importance of rights holders protecting their hardware-related IP is diminishing. As a result, IPR protection is shifting toward enforcing software and technology licensing and support. Software license agreements are an important part of purchase agreements, providing the buyer (end user) with the "right to use" the software (rights holders actually do not sell the software, only license its use). The right-to-use licenses vary from rights holder to rights holder and product to product. The right to use license can be perpetual or one-time (only the original buyer has the right to use the software), or time-based (annual, semiannual, or other), where users have to renew such licenses before the expiry of each term. Software license agreements therefore need clearly defined terms and conditions for the use of the software and need to provide remedies for rights holders to take appropriate actions when the licensee violates these agreements. A critical part of enforcing software licensing is monitoring and licensing reviews (audits). With current technology (software authentication, call-home, etc.), most of such monitoring can be done remotely. Software license reviews can be made part of basic software support (such as patching, upgrades, updates), which is also delivered remotely.

The following language is an example of how to request access to customer systems to verify the validity of all installed software to ensure there is no unauthorized software installed (used) or find out if there are any expired licenses that would require license renewal:

VIA E-MAIL and EXPRESS MAIL

[Date]

[Mr./Mrs. Name]

[Company]

[Address 1]

[Address 2]

[Telephone Number]

[E-mail]

Subject: *Software License Agreement Audit*

Dear [Partner/Customer Name],

This communication is to notify you that [Rights Holder] will be initiating an audit of Software Licenses and Support for our customers. Your company has been selected for an upcoming audit to ensure compliance to the terms of the End-User Software License and End-User Software Support License Agreement. The requirements of the audit are those specified in the "End-User Software License Agreement [insert Section(s) reference] document of your purchase agreement."

[Rights Holder/Auditing Firm] representative conducting the audit will require coordination with you to gain [remote/physical] access to the [system(s) name(s)]. The representative will call you to schedule the best time to obtain the access. Please respond to this e-mail, with the name and the telephone number of a contact person for this audit, at xyz@ rightsholder.com by [MM/DD/YYYY, 5 business days].

The review will not affect service. We thank you in advance for your cooperation.

If you have any questions, please contact me directly.

With best regards,

Officer Name

Title

_____

Signature

In the absence of a technical solution for tracking and authenticating software licensing, licensing reviews (audits) are the only tool to enforce compliance with the Licensing Agreement and recover potential losses from underreporting or nonreporting.

Warranty

"Warranty and service abuse can affect a company's profitability in a number of ways. According to survey participants, the areas most affected by warranty and service abuse are: financial loss from unentitled service costs; loss of service revenue; product failure rate distortion and resulting increase in R&D costs; and enforcement costs. Warranty and service abuse can also be detrimental to a company's relationships and reputation … ."[13] A warranty entitlement process using serial numbers or other means to track the products to the point of sales (POS), strong relationships with authorized partners, and regular audits are a few of the remedies that can help reduce unauthorized warranty claims. Companies that address warranty service abuse can generate enormous savings and create long-term value for their organizations, their investors, and their customers, without compromising customer service and satisfaction.[14]

Before taking any corrective or preventive actions, a rights holder needs to have clearly defined terms of warranty entitlement and a support policy that excludes grey market products and any other unauthorized products (counterfeits, stolen, pirated, reverse engineered, etc.). This warranty and service policy needs to be included in product literature (product and user manuals or packaging, etc.), communicated to authorized distributors, and available on company web pages, defining coverage terms provided to the original purchaser and providing a consumer guide to the warranty registration process. Making the warranty terms and policy available in multiple documents increases the chance of enforcing them. If a customer decides to favor less expensive grey market products and to forego the original warranty coverage, the rights holder who has a well-documented

---

[13] AGMA. October 20, 2009. "Price Waterhouse Coopers Expose Multi-Billion Dollar Threat to Technology Industry: Warranty and Service Abuse; New Study Defines Problem and Presents Methods to Effectively Manage Growing Threat." Available at https://agmaglobal.org/uploads/whitePapers/Final%20PwC%20Service%20Blues%20(10-26-09).pdf (accessed March 05, 2021).
[14] COMPTIA, AGMA. 2013. "IT Industry Warranty and Service Abuse: Stealing Profitability!" (2013), available at https://agmaglobal.org/uploads/whitePapers/CompTIA_WhitePaper-WarrantyAbuse-8%2027%2013.pdf (accessed March 05, 2021).

and communicated warranty policy that clearly articulates who is eligible for warranty coverage and when this warranty is void may use this to its benefit during litigation.[15]

Although a well-defined warranty and support policy is a must, specific terms and conditions included in such a policy, designed to protect the business from service and warranty fraud, may vary from business to business. What may work for one company may not necessarily work for another. "[T]he U.S. division of Japanese camera-maker Nikon will service products purchased only through an authorized retailer. It declines grey-market repairs even if a customer is willing to pay for them. On the other hand, Garmin evaluates service on a case-by-case basis for its Global Positioning System (GPS) devices. It tries to help customers but usually can't work on devices that have been tampered with … ."[16]

Listed in the following are some other companies, and the extent to which they warrant their grey-market products:

---

[15] In Hyundai Construction Equipment U.S.A., Inc. v. Chris Johnson Equipment, Inc., 2008 WL 4210785 (N.D. Ill. September 10, 2008), the defendant (grey marketer) purchased Hyundai heavy construction machines in Korea from Korean dealers that purchased the machines directly from the manufacturer (Hyundai-Korea). The grey marketer purchased those machines at a significant discount, and as a result, the grey marketer was able to sell this grey market equipment at prices significantly below the standard pricing of authorized Hyundai-U.S.A. dealers. However, since the equipment was authorized for sale and use in Korea and/or China, but not in the United States, it was not covered by the required standard U.S. warranty. The equipment also had non-English language safety, operational, and maintenance labels and manuals, unlike domestic Hyundai-U.S.A. machines, and was equipped with non-EPA-compliant engines. The court held that these differences were material and held that "the primary purpose of the Lanham Act is to protect consumers" and the goodwill of U.S. distributors, and went on to permanently enjoin the grey marketer from importing or selling any Hyundai heavy construction equipment with less than 100 hours of operational time. *Id.*

[16] M. Kessler. December 11, 2006. "Some See Red Over Gray-Market Goods." *USA Today.* Available at www.usatoday.com/tech/products/2006-12-10-gray-market_x.htm (accessed March 05, 2021).

- Company A: Leading Consumer Electronics company publishes limited warranty that covers all hardware products manufactured by or for Company A that can be identified by the "Company A" trademark, trade name, or logo affixed to them. This warranty covers all grey market products, as long as the serial numbers have not been removed or defaced.
- Company B: Provides the same warranty to grey market and legitimate hardware, provided the owner can prove the date the product was purchased, and provided the serial number has not been altered, defaced, or removed.
- Company C: Provides warranty coverage only for products purchased through an authorized dealer and accompanied by a warranty certificate stamped and signed by the authorized dealer, showing the date of purchase and model number.
- Inserting the following language into a product warranty may help to define clearly that the brand owner has "no obligation" to provide coverage under the following conditions:
- Defects/issues associated with product on which the serial number and/or month/year of manufacture have been removed or altered; or product purchased through an unauthorized dealer. For more information, please consult corporate brand protection website;
- Brand owner will not service any product that does not have an authentic manufacturer barcode label on the box, if applicable, and on the product itself. All products returned for warranty and repair reasons will be checked and inspected for authenticity. Warranty is voided on products that have been purchased through unauthorized channels, altered, and/or damaged;
- Defects or issues arising from:
  o Improper handling, storage, or service not performed by Authorized Brand Owner Partner;
  o Use in a manner not in conformance with Brand Owner's specifications, instructions, or license.

Another company ("Company D") made its global warranty policy publicly available to customers and resellers alike on its website. The policy was a great example of unauthorized product warranty void language in practice. It stated in a warranty exclusions section that no warranty was provided for (among others): (i) Failures caused by non-Company D products; (ii) failures caused by a product's inability to operate in conjunction with other customer products; (iii) performance *failures resulting from services, including installation, not performed by Company D or an authorized Company D representative or customer's use of unauthorized parts or components*; (vi) failure resulting from use other than expressly provided; (viii) lack of compliance with Company D technical operating procedures.

The Company D warranty was also void under these specific conditions: (i) Defects/issues associated with products on which the serial number and/or month/year of manufacture have been removed or altered; or products purchased through an unauthorized dealer. As a result, Company D did not service any product that did not have an authentic manufacturer barcode label on the box, if applicable, and the product itself. All products that were returned for warranty and repair reasons were checked and inspected for authenticity. Warranty was voided on products that had been purchased through unauthorized channels, altered and/or damaged; (ii) use of software with incompatible or unauthorized hardware or software.

The above is a great example of what companies could incorporate in official product documentation to enforce compliance.

Presale Due Diligence

Presale due diligence can be very effective by implementing just a few basic tasks:

- Resale channel selection process;[17]
- Purchase order verification, including buyer authentication;
- Sales trends monitoring.

---

[17] See 4.04[2][a] *infra*.

Buyer authentication is a presale activity (ensuring the product is sold to a valid business or consumer) and needs to be treated with the same significance as product authentication in the postsale phase (for warranty claims or other customer support or investigation of counterfeit or grey market incidents). Confirming that a buyer is not a phony or a suspicious entity/individual may save businesses a lot of headaches and money later. Sales personnel should use a compliance checklist and verify every new customer and even every new transaction to manage/avoid possible risks. This checklist should include:

- Verification of the business entity (incorporation, certification—i.e., licensed contractor, credit check, etc.);
- Business address verification (checking for PO Box or "unlikely address"—examples may include undeveloped or deserted sites, unrelated institutions such as retirement homes, and personal residences);
- Verification of e-mail address ownership and business URL ownership (hidden entities are suspects);
- In the case of an existing history of past orders, checking the typical order size and looking for unusual volumes or repetitive information (e.g., if the end user is a small business—a few small orders are not unusual, many orders or large volume could indicate noncompliance);
- If there is a valid supply agreement, verification of the agreement terms against the order;
- Checking the previous order(s) history (past payment collection issues); and
- Special pricing requests (whether the price has been used in the past and verification of validity; checking for double-dipping—ensuring the incentives and discounts and/or rebates are used as intended).

Businesses can compile their own compliance checklists that meet their specific needs. The basic idea, however, remains the same—customer/order verification is important. It is always easier and much, much cheaper to avoid deals with "bad" customers than it is to remedy them.

Ongoing monitoring of the sales orders—as many businesses use automated order processing—is an important part of identifying potential noncompliance. Any unusual spikes in order quantities may be an indication of grey market activity.

Partner Screening and Contracting

Business partners (resellers, distributors, licensees, etc.) are critical to the success of any business, local or global, and finding reliable and honest partners is very important, especially when a business operates in foreign markets. Taking corrective actions in some foreign markets or countries is often difficult and sometimes even impossible. There are certain steps that a business could follow when entering into business partnerships that may prevent future headaches.

Selecting Partners: Screening and Certification

A new partner selection process can be a lengthy and complex endeavor and each business has its own specific criteria, requirements, and priorities in selecting its business partners; yet the basic due diligence should never be omitted and the "screening checklist/questionnaire" should include the following items.

Credit History and Overall Financial Strength

Privately owned companies should be required to provide proof of solvency and credit rating. For publicly traded companies, this information should be readily available. Reviewing past years' financial statements and looking for trends and inconsistencies is plain common sense (especially in lieu of any significant deals).

Business Hierarchy

Complexity in a potential partner's organizational hierarchy, such as a proliferation of subsidiaries or affiliates, brand mark out-licensing, and so on, and an overall complex ownership structure, may be undesirable. Executing an agreement in such complex hierarchies may be complicated. The best practice when executing an agreement with a subentity is to have it executed or coexecuted by the parent to ensure legal and financial liability. Following this simple principle doubles the chance of financial recoveries. This best practice should be mandatory in high-risk countries, especially if a business wants to maintain longer-term relationships.

Credit Assurance or Security Deposit

Credit assurance in the form of a credit letter is a practical measure to dissuade entities that are not interested in continuous business from the beginning (like frauds, speculators, etc.). A credit letter in the amount stated in the agreement is an irrevocable standby and must meet the basic requirements of the agreement, such as identifying the rights holder as the beneficiary, and stating that the funds shall be readily available to the rights holder and in the event that the rights holder draws the funds, the credit amount must be restored to the full amount required under the agreement. The credit letter should have an automatic renewal term so that it automatically extends for additional terms, unless the agreement is terminated. If a rights holder reasonably believes that a financial institution is no longer a commercially viable entity, a credit letter should be established with another financial institution and issued in the amount stated in the agreement.

Instead of establishing a credit letter, a partner may provide the security deposit directly to the rights holder. The deposit can be withdrawn (in full or in part) if the rights holder reasonably believes the partner is delinquent in payments under the terms of the agreement, or is liable for quantifiable damages resulting from a breach of any provision of the agreement. If the rights holder withdraws any part of the deposit, the partner shall restore the deposit amount to the full amount required under the agreement no later than the first day of the calendar month immediately following such withdrawal. The rights holder shall refund the balance of the deposit within the period specified in the agreement after the expiration or termination of the agreement.

A history of the partner's past and present relationships with other businesses should be part of the due diligence investigation. This includes past or present disputes, litigation, longevity of other partners' relationships, major contracts or deals announcements, joint ventures, and so on—any relationships that may be a cause for concern, or otherwise.

Contracting With Partners to Prevent Grey and Counterfeit Goods From Coming Into the Supply Chain Through Partners

The contract with business partners should clearly define the source of products authorized by the rights holder and prohibited otherwise. Terms of use, sales, and applicable limitations (if any) need to be defined as well. The following are examples of language that can help to define these matters in agreements.

Scope and Grant of Rights

For authorized Products and subject to the terms herein, Reseller is hereby granted a personal, nontransferable, nonexclusive right to: (a) purchase from [Rights Holder] Distributors [products] ("Products") for Resale to Consumers within the [Territory] ("Territory"). [Rights Holder] may at its sole discretion authorize Reseller in writing to Resell Products to other authorized resellers within the Territory (who may then resell the Products to Consumers). In order to acquire Products or Services directly from [brand owner], Reseller must be approved by [Rights Holder] and agree to additional terms and conditions. Reseller may purchase authorized Products for its internal use within the Territory. Certain Products may not be available for resale and authorization to resell specific Products may be based upon the completion of accreditation/training requirements or such other requirements as may be specified by [Rights Holder].

Definitions

For the purpose of this Agreement, certain terms have been defined as follows:

"Authorized Reseller" means a person or entity that is authorized in writing by [Rights Holder] to distribute and resell [Rights Holder] branded Products and services in accordance with [Rights Holder] policies, procedures, and terms and conditions.

"Distribute," "Distribution," "Resale," or "Resell" means the offer or sale, lease, or rent of Products in accordance with the terms and conditions of this Agreement.

"Product(s)" means any Item provided under this Agreement that is authorized by [Rights Holder].

"Unauthorized Reseller" means a person or entity that acquires [Rights Holder] branded products that are identical to Products, or purported to be [Rights Holder] branded products, for resale and not for its internal business use and without permission or authorization in writing from [Rights Holder] to Resell or to use for its internal purpose.

Relationship

Reseller agrees to:

Distribute the Products and Services to Consumers within the Territory in accordance with the terms and conditions of this Agreement in a manner that will neither damage the quality or functionality of the Products nor require extraordinary support from [Rights Holder]. The pricing Reseller receives from [Rights Holder] is contingent on Reseller's agreement to (i) Resell Products solely to Consumers or purchase for the Reseller's internal use, (ii) purchase only Products directly from [Rights Holder] or [Rights Holder] Distributors, and (iii) refrain from purchasing or selling products purported to be [Rights Holder] products. Such activities are strictly prohibited. In the event [Rights Holder] discovers that Reseller has engaged in such activities, Reseller agrees that [Rights Holder] may submit an invoice to Reseller in an amount that is equal to [amount] percent ([amount]%) of the Retail Price for the respective Product. Reseller hereby agrees to and shall make payment for any such invoiced amount in accordance with Agreement Payment Terms. Reseller further agrees that the activities described above shall constitute a material breach of this Agreement, entitling [Rights Holder] to the remedy set forth above and all other available remedies including, but not limited to, termination of this Agreement.

Right to Audit

"Even though many companies never invoke them, most 'standard' agreements contain audit provisions …"[18] This statement with respect to a right to audit applies to a wide array of agreements. Even if a company chooses not to conduct audits, certain audit terms should always be included in the agreements, such as:

(a) A broad right to audit the contracted business partner's records and books (paper and/or electronic), with no restrictions placed on the scope of the investigation, including negative testing;[19]

(b) Appointing a third-party auditing firm (most resellers, distributors, or licensees will not agree to "in-house" auditing by the rights holder);

(c) Format of the reported data, which should contain (but not exclusively):

   i. Product numbers;

   ii. Units sold;

   iii. Sales dollars;

   iv. Country and currency translation used, if any;

   v. Details of any product returns;

   vi. Details of any promotional and demo units;

   vii. Details of amounts manufactured but not yet sold (inventory);

   viii. If any costs are deductible, details of the specific items.

     If applicable, any calculations based on the above (e.g., royalties or other payables) regular (at least quarterly) reporting and payments (where applicable);

(d) A provision that makes a partner liable for the full cost of the audit should an underreported amount or other applicable discrepancy exceed a specified allowable amount (5 percent is a typical allowable margin of error);

---

[18] Fulcrum Inquiry. January 2004. "Getting More Money From Licenses." Available at www.fulcrum.com/money_from_licenses/ (accessed March 06, 2021).

[19] Negative testing is usually defined as reverse conformance (compliance) testing, that is, testing in a negative way, checking whether a partner is doing what it is not supposed to do.

(e) Interest charged on late or underreported amounts;

(f) Require partners to keep all the sales and related records for minimum of the past three years.

If the cost of the audit is a concern, the company can choose to work with auditors who agree to work on a contingency basis. In this scenario, an auditor receives a premium if the audit findings are large. "If the auditor does not find anything, then you get peace of mind for free!"[20]

Incentives

If an agreement needs to specify certain incentives (discounts, special pricing, etc.), a rights holder should make sure the language in the agreement does not leave any room for misrepresentation and that it could be enforced. The following is an example of such language:

The price for the [Product(s)] shall be the price (or license fee schedule) at the level and currency specified in the Product Catalog(s) (or licensing agreements) for the ordered Products (technology) in effect on the date the purchase order (sale or other disposal) is accepted by [Rights Holder] (or customer), less any applicable discounts. The price may not include any applicable handling charges, interest charges, shipping charges, insurance charges, cancellation charges, or rescheduling charges, or any applicable sales, use, and/or privilege taxes, all of which will be additionally invoiced to [Partner].

Penalties

Penalties for late payments need to be expressly addressed in the agreements. Example language could read as follows:

Late payments bear interest at a rate of [___ percent] per month (but in no event more than the maximum legal rate) until paid.

It is important to enforce the penalties and to set up the back-end processes to collect the interest. Most of the penalties relate to results of audits.

---

[20] "Getting More Money From Licenses." N. 1 *supra.*

Record Keeping and Audit

The following is an example of an agreement "audit clause" and record-keeping requirements. Tighter language facilitates an easier audit:

[Partner] shall keep complete books and records about its operations relating to [Rights Holder]'s reporting obligations under this Agreement in accordance with generally accepted accounting principles, for a period of at least [Number] years from delivery of the [Periodic] Report to which the information relates. At [Rights Holder]'s expense, during business hours, on at least [Number] calendar days' notice, and not more often than once a year, [Rights Holder] or [Rights Holder]'s agent(s) may inspect and make abstracts of such books and records as well as any books or records of [Partner] or its Subsidiaries (including, but not limited to, production and purchasing records of components, finished Products and any Product work in process, inventory levels, including specification sheets and bills of materials, data about inventory movement and balances, sales and shipping data that tie to financial statements and/or management reports), wherever located and however stored, to verify the accuracy of [Partner's] [Quarterly] Reports and [Partner's] compliance with its obligations herein. [Partner] shall cooperate with this examination and provide reasonable access to all information (including information not related to Sales of Products to verify the integrity of [Partner's] records and accuracy of [Partner's] [Quarterly Reports]) and relevant personnel requested by [Rights Holder] or [Rights Holder]'s agent(s) that will allow the examination to be completed in a timely manner. Also, electronic records will be provided in an electronic format requested by [Rights Holder]. [Rights Holder] will cause [Rights Holder]'s agent(s) to sign a nondisclosure agreement attached as Appendix [#] prior to such inspection. [Partner] will not impose any nondisclosure or other obligations on [Rights Holder]'s agent outside those in such nondisclosure agreement.

Underreporting Sales

The definition of the penalties for noncompliance is as important as the definition of the rights to audit. Again, the tighter the language, the easier it will be to enforce the retribution and recovery. The following is an example of language applicable to a resale/distribution agreement follows:

If [Rights Holder's] inspection of the relevant records of [Partner] or otherwise reveals that [Partner] underreported the sales, failed to comply with [Partner's] obligations set forth in this Agreement; including selling Products outside [Partner's] approved Territory; and purchase of Products from sources other than [Rights Holder] or [Rights Holder]-authorized Distributors, then [Partner] shall pay [Rights Holder]: (i) all payments which were not paid in accordance with the terms set forth in this Agreement ("Unpaid Payments"), and (ii) interest on the Unpaid Payments from the date such Unpaid Payments were due at a rate of [amount%] per month (but in no event more than the maximum rate allowed by law). If the Unpaid Payments for any consecutive 4-quarter period of the inspected period exceed [amount%] of total payments due in such 4-quarter period, [Partner] will also pay [Rights Holder] for the full cost of any examination and collection undertaken by or for [Rights Holder], including accounting, audit and legal fees and costs (including, without limitation, travel and lodging costs) and such breach will be deemed to be a material breach of the Agreement.

Consent to Injunctive Relief

The following is an example of applicable language:

Any actual or threatened violation by [Partner] of Sections [A], [B] or any other actual or threatened infringement of [Rights Holder] intellectual property by [Partner] will irreparably injure [Rights Holder] and monetary damages would not be an adequate remedy and, in such event, [Rights Holder] may seek injunctive relief in any court or forum of competent jurisdiction, in addition to pursuing any other legal remedies.

Limitation of Liabilities and Damages

The following is an example of typical language that may be used in distribution agreements:

In no event shall [Rights Holder] or its agents or suppliers be liable to [Partner] for more than the amount of any actual direct damages up to the greater of [U.S. $100,000] (or equivalent in local currency) or the charges for the Products or Services that are the subject of the claim, regardless of the cause *and whether arising in contract, tort (including negligence), or otherwise. This limitation will not apply to (a) claims for damages for bodily injury (including death) and damage to real property and tangible personal property for which [Rights Holder] is legally liable and (b) payments as set forth in Section [#] Patents and Copyrights.* IN NO EVENT SHALL [Rights Holder] OR ITS AGENTS OR SUPPLIERS BE LIABLE FOR ANY OF THE FOLLOWING: (a) DAMAGES BASED ON ANY THIRD PARTY CLAIM EXCEPT AS EXPRESSLY PROVIDED HEREIN AND IN SECTION [#] PATENTS AND COPYRIGHTS; (b) LOSS OF, OR DAMAGE TO, [PARTNER'S] OR [PARTNERS'] END USERS' RECORDS, FILES OR DATA; OR (c) INDIRECT, SPECIAL, INCIDENTAL, PUNITIVE, OR CONSEQUENTIAL DAMAGES (INCLUDING LOST PROFITS OR SAVINGS), EVEN IF [Rights Holder] IS INFORMED OF THEIR POSSIBILITY.

Patents and Copyrights

This section of an agreement is important in complex supply chains transactions for products that may use multiple rights holders' intellectual property (IP). The following is suggested example language:

If a third party claims that [Rights Holder] [Product] purchased by [Partner] from [Rights Holder] authorized Distributors infringes that party's patent or copyright, [Rights Holder] will defend [Partner] against that claim at [Rights Holder]'s expense and pay all costs and damages that a court finally awards or are agreed upon in settlement, provided that [Partner] (a) promptly notifies [Rights Holder] in writing of the claim and (b) allows [Rights Holder] to control, and cooperates with [Rights Holder] in the defense and any related settlement negotiations. If such a claim is made or appears likely to be made, [Rights Holder] may, but agrees in the case in which an infringement has been found, at its option, to secure the right for [Partner] or [Partner's] End User to continue to use the [Product], or to modify it, or to replace it with one that is equivalent. If [Rights Holder] determines that none of these alternatives is reasonably available, [Partner] agrees to return the [Product] and/or require that [Partner's] End User return the [Product] to [Rights Holder] upon [Rights Holder]'s written request. [Rights Holder] will then give [Partner] a credit equal to

[Partner's] or [Partner's] End User's net book value as determined by generally accepted accounting principles for the [Product]. Any such claims against [Partner] or liability for infringement arising from use of the [Product] following a request for return by [Rights Holder] are the sole responsibility of [Partner]. This represents [Rights Holder]'s entire obligation to [Partner] regarding any claim of infringement. [Rights Holder] has no obligation regarding any claim based on any of the following: (a) anything [Partner] or any third party provides that is incorporated into or used with the [Product] or that the [Product] is incorporated into; (b) third [Product]; (c) compliance by [Rights Holder] or its authorized suppliers or resellers with [Partner] or End User specifications, designs or instructions or any modification, change or improvement made at the request of [Partner] or End User or for the benefit of [Partner] or End User; (d) the amount of revenues or profits earned or other value obtained by the use of the [Product] by [Partner] or End User, or the amount of use of the [Product]; (e) the lost revenues or profits of third parties arising from [Partner's] or End User's use of the [Product]; (f) [Partner's] or End User's modification of [Product]; (g) the combination, operation, or use of [Product] with other products or items; (h) [Partner's] failure to perform changes, revisions or updates as instructed by [Rights Holder]; or (i) improper use of the [Product] or use outside the scope of the licensed use.

In other situations, such as direct supply or licensing agreements, the agreement language could be as shown subsequently.

Indemnity

The following is example indemnity clause language:

Licensee shall indemnify, defend, and hold harmless [Rights Holder], its affiliates, their respective successors, and their respective officers, directors, employees, agents, and representatives from any claim, loss, or damage (and expenses incurred in their investigation and defense, including attorney fees), arising from making or Selling by or for [Partner] of any product containing any [Rights Holder] intellectual property, except third-party claims alleging that the [Rights Holder] intellectual Property as delivered to [Partner] by [Rights Holder] infringes a third-party intellectual property right.

If [Partner] is required to defend [Rights Holder] pursuant to this Section, [Rights Holder] shall promptly notify [Partner] of any claim upon becoming aware of it and permit [Partner] at [Partner's] cost and expense to control the defense and disposition (including all decisions to litigate, settle [with [Rights Holder]'s consent for any settlement requiring any obligation for [Rights Holder]] or appeal) of such claim. [Rights Holder] shall reasonably cooperate in the defense thereof. [Rights Holder] may, at its option and expense, retain its own counsel to participate in any proceeding. [Partner] shall promptly advise [Rights Holder] of any significant events about such actions, including, but not limited to, any issues that could affect [Rights Holder]'s interests or where [Partner] and [Rights Holder] may have potentially adverse interests, such as issues relating to discovery from Licensor and any settlement that may include any obligation by [Rights Holder].

Arbitration

Most agreements also include language specifying terms regarding arbitration—such as the following example:

In any action brought to resolve a dispute under this Agreement, the prevailing Party will be entitled to recover from the other Party all costs and expenses incurred in that action or any appeal therefrom, including, but not limited to, court or arbitration costs and fees, all reasonable attorney fees, and other related costs.

Jurisdiction and Venue

Jurisdiction and venue language that may relate to an agreement in the United States follows:

This Agreement will be construed according to the substantive law, but not the choice of law rules, of the State of [State] and of applicable federal law of the United States. If any dispute arises under this Agreement, the venue for such dispute will be in the [State] Superior Courts and the Federal District Court for the [District of State] located in [City, State], and [Partner] hereby submits to the jurisdiction of such courts. However, this Section will not preclude either Party from seeking equitable relief in any court of competent jurisdiction. Any judgment issued by a court or other tribunal may be enforced to the fullest extent of the law in the country in which a Party resides, is located or owns assets.

Identifying the Perpetrators

As stated at the beginning of this chapter, even if IPR holders dedicate significant global resources to their brand protection efforts, they cannot possibly be everywhere and address every incident or concern. Selection of the right enforcement targets should be based on specific selection criteria consistent and in balance with the suite of strategic objectives as determined in the rights holder's brand protection program. The targets can be manufacturers, individuals, groups, importers, brokers, distributors, retailers, or other rights holders and other constituents in the supply chain. A rights holder's intelligence investigation is critical and should be the fundamental component of a successful brand protection program. The most resources should be dedicated to this section of the brand protection team. Without good investigative intelligence, the brand protection program can be derailed, or result in fishing-out "small fish" while missing the worse perpetrators.

There is not a single approach or investigative method for identifying the enforcement targets. Much of it depends on the industry, supply chain structure, business deliverables (product, service, other). There is usually one common element all rights holders want to protect—their trademarks. Custom-built Internet search engines that can identify unauthorized use of trademarks by online retailers, auction sites, or other businesses and individuals are the predominant intelligence tool deployed by most rights holders monitoring the Internet. These search engines can also search for use of trademarked names by web domain names (Uniform Resource Locator or URL). The approach to cease and desist or take-downs, or both, of unauthorized use of brand names can be either aggressive, which ultimately can be an expensive undertaking, or less aggressive but more pragmatic. The really aggressive approach is targeting registration of all URLs with the brand name included in part or whole within the URL, and other infringement that incorporates in any shape or form the trade name. Businesses can either preregister all such URLs or address every instance of perceived infringement via a Uniform Dispute Resolution Policy (UDRP) complaint, and have the infringing URL registered with a company. Even such an aggressive approach, however, will not prevent future infringements (as there are infinite potential variations of any trademark name) and may deliver low returns on investment.

A more pragmatic approach is to take action with infringing URLs that present a real risk to the business or products and acquire only the URL(s) registered by these serious offenders, unauthorized resellers, counterfeiters, offensive-content websites, and so on, that may tarnish the brand name or mislead customers and cause deterioration of the value of the brand.

Other common techniques in identifying perpetrators include investigations at point of purchase (POP), tradeshow canvassing, and monitoring retail stores and online sites for products bearing the company's brand. Monitoring auction sites and submitting "daily" take-down requests is now possible as many well-known auction sites offer a process to remove counterfeit (or otherwise infringing) articles.

The following is an example of a take-down letter used in these circumstances:

VIA E-MAIL and EXPRESS MAIL

[Date]

[Mr./Mrs. Name]

[Company]

[Address1]

[Address 2]

[Telephone]

[E-mail]

Subject: *Unauthorized use and distribution of [trademark(s), patent(s)]*

Dear [Name],

This is to inform you that we are aware of [product] on your website ([www.xyz.com]), which use(s) [trademark(s), patent(s)].

Our company is the rights holder to the [trademark(s), patent(s)]. From your website we were able to [obtain unauthorized product, download unlicensed software, etc.] containing our [trademark(s), patent(s)]. The distribution of this [product], whether directly or indirectly (via link to remote URL), without [authorization or license] is unlawful as it infringes on the intellectual property rights of [rights holder]. Accordingly, we request the unauthorized [product] accessible from your site to be removed from public access immediately.

The [trademark, patent] is the exclusive property of [rights holder] and is registered as such with the United States Patent and Trademark Office. Use and distribution of the [trademark, patent] whether for commercial distribution or other personal interest requires a valid [rights holder] license. Without the license, you may not distribute or use the [trademark, patent] and doing so exposes you to civil liability, including monetary damages.

If you are interested in obtaining a license, we encourage you to contact [rights holder] at [xyz@rightsholder.com].

We consider the unauthorized use and distribution of our intellectual property a direct threat and we will pursue our legal rights to the extent permissible by law. Please immediately remove all of our intellectual property from your website (including all mirror sites, and links to off-site content) as well as all links directing click-through traffic to known unauthorized, until such time a valid license is issued to you by [rights holder].

Please acknowledge your removal of [product(s)] and all related links providing direct access to [product(s)], no later than 5 business days from receiving this letter or 15 days from the date of this letter, whichever comes first. We thank you in advance for your cooperation, and encourage you to contact us to discuss licensing options.

With best regards,

Officer Name

Title

--

Signature

Monitoring internal databases and systems is as effective as any other investigative techniques—looking for unusual patterns, phony business/customer addresses (such as a PO Box), volumes, pricing (overusage of special pricing program), repetition and multiple-entry (repetitive use of the same serial number), and so on—and can yield the best results.

Warning Signs of Grey Market and Counterfeiting Activity

Each holiday season features new "must-have" gifts or toys a child just cannot live without, or that highly anticipated next-generation video game or console, or one special fashionable article. Such "hot" products attract the attention of consumers but they also attract unwanted attention. Counterfeits, pirated copies, and grey-market goods often closely follow a new hot product in the marketplace. Of course, these knock-offs mean lost sales as well as the cannibalization of the hard-earned goodwill associated with valued brands and products.

Rights holders can protect the integrity of their products, brands, and IPR by preparing early for an efficient and effective enforcement program.

Pricing Anomalies and Requests for Special Discounts

Most rights holders provide incentives to distributors and end users in order to increase sales opportunities or when facing stiff competition, introducing new products or technologies, or entering new markets. However, "channel incentives (such as SPIFFs,[21] product promotions, channel partner program discounts, etc.)—designed to boost sales by increasing loyalty and motivating channel partners to sell products—are vulnerable to abuse which may cost high tech companies an estimated $1.4 billion in lost profits each year. In addition to this lost profit, the abuse of channel incentives helps fuel the high tech grey market."[22]

---

[21] An acronym for immediate bonus for a sale. Typically, "spiffs" are paid, either by a manufacturer or employer, directly to a salesperson for selling a specific product.

[22] These are two key findings of research conducted by Deloitte & Touche® LLP and the Alliance for Gray Market and Counterfeit Abatement (AGMA®)

"However, the risks and rewards introduced by incentive programs must be balanced by creating consistent processes to administer, monitor and verify compliance, while enforcing protocols when dealing with identified non-compliance."

"Strong channel incentive management programs may significantly reduce exposure to the grey market and capture billions in what might otherwise be lost profit. Effective channel management programs enable companies to gain greater visibility into cross-functional incentive programs, and establish globally consistent policies through increased interaction with business and channel partners. Not only can these efforts reduce the number of grey market products in the market, but they can facilitate a better functioning distribution channel environment, reduce costs, and ultimately create stronger, more profitable brands."[23]

Changes in Ordering Habits

Frequent or significant changes in ordering or unusual swings in quantities could also be indicators of potential fraudulent behavior. These changes may include frequent or large orders for a small customer, an address that is not conditioned to receive such large amounts of goods (private address or small business), significant changes in pricing for the same customer, frequent changes to shipping addresses, and so on.

Changes in Delivery

Drop-ship orders should be exceptions, so any requests for drop-ship orders or changes in delivery addresses for the same customer from the same customer should raise a red flag and these incidents should be investigated immediately.

---

in November 2010, Available at https://agmaglobal.org/uploads/whitePapers/ KPMG-AGMA%20Effective%20Channel%20Management..pdf (accessed March 05, 2021).

[23] *Id.*

Spike in Returns or Warranty Requests

A warranty and support entitlement process needs to be an integral part of a brand protection program. Adherence to clear guidelines and procedures in entitlement is a best preventative tool. Any time a warranty or support claim is received, it should be matched with a valid customer contract, related serial number(s), and past history—looking for potential discrepancies, and trends. If the same serial number is claimed in more than one instance, there may be a problem. When there is a spike in claims when compared to previous periods, there may be a problem, either with the quality of the products or the customer.

Monitoring

Brand reputations can erode in a matter of days or weeks if customers start associating your brands with fraudulent online sales practices, therefore brand monitoring is the only defense that helps different enterprises combat any kind of reputation erosion. One can never overemphasize the need to implement efficient brand-monitoring solutions to ensure protection of revenue by identifying and shutting down sites selling grey market, pirated or counterfeited goods.

Internet

Most grey market sellers use the Internet to conduct their transactions, and so rights holders should closely monitor the Internet. Although some websites may blatantly advertise grey market goods that are clearly different from the authorized goods, most grey marketers take precautions to hide this. Since the grey market goods are usually priced well below authorized retail price levels, to hide this "obvious rapport," grey marketers may choose not to show prices and request potential purchasers to telephone or e-mail for the price instead. "When asked about product serial numbers, grey market sellers often claim that they do not know this information because the good 'is on the boat' or 'on the water.' Such answers are a sure sign of grey goods … ."[24]

---

[24] F.A. Mendelsohn, and A.H. Stanton. 2010. "Combating Gray Market Goods in an Economic Downturn with the Lanham Act." *Computer & Internet Law* 27, no. 8.

Even as companies spend millions to build global brands, the Internet with its wide reach can easily put such brands at risk—resulting in not just undermining the marketing investments [the companies] have made, but also eroding the brand and its reputation and losing customer trust.

Stings and Active "on the Street" Investigations

The best brand protection programs do not rely solely on "desk research" but also use either in-house or contracted investigators for monitoring what is sold on the shelves at POS (brick and mortar retail) and what is listed for sale at online auctions and industry-specialized trade exchanges, and for product acquisitions (test purchases) for forensic testing. In instances when a company may want to pursue a legal action, to maintain the "chain of evidence" or "chain of custody," these investigators should be commissioned/contracted by the law firm that will be representing the company in legal proceedings.

Where a company has a good product-tracking system in place, such investigative purchases can be a very helpful tool in identifying the actual sources of grey market goods. Brand protection teams need constantly to monitor market and sales trends, and adjust targets of these investigations to make sure the teams identify and address the products that have the most negative impact on the company at that time.

In the case of counterfeits, this still applies where counterfeits contain authentic components that can be traced. Otherwise, investigative purchases of counterfeits are mostly used for building the evidence in future legal action.

Tradeshow Canvassing

Many rights holders realize the seriousness of their situation and begin to take measures to protect their IPR only after the infringements of their IPR are widespread. Tradeshow canvassing is a proactive way to identify these threats early before they become entrenched and while they still represent a relatively manageable problem. Canvassing also allows rights holders' enforcement teams to interact personally with infringers and obtain valuable intelligence that helps to provide potential evidence and helps in shutting down infringers' operations.

Because of the high concentration of vendors in attendance, trade-shows are excellent platforms from which to survey the types of potential IPR infringements and gather extensive information (about counterfeit merchandise, unauthorized use of trademarks and patents, unauthorized resale, unlicensed/royalty owing products, etc.). For the same reason, tradeshows are ideal venues for serving cease and desist letters to both newly identified infringers and previously known infringers, or serving injunctions—all in a very cost-effective manner.

Preparing for a tradeshow can be a significant task that can tie up an enforcement team's resources for an extensive period of time (selecting enforcement and investigation targets based on collected data from the tradeshow website or other media, sifting through and capturing this in a manageable format, preparing and sending notifications, etc.), and most rights holders use processes and tools such as spreadsheets or some partial and specialized solutions, often making the overall process cumbersome, inefficient, and very lengthy. It does not have to be.

Monitoring Sales Trends and Channel and Supplier Audits

According to the KPMG and AGMA white paper "Managing the Risks of Counterfeiting in the Information Technology Industry," "[N]early all interviewees agreed that contract manufacturing poses greater counterfeiting risks than internal manufacturing. More stringent contracts and audit-ing, however, can help reduce the risk. They enhance both prevention and detection, and they spell out specific remediation plans. It is also important to consider the supply chain. Here, too, better monitoring enables preven-tion and detection. As KPMG notes, Counterfeiters do not announce their intention to copy branded products, and discovery often occurs by chance. But there are early indications that can signal when a company has a coun-terfeiting problem such as a sudden drop in raw-materials orders increased orders for proprietary components increased grey market availability increase in service returns and large volume of discounted product available. [25]

---

[25] KPMG. 2016. "Gray Markets: An Evolving Concern. Unauthorized Sales Continue to Raise Costs and Damage Brand Reputation." Available at https://agmaglobal.org/uploads/whitePapers/2-25-16%20Gray%20Market%20Sur-vey-2015%20KPMG%20AGMA.pdf (accessed March 05, 2021).

Auditing Sales Activity: Ensuring Volume Discounts Going to Proper Place

The purpose of an audit is to assess a business partner's compliance with the requirements of the existing agreement(s) and to gain an understanding of a partner's processes and controls to enable compliance with the requirements outlined in the agreement(s), including the completeness and accuracy of the partner's reporting and accuracy of applicable contractual incentives. Auditing of sales records (POS) is often the only way to uncover an abuse of incentive programs—the partner's reporting of sales to an entity eligible for special incentives while transacting with (actual sales to) another entity—to unfairly benefit from larger, aggregated volume discounts.

Product Tracking

Serialization or other authentication is an important enabler of product tracking. POS reports can be compared to a partner's sales records to uncover any discrepancy between quantities of product reported and actually sold, but they will not uncover any unauthorized purchases and subsequent sales, unless the products' unique identifiers can be matched with the POS. For example, resellers and distributors may source unauthorized grey market products and mix them with authorized products, and in the absence of vendor's product tracking, the resellers and distributors may be able to claim warranty or service support for these products.

In order to succeed, a business initiative requires appropriate resources; in order to get such resources, the benefits these resources will bring to the business have to be clearly defined. Many benefits of brand protection are hard to convert to financial metrics because they include preserving brand value, customer loyalty, or customer perception, which convert to financial gains but there is no unique formula to measure these benefits. There are, however, benefits that can be clearly measured, financial recoveries resulting from enforcing agreement(s) terms, via either audits or other brand protection or compliance initiatives. The following is an example of recoveries from such activities. The best brand protection programs are often self-funding and profit generating.

Brand Protection Program—Self-Sustained Profit Center

Action	Key Deliverables	Costs	Revenue Oprotunities	Contribution
Prevention and Education	• Intelligence and Investigations • Counter-Measures • Infringement Reconciliation • Training • Policies and Tools	< $5M	$31M	$51M

Enforcement	• Enforce Collection From Infringing Parties
	  o Un-Entitled Service
	  o Unearned Discounts
	  o Underreporting
	  o Other Infringements
	• Audits
	• Litigation
	• Other Remedies and Deterrents
	Policies and Tools
			$20M	

Continuance	• De-Tiering Data • Collection and Integrity • Process and Policies • Continuous Intelligence • Publicity and Tools		N/A	

Discounting Programs

In a survey conducted by Deloitte LLP and the AGMA, "respondents estimated that incentive abuse may affect up to 25 percent of all channel sales and result in significant lost profits; they also stated that it often goes largely undetected due to a lack of active program management and inadequate internal controls related to channel incentives ... ."[26] According to this research, "[I]t is a case of unintended consequences. In an effort to boost sales by increasing loyalty and motivating channel partners to sell products, technology companies around the world commonly use incentives—such as end-user pricing, volume incentive rebates, product promotions, and authorized channel partner program discounts. However, the unfortunate reality is that these same programs may actually cost high tech companies an estimated $1.4 billion in lost profits each year ... ."[27]

Deloitte and AGMA also identified a clear connection between channel incentive abuse and the grey and counterfeit markets. For example, in some instances, buyers who receive special pricing for a specific customer do not sell only to this specific customer, and divert the products to the open market, which results in a "potentially significant flow of grey market products ... ."

The study also found that 84 percent of the surveyed vendors agreed that some channel incentives are responsible for grey market activity causing profit margin erosion and cash drain because of payout of unearned incentives.

---

[26] Deloitte LLP. 2016. "When Channel Incentives Backfire: Strategies to Help Reduce Gray Market Risks and Improve Profitability." Available at www.agma-global.org/cms/uploads/whitePapers/AGMA%20Deloittte%20When%20channel%20incentives%20backfire%20FINAL%204-14-11.pdf (accessed March 05, 2021).

Channel incentives "[a]re defined as end-user pricing, channel partner accreditation and programmatic incentives (such as SPIFFs, product promotions, channel partner program discounts, etc.)."

[27] *Id.*

Vendors need to communicate more frequently with their channels, especially if they allow stacking of incentives, which is the most frequent form of noncompliance or abuse.[28]

Improving Warranty and Service Process

The best practices against service abuse and fraud are the exact opposite of the control weaknesses.[29] Additional best practices may include providing access or validation of the product unique identifiers (such as serial numbers, MAC address, software key, etc.) to the partners, other business partners, and even to the public. Online tools that can verify the authenticity of the serial number in question and provide basic information about what product is related to this serial number and what is the release (manufacture date) can assist customers to identify counterfeit or misrepresented products. Because of advances in technology, the counterfeits or "Frankenstein engineered" products often carry product labels that are almost identical to authentic product labels, including serial number sequencing. Only when such serial numbers are verified against manufacture records or shipping information and product type, the fraud is revealed.

---

[28] "Bent, Shades Of Gray: When Channel Incentives Go Wrong." *CRN.com,* November 11, 2013. Available at www.crn.com/news/components-peripherals/240163726/shades-of-gray-when-channel-incentives-go-wrong.htm (accessed March 05, 2021).

[29] Control weaknesses enabling service abuse are (not exclusively): (i) business cultures that allow or disregard service abuse; (ii) poorly designed contract terms; (iii) lack of monitoring; (iv) lack of appropriate entitlement tracking; (v) poor serial numbers tracking related to service entitlement; (v) system controls that do not prevent the download of unauthorized software or its registration before its activation; (vi) poor product data management; (v) manual and decentralized processes leading to lack of data analytics related to product sales and service claims; (vi) lack of product/customer service history tracking; and so on.

For more details on service abuse, see the PricewaterhouseCoopers/AGMA Whitepaper. 2009. "Service blues: Effectively Managing the Multi-Billion Dollar Threat from Product Warranty and Support Abuse." Available at www.pwc.com/cz/en/fraud-forum/assets/warranty_service_blues.pdf (accessed March 05, 2021).

So, what does all this mean in real life? On October 14, 2009, three people were sentenced to jail followed by three years' supervised release and were ordered to pay $21,715,844.00 in restitution for defrauding Cisco of $23M. A GPS tracking sting helped to determine that the accused used dozens of fake names and fictitious companies to obtain replacement parts from Cisco, a leading manufacturer of routers and other computer network equipment. The parts were shipped to private mailboxes at UPS stores in eight states between January 2003 and July 2005, authorities said. The replacement parts were provided under a Cisco program that allows customers to obtain technical support and parts without first returning a failed or defective part.[30]

Nortel won a $10 million court judgment against two U.S. companies it accused of selling its equipment through a warranty-fraud scheme. The two companies claimed to be operating a network under a Nortel warranty and received replacement parts for free and then resold the warranty parts. Nortel's claims included trademark infringement, fraud, breach of contract, and deceptive acts and practices.[31]

Reducing the risks of warranty and service fraud requires patience, knowledge, and commitment. The right prevention program includes commitment to change; intensive communication; commitment to compliance, risk management, and enforcement; and implementation of controls to reduce vulnerabilities and limit implications.[32]

---

[30] The United States Attorney's Office Eastern District of North Carolina "Husband, Wife and Co-Conspirator Sentenced for Participation In $23 Million Mail Fraud And Money Laundering Scheme." (September 29, 2010), available at www.justice.gov/archive/usao/nce/press/2010/2010-sep-29_04.html (accessed March 05, 2021).

[31] Reuters. September 07, 2007. "Nortel wins $10 Mln Judgement in Warranty Case." Available at www.reuters.com/article/idUKN0746658620070907 (accessed March 05, 2021).

[32] Price Waterhouse Coopers LLP. "Service blues: Effectively Managing the Multi-Billion Dollar Threat from Product Warranty and Support Abuse." Available at www.pwc.com/cz/en/fraud-forum/assets/warranty_service_blues.pdf (accessed March 05, 2021).

Global Versus Regional Price and Control

Although establishing practical and effective pricing (strategy, policies, and processes) is one of the most difficult and fundamental key success factors of any business, understanding, and eliminating potential weaknesses is an absolute cornerstone of grey market prevention, especially for a company with a global presence.

When establishing a commercial strategy, a company (especially when pursuing expansion into international markets) needs to conduct due diligence related to:

- Country market and economic conditions (purchasing power).
- Main competitors in the particular region.
- Market and consumer culture—buying behavior, decision making, demand.
- Characteristics of local distribution channels.
- Market integration.
- Company internal organization/structure fit.
- Federal and regional government policies, regulations, customs and duties, and taxation.
- Countries' pan-alignment (countries with similar conditions).
- Perceived brand and product value and potential product differentiation in a specific region.

Businesses need to consider all the contributing factors, balancing the facts, requirements, opportunities, strengths, and weaknesses that drive the final pricing strategy. Good analysis may yield dramatic differences among geographies or customer segments, and may suggest the necessity of differentiated pricing or a differentiated product. There are many pricing structures and processes to choose from, depending on the business requirements, but there are only two fundamental types of pricing:

- Global
- Regional

Implementing regional pricing (policy, tools, and systems) requires significantly more effort and resources on the "front-end": establishing, managing (depending on the type of goods and markets—frequent changes), and monitoring the pricing that varies per region, per distributor, per product, and so on. The complexity increases with the number of products and countries where the differentiation is required. The "back-end" (pricing waterfall, special pricing, special discounting, and promotions) still exists but it should be rare and required only sporadically. The regionalized pricing (if done well) should be continuously adjusted to meet the specific regional requirements and there should be no need for additional discounting.

"Pan-Regional" pricing (where pricing is common among multiple countries) is possible for certain groups of countries but simple sharing of borders does not automatically present an opportunity to apply the Pan-Regional concept. Countries should be grouped according to specific criteria (such as currency, market, and economic conditions; competition in the particular country; culture—buying behavior, decision making; demand and potential product differentiation; characteristics of distribution channels; and so on).

Within the European Union, for example, pricing is becoming more transparent because of a single standardized currency and trade legislation allowing "free trade" of products among the member countries. This does not necessarily mean the prices are also unilateral; however, a cross-border product flow among the EU countries is legitimate even without vendors' consent, so vendors have to be careful not to set significant price disparities.

With regionalized pricing, it is essential that a company implement additional sets of "front-end" tools (usually within enterprise resource planning (ERP)), such as tracking and monitoring the product flow by serial numbers, POS, and end-user information reporting, so it can identify potentially speculative trends and activities. With respect to the "back-end," some simple policies and controls are usually sufficient, as special discounting should be rare and highly visible.

A company may decide to approach all markets equally, with global pricing. Implementing global pricing requires less effort on the "front-end" but significantly more effort on the "back-end," managing and controlling the pricing waterfall (special discounting, promotions, rebates, etc.) for all opportunities that require some price incentive. Global prices are less complex to establish and the pricing tools are also less complex. The difficulty lies in establishing really robust pricing controls, policies, and procedures (and discounting guidelines) that can handle a large volume of deals while ensuring efficiency, with proper due diligence (tracking and monitoring that may not be incorporated in the ERP), and enforcement—companywide. As long as there are robust controls preventing abuse in place (end-user authentication, opportunity analysis, etc.), and company culture evolved to enforce compliance, the risk of grey marketing that leverages price differentials could be kept to a minimum. Additional controls such as serial number tracking, POS, and so on, add an additional layer of security and enable corrective actions.

Because the economy, technology maturity, shortening product life-cycles in technology industries, markets, customers, and other factors are constantly changing, the pricing has to be constantly adjusted. There is usually not much room for error when setting or changing the pric-ing—even small opportunities for arbitrage can be immediately exploited by grey marketers. Businesses have to weigh the pros and cons of global and regional pricing and decide which one is more appropriate for their business. In many instances, businesses implement one or the other or a hybrid, leveraging the strengths of both strategies for different sets of products.

There are also other ways to implement differentiated regional offer-ings that enable regionalized pricing but are much more resistant to grey market speculation:

- De-featuring products by reducing functionality to meet regional demand (and make the extras optional or not available).
- Adjusting the product pricing structure to reduce the impact of tariffs and import taxes (in some countries import taxes on software are less than hardware taxes).
- Shortening distribution channels (reduce the number of resale tiers).
- Using regional distributors or global distributors that have a regional presence.

Does a global market require global products? Many hi-tech products, for example, are designed for markets with technically savvy customers, but some product features required by customers in North America may not be required or even desired by customers in Asia. Vendors may consider localizing (de-featuring) their products by a redesign adhering to regional specifications and legislation, or differentiating product features and functionality.

Product differentiation provides another means of combating the grey market problem locally. Products sold in a specific region or market must be compliant with regional legislation, health and safety standards and certifications. Vendors of products that intentionally lack specific standards and certifications are in a much better position to pursue grey marketers and counterfeiters that sell these products in regions where the products are noncompliant. One negative aspect of this solution is that it adds more complexity to supply operations because it can significantly increase the number of differentiated stocking units (SKUs).

Today, besides the warranty and service abuse, the price differential between regional markets is still the most significant contributor to triggering grey market speculation. This usually involves initial and legitimate sale of genuine goods in one region and subsequent unauthorized resale in another. Internal business controls, brand protection, and compliance programs could prevent product leakage to grey markets and rehabilitate distributors. Deciding on the best pricing strategy depends on many factors as well as a business's ability to implement front-end and back-end processes that are required for either regional or global pricing.

Building Corporate Awareness

"An organization can only 'walk the talk' when its managers deliberately shape its internal reality to align with its brand promise … (the brand's) values must be internalized by the organization, shaping its instinctive attitudes, behaviors, priorities, etc."[33]

---

[33] Mitchell. January-April 1999. "Out of the Shadows." *15 J. Marketing Management* no. 1–3, pp. 25–42.

Corporate awareness is critical for the success of a brand protection program. It starts at the top and ends with every employee, partner, suppliers, contractor, and so on.

Sales Force Education and Due Diligence: Training Salespersons to Spot Red Flags

The first target of IPR protection and compliance programs should be a company's sales force. These individuals are in the trenches, speaking to customers, partners, and other third parties on a daily basis. If they are ambassadors of a company's IPR protection and compliance policies, they are carrying the message to the field, and can also be an unequaled source of information from the field. There should be IPR protection and compliance training specifically designed for the sales force, to ingrain best practices for customer and partner verification, problem spotting, deal due diligence, and other vital tasks that can prevent a negative effect on revenues, on costs, or create potential liabilities. Only prevention can keep a company's brand name untarnished. Reactive countermeasures will not avert a negative effect on brand recognition.

Best practices in training a sales force and other key employees include:

- Completion of mandatory annual ethics and compliance training;
- Establishing and updating policies and procedures regarding intellectual property protection;
- Regular communications and updates about the company's efforts, legal wins, and actions taken with infringers;
- Use of such tools as compliance and IPR protection websites providing access to documents used in daily activities, such as red flags, due diligence, customer authentication, and so on; and
- Check-sheets, inbox for sales comments, complaints, action requests, and so on.

Educate Dealer Network Regarding Differences and Steps Taken to Stop Grey Marketing

The first step in enforcing any policy is the communic*ation and clear definition of the policy. An example of such a communication follows.*

Grey Market Policy for Channel Partners

Global Distribution Management Notice

To: All Channel Partners:

[Rights Holder] is committed to ensuring the integrity of its products in the marketplace.

The grey marketing of [Rights Holder's] products is a serious problem that has serious consequences not only for our customers but also for our authorized Resellers. [Rights Holder] is dedicating its full attention to enforcing the integrity of its channel agreements and protecting the interests of our customers and our Resellers alike.

[Rights Holder] defines grey marketing as:

New [Rights Holder branded] products being sold by unauthorized resellers. Unauthorized resellers are those who do not have a valid [brand owner] reseller agreement or are selling products not authorized by their agreement with [Rights Holder].

[Rights Holder] products being sold in violation of a distribution agreement, i.e., selling to unauthorized resellers, selling outside a Reseller's authorized territory, or selling products to "customers" that are not end users.

Authorized Resellers who buy [Rights Holder] products from sources other than [Rights Holder] or an authorized Distributor. These partners are also engaged in "grey market" activity since the quality and functionality of these products cannot be verified. Grey market products are not eligible for support and warranty service from [Rights Holder] and the resale of such products is wholly inconsistent with the value and goodwill associated with the [Rights Holder] trademarks authorized for use by our Resellers and relied upon by our customers.

> *This policy is intended to communicate clearly to our customers and our Resellers, [Rights Holder's] long-standing position on the sale of grey market products. [Rights Holder] will not support any Reseller who engages in the grey marketing of our products.*
>
> *At [Rights Holder], we are taking the grey market problem very seriously. Your continued efforts to assist us are invaluable. Please continue to report details of suspected grey market activity to greymarket@rightsholder.com*

Tools and Processes to Enforce the Strategy

The following is an example of a communication that should be sent to all business partners that use systems or processes that require access to brand owner systems and tools and could potentially be abused or breached and used for unauthorized use. Without such communication, any enforcement of compliance with terms and conditions of use of such systems and tools is almost impossible to enforce. It is generally a good idea to send updates or just reiterate this policy annually.

e-Business Applications

> *Business Partner Notice*
>
> *To: Global contracted [Rights Holder] Resellers, Distributors (collectively referred to herein as "Partner") authorized by [Rights Holder] to resell [Rights Holder] products.*
>
> *Details:*
>
> *[Rights Holder] e-Business applications, including but not limited to [XYZ], ABC (ABC), Ordering Centre (OC) and Customer Price List (CPL) and other [Rights Holder] proprietary applications available for business Partner use, are provided to [Rights Holder] authorized Partners to ensure streamlined and efficient product ordering and support. So that Partners may get the full benefit for which these systems were*

designed, it is imperative for each Partner to follow the policies and procedures for use of these systems.

Upon accessing these applications, either online or through incorporating the system into the Partner's electronic data interface (EDI) for ordering [Rights Holder] product, the Partner has agreed to comply with certain terms and conditions, such as software licensing, confidentiality, warranty, and registration.

For convenience, this notice outlines some of the obligations the Partner has agreed to for use of [Rights Holder] e-Business applications and options available for maintaining the Partner's records. This notice formally addresses an existing practice.

1. *Partner is responsible for maintaining its employees' access and passwords to the tools. A Partner must notify [Rights Holder] within three (3) business days of an employee's termination from the company by one of the following methods:*
   i. *Calling 1-800-eBUSSNS.*
   ii. *E-mailing changes2ebusiness@rightsholder.com with the employee's name, contact information, and date of termination.*
   iii. *Accessing the shared-administration functionality whereby the Partner has the ability to update the registration directly online. To use this functionality, the Partner will need to send an e-mail to registration2shared-admin@rightsholder.com, identifying the person who will be accountable for the updates along with availability dates for training and requesting that the administrator function be turned on.*
2. *Partner has agreed, per the original terms and conditions for use of the applications, to hold all information and contents of these applications as proprietary and confidential; and to only use for each application's intended purpose.*
3. *Partner has been granted a nonexclusive right to use these applications. All pricing, configuration, and electronic order placement is governed under the terms and conditions for which the Partner has agreed to resell [Rights Holder] products.*

> *Violations of use of any of these applications by the Partner may result in revocation of access to these applications or possible termination of the resale agreement in its entirety.*
>
> *Additional Information:*
>
> *For additional information, contact eBusiness@rightsholder.com.*

There are other communication vehicles—choice of which depends on the purpose and content—newsletters, training manuals, brochures, communiqués, guidelines, web pages, e-mail inbox, and so on. Below is how the actual brand protection program schedule may look:

IPR Protection Program Communications Schedule		
Internal Awareness	**Partner Awareness**	**Customer Awareness**
(January 01–March 31, 20__)	(April 01–April 30, 20__)	(April 01–April 30, 20__)
Executive newsletter	Sales bulletins and guidelines	Social media (Twitter, LinkedIn, blogs, etc.
Sales newsletter	Emphasis on	User associations (news-
Sales training	new (renewal)	letters, websites, executive
General information	Distribution and services	sessions, conferences)
Sales	agreements	Media contributed articles
Services	Partner mentoring	and whitepapers, interviews
Product	Partner hot-line	Emphasis on renewal agree-
IPR protection	(dedicated inbox)	ments
corporate-wide	Partner newsflash	Regular reach-out—emails,
IPR protection website	(newsletter, alerts, cases,	bulletins (alerts, cases, settle-
launch—clear link from	settlements)	ments, etc.)
www.company.com page	External websites	Industry association member-
Links to new global	(partner, services, product	ships and participation
warranty policy	portals)	

Public Relations: Inform Public and Customers Regarding Differences and Dangers of Grey/Counterfeit Goods

The first public relations step should be publication of a company policy that is communicated to customers and business partners. This policy could be as simple as:

Resale Policy   *Date/issue*

"Territory" Resale Policy

To: "Territory" contracted Resellers, Partners (collectively referred to herein as "Partner") and Distributors authorized by [Rights Holder] to resell [Rights Holder] products.

[Rights Holder]'s distribution strategy has included a restriction that authorizes products purchased under a resale agreement to be sold to end users only. Purchases by Distributors have been authorized for resale to [Rights Holder]-accredited Partners only. Resale of such products among Partners or to nonauthorized parties has been, and continues to be, prohibited.

The above authorizations are governed under the terms and conditions under which Partners and Distributors have agreed to resell [Rights Holder] products. Exceptions to these authorizations may be granted on a case-by-case basis where necessary to address the market. Violations by Distributors or Partners may result in revocation of product authorization or termination of the agreement in its entirety.

[Rights Holder] appreciates each Partner's and Distributor's adherence to the current distribution strategy. It is [Rights Holder]'s intent to ensure that the Distributors engaged in wholesale distribution are the best in the industry and committed to delivering superior value to all [Rights Holder] Partners. Through sales and marketing efforts, brand owner will ensure its Partners are equipped to provide the highest quality sales and support to their end users.

Any questions or clarifications regarding this matter should be directed to your Account Representative or Distribution Management.

Officer Name

Title

_____

Signature

It is beneficial to send such notice once a year to all resellers, reiterating this resale policy.

Another vehicle is product bulletins informing about changes, including requirements for warranty and support entitlement:

Repair and Return Policy and Procedure Update

"Territory" Repair and Return Policy and Procedures Update

Date/issue

To: "Territory" contracted Resellers, Partners (collectively referred to herein as "Partner") and Distributors authorized by [Rights Holder] to resell [Rights Holder] products.

In addition to current Repair Policies and Procedures:

- *Starting on date, year, warranty for Products (as detailed in this notice) will be honored on Products identified with a valid authentic product code (Serial Number) and a valid warranty entitlement label.*
- *The warranty entitlement label is present on Products manufactured on or after date, year (as identified further in Section Y, of this notice).*
- *Out-of-warranty support will be available according to the current out-of-warranty pricing schedule.*
- *Warranty will be provided to authorized Partners and customers who purchase the new products from authorized Partners only.*

Note: Current Repair Policies and Procedures are available on the Policy and Procedures link containing current warranty and repair policies and procedures.

Officer Name

Title

Signature

Website Disclaimer: Detailing Above and That No Service on or Return of Grey/Counterfeit Goods

During litigation, the rights holder may need to demonstrate that it established clear and well-documented policies and procedures and raised public awareness of these policies and procedures. The appropriate place for a business to present these policies is on the actual product web pages. The business should also have generic warranty and support documents aggregated to a single Service and Support-designated web page that is available to partners and consumers. Short statements, disclaimers, or warnings can be inserted at various points of interest with high user traffic, to highlight the policies.

Website With Policy, Processes, Tools, and Examples of Actions Taken (Communication Hub)

Some companies state on their web pages that they will not service grey market products.[34] Many brand owners publicize their activities related to grey market and counterfeiting, and communicate their activities in a matter, showing their customers and business partners the owners' commitments to protect their customers and partners against the potential risks of acquiring unauthorized products. Hewlett Packard, for example, released news on its website regarding a suit it filed in federal court to recover more than $8.6 million in pricing discounts for computer equipment that defendants falsely claimed were purchased for resale. The complaint states claims for damages including civil conspiracy, common-law fraud, and breach of contract.[35] An industry study by KPMG and the

---

[34] See, e.g., Nikon USA, "What is Gray Market?" Available at https://support.nikonusa.com/app/answers/detail/a_id/331/~/what-is-gray-market%3F (accessed March 05, 2021).

[35] HP. September 02, 2004. "HP Continues to Combat the Gray Market, Files Suit for Fraud, Breach of Contract and Conspiracy." Available at https://e-channelnews.com/hp-continues-to-combat-the-gray-market-files-suit-for-fraud-breach-of-contract-and-conspiracy/ (accessed March 05, 2021).

AGMA reported that $58 billion worth of information technology (IT) products are resold on the worldwide grey market annually.[36]

Microsoft provides customers with a "How to Tell" web page advising consumers on how to identify counterfeit or pirated software, and provides tools for authentication.[37]

Engineering and Supply Chain Process Controls

If rights holders are not prepared to protect their IP and do not take precautions, somebody will take advantage of their weaknesses. All rights holders, and especially those that hold globally recognized (well-known) trademark(s), need to have controls in place that could prevent and discourage anyone from taking unfair advantage of one of their most valuable asset(s). Depending on where such controls make the most sense and where they would be most effective, businesses can implement specific measures in various parts of their business operations—research and development, manufacturing, logistics, and so on.

Shipping Controls

Despite investing heavily in ERP, warehouse management (WM), supply chain management (SCM), or an alphabet soup of other business systems, many businesses are finding that they lack the real-time visibility and situational awareness needed to identify threats from counterfeiting and grey marketing, because the information is gathered from the same sources that are engaging in grey marketing or counterfeiting. Inconsistent product volumes, suspicious addresses, or multiple customers (business of names of individuals) with identical coordinates should be the initial red flags of suspicious activities, but in order to get to the

---

[36] KPMG. 2016. "Gray Markets: An Evolving Concern. Unauthorized Sales Continue to Raise Costs and Damage Brand Reputation." Available at https://agmaglobal.org/uploads/whitePapers/2-25-16%20Gray%20Market%20Survey-2015%20KPMG%20AGMA.pdf (accessed March 05, 2021).

[37] See www.microsoft.com/howtotell/default.aspx?displaylang=en (accessed March 05, 2021).

bottom of the problem, a business needs to have more detailed product information; it needs product tracking.

Tracking

The sale of unauthorized products or the unauthorized sale of authentic products, either diverted from an intended authorized distribution channel or imported into a country for unapproved sale, has led to a serious need for tighter product-level tracking and traceability along the entire supply chain. Successful brand owners are developing enterprisewide tracking strategies encompassing packaging, IT, and other disciplines and addressing the organization's product serialization from the standpoint of consumer safety, IPR protection, and supply chain operations. Companies with solid serialization strategy have more control of their destiny and will likely be positioned to unlock other potential future benefits.

Safeguarding Products and Serial Numbers

With authentication technologies available today, each single item (product or package or both) can have its own identity through an individual, unique number that is recorded in a secured database, and is usually not publicly accessible. This unique number can be encoded in a machine-readable form, for example as a barcode or RFID (Radio Frequency Identification Device). These serial numbers can be printed directly on products, packages, or serialized labels.

A product tracing system provides benefits in protection against grey market diversion and counterfeiting along the supply chain, such as:

- Warranty and Support of products can be managed in a cost-effective manner and help avoid servicing unauthorized products.
- Identification of manufacturing sites and POS through the tracing system. This allows for easy correlation to a specific subcontractor or manufacturing site, and distributors who may be selling products outside of the authorized supply chain.

- Providing product specific information such as date of manufacture. This is important for goods with a limited shelf life, such as pharmaceuticals, batteries, and food.
- Generating intelligence such as customer sales data at the end of the supply chain can be done centrally and "online." Moreover, analysis of a marketing campaign's effectiveness can be managed centrally.

Making the right investments in serialization can protect customers, brands, and supply chains from counterfeit threats.[38]

Product Enhancements

Technical solutions by which products are serialized are generally not exclusive to one product or one rights holder. Aside from the unique product coding sequence, such solutions are usually in the form of alphanumeric or numeric codes or barcodes, or RFIDs. In addition to such unique identification, businesses have the opportunity to incorporate their own unique and proprietary features or enhancements in products so they are differentiated based on price, on where they are sold,

---

[38] Potter and Pequignot. 2009. "Actionable Trademark Infringement; Unauthorized Removal of Quality Control, Anti-counterfeiting Devices from Genuine Trademarked Products." *The Intellectual Property Strategist*, no. 12, © 2009 ALM Media Properties, LLC. All rights reserved. See also, www.kilpatrick-townsend.com/~/media/Files/articles/RPotterAPequignotLJN09.ashx (accessed March 05, 2021). The authors are discussing Davidoff's use of unique code on the packaging and bottle that contains the date and time the unit was produced and the specific production line information and its importance to Davidoff's quality control as well as anticounterfeiting efforts. This helped Davidoff in 1998, and subsequently in 2005, when Davidoff learned that counterfeited DAVIDOFF COOL WATER fragrances were sold at CVS, which is not one of DAVIDOFF authorized retailers, but in both instances CVS agreed to eliminate counterfeit products. However, in 2006, Davidoff discovered counterfeit fragrances for sale at CVS for the third time and brought suit (Zino Davidoff SA v. CVS Corp., 2009 WL 1862462 (2d Cir. June 19, 2009) against CVS specifically in the Southern District of New York, alleging, among other things, trademark infringement, unfair competition, and trademark dilution under the Lanham Act.

or in ways that would require significant rework that would dissuade counterfeiting and grey marketing. For example, changes may be made to the product design (external or internal) associated with a specific application or market, or to the level of functionality—products can be de-featured (limited software functionality, lower performance, or quality standards). These are ways to differentiate products sold in various markets so there are significant material differences that can affect or confuse customers.

Authentication Technologies

The efforts of rights holders to protect their rights against counterfeiting and grey marketing led to the birth of many new businesses that provide rights holders with authentication solutions. There are probably as many authentication solutions as there are types of products using them. Many well-known brands use at least a few of these solutions. According to the World Intellectual Property Organization (WIPO):

"The function of authentication technology is to help examiners—customs, police and consumer protection agencies—identify the genuine product in ways that are *not obvious* to counterfeiters, who have become adept at accurately copying products and packaging. It enables the examiner to look beyond the obvious characteristics of the product in order to determine to a reasonable level of certainty whether the item is genuine. Conversely, the absence of the nonobvious characteristics will betray a fake, even though it may look exactly like the genuine product … .

"The layering of an authentication device is achieved through combinations of technologies which are characterized as follows:

- *Overt devices.* These are visible to the naked eye under standard viewing conditions, including holograms, color-change inks, iridescent thin films and retro-reflective materials.
- *Hidden (also semicovert) devices.* These are revealed to the human eye through use of a handheld inspection tool, such as a plastic film overlay, a UV light, a magnifying glass or a laser pointer. Includes ultraviolet/infrared-sensitive inks, microtext, scrambled images, holograms.

- *Covert devices.* These require a more sophisticated detection tool or kit. They may be chemical-based, such as chemical tag-gants and markers incorporated in the product or the packaging; or electronic, such as a code number or similar identifier (which may require connection to a central database). Covert devices also include DNA and molecular taggants, magnetic labels, and embedded codes.
- *Forensic devices.* These require laboratory analysis, which can include analysis of the composition of the product as well as forensic analysis of the authentication marker."

"These elements may be found separately or incorporated into a single authentication device. For example, a hologram, the most commonly used device, is an overt feature that can contain hidden and covert images, and the optical 'fingerprint' of the original hologram, which can be examined in a laboratory."

"Research conducted by Reconnaissance or by the IPR owners themselves–including case-studies on Allied Domecq, Microsoft, Chanel, Epson and the Turkish Caykur Tea Company—indicate that the properly applied use of authentication devices within a comprehensive anti-counterfeiting strategy can make an effective contribution to reducing counterfeiting and more than recover their cost."[39]

There are also digital authentication technologies that may be either overt or covert that require an electronic means for detection and validation. Some commonly known digital authentication technologies are RFID tags, which can be linked to product serial numbers or compared to a remote identification database.

Each authentication solution has its advantages and disadvantages. Many authentication solution vendors use a combination of various technologies (also called "layering") that allows them to provide rights holders with a single solution that can address multiple objectives of their brand protection strategy.

---

[39] Lancaster. April 2006. "The Role of Authentication Technologies in Combating Counterfeiting." *Wipomagazine*, available at www.wipo.int/wipo_magazine/en/2006/02/article_0004.html (accessed March 05, 2021).

New technologies used to combat anti-counterfeiting and grey market are discussed in Chapter 8: New Technologies and Alternative Methods to combat Counterfeiting and Grey Market.

Government and Law Enforcement Agencies and Organizations

Public policy coverage is integral to advancing an organization's IPR protection agenda. Not being "at the table" translates into lost opportunities and narrows the organization's scope and effectiveness.

Historically, the high-tech industry has chosen self-help solutions (supply chain security, technological protection measures, and the like) over government recourse in combating IPR violations such as counterfeiting, piracy, and grey market practices. Many IPR protection professionals do not devote much time or attention to governmental liaison. They may believe that they cannot affect policy outcomes or that there is someone else who shares their interests (e.g., perhaps within their organization's government affairs department) who has these matters covered. In point of fact, a measure of focused engagement in governmental matters by everyone involved in brand protection is both productive and necessary.

For better or worse, government has a monopoly on certain services vital to IPR protection. Only government has the authority and ability to:

- Enact law reform.
- Police the border.
- Conduct federal investigations and bring federal prosecutions.
- Use trade incentives to pressure foreign governments to protect IP.

On a less exclusive basis, government plays a key role in:

- Educating and influencing foreign policy makers.
- Training foreign law enforcement officers and supporting IP capacity-building efforts.
- Quantifying, analyzing, and validating the problem.
- Raising public awareness.

There is also an opportunity to participate in industry groups that actively work with government on a range of brand protection matters to:

- Strengthen or close gaps in the law and augment and more effectively deploy governmental resources.
- Increase the level of IPR enforcement and improve the exchange of information between industry and enforcement agencies.
- Share industry experiences regarding IPR protection in foreign countries and help direct government efforts to effect change (e.g., through the "Special 301"[40] process and several international frameworks).
- Contribute to various studies and reports seeking to provide authoritative data on the scope and nature of the problem, to assess governmental efforts, and to identify effective initiatives.
- Leverage the collective resources and power of like-minded businesses and industry groups through umbrella organizations (such as the U.S. Chamber of Commerce's Coalition Against Counterfeiting and Piracy).

Government studies of the problem can support an IPR protection professional's ability to make a business case for devoting company resources to anti-counterfeiting or antigrey market efforts. "Official" recognition of a problem (and the scope and nature of its economic impact) not only becomes a basis upon which government resources can be deployed but it also can serve to validate the existence of a problem and the business imperative to take action to address it. Conversely, lack of government awareness or recognition that a particular industry is affected by a problem does not help internal efforts to win executive support for brand protection programs.

---

[40] Office of the United States Trade Representative. April 2015. "USTR Releases Annual Special 301 Report on Intellectual Property Rights." Available at https://ustr.gov/about-us/policy-offices/press-office/press-releases/2015/april/ustr-releases-annual-special-301 (accessed March 05, 2021).

Overview of a Basic Public Policy Program

In general, protection of IP needs to draw upon a variety of resources, internal and external. Essentially, these efforts fall into four categories:

- Informing. Company public policy resources need continuously to monitor, filter, and report to company leadership on government actions affecting the company's core concerns; they need to stay abreast of developments, and understand their significance in a real-time and efficient manner.
- Educating. Public policy resources articulate a company's views on policies and issues to other stakeholders (industry, consumer advocates, etc.) in a persuasive manner and effective dissemination. Where no opinion exists, public policy resources can help forge one.
- Leveraging relationships. Public policy resources can keep abreast of work being done on relevant issues by like-minded rights holders (to conserve resources and to influence and take advantage of that work). As many rights holders operate out of Washington, DC, DC-based public policy resources are well positioned to participate in deliberations and represent their members' interests.
- Influencing policy formation. Public policy resources seek to influence policy outcomes through a range of actions—from meetings with policy makers to educate them on key issues to mounting campaigns to achieve particular law reforms. They assess opportunities, formulate strategy, and serve as lead advocates for their members' views.

Establishing a Basic Public Policy Program

To put such a plan into effect, a rights holder needs to:

1. Attain consensus among leadership on policy views and priorities.
2. Raise general awareness and understanding of policy matters.

3. Ensure that rights holder executive leadership has relevant and timely information regarding domestic policy matters, including potential opportunities and threats.
4. Form relationships with other organizations with similar interests that can be leveraged.
5. Increase the rights holder's visibility and "a seat at the table" in both legislative and executive branches of government.

Primary tasks:
To achieve these goals, a rights holder Public Policy Program (resources) needs to pursue the following actions:

- Establish policy priorities and policy positions.
- Create and disseminate a policy primer and guide to initiate policy-related discussions.
- Monitor relevant policy matters and institute a system for providing executive leadership with updates on developments.
- Provide key resources on an ongoing basis.
- Alert executive leadership to upcoming opportunities of special interest, for example, opportunities to participate in government-sponsored training programs and industry-outreach sessions (such as the U.S.–EU IPR working group session devoted to seeking private sector input).
- Report on federal investigations and prosecutions of special interest, executive branch deliberations relating to the deployment of federal resources, and pending court cases of potential interest.
- Enroll the company in the U.S. Chamber of Commerce's Coalition Against Counterfeiting and Piracy (CACP) and other organizations, and attend and report on meetings of these organizations and their task forces:
  o Legislative
  o International
  o Enforcement and detection
  o Authentication and technology
  o Internet.

- Identify and, with executive leadership guidance and approval, pursue opportunities to participate in governmental task force initiatives as appropriate.
- Explore opportunities to contribute to or be identified with pending studies, such as having the rights holder included in the list of associations contained in the OECD study on the economic impact of piracy and counterfeiting.[41]

Advanced activities:

The previously mentioned initial activities will measurably advance a rights holder toward attainment of the public policy goals initially outlined. After the Program establishment and initial period, the rights holder should investigate the opportunity for additional activities that could include:

- Direct outreach to lawmakers and government officials ("lobbying"). The rights holder could begin to explore opportunities to educate policy makers indirectly (through reports) and directly (e.g., hold a meeting and have a policy makers attend).
- Developing a rights holder "training module" that could be presented by the company's public policy resource at certain government training programs, such as the PTO IP Enforcement Academy.[42]
- Developing a plan for having Congress or the Administration commission a useful governmental study, for example of the economic impact of IPR violations, theft, and so on.

Federal Bureau of Investigation (FBI)

Part of the FBI's mission as a law enforcement agency is to uphold and enforce the criminal laws of the United States, and to provide leadership

---

[41] See www.oecd.org/sti/industryandglobalisation/theeconomicimpactofcounterfeitingandpiracy.htm (accessed March 05, 2021).

[42] U.S. Patent and Trademark Office, Training and Education: Global Intellectual Property Academy. Available at www.uspto.gov/ip/training/index.jsp (accessed March 05, 2021).

and criminal justice services to other agencies and partners. As part of this effort, the FBI has investigated cases of trafficking in counterfeit goods and related charges.

Internal Revenue Service (IRS)

The IRS's Criminal Investigation (CI) unit has worldwide jurisdiction to investigate potential criminal violations of the Internal Revenue Code. These CI agents are specially trained to deal with complex and often encrypted or otherwise protected financial records. "Criminal Investigation's conviction rate is one of the highest in federal law enforcement. Not only do the courts hand down substantial prison sentences, but those convicted must also pay fines, civil taxes and penalties … ."[43] For example, in one case, a man was sentenced to prison for trafficking in counterfeit goods, tax fraud, and mail fraud.[44]

Immigration and Customs Enforcement (ICE)

ICE is one of the largest investigative agencies in the federal government. Its primary mission is to promote homeland security and public safety through the criminal and civil enforcement of federal laws governing border control, Customs, trade, and immigration.[45] The agency has investigated cases dealing with counterfeit drugs, among others, and those convicted of these crimes face imprisonment and substantial fines.[46]

---

[43] USPTO, The Global Intellectual Property Academy, Available at www.uspto.gov/ip-policy/global-intellectual-property-academy (accessed March 05, 2021).

[44] "Birmingham Man Sentenced for Trafficking Counterfeit Nike Shoes, Filing False Tax Return and Mail Fraud." Available at www.fbi.gov/birmingham/press-releases/2011/birmingham-man-sentenced-for-trafficking-counterfeit-nike-shoes-filing-false-tax-return-and-mail-fraud (accessed March 05, 2021).

[45] See www.ice.gov/ (accessed March 05, 2021).

[46] "Chinese National Pleads Guilty to Trafficking Counterfeit Pharmaceutical Weight-Loss Drug." January 28, 2011. Available at www.justice.gov/archive/usao/co/news/2011/January2011/1_28_11.html (accessed March 05, 2021). According to court documents, between December 2008 and March 2009, the FDA issued a series of alerts about serious health risks to consumers, regarding drugs

National Intellectual Property Rights Coordination Center

The National Intellectual Property Rights Coordination Center (IPR Center) serves as the vanguard of the U.S. government's response to global IP crimes. The IPR Center and its member agencies share information, develop initiatives, coordinate enforcement actions, and conduct investigations associated with IP crimes. The Center employs a task force model to optimize the roles and enforcement efforts of each of the member agencies, while fostering government–industry partnerships in support of ongoing IPR enforcement initiatives such as counterfeiting and piracy—IP crimes that endanger public health and safety, and fair competition.[47] The IPR Center encourages rights holders, trade associations, law enforcement, and government agencies, as well as general public, to report instances of IPR theft.[48]

Industry Cooperation

Increasing numbers of rights holders have found that it makes sense to tackle the global threats of grey marketing, counterfeiting, software piracy, and other IPR violations together with other industry peers and even beyond their industry boundaries. They are also willing to educate

---

containing undeclared active pharmaceutical ingredients, one of which can cause severe side effects and had been withdrawn from the market in the United States and other countries. In subsequent alerts, the FDA warned the public about counterfeit versions of a popular over-the-counter brand-name weight-loss drug manufactured by GlaxoSmithKlein. The alerts indicated that these counterfeit drugs did not contain the proper active pharmaceutical ingredients present in the authentic product, but instead contained dangerous levels of the withdrawn drug. These counterfeits were sold, among other ways, through Internet websites, including online auction websites, and imported to the United States from China.

A number of U.S. consumers reported adverse physical effects from taking one of the counterfeit drugs they had purchased from the defendant's web page or through a redistributor.

[47] See www.iprcenter.gov/ (accessed March 05, 2021).

[48] See www.iprcenter.gov/reports/library?filter=p1 (accessed March 05, 2021). Reports of investigations by the IPR Center of counterfeit goods can be found at www.iprcenter.gov/reports/library?filter=p0 (accessed March 05, 2021).

others and share their experiences and best practices either directly or by participating in various industry groups or nonprofit organizations. A growing number of organizations, alliances, and groups of companies around the globe are established for the sole purpose of addressing these threats, and any brand owner looking for expertise, advice, or help should be able to find one or more organizations that fit its focus and purpose.

Many of these organizations cooperate closely with law enforcement agencies and may provide opportunities for any business that is starting its brand protection program to leverage these well-established connections. Some IPR protection organizations also work with other peer organizations—sharing best practices, hosting joint events, and so on. Following are a few examples of some of the leading IPR brand protection organizations:

The International Anti-Counterfeiting Coalition (IACC) (www.iacc.org/) is a global nonprofit organization headquartered in Washington, DC that solely focuses its efforts on combating counterfeiting and piracy. Formed in 1979, it is the longest standing organization of this kind. IACC members, whose combined annual revenues exceed $650 billion, come from a variety of businesses and industries, including automotive, apparel, luxury goods, pharmaceuticals, food, software, and entertainment. Among other activities, the IACC globally develops and conducts training for law enforcement officials, collaborates with payment processors and rights holders targeting transactions associated with sales of counterfeit goods, takes part in regional and international programs directed at improving IP enforcement standards, and provides comments on proposed IP enforcement laws and regulations in the United States and abroad.

AGMA (www.agmaglobal.org) is a nonprofit organization focused on curbing grey market fraud, counterfeit crime, and service fraud affecting the technology sector throughout the world and on developing IP protection activities. Incorporated in 2001, current members include hi-tech heavyweights whose combined annual revenue exceeds $425 billion and who all recognize that IP protection is a fundamental element of innovation and economic growth. AGMA's members are some of the most innovative technology companies in the world. The organization's goals are to protect rights holders' IP and authorized distribution channels, improve customer satisfaction, and preserve brand integrity.

Quality Brands Protection Committee (QBPC) (www.qbpc. org.cn) was established in March 2000 and registered under the China Association of Enterprises with Foreign Investment (CAEFI). QBPC is supported by the former Ministry of Foreign Trade and Economic Cooperation. The QBPC membership comprises more than 190 multinational companies representing nearly $80 billion in investment in China. QBPC assists Chinese law-enforcement agencies in combating counterfeiting and safeguarding fair competition, organizing activities such as training, workshops, and sharing IPR protection practices. QBPC is also actively involved in legislative reform and regulation revisions focused on IPR protection in China.

REACT (European Anti-Counterfeiting Network) (www.react. org) is a nonprofit organization with more than 20 years of experience in investigating and combating counterfeit trade. REACT has more than 190 members from a variety of industries, including fashion and merchandising, tobacco, electronics and mobile phones, pharmaceuticals, toys, and so on. REACT has a large international network, with strategically placed offices and partners around the world, allowing it to fight the global counterfeit trade more efficiently.

UNECE Committee on Economic Cooperation and Integration (CECI) (www.unece.org/ceci/ip.html). CECI has established the Team of Specialists on Intellectual Property (TOS-IP) in order to support its IP efforts. The TOS-IP acts to facilitate effective regulatory IPR protection and enforcement and strengthen the role of IP as a basis for innovative development. TOS-IP responds to the needs of governments while taking into consideration the needs of the private sector, consumers, and researchers.

Canadian Anti-Counterfeiting Network (CACN) (www.cacn.ca) is an alliance of individuals, companies, firms, and associations fighting counterfeiting and piracy in Canada and internationally. The key initiatives include lobbying policy makers at the federal and provincial levels in support of legislative changes and resources needed to raise awareness of the negative impact of counterfeiting and piracy on the economy and society. CACN facilitates training of law enforcement and shares information regarding counterfeit cases, developments, and emerging trends among law enforcement and the private sector.

World Customs Organization (WCO) (www.wcoomd.org) is the only intergovernmental organization focused exclusively on Customs matters. WCO focuses on (among other initiatives) development of global standards, simplification, and harmonization of Customs procedures, facilitation of international trade, enhancement of Customs enforcement and compliance activities, anti-counterfeiting and piracy initiatives, and supply chain security. WCO also facilitates public–private partnerships and maintains the international Harmonized System goods nomenclature.

There are many other alliances or business-oriented initiatives established under umbrellas of various governmental agencies, such as Business Action to Stop Counterfeiting and Piracy (BASCAP) and the International Chamber of Commerce (ICC) initiative. The purpose of BASCAP Connections Gateway is to facilitate better coordination of industry efforts, both by companies and by the associations, in order to improve effectiveness in implementing efforts and better use of available resources and to create greater transparency of the strategic activities to IP-focused organizations with global memberships, so they may pursue a variety of international activities.[49]

Disciplining Channel Partners

Many businesses depend on channel partners to perform the selling function with the end customers. These channel partners could be dealers, distributors, brokers, value-added resellers, agents, and so on. The effective business understands that it must create value for the end customer because without such value neither the brand owner nor the channel partner has anything to sell. There also has to be a value created for the channel partner to make the business relationship work. It is very common

---

[49] See https://iccwbo.org/global-issues-trends/bascap-counterfeiting-piracy/bascap-global-engagement/ (accessed March 05, 2021); BASCAP Members are Listed by their Geographic Base of Operations at www.iccwbo.org/worldwide-membership/national-committees/ (accessed March 05, 2021).

for businesses to enforce some contractual terms and conditions, such as standard payment terms, and punish delinquency. It is less common to really enforce and remedy some other contractual terms, such as audits and resale restrictions, even though it may be more important to discipline channel partners for noncompliance with these "other" contractual terms to deter or prevent grey market or black market activities, unsanctioned purchasing or selling of unauthorized products, violations of software licensing terms or IPR such as patents, trademarks, and copyrights.

In the presence of the robust brand protection program and the supporting framework previously discussed, a business will be in a good position to discipline noncompliant channel partners. Depending on a contractual breach, the relationship history, and other decision criteria, a business should have specific remedies at hand that may vary from a "slap on the wrist" to a suspension, probation, financial retributions, and even litigation or termination of the contract. Establishing effective remedies is, however, meaningless unless the business is enforcing them. The rights holders are only successful in protecting their brands as long as they enforce their rights swiftly, aggressively, and persistently.

Probation

When the rights holder identifies a breach or problem(s) with a channel partner otherwise in good standing and with a history of a nonproblematic, long-term relationship, depending on the type and size of the breach, a business may decide to request a corrective action(s) without significantly affecting ongoing business with this channel partner. For example, where the identified breach relates to a rogue employee who acted without the channel partner's knowledge or consent, the rights holder may choose to notify the channel partner about probation (conditional suspension) of some activities in accordance with the terms of the contract. This may include a request for immediate corrective actions (change in processes or business controls) to be implemented to prevent similar future incidents, and (if applicable) reconciliation of any financial or inventory or other discrepancies that were caused by the breach (again, in accordance with the contract), with a specific deadline. If the channel partner does not comply or respond, the rights holder may suspend the activities applicable under the contract, or may decide to implement more aggressive remedies such as litigation or termination of the contract. An example of such a notification is the following.

Where the breaches are more complex or serious (long-term, significant amounts, more individuals, and intentional breaches), the language

---

VIA E-MAIL & EXPRESS MAIL   *[Date]*

[Mr./Mrs. Name]

[Company]

[Address1]

[Address 2]

[Telephone]

[E-mail]

Subject: *Probation Notice*

Dear [Name],

Further to our correspondence with Subject: Breach of the Agreement sent to you on [Date], as a result of the breach of the [Agreement] between [Rights Holder] and [Company], we would like to notify you that [Rights Holder] will suspend certain activities in accordance with [Section(s) ##] of the Agreement, effectively from [Date], unless the following conditions are met by [Date].

1. *[Rights Holder] will furnish [Company] with an invoice and [Company] will pay immediately the amount of [$###] representing [unearned sales incentives, rebates, underreported sales, etc.], and related applicable interest charges; and*
2. *[Rights Holder] and [Company] will agree on and implement improvements to their business processes to prevent future breaches by [Date].*

Please acknowledge you received this letter and will comply with the above requirements by signing below and sending us back a copy within next five (5) business days.

We consider the breach of Agreements a direct threat and we will pursue our legal rights to the extent permitted by law.

Regards,

Acknowledgment:

Rights Holder	*Company*
Officer Name	*Officer Name*
Title	*Title*
Signature	*Signature*

may be more aggressive, and vice versa, with good-standing partners, the language may be softer than in the previous example.

Suspension

In the event that a contracted partner does not cooperate or comply with the contractual remedies deployed to correct a breach, a rights holder could move to suspend an agreement by way of a formal Notification of Suspension containing specific requirements and the timeframe for a partner to achieve compliance, after which the suspension may be lifted or (in the event on failure to comply) other remedies may apply.

An example of such a suspension notice follows (in the context of a contractual breach related to a refusal to allow an audit):

Monetary Penalties or Reduction in Allotment

VIA E-MAIL AND COURIER   [Date]

[Mr./Mrs. Name]

[Company]

[Address1]

[Address 2]

[Telephone]

[E-mail]

Subject: Suspension Pursuant to the Agreement entered into between [Rights Holder] and [COMPANY], effective [Agreement Date] (the "Agreement")

Dear [Name],

As a result of [Company's] breach of the Agreement by failing to cooperate with [Rights Holder's] review of the records and to provide reasonable access to all information that would allow the review to be completed in a timely manner, [Rights Holder] has no alternative but to exercise its right under [Section(s) ##] of the Agreement to suspend [Company] as defined under the Agreement.

As a result of the suspension you are hereby instructed to: (i) immediately cease to procure…, (ii) immediately cease to sell …, and (iii) provide within 30 days of the date of this letter a report of Sales through (date).

If [Company] does not remedy its breach of the Agreement within 30 days of the date of this letter, [Rights Holder] will have no alternative but to terminate the Agreement as well as pursue available legal options to the extent permitted by law.

Regards,

Officer Name

_____

Signature

A majority of contractual remedies incorporate some monetary recoveries such as penalties, interest charges, repayment of unearned discounts, compensation, and so on. Aggressive enforcement of these remedies makes good business sense. One might take an example from the banking industry—late payments or overdraft charges are never pardoned.

Unfortunately, although interest charges are present in a majority of agreements, often they are not enforced and, as a result, the rights holders that do not enforce interest charges struggle more frequently with late payments, underreporting, and collection efforts.

There are also other than direct financial remedies at a rights holder's disposal. When a business identifies that its channel partners are artificially bumping up their sales forecast in order to reach the bigger discount thresholds while dumping the products into grey market, the business may reduce product allotments and associated marketing funds for these partners.

CHAPTER 6

Trademark Infringement: Diminishing the Value of Brand Equity

Trademarks often serve as a brand's most important means for communicating with a consumer. Trademarks are the vehicles by which consumers can develop a range of perceptions related to a product or service attributes. Trademarks are not only identifiers of where or who has produced the product or service, but are the consumer touchpoints that strengthen a brand's equity. Equity is built upon brand loyalty, awareness, quality associations, and relevance, as well as a brand's engagement and leadership in the marketplace.

Trademark infringement of goods that neither are grey market nor bear counterfeit marks can be the cause of serious harm to rights holders. Damage comes in the form of lost sales, loss of goodwill, customer confusion and, ultimately, the loss of confidence in the brand by consumers. Trademark infringement carves into the equity of a brand that is so key to its sustainability. Although the infringement may be completely innocent and stem from independent, unknowledgeable or unaware use and creation, it can also be intentional and a willful effort to "commercially hitchhike" on another's brand. In the latter situation, the infringer takes advantage of the rights holder's goodwill and causes confusion among the consuming public by creating an impression that the rights holder is associated with the particular goods. This confusion by the consumer may lead to lost sales and profits for the rights holder when consumers end up buying the infringer's goods instead. However, even if a lost sale does not immediately result from the public's identifying the infringing goods as those of the rights holder, the rights holder may yet suffer as a result of postsale confusion and thereby diminishment of the marketing power of the brand, not only among consumers but among retailers and commentators as well. Moreover, the particular infringing goods will often fail to meet the quality standards associated with the rights holder's product, resulting in a loss of goodwill and esteem for the brand.

The Lanham Act contains the federal statutes that govern trademark law in the United States, and the infringement aspects of the Lanham Act, other than those pertaining to counterfeiting and grey market goods, should be considered a significant part of the tool box for combating unauthorized use of or association with a rights holder's brand identification. At the same time, it should be noted that common law and state statutes also control aspects of trademark regulation.

Elements of Trademark Infringement

A trademark infringement claim is built upon a standard prima facie analysis. First, while registration is not required to raise a cause of action under the Lanham Act, it does provide the plaintiff with significant benefits should a dispute arise.[1] In particular, registration provides a rights holder with proof of ownership and validity, which is required for recovery in an infringement action.[2] Second, upon filing a claim for trademark infringement, the plaintiff will need to show that the defendant's use of the mark is actionable in that it violated the Lanham Act. The plaintiff will then need to establish that such use is in commerce, that it is in relation to goods or services, and that it is likely to cause confusion to the consuming public.

---

[1] Lanham Act Section 32 provides a cause of action for registered marks; Lanham Act Section 43 provides a cause of action for unregistered marks.

[2] 15 U.S.C. § 1057(b) ("A certificate of registration of a mark upon the principal register provided by this chapter shall be prima facie evidence of the validity of the registered mark and of the registration of the mark, of the owner's ownership of the mark, and of the owner's exclusive right to use the registered mark in commerce on or in connection with the goods or services specified in the certificate, subject to any conditions or limitations stated in the certificate.").

Registered Mark

Registration of a mark is not required to combat trademark infringement in the United States. Trademark rights are acquired through use and unregistered rights are enforceable in Federal Court under Section 43 of the Lanham Act.[3] Nevertheless, registration becomes important in a trademark dispute because it provides notice to the public of the trademark owner's rights and creates a presumption of validity, ownership, and exclusivity in the use of the mark.[4] Moreover, these presumptions become conclusive if the registration becomes incontestable. Unlike most trademark law that derives primarily from common law, the registration process is largely embodied in Lanham Act provisions. Trademark examiners at the United States Patent and Trademark Office (USPTO) review registration applications for their compliance with formal requirements (most of which are found in Section 1) and substantive requirements (found in Section 2) that are enumerated in the Lanham Act.[5]

The USPTO may refuse registrations or renewals of registrations under Title 15, Section 1052 of the United States Code, which provides for refusals to register marks "… which may disparage … persons living or dead, institutions, beliefs, or national systems … ."[6] In one case, a Native American persuaded the U.S. District Court for the Eastern District of Virginia to cancel the registrations of the Washington Redskins Football Club, whose mark, she argued, disparaged Native Americans. The judge indicated that trademarks were government speech, not constitutionally

---

[3] 15 U.S.C. § 1125.

[4] 15 U.S.C. § 1115 ("Any registration … of a mark registered on the principle register … shall be prima facie evidence of the validity of the registered mark and of the registration of the mark, of the registrants ownership of the mark, and of the registrant's exclusive right to use the registered mark."); see also, 15 U.S.C. § 1057.

[5] 15 U.S.C. § 1051 ("Application for registration; verification"); 15 U.S.C. § 1052 ("Trademarks registrable on principle register; concurrent registration"). Section 2(a) regarding registration of disparaging marks held unconstitutional. In re Tam, 808 F.3d 1321 (Fed. Cir. 2015).

[6] "Pro Football Inc. v. Blackhorse,. No. 14-1043, 2015 WL 4096277 (E.D. Va. July 08, 2015).

protected private speech, and therefore the government could determine what messages it wanted to afford special protection.

Since 1989, the Lanham Act has provided four separate bases for the registration of a mark: (1) a Section 1(a) use-based application;[7] (2) a Section 1(b) Intent to Use application;[8] (3) a Section 44(d) application filed by a qualified foreign firm;[9] and (4) a Section 44(e) application based on the registration of the mark in the applicant's country of origin.[10] Additionally, the Madrid Protocol now provides for a fifth filing basis referred to as a Section 66(a) Extension of Protection to the United States under the Madrid Protocol.[11] However, because United States trademark law is a use-based system, a mark, whether it be a symbol, a word, a term, a name, or a device, must be in actual use as a trademark before it can be registered.[12]

The United States trademark system requires that any individual seeking to register his mark prove actual use or constructive use of the trademark before registration shall be issued.[13] In order to satisfy this requirement, individuals must either establish that they have actually used the mark in the sale of goods or services, or that they have constructively used the mark by filing an application of their intention to use the

---

[7] 15 U.S.C. § 1051(a)(1) ("owner of a trademark used in commerce may request registration").

[8] 15 U.S.C. § 1051(b)(1) ("A person who has a bona fide intention ... to use a trademark in commerce may request registration").

[9] 15 U.S.C. § 1126(d) (an application for registration of the same mark in one of the countries described in subsection (b) shall be accorded the same force and effect as would be accorded had the application been filed in the United States on the same date).

[10] 15 U.S.C. § 1126(e) ("A mark duly registered in the country of origin of the foreign applicant may be registered").

[11] 15 U.S.C. § 1141f (a) ("request for extension of protection of an international registration to the United States ... shall be deemed to be properly filed in the United States").

[12] "Grand Canyon West Ranch, LLC v. Hualapai Tribe." 78 U.S.P.Q.2d 1696 at 2 (T.T.A.B. 2006) ("It is clear that an applicant cannot obtain a registration under Section 1 of the Trademark Act for goods or services upon which it has not used the mark").

[13] *Id.*

mark at some time in the future.[14] However, an "intent-to-use" application only reserves a mark based on the applicant's good faith plan to use the mark to represent its goods and services.[15] Therefore, registration itself will be issued only upon the applicant's filing of a "verified statement that the mark is in use in commerce."[16] Moreover, since the 1989 revisions to the Lanham Act, the required actual use must be in commerce.[17]

With the U.S. dual system of registration and the growth of digital platforms, the issue of when "use" has taken place has become of greater importance. Prior to a trademark application proceeding to registration, there must be actual use.[18] Practically, this means that a photograph on a website or the advertising of a product on a site is not sufficient to establish "use." A consumer must be able to purchase the goods or services on the website. A product must be shipped in commerce; therefore, the rights holder should maintain documentation of the earliest shipments. Token shipments across state lines do not suffice. Similarly, a service offered on a website or simply advertised as being offered is not sufficient to establish "use." The service must be provided in commerce. Again, maintaining records showing the earliest provision of services will be important.

With the extensive use of the digital platform Twitter, "hashtags" as part of composite marks have been increasingly the subject of applications to the USPTO. However, merely placing a "#" symbol in front of an otherwise generic or highly descriptive term will not likely pass the scrutiny of the trademark office examining attorney. Furthermore, use of a hashtag on social media with a Twitter message or other text message is not sufficient to show "use" for purposes of establishing a trademark. In such a case, the "#" symbol is merely viewed as a data tag. Those seeking to protect hashtags must use them as they would other marks, as source

---

[14] 15 U.S.C. § 1057(c) ("Contingent on the registration of a mark on the principal register provided by this chapter, the filing of the application to register such mark shall constitute constructive use of the mark").

[15] 15 U.S.C. § 1051(b).

[16] 15 U.S.C. § 1051(b) & (d).

[17] 15 U.S.C. § 1127 (As of 1988, under Section 45 of the Lanham Act, actual use requires a bona fide use of a mark in the ordinary course of trade.). For a discussion of this "use in commerce" requirement, see § 7.02 *infra*.

[18] 15 U.S.C. § 1051.

indicators, by applying them to the goods, advertising, or an active website that is actually engaged in commerce. However, the U.S. Supreme Court recently held that in certain circumstances the addition of a generic top-level domain (gTLD) (e.g., ".com") to an otherwise generic term can create a protectable trademark.[19]

In the use-based system, federal registration does not create a trademark.[20] In fact, the United States has a rule of priority that says the rightful owner of a trademark is the one who first puts the mark to use in commerce.[21] Therefore, neither application nor registration of a mark invalidates the prior common law rights of others; and neither cancellation nor lack of registration invalidates a trademark.[22] Under the first-to-use doctrine, an early user's rights in an unregistered mark are not trumped by a later user's registration.[23] However, registration on the principal register provides the registrant with a presumption of validity owing to the registration and examination process the mark underwent in the USPTO.[24]

---

[19] "United States Patent and Trademark Office v. Booking. Com B.V." 140 S. Ct. 2298 (2020). In this matter, the Court recognized that the otherwise generic term "BOOKING.COM" was perceived by consumers as a recognizable brand.

[20] Couture v. Playdom, 778 F.3d 1379 (Fed. Cir. March 02, 2015).

[21] "Eighth Circuit: Flavor Corp. of America v. Kemin Industries, Inc." 493 F.2d 275, 284 (8th Cir. 1974) (trademark rights are acquired only by actual use of a mark in commerce in connection with the goods).

Eleventh Circuit: Cotton Ginny, Ltd. v. Cotton Gin, Inc., 691 F. Supp. 1347, 1352 (S.D. Fla. 1988) ("It is axiomatic that a trademark is acquired through appropriation and use."); ("the rights to a mark accrue ... from prior use to the one who first uses the marks in connection with a particular line of business.").

[22] Cotton Ginny, Ltd. v. Cotton Gin, Inc., 691 F. Supp. 1347, 1352 (S.D. Fla. 1988) ("The mark need not be registered under the Lanham Act ... in order to be protected against infringement. The appropriation and use of the mark itself establishes one's exclusive right to its utilization."); ("The fact that [Plaintiff] eventually registered its mark does not expand its rights and entitle it to exclusive use if it did not establish priority of use.").

[23] *Id.*

[24] 15 U.S.C. § 1051(a)(3) ("The statement shall be verified by the applicant and specify that (A) the person making the verification believes that he or she, or the juristic person in whose behalf he or she makes the verification, to be the owner of the mark sought to be registered; (B) to the best of the verifier's knowledge and

Registration also provides a potential cause of action under Section 32 of the Lanham Act, and is thus particularly useful should a dispute arise over the use of a trademark.

A trademark may be registered on either the principal register or the supplemental register. Registration on the principal register provides the registrant with several valuable rights. Such registration creates federal jurisdiction for infringement without a required minimum amount in controversy;[25] and federal jurisdiction subsequently allows the plaintiff to recover profits, damages, and costs as well as treble damages and attorney fees. Perhaps most important, a registration on the principal register provides an owner with prima facie evidence of the mark's validity and registration as well as the registrant's ownership.[26] Furthermore, this registration acts as constructive notice of the registrant's ownership of the mark, thus eliminating any good-faith defense offered by others who might adopt or use the mark post registration.[27]

Registration on the supplemental register, however, does not confer any of these rights to the owner, and, therefore, as a practical matter is generally not useful in combating trademark infringement. In fact, the purpose of the supplemental register is to facilitate foreign registration by allowing registrants to satisfy the domestic registration requirement without having to gain principal registration. The supplemental register is also used for those marks that have been initially found to be descriptive and therefore not capable of serving as a trademark, as, for example, the use of a person's surname as a trademark. Allowing a mark to be placed

---

belief, the facts recited in the application are accurate; (C) the mark is in use in commerce ... .").

[25] 15 U.S.C. § 1121 ("The district and territorial courts of the United States shall have original jurisdiction ... without regard to the amount in controversy or to diversity.").

[26] 15 U.S.C. § 1115 ("Any registration ... of a mark registered on the principle register ... shall be prima facie evidence of the validity of the registered mark and of the registration of the mark, of the registrant's ownership of the mark, and of the registrant's exclusive right to use the registered mark."); see also, 15 U.S.C. § 1057(b).

[27] 15 U.S.C. § 1072 ("Registration of a mark on the principal register ... shall be constructive notice of the registrant's claim of ownership thereof.").

on the supplemental register may actually hinder the registrant's ability to enforce its common law rights, since it may be viewed as an admission of the mark's weakness to serve as a source identifier.[28]

Although registration on the principal register is beneficial when bringing suit for trademark infringement under Section 32 of the Lanham Act, Section 43(a) still provides the rights holder of an unregistered mark with a cause of action. Nevertheless, obtaining registration of a trademark on the federal register gives rights holders a valuable tool when looking to the Lanham Act for protection of their brands.

U.S. Intent to Use Requirement

With the adoption of the dual application system for registering a trademark in the United States, one area that has seen increased enforcement activity at the U.S. Trademark Trial and Appeals Board is the attack on the claimed applicant's "intent to use" a mark in the near future. It is critical that the applicant be able to demonstrate that there was a bona fide intent to use the mark in commerce at the time the application was filed. This issue is also increasingly used as an avenue of attack on the applications of foreign registrants in the United States under Sections 44(d) or 66(a). It is not unusual for a foreign applicant to have used the mark in its home country and simply file an application in the United States claiming treaty priority for a "laundry list" of goods and services. Another applicant for the same or similar mark may challenge the foreign application with respect to a "*bona fide* intent-to-use" one or more of the listed goods or services, and the foreign applicant will have to prove up that it in fact did have a bona fide intent-to-use the mark with such goods or services in the United States. Often the foreign applicant has no evidence with respect to use in the U.S. market except that it decided it should file an application in the country to secure protection.

There are two requirements for meeting the standard "*bona fide* intent to use": (1) the intent must be more than a subjective belief that the use

---

[28] "Quaker State Oil Refining Corp. v. Quaker Oil Corp," 453 F.2d 1296, 1299 (CCPA 1972).

will take place and (2) there must be good evidence of this intent.[29] These standards may be viewed under the totality of all of the facts and circumstances in the matter. It is important that a rights holder demonstrate through documentation that there was serious internal consideration or discussion regarding use of the mark in the United States in the future. An interest in "place-holding" the mark is not sufficient. Applicants should have documents memorializing discussions at, for example, marketing or board of directors meetings. In addition, artwork, promotional materials, licensing plans, and the like will be useful evidence.

Tacking

A related issue known as "tacking" arises where modifications are made to a mark over time. Litigants will allege that the mark has been modified one or more times in such a manner that there is a material difference in the mark and its priority date should be aligned with its current modified form rather than with the date of the original mark. For example, the visual depiction of the character "Betty Crocker" used in connection with baking supplies has changed a number of times since the mark was first introduced. Another example is the transformation of financial services marks such as "City Bank of New York" founded in 1812, into its present trademark "Citigroup." "Tacking" is a trademark mechanism whereby, in certain cases, a rights holder with a recently modified mark wants to enforce its rights against a junior user of a similar mark based on seniority of adoption and use, claiming that its rights commence on the date of the adoption of the mark as it was originally used. Whether "tacking" should be recognized in a particular case has been determined by the U.S. Supreme Court to be a decision for a jury rather than a judge.[30]

---

[29] M.Z. Berger & Co. v. Swatch AG, 787 F.3d 1368 (Fed. Cir. 2015).
[30] "Hana Financial, Inc. v. Hana Bank." __ U.S. __, 135 S.Ct. 907, 190 L.Ed.2d 800 (2015).

Use Without Consent of Owner of Mark

Section 32 of the Lanham Act provides a cause of action for trademark infringement of a registered mark and Section 43(a) provides a cause of action for infringement of common law trademarks. Both causes of action require that the alleged infringer actually "used" the mark "in commerce" without the consent of the registrant and in a way that is "likely to cause confusion."[31] This section will address the "use" element of trademark infringement.

The inclusion of this requirement serves the Lanham Act's purpose of securing to the owner of the mark "the goodwill of his business and" to protect the ability of consumers "to distinguish among competing producers."[32] Although litigation outside of the Internet context regarding this "use" element is at present rare, it remains important because without it no activity is actionable under the Lanham Act.[33] Nevertheless, this element is often addressed in the Internet context and there are various approaches to what constitutes actionable use by a defendant under the Lanham Act.

---

[31] 15 U.S.C. § 1114 ("Any person who shall, without the consent of the registrant, use in commerce any reproduction, counterfeit, copy, or colorable imitation of a registered mark ... in connection with which such use is likely to cause confusion ... shall be liable in a civil action."); 15 U.S.C. § 1125(a) ("Any person who, on or in connection with any goods or services, or any container for goods, uses in commerce any word, term, name, symbol, or device ... or any false designation of origin ... which is likely to cause confusion ... shall be liable in a civil action.").

[32] "Two Pesos, Inc. v. Taco Cabana Inc," 505 U.S. 763, 774, 112 S.Ct. 2753, 120 L.Ed.2d 615 (1992).

[33] See Holiday Inns, Inc. v. 800 Reservations, Inc., 86 F.3d 619 (6th Cir. 1996) ("the defendant's use of a protected mark or their use of a misleading representation is a prerequisite to the finding of a Lanham Act violation."). See also, 1-800 Contacts, Inc. v. Whenu.com, Inc., 414 F.3d 400 (2d Cir. 2005) ("Not only are 'use,' 'in commerce,' and 'likelihood of confusion' three distinct elements of a trademark infringement claim but 'use' must be decided as a threshold matter because, while any number of activities may be 'in commerce' or create a 'likelihood of confusion,' no such activity is actionable under the Lanham Act absent the 'use' of a trademark.").

Actionable use exists where a defendant actually uses the protected mark itself or a similar representation in such a way that is likely to cause confusion as to the source of the goods or services being offered under the mark. Conversely, if a defendant does not use the plaintiff's actual mark or create any confusion by putting forth a similar representation of a protectable mark, there is no infringement under the Lanham Act and defendant's activity is not actionable.[34] This was clearly the case where a plaintiff owned a telephone number corresponding to the alphanumeric 1-800-holiday [465-4329] and the defendant owned a similar number of 405-4329.[35] The plaintiff sued, alleging the defendant violated the Lanham Act by using plaintiff's trademark. The court, however, determined that there was no actionable use because the defendant did not use the plaintiff's actual trademark, nor did the defendant advertise its similar number in such a way that created confusion.[36]

Another case demonstrates how actionable use fails to exist where the defendant's use is not in connection with goods or services. In this instance, the plaintiff, the owner of a website and the mark "1-800CON-TACTS," sued the defendant, seeking to enjoin the defendant from delivering to computer users competitive pop-up advertisements.[37] The defendant provided software that when downloaded automatically generated pop-up advertisement windows relevant to the computer user's specific activities. In order to deliver the contextually relevant advertisements, defendant's software employed an internal directory comprising key words and search terms that included plaintiff's website address. The Court of Appeals held that the defendant did not use the plaintiff's trademark by including plaintiff's website address, which is almost identical to plaintiff's trademark, in an unpublished directory of terms triggering

---

[34] See "Holiday Inns, Inc. v. 800 Reservations, Inc." 86 F.3d 619 (6th Cir. 1996) (defendants never used plaintiff's trademark nor any facsimile of plaintiff's marks, nor did they create any confusion; the confusion already existed among the mis-dialing public; therefore, because defendant neither used the offending mark nor created the confusion, no infringement occurred).

[35] *Id.*

[36] *Id.*

[37] 1-800 Contacts, Inc. v. Whenu.com, Inc., 414 F.3d 400 (2d Cir. 2005).

delivery of defendant's advertising to the relevant public.[38] Such use was not actionable because the defendant did not use plaintiff's trademark on any goods or services in order to pass them off as emanating from or authorized by the plaintiff.[39] Furthermore, the manner of defendant's use did not reproduce or display plaintiff's trademark in any way.[40] The defendant also did not use plaintiff's trademark when it caused separate, branded pop-ups to appear on computer screens above, below, or along the bottom edge of plaintiff's website window because defendant's ads did not display the trademark and had no tangible effect on the functionality of plaintiff's website.[41] Use is not actionable, then, when the defendant's use of the mark is not in connection with any goods or services.

Use is actionable when an alleged infringer uses a protected mark in a way that identifies his or her goods or services. One plaintiff's claims arose from the defendant's alleged use of plaintiff's trademarks through Google's AdWords program and in the meta tags for defendant's website.[42] The defendant's use of plaintiff's marks to trigger an advertisement for itself was consistent with the language of the Lanham Act and thus constituted actionable use because it was tied to the promotion of the defendant's goods and services.[43] By using a protected mark to identify

---

[38] *Id.*, 414 F.3d at 403.

[39] *Id.*, 414 F.3d at 408 ("[defendant] does not 'use' [plaintiff's] trademark in the manner ordinarily at issue in an infringement claim.").

[40] *Id.*, 414 F.3d at 408–409 ("the difference between [plaintiff's trademarks and the website address utilized by [defendant] ... [is] quite significant because [it] transform[s] [plaintiff's] trademark—which is entitled to protection under the Lanham Act—into a word combination that functions more or less like a public key to [plaintiff's] website.").

[41] *Id.* ("[Defendant's] pop-up ads appear in a separate window that is prominently branded with its mark; they have absolutely no tangible effect on the appearance or functionality of the [plaintiff's] website.").

[42] J.G. Wentworth, "S.S.C. Limited Partnership v. Settlement Funding LLC." 2007 WL 30115 at *1 (E.D. Pa. 2007).

[43] *Id.* at *6 ("the alleged purchase of the keyword was a commercial transaction that occurred 'in commerce' ... [and] alleged use was ... 'in connection with any goods or services' in that Plaintiff's mark was allegedly used to trigger commercial advertising which included a link to Defendants' [retail services] ... through which the user could make ... purchases.").

goods or services, an alleged infringer usurps the good will of the owner and the activity is actionable.

A Ninth Circuit case demonstrates how noncommercial use in commerce does not constitute actionable use. The defendant in this case used the plaintiff's trademark as the domain name of a website, the subject of which was consumer commentary about the products and services represented by the mark.[44] Because the defendant earned no revenue from or sold any goods on the website, and no links to any of plaintiff's competitors appeared there, the defendant's use was not in connection with the sale of goods or services and thus could not mislead consumers into buying a competing product.[45] Accordingly, such use is noncommercial and therefore not actionable.

The ability of a rights holder to demonstrate actionable use is imperative if the trademark owner seeks protection for its mark and brand under the Lanham Act. A rights holder must be able to show that the alleged infringer used the rights holder's mark without consent and in connection with goods or services.[46] Upon a showing of actionable use, in order to prevail and thus protect its brand, a rights holder will need to establish the elements of "use in commerce" and "likelihood of confusion" if the provisions of the Lanham Act are to support its claim of trademark infringement. Rights holders need to show that the infringing product: (a) is used in commerce; (b) constitutes a reproduction, counterfeit, copy, or imitation of the registered mark; and (c) is used in the sale of goods or service.

Use in Commerce

The Lanham Act requires that the infringing mark be used in commerce. This requirement applies to both registered and unregistered marks and ensures that the federal trademark regime remains within Congress's

---

[44] "Bosley Medical Institute, Inc. v. Kremer." 403 F.3d 672 (9th Cir. 2005).

[45] *Id.*

[46] The "connection with goods and services" aspect of such use is further discussed in § 7.03 *infra*.

Commerce Clause powers.[47] According to the Lanham Act, "use in commerce" encompasses all commerce that may lawfully be regulated by Congress.[48] Thus, the "use in commerce" element "is simply a jurisdictional predicate to any law passed by Congress under the Commerce Clause."[49]

Essentially, "use in commerce" is understood as requiring the alleged infringer's use of a protected mark to be in connection with the sale of goods or services.[50] In fact, the Lanham Act defines "use in commerce" as "the bona fide use of a mark in the ordinary course of trade, and not made merely to reserve a right in a mark."[51] "A mark shall be deemed to be in use in commerce on goods when it is placed in any manner on goods or their containers or the displays associated therewith or on the tags or labels affixed thereto, or if the nature of the goods makes such placement impracticable, then on documents associated with the goods or their sale."[52] A mark is used in commerce regarding services "when it is displayed in the sale or advertising of services and the services rendered are in commerce, or the services are rendered in more than one State or in the United States and a foreign country and the person rendering the services is engaged in commerce in connection with the services."[53]

---

[47] Dinwoodie and Janis, *Trademarks and Unfair Competition*, at 215 (2d ed. 2007).

[48] 15 U.S.C. § 1127.

[49] "Bosley Medical Institute, Inc. v. Kremer." 403 F.3d 672, 676–677 (9th Cir. 2005).

[50] *Ninth Circuit:* Bosley Medical Institute, Inc. v. Kremer, 403 F.3d 672, 677 (9th Cir. 2005) ("'[u]se in commerce' is simply a jurisdictional predicate to any law passed by Congress under the Commerce Clause ... [t]he word "commerce" means all commerce which may lawfully be regulated by Congress.' Therefore, the district court should have determined instead whether [defendant's] use was 'in connection with a sale of goods or services' rather than a 'use in commerce.'").

Tenth Circuit: Clearly Building Corp. v. David A. Dame, Inc., 674 F. Supp.2d 1257, 1267 (D. Col. 2009) ("plaintiff must plead facts sufficient to [demonstrate] that Defendant used Plaintiff's mark 'in connection with any goods or services.' This is commonly described as the commercial use requirement.").

[51] 15 U.S.C. § 1127.

[52] *Id.*

[53] *Id.*

According to the Supreme Court, the "use in commerce" requirement serves to ensure that "trademark infringement law prevents only unauthorized uses of a trademark in connection with a commercial transaction in which the trademark is being used to confuse potential customers."[54] Therefore, the real inquiry regarding this element is whether a plaintiff can demonstrate that a defendant has used the trademark in connection with any goods or services.

Sale of Goods or Services

Both, Section 32 and Section 43 of the Lanham Act, protect trademarks from infringement by prohibiting a person other than the rights holder from using the mark in connection with any goods or services.[55] "This is commonly described as the commercial use requirement."[56] In fact, liability for trademark infringement attaches when an unauthorized person uses a protected mark in connection with any goods or services in a way that is likely to cause confusion regarding the source of the goods or services.[57] Therefore, in order to establish trademark infringement, a

---

[54] "Bosley Medical Institute, Inc. v. Kremer." 403 F.3d 672, 676–677 (9th Cir. 2005).

[55] 15 U.S.C. § 1114 ("Any person who shall … use in commerce any reproduction, counterfeit, copy, or colorable imitation of a registered mark in connection with the sale, offering for sale, distribution, or advertising of any goods or services … or reproduce, counterfeit, copy, or colorably imitate a registered mark and apply such reproduction, counterfeit, copy, or colorable imitation to labels, signs, prints, packages, wrappers, receptacles, or advertisements intended to be used in commerce upon or in connection with the sale, offering for sale, distribution, or advertising of goods or services … shall be liable …"); 15 U.S.C. § 1125 ("Any person who, on or in connection with any goods or services, or any container for goods, uses in commerce … shall be liable …").

[56] "Clearly Building Corp. v. David A. Dame, Inc." 674 F. Supp.2d 1257, 1267 (D. Col. 2009).

[57] "*Ninth Circuit:* Jarritos, Inc. v. Reyes." 345 Fed. Appx. 215, 218 (9th Cir. 2009) ("Liability for trademark infringement attaches when a person uses, 'in connection with any goods or services … any [protected mark] … which is likely to cause confusion as to the origin, sponsorship, or approval' of the goods or services.").

plaintiff must prove that a defendant has used the trademark in connection with goods or services.[58] If the plaintiff cannot prove this, no trademark infringement has occurred.[59]

In one case, where the plaintiff sued a former customer for the use
of plaintiff's trademark as the name of the defendant's website, whether
the defendant used the plaintiff's mark in connection with any goods or
services was a determinative issue. However, the website content merely
expressed the defendant's opinions about the plaintiff's goods and services, and did not employ plaintiff's mark in connection with any sales.
Therefore, in this instance, the plaintiff was unable to establish that the
defendant was using the mark in connection with any goods or services, and the trademark infringement claim was dismissed. Accordingly,
because "the Lanham Act is intended to protect the ability of consumers to distinguish among competing producers,"[60] it cannot be used to

---

Tenth Circuit: Utah Lighthouse Ministry v. Foundation for Apologetic, 527
F.3d 1045, 1054 (10th Cir. 2008) ("It is important to distinguish between the
merely jurisdictional 'in commerce' requirement and the 'in connection with any
goods and services' requirement that establishes a violation of section 43 of the
Lanham Act.").

[58] *Third Circuit*: AcademyOne, Inc. v. College Source, Inc., 2009 WL 5184491
at *7 (E.D. Pa. 2009) ("a plaintiff who seeks to establish trademark infringement
… must prove … that the defendant's use of the mark to identify goods or services is likely to create confusion.").

Tenth Circuit: Triple-I Corp. v. Hudson Associates Consulting, Inc., 713 F.
Supp.2d 1267, 1281 (D. Kan. 2010) ("a plaintiff must demonstrate that Defendants used the trademark 'in connection with any goods or services' to establish
trademark infringement."); Clearly Building Corp. v. David A. Dame, Inc., 674
F. Supp.2d 1257 (D. Col. 2009) ("in order to survive a motion to dismiss, a
plaintiff must plead facts sufficient to state a plausible claim that Defendant used
Plaintiff's mark 'in connection with any goods or services.'").

[59] See Utah Lighthouse Ministry v. Foundation for Apologetic, 527 F.3d 1045,
1054 (10th Cir. 2008) ("Defendant's use of [plaintiff's] trademark is not in connection with any goods or services, and therefore the district court properly
granted summary judgment on [plaintiff's] trademark infringement and unfair
competition claims [in favor of defendant].").

[60] "Clearly Building Corp. v. David A. Dame." *Inc.*, 674 F. Supp.2d 1257, 1268
(D. Col. 2009).

prevent someone from using a mark strictly to communicate ideas or express points of view.[61] This rationale comports with the underlying purpose of the Lanham Act, which is "to prevent the defendant from unfairly profiting or capitalizing on the plaintiff's goodwill and established reputation through the unauthorized use of a trademark."[62]

This element does not require that a defendant actually caused goods or services to be placed in the stream of commerce.[63] In fact, the use of a trademark is in connection with goods or services when it affects a plaintiff's business.[64] For instance, a defendant's use of a misleading domain name that includes a plaintiff's mark is in connection with goods or services, because it is likely to prevent relevant consumers from reaching the plaintiff's own website.[65] Activities of the defendant are also in connection with goods or services when the activities encourage the purchase of a product or service, or prevent consumers from reaching the plaintiff's product or services.[66]

Litigation over this issue has occurred when a trademark has been used in the Internet context, such as in a domain name or a website. In these circumstances, a mark is used in connection with goods or services when the defendant's website carries commercial content that is directly present on the website.[67] A website simply carrying a link that leads to

---

[61] *Id.* ("trademark rights cannot be used to quash an unauthorized use of the mark by another who is communicating ideas or expressing points of view").

[62] "Savannah College of Art and Design." *Inc. v. Houiex,* 369 F. Supp.2d 929, 945 (S.D. Ohio 2004).

[63] "Jews for Jesus v. Brodsky." 993 F. Supp. 282, 309 (D.N.J. 1998).

[64] "People for the Ethical Treatment of Animals." *Inc. v. Doughney,* 113 F. Supp.2d 915, 919 (E.D. Va. 2000) ("Defendant's use of [plaintiff's] [m]ark was 'in connection' with goods and services because the use of a misleading domain name has been found to be in connection with the distribution of services when it impacts on the Plaintiff's business.").

[65] *Id.*

[66] *Jews for Jesus v. Brodsky,* N. 9 *supra,* 993 F. Supp. at 309.

[67] "*Savannah College of Art and Design.*" *Inc. v. Houiex, N. 8 supra,* 369 F. Supp.2d at 945 ("the commercial content on those sites is one step removed from [defendant's] own websites. Further, [defendant] is not engaged in his own business enterprise through his websites."); *Id.* at 946 ("[defendant's] website [does] not constitute a use of the [plaintiff's] mark in connection with advertising or sale of goods or services.").

commercial content, however, is insufficient to infuse a defendant's site with a commercial purpose.[68]

This element of trademark infringement is fundamental to properly using the Lanham Act to protect a rights holder's mark. Without demonstrating that a defendant has used a trademark in connection with the sale of goods or services, a claim for trademark infringement will not succeed.

Reproduction, Counterfeit, Copy, or Colorable Imitation

In order for there to be a valid Section 32 trademark infringement claim, the Lanham Act requires that the infringing mark be a "reproduction, counterfeit, copy, or colorable imitation"[69] of a registered mark. Section 43, however, only requires the infringing mark to be "any word, term, name, symbol, or device, or any combination thereof"[70] that is likely to cause confusion. Although the language of Section 43 differs from that of Section 32, both sections require and apply the same likelihood of confusion test.[71] This test essentially allocates the "reproduction, counterfeit, copy, or colorable imitation" language to a Section 43 claim through the fundamental "similarity of marks" factor considered in the likelihood of confusion test. This factor determines whether the mark used by the defendant is a "reproduction, counterfeit, copy, or colorable imitation," and whether it may be protected by the Lanham Act. An important distinction among these four terms is that the presence of a counterfeit presumes consumer confusion, whereas the use of reproduction, copy, or colorable imitation requires consideration of further factors in order to establish likelihood of confusion.

The Lanham Act defines a counterfeit as "a spurious mark which is identical with, or substantially indistinguishable from, a registered

---

[68] *Id.*, 369 F. Supp.2d at 945 ("The fact that [defendant's] sites link to another site which in turn includes commercial links is insufficient to infuse [defendant's] sites with a commercial purpose.").

[69] 15 U.S.C. § 1114.

[70] 15 U.S.C. § 1125(a).

[71] For a discussion of this test, see § 7.05 *infra*.

mark."[72] Counterfeiting involves using a false "trademark that is an intentional and calculated reproduction of" a protected mark in order to produce or sell a product.[73] A counterfeit requires a closer degree of similarity than traditional trademark infringement. For instance, a counterfeit mark must be identical or substantially similar to a registered mark, whereas a colorable imitation need only resemble a mark in a way that is likely to cause confusion.[74] Therefore, the presence of a counterfeit mark allows the court to presume that consumer confusion exists.[75] It should also be noted that while goods are often referred to as being "counterfeits" or "bootlegs," it is the counterfeiting of the mark, not the product that is prohibited by the Lanham Act.

In one case in which a trademark owner sued an unlicensed manufacturer, alleging counterfeiting in violation of the Lanham Act,[76] the plaintiff claimed that the defendant violated both Section 32 and Section 43 of the Lanham Act. The plaintiff, therefore, needed to demonstrate that its mark was valid and entitled to protection and that defendant's actions were likely to cause confusion.[77] The parties did not dispute the validity of the mark, and so the resolution of the case turned on the presence of likelihood of confusion.[78] Although courts generally undertake a factor-by-factor analysis,[79] the court in this case determined that such action

---

[72] 15 U.S.C. § 1127 ("A 'counterfeit' is a spurious mark which is identical with, or substantially indistinguishable from, a registered mark.").

[73] *McCarthy on Trademarks and Unfair Competition* (4th ed. 2010) ("Counterfeiting is the act of producing or selling a product with a sham trademark that is an intentional and calculated reproduction of the genuine trademark.").

[74] 15 U.S.C. § 1127 ("The term 'colorable imitation' includes any mark which so resembles a registered mark as to be likely to cause confusion or mistake or to deceive."); ("A 'counterfeit' is a spurious mark which is identical with, or substantially indistinguishable from, a registered mark.").

[75] "Gucci America." *Inc. v. Duty Free Apparel, Ltd.*, 286 F. Supp.2d 284 (S.D.N.Y. 2003) (court determined that likelihood of confusion analysis was unnecessary because counterfeits automatically create confusion).

[76] *Id.*

[77] *Id.*, 286 F. Supp.2d at 287.

[78] *Id.*

[79] See § 7.05 *infra* for a discussion of these factors.

was unnecessary because counterfeits automatically cause confusion.[80] In fact, the whole purpose of creating a knock-off product with a counterfeit mark is to confuse the customer.[81] Accordingly, once a court determines that a counterfeit mark exists, likelihood of confusion is presumed.

Because items bearing counterfeit marks are by their nature intended to be highly similar to the authentic product, they provide no means for the public to distinguish between the products.[82] Therefore, consumer confusion may be inevitable and a factor-by-factor analysis assessing likelihood of confusion unnecessary.[83]

The presence of a counterfeit mark essentially does away with the likelihood of confusion test because it allows the court to assume that confusion exists. Moreover, should the court choose to apply the likelihood of confusion test to a counterfeit mark, the factors considered in the test are highly likely to favor the plaintiff. Thus, the Lanham Act provides rights holders with particularly strong protection against counterfeits.

Likelihood of Confusion: Balance of Factors

Likelihood of confusion is the result of the analysis required under the Lanham Act and must be established for both Section 43 common-law trademark infringement and Section 32 federal statutory trademark infringement.[84]

---

[80] "Gucci America." *Inc. v. Duty Free Apparel, Ltd.*, 286 F. Supp.2d 284 (S.D.N.Y. 2003).

[81] *Id.*, 286 F. Supp.2d at 287 ("Indeed, confusing the customer is the whole purpose of creating counterfeit goods.").

[82] "Romag Fasteners." *Inc. v. J.C. Penney, Inc.*, 2007 WL 4225792 at *3 (D. Conn. 2007) ("In the circumstances of counterfeit products, the *Arrow Fastener* mandate is met as to the actual-confusion and similarity-of-the-marks tests, since counterfeit items are intended to be highly similar to the authentic product by their nature, and provide no means for the public to distinguish between manufacturers.").

[83] *Id.* at *4 ("On this record, consumer confusion as to the source of the snaps is virtually inevitable").

[84] 15 U.S.C. § 1114 ("Any person who shall ... use ... with which such use is likely to cause confusion, or to cause mistake, or to deceive;"); 15 U.S.C. § 1125 ("any person who ... uses ... any word, term, name, symbol, or device ... which is likely to cause confusion, or to cause mistake, or to deceive as to the affiliation,

"The test for likelihood of confusion is whether a 'reasonably prudent consumer' in the marketplace is likely to be confused as to the origin of the good or service bearing one of the marks."[85] At least one court has opined that confusion need not be limited to a consumer; confusion by another company selling the disputed product or service might be sufficient.[86]

A Section 32 cause of action requires the defendant's use to be "likely to cause confusion, or to cause mistake, or to deceive."[87] Similarly, a Section 43 cause of action requires the defendant's use to be "likely to cause confusion, or to cause mistake, or to deceive as to the affiliation, connection, or association" with the actual owner of the mark.[88] Therefore, courts apply the same confusion theories regardless of whether the case involves registered marks.[89] Today, all federal circuit courts employ a likelihood-of-confusion test that relies on the balance of several factors, a typical version of which can be found in both *AMF, Inc. v. Sleekcraft Boats*[90] and *Polaroid Corp. v. Polarad Electronics.*[91] Applying the *Sleek-*

---

connection, or association of such person with another person, or as to origin, sponsorship, or approval of his or her goods, services, or commercial activities by another person").

[85] Dreamworks Production Group, Inc. v. SKG Studio, d/b/a Dreamworks SKG, 142 F.3d 1127, 1129 (9th Cir. 1998).

[86] Rearden LLC v. Rearden Commerce, Inc., 683 F.3d 1190 (9th Cir. 2012).

[87] 15 U.S.C. § 1114(1)(a).

[88] 15 U.S.C. § 1125(a)(1)(A).

[89] Dinwoodie and Janis, *Trademarks and Unfair Competition*, at 443 (2d ed. 2007) ("The same confusion theories apply irrespective of whether the case involves registered rights.").

[90] AMF, Inc. v. Sleekcraft Boats, 599 F.2d 341, 348–349 (9th Cir. 1979).

[91] *Second Circuit:* Polaroid Corp. v. Polarad Electronics Corp., 287 F.2d 492, 495 (2d Cir. 1961) ("[Likelihood of confusion] is a function of many variables: the strength of [the mark], the degree of similarity between the two marks, the proximity of the products, the likelihood that the prior owner will bridge the gap, actual confusion, and the reciprocal of defendant's good faith in adopting its own mark, the quality of defendant's product, and the sophistication of the buyers.").

Ninth Circuit: AMF, Inc. v. Sleekcraft Boats, 599 F.2d 341, 479 (9th Cir. 1979) ("All circuits today employ a likelihood of confusion test, which rests on a balance of multiple factors. A typical recitation of factors can be found in Polaroid Corp. v. Polarad Electronics Corp., 287 F.2d 492 (2d Cir. 1961).").

craft test, the eight factors the courts consider in determining whether a likelihood of confusion exists are: (1) strength of the plaintiff's mark; (2) proximity and relatedness of the plaintiff's and defendant's goods; (3) similarity of the plaintiff's and defendant's marks; (4) evidence of actual confusion; (5) the degree to which the parties' marketing channels converge; (6) the type of goods and the degree of care customers are likely to exercise in purchasing them; (7) evidence of the defendant's intention in selecting and using the allegedly infringing mark; and (8) the likelihood that the parties will expand their product lines.[92] "The[se] factors should not be rigidly weighed, but rather are intended to guide the court in assessing the basic question of likelihood of confusion."[93]

Strength of Marks

The strength of a trademark encompasses two concepts: the inherent strength of the mark and the acquired distinctiveness of the mark.[94] Both these concepts are substantially related to the likelihood of confusion test.[95]

The first, and most important, concept is whether the mark is considered inherently strong. In order to determine this, one must distinguish whether the mark is arbitrary or fanciful in relation to the products or services for which it is used, or is generic, descriptive, or suggestive as to those goods or services.[96] A mark that is arbitrary or fanciful is inherently

---

[92] AMF, Inc. v. Sleekcraft Boats, 599 F.2d 341, 479 (9th Cir. 1979).

[93] Glow Industries, Inc. v. Lopez, 252 F. Supp.2d 962, 986 (C.D. Cal. 2002).

[94] Virgin Enterprises Ltd. v. Nawab, 335 F.3d 141, 147 (2d Cir. 2003) ("The strength of a trademark encompasses two different concepts, both of which relate significantly to likelihood of consumer confusion."); ("The first and most important is inherent strength, also called inherent distinctiveness."); ("The second sense of the concept of strength of a mark is "acquired distinctiveness," i.e., fame, or the extent to which prominent use of the mark in commerce has resulted in a high degree of consumer recognition.").

[95] *Id.*

[96] *Id.* ("This inquiry distinguishes between, on the one hand, inherently distinctive marks—marks that are arbitrary or fanciful in relation to the products (or services) on which they are used—and, on the other hand, marks that are generic, descriptive or suggestive as to those goods. The former are the strong marks.").

distinctive and is accorded "broad, muscular protection."[97] The justification behind according such protection to these marks is directly related
to the likelihood of confusion, because consumers who see an arbitrary
mark on different products in the marketplace will likely assume that the
products come from the same source.[98] Therefore, "the more distinctive
the mark, the greater the likelihood that the public, seeing it a second
time, will assume that the second use comes from the same source as the
first."[99] Accordingly, in an effort to protect and avoid consumer confusion, inherently strong marks (i.e., arbitrary or fanciful) receive broader
protection than weak marks that are merely descriptive or suggestive of
the products on which they are applied.[100]

The second concept of trademark strength, known as "acquired
distinctiveness" (i.e., the fame of a mark), is also relevant to customer
confusion.[101] A mark is considered famous "if it is widely recognized by
the general consuming public of the United States as a designation of
source of the goods or services of the mark's owner."[102] If a mark has
been used prominently and notoriously in commerce for an extended

---

[97] *Id.* ("The law accords broad, muscular protection to marks that are arbitrary or
fanciful in relation to the products on which they are used, and lesser protection,
or no protection at all, to marks consisting of words that identify or describe the
goods or their attributes."); ("trademark law accords broader protection to marks
that serve exclusively as identifiers and lesser protection where a grant of exclu-
siveness would tend to diminish the access of others to the full range of discourse
relating to their goods.").

[98] *Id.*, 335 F.3d at 148 ("If a mark is arbitrary or fanciful, and makes no reference
to the nature of the goods it designates, consumers who see the mark on different objects offered in the marketplace will be likely to assume, because of the
arbitrariness of the choice of mark, that they all come from the same source.").

[99] Virgin Enterprises Ltd. v. Nawab, 335 F.3d 141, 148 (2d Cir. 2003).

[100] *Id.* ("The goal of avoiding consumer confusion thus dictates that the inherently distinctive, arbitrary, or fanciful marks, i.e.[,] strong marks, receive broader
protection than weak marks, those that are descriptive or suggestive of the products on which they are used.").

[101] *Id.* ("The second sense of trademark strength, fame, or 'acquired distinctiveness,' also bears on consumer confusion.").

[102] 15 U.S.C. § 1125(a).

period of time, consumers are likely to recognize it.[103] This widespread recognition of the mark increases the likelihood of confusion because of the high probability that consumers will assume that any product bearing the familiar mark originates from the same source.[104] Therefore, the unauthorized use of a famous mark (i.e., a mark with "acquired distinctiveness") increases the likelihood of consumer confusion. Accordingly, famous marks are granted a broader scope of protection.[105]

A Second Circuit case demonstrates how the strength of a mark is factored into the likelihood of confusion test. The plaintiff, holder of the VIRGIN trademark, sought a preliminary injunction against the defendant using the mark VIRGIN WIRELESS in conjunction with sales of wireless telephones. Plaintiff's VIRGIN mark was inherently distinctive because it was arbitrary and fanciful in relation to the consumer electronic equipment it was selling.[106] This lack of an intrinsic relationship between VIRGIN and its products increased the likelihood of confusion because consumers seeing VIRGIN, or a similar mark, used in separate stores selling similar equipment would likely assume that the stores and products were related.[107] Furthermore, the VIRGIN mark was also famous, that is, it had "acquired distinctiveness," because it was recog-

---

[103] *"Virgin Enterprises Ltd. v. Nawab,* N." 16 *supra,* 335 F.3d at 148 ("If a mark has been long, prominently and notoriously used in commerce, there is a high likelihood that consumers will recognize it from its prior use. Widespread consumer recognition of a mark previously used in commerce increases the likelihood that consumers will assume it identifies the previously familiar user, and therefore increases the likelihood of consumer confusion if the new user is in fact not related to the first.").

[104] *Id.*

[105] "Virgin Enterprises Ltd. v. Nawab." 335 F.3d 141, 148 (2d Cir. 2003) ("The added likelihood of consumer confusion resulting from a second user's use of a famous mark gives reason for according such a famous mark a broader scope of protection, at least when it is also inherently distinctive.").

[106] *Id.*, 335 F.3d at 149 ("The word 'virgin' has no intrinsic relationship whatsoever to selling such equipment. Because there is no intrinsic reason for a merchant to use the word 'virgin' in the sale of consumer electronic equipment, a consumer seeing VIRGIN used in two different stores selling such equipment will likely assume that the stores are related.").

[107] *Id.*

nized worldwide as the mark of an airline and megastore selling consumer electronic equipment. Accordingly, the fame of the mark increased the likelihood of consumer confusion.[108] Therefore, there was no doubt that the mark VIRGIN, when used on consumer electronic equipment, was a strong mark and thus entitled to a broad scope of protection.[109] In this instance, the strength of the mark weighed in favor of a likelihood that consumers would be confused as to the source of the goods and services offered under the trademark.

The ability of a rights holder to demonstrate that his or her mark is strong is important when using the Lanham Act to combat trademark infringement. Although weak marks are also granted a certain amount of protection, because the scope of protection is not as broad, a rights holder will more likely succeed in a trademark infringement claim if his or her trademark meets the strong mark criteria.

Degree of Similarity

Marks do not have to be identical for the likelihood of confusion to exist.[110] In fact, a defendant often will not blatantly copy a mark, but will instead make slight variations to the mark that do not amount to a substantive difference. The similarity between the protected mark and the alleged infringing mark must be considered when assessing the likelihood of consumer confusion. "When the secondary user's mark is not identical but merely similar to the plaintiff's mark, it is important to assess the degree of similarity between them in assessing the likelihood that

---

[108] *Id.*, 335 F.3d at 149 ("The fame of the mark increased the likelihood that consumers seeing defendants' shops selling telephones under the mark VIRGIN would assume incorrectly that defendants' shops were part of plaintiff's organization.").

[109] *Id.*

[110] "American Steel Foundries v. Robertson." 269 U.S. 372, 381, 46 S.Ct. 160, 70 L.Ed. 317 (1926) ("The general doctrine is that equity will not only enjoin the appropriation and use of a trademark or trade name, where it is completely identical with the name of the corporation, but will enjoin such appropriation and use where the resemblance is so close as to be likely to produce confusion as to such identity, to the injury of the corporation to which the name belongs.").

consumers will be confused."[111] In conducting this inquiry, it is important to examine each mark in its entirety because a mere side-by-side comparison is not how most consumers will experience the marks.[112] For instance, a consumer may hear an advertisement of the protected mark on the radio and later see the secondary mark and have no way of knowing that the two marks look different from each other.[113] Moreover, a consumer who has previously seen the protected mark may only remember the name and not necessarily the color or typeface. Therefore, when assessing the degree of similarity between marks, "courts look to the overall impression created by the logos and the context in which they are found and consider the totality of factors that could cause confusion among prospective purchasers."[114] This inquiry is essential because a greater degree of similarity between the marks increases the likelihood of consumer confusion.[115]

The degree of similarity needed to show that consumer confusion is likely varies, depending on whether the goods to which each respective mark is attached are different. Where the goods or services attached to

---

[111] "Virgin Enterprises Ltd. v. Nawab." 335 F.3d 141, 149 (2d Cir. 2003).

[112] Most consumers will not experience both marks side-by-side. They are likely to view them separately, at different times, in different contexts (i.e., radio advertisements); *Id.*, 335 F.3d at 150 ("Advertisement and consumer experience of a mark do not necessarily transmit all of the mark's features.").

[113] See *id.*, 335 F.3d at 149 (plaintiff advertised its Virgin Megastores on the radio. A consumer who heard those advertisements and then saw the defendants' installation using the name VIRGIN would have no way of knowing that the two trademarks looked different; "the reputation of a mark also spreads by word of mouth among consumers. One consumer [who] hears from others about their experience with Virgin Stores and then encounters defendants' Virgin store will have no way of knowing of the differences in typeface.").

[114] De Beers LV Trademark Ltd. v. DeBeers Diamond, 440 F. Supp.2d 249, 275 (S.D.N.Y. 2006) ("… it is important to assess the degree of similarity between [the marks]. In making that assessment courts look to the overall impression created by the logos and the context in which they are found and consider the totality of the factors that could cause confusion among prospective purchasers.").

[115] See "Virgin Enterprises Ltd. v. Nawab." N. 28 *supra*, 335 F.3d at 149 ("In view of the fact that defendants used the same name as plaintiff, we conclude the defendants' mark was sufficiently similar to plaintiff's to increase the likelihood of confusion. This factor favored the plaintiff as a matter of law.").

each mark are in direct competition, the degree of similarity required of the marks is less than if the products are not similar.[116] Conversely, if a great degree of similarity between the marks exists, a lesser degree of similarity is required between the goods or services to support a finding of likelihood of confusion.[117] In fact, if a great degree of similarity between the marks exists, "it is sufficient that the goods and services are related in some manner, or that the circumstances surrounding their marketing are such, that they would be likely encountered by the same persons in situations that would give rise ... to a mistaken belief that they originate from or are in some way associated with the same source."[118] Accordingly, the relative similarity between the goods and services attached to each mark is considered when determining the degree of similarity of the marks themselves.[119]

---

[116] *"First Circuit: Attrezzi, LLC v.* Maytag Corp." 436 F.3d 32 (1st Cir. 2006) ("This is not a case in which two products are so dissimilar as to make confusion highly unlikely; and the more similar the marks are, the less necessary it is that the products themselves be very similar to create confusion.").

Trademark Trial and Appeal Board: Fossil Inc. v. Fossil Group, 1998 WL 962201 at *5 (TTAB 1998) ("As the degree of similarity of the goods of the parties increases, the degree of similarity of the marks necessary to support a conclusion of likely confusion declines.").

[117] In re Opus One, Inc., 2001 WL 1182924 at *3 (TTAB 2001) ("The greater the degree of similarity between the applicant's mark and the cited mark, the lesser the degree of similarity between the applicant's goods or services and the registrant's goods or services that is required to support a finding of likelihood of confusion.").

[118] *Id.* **3–4 (Applicant's "restaurant services" and registrant's "wine" were clearly found to be complimentary goods and services that could be encountered together by the same purchasers; accordingly, this factor weighed in favor of a likelihood of confusion).

[119] Rodgers v. Wright, 544 F. Supp.2d 302 (S.D.N.Y. 2008). In this case, the founder of a music group and owner of the mark CHIC brought an infringement action against two former group members for performing under the marks LADIES OF CHIC and FIRST LADIES OF CHIC. In assessing the likelihood of consumer confusion, the court used the traditional *Polaroid* test and considered the similarity of the marks. *Id.*, at 311 ("When the secondary user's mark is not identical but merely similar to the plaintiff's mark, it is important to assess the degree of similarity between them in assessing the likelihood that consumers will

One court examined the similarity between the plaintiff's mark DE BEERS and the defendant's name DEBEERS DIAMOND SYNDI-CATE by assessing the overall impression created by the marks.[120] The defendant's slight variation of the omitted space in the word DEBEERS did not create a legally recognizable distinction between the two marks.[121] Moreover, DEBEERS was clearly the dominant element in the defendant's name and neither the words "diamond" nor "syndicate" amelio-rated the likelihood of confusion.[122] Such similarities between the marks favored a finding of consumer confusion.[123]

The similarity between the senior and junior marks is very import-ant in the balance of factors leading toward the conclusion of whether a likelihood of confusion exists. In deciding whether two marks are similar enough to weigh in favor of consumer confusion, the basic principle is that the "marks must be compared in their entireties and must be consid-ered in connection with the particular goods or services for which they are used."[124] Therefore, likelihood of confusion cannot be predicated on the similarity or difference regarding only one part of the mark.[125] Nev-ertheless, more or less weight may be given to particular features of the mark depending on whether they are considered dominant elements of that mark.[126] In the end, however, the determination of this factor rests on

---

be confused."). The court found that defendants' marks were sufficiently similar to plaintiff's mark so as to cause confusion. *Id.*, 544 F. Supp.2d at 311 ("Here, defendants sometimes used the identical mark but other times performed as the "First Ladies of Chic" or the like. The court finds that the latter formulation and those like it are sufficiently similar to Chic so as to cause confusion.").

[120] "De Beers LV Trademark Ltd. v. DeBeers Diamond." 440 F. Supp.2d 249, 276 (S.D.N.Y. 2006).

[121] *Id.* ("A variation as slight as an omitted space does not serve to create a legally recognizable distinction between De Beers and DeBeers.").

[122] *Id.*

[123] *Id.*

[124] In Re National Data Corp., 753 F.2d 1056, 1058 (Fed. Cir. 1985).

[125] *Id.* ("Likelihood of confusion cannot be predicated on dissection of a mark, that is, on only one part of a mark.").

[126] *Id.*, 753 F.2d at 1058 ("On the other hand, in articulating reasons for reach-ing a conclusion on the issue of confusion, there is nothing improper in stat-ing that, for rational reasons, more or less weight has been given to a particular

the consideration of the marks in their entirety. Accordingly, the ability of a rights holder to demonstrate a great degree of similarity between his or her mark and another user's same or similar mark provides the rights holder with valuable evidence that consumer confusion is likely.

Proximity of Products and Likelihood of Bridging the Gap

This factor has an obvious influence on the likelihood of confusion. On the one hand, two marks that are operating in completely different areas of commerce are less likely to cause consumers mistakenly to assume that the similarly branded products come from the same source.[127] On the other hand, the closer in proximity the secondary mark's products are to those of the protected mark, the more likely the consumer is to mistakenly assume that the products have a common source.[128] This inquiry considers whether the products associated with both marks are sold in the same channels of commerce and, even if plaintiff's products are not close to defendant's products when defendant begins marketing them, whether there is a reasonable likelihood that plaintiff will enter that market.[129]

---

feature of a mark, provided the ultimate conclusion rests on consideration of the marks in their entireties.").

[127] "Virgin Enterprises Ltd. v. Nawab." 335 F.3d 141 (2d Cir. 2003) ("[Proximity of products] has an obvious bearing on the likelihood of confusion. When the two users of a mark are operating in completely different areas of commerce, consumers are less likely to assume that their similarly branded products come from the same source. In contrast, the closer the secondary user's goods are to those the consumer has seen marketed under the prior user's brand, the more likely that the consumer will mistakenly assume a common source.").

[128] *Id.*

[129] *Id.*, 335 F.3d at 150 ("They are sold in commerce. Our classic *Polaroid* test further protects a trademark owner by examining the likelihood that, even if the plaintiff's products were not so close to the defendants' when the defendants began to market them, there was already a likelihood that plaintiff would in the reasonably near future begin selling those products.").

Second Circuit: Arrow Fastener Co., Inc. v. Stanley Works, 59 F.3d 384, 396 (2d Cir. 1995) ("The question is whether a purchaser could easily assume that, while the [products] themselves are different, they belong to the same genre of products and might well have the same source.").

A Second Circuit case demonstrates the proper application of this factor. There, the defendant was selling telephones and the plaintiff was selling consumer electronic equipment.[130] Although plaintiff had not sold telephones, its products were like telephones because they were small consumer electronics making use of computerized audio communication.[131] Therefore, consumers would have a high expectation of finding plaintiff's and defendant's products in the same stores because they were sold in the same channels of commerce.[132] This proximity in commerce of plaintiff's and defendant's products substantially increased the likelihood of consumer confusion.[133]

This factor may favor a finding of consumer confusion even "when the secondary user is not in direct competition with the prior user, but is selling a somewhat different product or service"[134] because "direct competition between the products is not a prerequisite to relief."[135] Therefore, "a trademark owner does not lose merely because it has not previously sold the precise good or service sold by the secondary user."[136] Although the plaintiff was selling a different product, it was likely to enter the defendant's market, likely resulting in consumer confusion.[137] Accordingly, the proximity of products factor turns on whether the consumer could

---

[130] "Virgin Enterprises Ltd. v. Nawab" 335 F.3d 141, 150 (2d Cir. 2003).

[131] *Id.* ("Like telephones, many of these are small consumer electronic gadgets making use of computerized audio communication.").

[132] *Id.* ("They are sold in the same channels of commerce."); ("Consumers would have a high expectation of finding telephones, portable CD players, and computerized video game systems in the same stores.").

[133] *Id.* ("We think the proximity in commerce of telephones to CD players substantially advanced the risk that consumer confusion would occur.").

[134] *Id.*, 335 F.3d at 150.

[135] Arrow Fastener Co., Inc. v. Stanley Works, 59 F.3d 384, 396 (2d Cir. 1995).

[136] Virgin Enterprises Ltd. v. Nawab, 335 F.3d 141, 151 (2d Cir. 2003).

[137] *Id.*, 335 F.3d at 151 ("Plaintiff already had plans to bridge the gap by expanding its sales of consumer electronic equipment to include those very goods and services in the near future. Consumer confusion was more than likely; it was virtually inevitable.").

assume that the products belong to the same genre and originate from the same source.[138]

Evidence of Actual Confusion

"Actual confusion occurs when the source of the copy is mistaken for the source of the original."[139] It is obvious that the existence of actual consumer confusion indicates a likelihood of consumer confusion.[140] On the one hand, if an allegedly similar secondary mark enters the marketplace for an adequate period of time and no actual confusion results, this factor favors a finding that the secondary mark does not create consumer confusion.[141] On the other hand, if consumer confusion actually occurs under such circumstances, this supports a finding of likelihood of confusion.[142]

---

[138] See: Virgin Enterprises Ltd. v. Nawab, 335 F.3d 141, 150 (2d Cir. 2003) (proximity in commerce between the products advances risk that consumer confusion will occur. Likelihood of bridging the gap makes consumer confusion likely.); Arrow Fastener Co., Inc. v. Stanley Works, 59 F.3d 384, 396 (2d Cir. 1995) ("The question is whether a purchaser could easily assume that, while the [products] themselves are different, they belong to the same genre of products and might well have the same source.").

[139] Brunswick Corp. v. Spinit Reel Co., 832 F.2d 513, 521 (10th Cir. 1987).

[140] "Virgin Enterprises Ltd. v. Nawab." 335 F.3d 141, 151 (2d Cir. 2003) ("We have deemed evidence of actual confusion particularly relevant to the inquiry [of a likelihood of consumer confusion]."); Nabisco, Inc. v. PF Brands, Inc., 191 F.3d 208, 228 (2d Cir. 1999) ("The presence or absence of actual confusion can be highly effective in showing a high, or a low, likelihood of confusion if there has been ample opportunity for consumer confusion.").

[141] "Virgin Enterprises Ltd. v. Nawab." 335 F.3d 141, 151 (2d Cir. 2003) ("If consumers have been exposed to two allegedly similar trademarks in the marketplace for an adequate period of time and no actual confusion is detected either by survey or in actual reported instances of confusion, that can be powerful indication that the junior trademark does not cause a meaningful likelihood of confusion.").

[142] "Virgin Enterprises Ltd. v. Nawab." 335 F.3d 141, 151 (2d Cir. 2003) (plaintiff submitted evidence of actual confusion, which weighed in favor of a likelihood of consumer confusion); Nabisco, Inc. v. PF Brands, Inc., 191 F.3d 208, 228 (2d Cir. 1999) ("in contrast, if numerous instances of consumer confusion have occurred, that suggests a high likelihood of continuing confusion."); McDonald's

In fact, evidence of actual confusion is commonly considered the best evidence of likelihood of confusion.[143]

Evidence of actual confusion is generally introduced by conducting surveys, although their evidentiary value depends on the methods used.[144] Such evidence must meet the *Daubert* standard and "is trustworthy if it is shown to have been conducted according to generally accepted survey principles."[145] In one case in which a retailer and manufacturer of hair care products sold under the mark GENERIC VALUE PRODUCTS alleged trademark infringement against a competitor selling products under the mark GENERIX, evidence of actual confusion weighed in favor of finding likelihood of confusion.[146] The plaintiff presented a survey indicating

---

Corp. v. Druck and Gerner, D.D.S., P.C., d/b/a McDental, 814 F. Supp. 1127, 1131 (N.D.N.Y. 1993) (plaintiff presented evidence of actual confusion via survey and testimony, which supported a finding of likelihood of confusion).

[143] Brunswick Corp. v. Spinit Reel Co., 832 F.2d 513, 521 (10th Cir. 1987) ("Evidence of actual confusion which, although not necessary for a finding of likelihood of confusion, may be the strongest evidence to support such a determination."); 1-800 Contacts, Inc. v. Lens.com, Inc., 2010 WL 5150800 at *16 (D. Utah 2010) ("Actual confusion in the marketplace is often considered the best evidence of likelihood of confusion.").

[144] *Third Circuit:* Facenda v. N.F.L. Films, Inc., 542 F.3d 1007, 1020 (3d Cir. 2008) ("A common way of providing such evidence of actual confusion is to conduct a survey.").

Tenth Circuit: Vail Associates, Inc. v. Vend-Tel-Co., Ltd., 516 F.3d 853, 864 (10th Cir. 2008) ("Evidence of actual confusion is often introduced through the use of surveys, although their evidentiary value depends on the methodology and questions asked.").

[145] "Brunswick Corp. v. Spinit Rell Co." 832 F.2d 513, 522 (10th Cir. 1987). See Vail Associates, Inc. v. Vend-Tel-Co., Ltd., 516 F.3d 853, 864 (10th Cir. 2008) ("Court exercises its *Daubert* gatekeeping role in deciding whether to admit or exclude survey evidence.") ("Following a *Daubert* hearing, the district court concluded flaws in the methodology made [Plaintiffs] survey data and supporting expert testimony unreliable as a basis for drawing conclusions about confusion or the likelihood of confusion in the relevant market of potential purchasers." Decision held up on appeal).

[146] Sally Beauty Co., Inc. v. Beautyco, Inc., 304 F.3d 964, 979-980 (10th Cir. 2002) ("Survey is strong evidence of actual confusion between [plaintiff] and [defendant's] trade dresses. Accordingly, this factor weighs heavily in favor of [plaintiff]").

26 percent of participants believed that the defendant's and the plaintiff's products had the same source.[147] Because such surveys are substantial evidence of actual confusion, this factor weighed heavily in favor of the plaintiff.[148]

Evidence of actual confusion need not be limited to evidence of mistaken completed transactions. In fact, evidence of actual confusion regarding affiliation, sponsorship, and goodwill are also entirely relevant to the likelihood of confusion inquiry.[149] Furthermore, while very little proof of actual confusion is necessary to favor a finding of likelihood of confusion, an overwhelming amount of proof is necessary to refute such a finding.[150] Accordingly, the ability of a trademark owner to demonstrate the existence of actual confusion is highly valuable when using the Lanham Act to protect one's brand. The absence of actual confusion, however, is not fatal to a plaintiff's case.[151]

---

[147] *Id.*, 304 F.3d at 979–980 (expert survey reported that fifty-one out of 180 participants, 26 percent, believed that products bearing defendant's mark were manufactured by plaintiff).

[148] *Id.*, 304 F.3d at 980.

[149] Connecticut Community Bank v. The Bank of Greenwich, 578 F. Supp.2d 405, 418–419 (D. Conn. 2008) ("Evidence of actual confusion need not be limited to evidence of mistaken completed transactions ... instead, evidence of actual confusion regarding affiliation or sponsorship is also entirely relevant to the ultimate likelihood of confusion inquiry.").

[150] *Id.*, 578 F. Supp.2d at 419 ("While very little proof of actual confusion would be necessary to prove the likelihood of confusion, an almost overwhelming amount of proof would be necessary to refute such proof"). Generally, a finding of 8 to 10 percent of actual confusion in a survey is sufficient.

[151] *"Third Circuit:* Facenda v. N.F.L. Films, Inc.." *"*542 F.3d 1007, 1020 (3d Cir. 2008) ("Even though the actual confusion factor can be important, survey evidence is expensive and difficult to obtain, leading some courts not to penalize plaintiffs for failing to obtain it.").

Sixth Circuit: Standard Coffee Co., Inc. v. William B. Reily, 210 F.3d 372, at *4 (6th Cir. 2000) ("Evidence of actual confusion is but one factor to consider in determining infringement; the lack of evidence of actual confusion is not necessarily fatal to a plaintiff's claim.").

Intent to Copy/Infringe

When considering a defendant's intent to copy or infringe upon a rights holder's mark, the relevant inquiry is whether the defendant intended to deceive consumers. The presence of such intent to copy a protected mark is generally not highly relevant to the issue of likelihood of confusion.[152] Although the secondary user's bad faith may affect the court's remedial decisions, "it does not bear directly on whether consumers are likely to be confused."[153] However, although intentional copying is not a requirement under the Lanham Act, some courts hold that such evidence does weigh in favor of finding a likelihood of confusion.[154] Nevertheless, "a defendant's mere intent to copy, without more, is not sufficiently probative of the defendant's success in causing confusion."[155] In fact, the secondary user's intent to copy or infringe upon a protected mark indicates a likelihood of confusion only if the secondary user intends to confuse relevant consumers by purposefully manipulating his mark to resemble the protected mark.[156]

Where the owner of a protected mark brought action against its competitor alleging that the competitor's similar mark infringed, defendant's

---

[152] Virgin Enterprises Ltd. v. Nawab, 335 F.3d 151 (2d Cir. 2003) ("The existence of bad faith on the part of the secondary user … [is not] of high relevance to the issue of likelihood of confusion."); Lois Sportswear, U.S.A., Inc. v. Levi Strauss & Co., 799 F.2d 867, 875 (2d Cir. 1986) ("intent is largely irrelevant in determining if consumers likely will be confused as to source.").

[153] *Virgin Enterprises Ltd. v. Nawab*, N. 69 *supra*, 335 F.3d p. 151.

[154] "*Second Circuit:* Lois Sportswear, U.S.A., Inc. v. Levi Strauss & Co." 799 F.2d 867, 875 (2d Cir. 1986) ("It must be remembered … that intentional copying is not a requirement under the Lanham Act.").

Third Circuit: Sabinsa Corp. v. Creative Compounds, LLC, 609 F.3d 175, 187 (3d Cir. 2010) ("Evidence of a defendant's intent is not a prerequisite for finding a Lanham Act violation; such evidence, however, weighs heavily in favor of finding a likelihood of confusion.").

[155] Sabinsa Corp. v. Creative Compounds, LLC, 609 F.3d 175, 187 (3d Cir. 2010).

[156] *Id.*, 609 F.3d at 187 ("Defendant's intent will indicate a likelihood of confusion only if an intent to confuse consumers is demonstrated via purposeful manipulation of the junior mark to resemble the senior's.").

intent favored a finding of likelihood of confusion.[157] Considering this factor required examining defendant's trademark searches prior to adopting its mark, false claims regarding this search, and the timing of the adoption. The intent factor, however, involved disputed factual issues and therefore did not favor either party.[158] Nevertheless, the court explained that the presence of "intent to confuse consumers demonstrated via purposeful manipulation of the [secondary] mark to resemble the [protected mark]" favors a likelihood of consumer confusion.[159]

Intent to cause confusion is proved by circumstantial evidence.[160] Circumstances favor a finding of intent or bad faith when a defendant deliberately adopts a similar mark.[161] Additionally, in determining a defendant's intent, actual or constructive knowledge of the prior user's mark may indicate bad faith.[162] Moreover, an inference of intent is particularly strong when the parties have also had a prior relationship.[163] The absence of such intent to copy or infringe furnishes no defense to a trademark infringement claim.[164] Although this innocent state of mind provides no evidentiary value, a guilty state of mind may be considered

---

[157] Id., 609 F.3d at 187–188 ("There was ample evidence that [defendant] attempted to pass off its products as [plaintiff's].").

[158] Id., 609 F.3d at 188 ("Accordingly, unlike the other factors, the intent factor involves disputed factual issues, and we are unable to hold that it favors either party as a matter of law.").

[159] Id., 609 F.3d at 187.

[160] Sensient Technologies Corp. v. SensoryEffects Flavor, 613 F.3d pp. 754–771 (8th Cir. 2010).

[161] Id., 613 F.3d at 772 ("Deliberate adoption of a similar mark may lead to an inference of intent to pass off goods as those of another and the inference of intent is especially strong when the parties have had a prior relationship.").

[162] New York City Triathlon, LLC v. NYC Triathlon Club, LLC, 704 F. Supp.2d 305, 339 (S.D.N.Y. 2010) ("In determining a defendant's intent, actual or constructive knowledge of the prior user's mark or dress may indicate an absence of good faith or bad faith.").

[163] Id.

[164] "Polo Fashions, Inc. v. Fernandez." 655 F. Supp. 664, 666 (D.P.R. 1987) (defendant was liable for infringement even though it made good faith effort to determine goods were not counterfeit, and upon discovering goods were counterfeit, immediately withdrew its remaining stock from sale).

probative of the existence of a likelihood of consumer confusion.[165] This is because actively pursuing an objective increases the chances that the objective will be achieved.[166] The ability of a rights holder to present circumstances that demonstrate a defendant's intent to copy or infringe on a mark is a valuable tool toward protecting a trademark and, just as important, the brand attached to it.

Quality of Infringing Product

The quality of the junior user's infringing product or service is not highly relevant to the likelihood of consumer confusion.[167] Instead, this factor relates more to the type of harm that consumer confusion can cause the plaintiff's mark.[168] In rare circumstances, however, similarity in the quality of the products may increase consumer confusion.[169]

---

[165] "Markel v. Scovill Manufacturing Co." 471 F. Supp. 1244, 1252 (W.D.N.Y. 1979) ("Although a showing of wrongful intent is not required, the existence of a purpose to foster the impression that it was the distributor of the same heaters as [plaintiff] is strong indication that confusion will occur in fact.").

[166] Sensient Technologies Corp. v. SensoryEffects Flavor, 613 F.3d 754, 772 (8th Cir. 2010) ("The fact that one actively pursues an objective greatly increases the chances that the objective will be achieved, and for this reason, a defendant's intent is an important factor, and can be weighed more heavily than other factors.").

[167] "Virgin Enterprises Ltd. v. Nawab." 335 F.3d 151 (2d Cir. 2003) ("Two factors remain of the conventional *Polaroid* test: the existence of bad faith on the part of the secondary user and the quality of the secondary user's products or services. Neither factor is of high relevance to the issue of likelihood of confusion.").

[168] Virgin Enterprises Ltd. v. Nawab, 335 F.3d 151, 152 (2d Cir. 2003) ("The issue of the quality of the secondary user's product goes more to the harm that confusion can cause the plaintiff's mark and reputation rather than to the likelihood of confusion."); Arrow Fastener Co., Inc. v. Stanley Works, 59 F.3d 384, 398 (2d Cir. 1995) ("This factor is primarily concerned with whether the senior user's reputation could be jeopardized by virtue of the fact that the junior user's product is of inferior quality.").

[169] "Arrow Fastener Co., Inc. v. Stanley Works." 59 F.3d 384, 398 (2d Cir. 1995) ("Similarities in quality may actually heighten the confusion of consumers after purchase.").

The good quality of products may be relevant to the likelihood of confusion because the products match the quality expected by the consumers.[170] Particularly in the post sale context, similarities in the quality of products may increase the likelihood that consumers could assume two different products had the same source.[171]

Congruently, the inferior quality of a junior user's goods or services weighs in favor of a likelihood of confusion. But this approach relies on the factor's consideration of whether the senior user's reputation could be tarnished by inferior merchandise or services of the junior user.[172] This manner of examining the factor focuses more on the damage caused by a secondary mark than on the likelihood of confusion created.

As a practical matter, this factor is generally not given much weight in considering a likelihood of consumer confusion. However, it may help shift the balance of factors in a rights holder's favor if he or she is able to demonstrate that the quality of defendant's goods or services does result in consumer confusion.

Sophistication of Buyer

This factor can have an important bearing on the likelihood of confusion.[173] The degree of sophistication of a consumer is relevant because it relates to the consumer's familiarity with the market. This familiarity bears

---

[170] Lois Sportswear, U.S.A., Inc. v. Levi Strauss & Co., 799 F.2d pp. 867–875 (2d Cir. 1986) ("It must be noted, however, that under the circumstances of this case the good quality of appellants' product actually may increase the likelihood of confusion as to source.").

[171] *Id.*, 799 F.2d at 875 ("Particularly in the post-sale context, consumers easily could assume that quality jeans bearing what is perceived as appellee's trademark stitching pattern to be a Levi's product.").

[172] New York City Triathlon LLC v. NYC Triathlon Club, Inc., 704 F. Supp.2d 305, 340 (S.D.N.Y. 2010) ("The quality of goods and services factor generally considers whether the senior user's reputation could be tarnished by inferior merchandise or services of the junior user.").

[173] Virgin Enterprises Ltd. v. Nawab, 335 F.3d 141, 152 (2d Cir. 2003). ("The degree of sophistication of consumers can have an important bearing on likelihood of confusion.").

on the consumer's propensity to be misled or confused by the similarity of different marks. Purchasers of a product who are highly trained professionals know the market and are less likely than untrained consumers to be confused regarding the source of a product.[174] On the other hand, "retail customers are not expected to exercise the same degree of care as professional buyers."[175] Therefore, the more sophisticated the consumers, the less likely they are to be misled by a secondary user's similar mark.[176] However, if the group of relevant consumers happens to be a combination of professionals and ordinary buyers, "the class as a whole is not held to a higher standard of care."[177]

In a case in which the products at issue were consumer electronics, the court noted that the relevant consumers were "likely to give greater care than self-service customers in a supermarket"[178] but were not professional buyers "expected to have greater powers of discrimination."[179] Because neither plaintiff nor defendant submitted evidence regarding the sophistication of consumers, this factor was found to be neutral. Nevertheless,

---

[174] "*Second Circuit:* Virgin Enterprises Ltd. v. Nawab." 335 F.3d 141, 152 (2d Cir. 2003) ("Where the purchasers of a product are highly trained professionals, they know the market and are less likely than untrained consumers to be misled or confused by the similarity of different marks.").

Third Circuit: Sabinsa Corp. v. Creative Compounds, LLC, 609 F.3d 175, 186 (3d Cir. 2010) ("Where the relevant ... buyer class consists of sophisticated or professional purchasers, courts have generally not found Lanham Act violations.").

[175] Sabinsa Corp. v. Creative Compounds, LLC, 609 F.3d 175, 186 (3d Cir. 2010).

[176] Savin Corp. v. Savin Group, 391 F.3d 439, 461 (2d Cir. 2004) ("The more sophisticated the purchaser, the less likely he or she will be confused by the presence of similar marks in the marketplace."); TCPIP Holding Co., Inc. v. Haar Communications, Inc., 244 F.3d 88, 102 (2d Cir. 2001) ("The more sophisticated the consumers, the less likely they are to be misled by similarity in marks.").

[177] Sabinsa Corp. v. Creative Compounds, LLC, 609 F.3d 175, 186 (3d Cir. 2010) ("Where the group of buyers is a combination of professionals and ordinary consumers, the class as a whole is not held to the higher standard of care.").

[178] "Virgin Enterprises Ltd. v. Nawab." 335 F.3d pp. 141–152 (2d Cir. 2003).

[179] *Id.*

a showing of a nonsophisticated consumer base supports a likelihood of consumer confusion.[180]

In a case in which the customers were sophisticated purchasers, this factor weighed against a finding of likelihood of confusion. Here, the consumers were generally repeat customers who exercised a high level of care.[181] Moreover, the relevant consumers regularly asked technical questions about the nature and merits of the product prior to purchase.[182] This high level of care exercised by relevant consumers was found to eliminate the likelihood of confusion.[183] Accordingly, this factor favored the defendant.

The question here is whether the relevant consumer class is classified as ordinary buyers or experienced professional purchasers. If the relevant consumers are found to be ordinary, then this factor is likely to weigh in favor of a likelihood of confusion. If the relevant consumers are found to be sophisticated and experienced professionals, this factor will not support a finding of likelihood of confusion.

Initial Interest, Post Sale, and Reverse Confusion

The likelihood of "confusion" that the Lanham Act attempts to prevent can take many forms. It is for this reason that the factual details of every potential infringement case become critical to the outcome. The courts—not the Lanham Act—have fashioned these various forms of confusion based on their analyses of the facts in each case.

In addition to the confusion by a consumer when viewing two products bearing the same or similar trademarks in the marketplace, courts in many circuits have recognized "initial interest confusion," which can arise

---

[180] See TCPIP Holding Co., Inc. v. Haar Communications, Inc., 244 F.3d 88, p. 102 (2d Cir. 2001) ("In this case, there is no reason to expect that plaintiff's consumers and users of defendant's portal will be particularly sophisticated. [Therefore,] there is no reason to expect that a degree of sophistication will protect consumers from confusion resulting from confusingly similar marks.")

[181] "Sabinsa Corp. v. Creative Compounds." LLC, N. 94 supra, 609 F.3d. at 186.

[182] Id.

[183] Id. ("These customers exercise a high level of care, and, therefore, eliminate the likelihood of confusion.").

when a potential buyer is misled by the association of the source of one product with the source of a similar product. Liability is created by initial interest confusion even when the consumer subsequently learns that the two products are not associated. Although the scope of this type of consumer confusion is fairly well settled in connection with hard goods, such liability is still evolving with respect to the Internet. Early in the life of the Internet, initial interest confusion was found to lie in the use of meta tags (meta tags are HTML codes inserted into the header of a web page to give web browsers and search engines information about the content of a web page) composed of the trademark owner's trademark.[184] However, now that meta tags are not as frequently used, the issue is of less importance. In fact, several circuits have ruled that use of a metatag is not likely to lead to confusion.[185]

The "confusion" may also happen at a point in time after the consumer sale or viewing has taken place and a third party may be the victim of the confusion. This is characterized as "post-sale confusion," and is recognized by many of the circuits. Post-sale confusion can occur even if the actual buyer knows that he or she is buying an infringement or counterfeit product because a third party viewing the product and not having the buyer's knowledge may, in fact, believe it to be from the legitimate rights holder. A classic example is demonstrated where a consumer buys a counterfeit watch or handbag and, because the consumer is only paying $50 for the ordinarily far more expensive product, it is or should be obvious to the consumer that the watch or handbag is not genuine. However, should a third party receive the counterfeit as a gift it is possible, if not likely, that the recipient is not aware that the product is not genuine and,

---

[184] "Brookfield Communications." *Inc. v. West Coast Entertainment Corp.*, 174 F.3d 1036 (9th Cir. 1999).

[185] "In Southern Snow Manufacturing v. Sno Wizard Holdings." Inc., 2:10-cv-00791 (E.D. La. February 16, 2011), a Louisiana district court granted summary judgment to a third-party defendant (Parasol Flavors LLC), citing the lack of evidence by plaintiff (Sno Wizard Holdings, Inc.) to demonstrate a likelihood of confusion between Parasol's use of the term "Snow Wizard" in its meta tags and Sno Wizard's registered trademark Sno Wizard and establishing how the "Snow Wizard" meta tag influences search engine results and whether the difference between "Snow Wizard" and Sno Wizard is influential in that result.

therefore, is likely to be confused as to its authenticity and source.[186] Even where a disclaimer is used in connection with the sale of the product, courts have found that such a disclaimer has no ameliorative effect on a third party who may still experience confusion at a later point in time.[187]

Cases of infringement such as those involving counterfeiting where there is "forward confusion," in which a consumer believes that the infringer's goods are the same or from the same source as the genuine rights holder or senior user of a trademark, are familiar. In a "reverse confusion" situation, the junior trademark user or counterfeiter markets its product in such a way as to exceed the goodwill (sales, advertising, and public relations) established by the genuine senior user so that consumers believe that the junior user is actually the source for, has approval of, or has licensed the genuine senior user's goods or services. This damages the good will of the senior user since consumers may believe that the senior user is itself the infringer or is commercially hitchhiking on the junior user.[188] As in the seminal *Gatorade* "Thirst Aid" case,[189] a larger company with resources can simply out market and out sell a smaller individual or entity and, in the process, cause significant injury to the smaller prior user of a mark.[190]

Trademark Dilution

Claims for trademark dilution provide a useful basis for rights holders to attack instances of infringement on noncompetitive goods and services.[191] Trademark dilution claims have increased in popularity as famous marks have come to be used on a wide range of products and services not authorized by the rights holder. In many of these situations, the rights holder

---

[186] United States v. Torkington, 812 F.2d 1347 (11th Cir. 1987).

[187] Au-Tomotive Gold, Inc. v. Volkswagen of America, Inc., 457 F.3d 1062, 1077 (9th Cir. 2006), *cert. denied* 549 U.S. 1282 (2007).

[188] Sands, Taylor & Wood Co. v. Quaker Oats Co., 978 F.2d 947 (7th Cir. 1992).

[189] *Id.* ("Gatorade is Thirst Aid" infringes on plaintiff's "Thirst-Aid").

[190] Big O Tire Dealers, Inc. v. Good Year Tire & Rubber Co., 408 F. Supp. 1219, *aff'd and award modified* 561 F.2d 1365 (10th Cir. 1977), *cert. dismissed* 434 U.S. 1052 (1978).

[191] See 15 U.S.C. § 1125(c).

cannot bring a claim of counterfeiting because the unauthorized mark is not being used on goods for which the rights holder has obtained a federal registration.[192] Nevertheless, brand holders who are the victims of inferior-quality products bearing counterfeits of their mark have included claims for trademark dilution by tarnishment, alleging that the "inferior" counterfeit good tarnishes the genuine product's reputation for quality.[193] Some commentators have argued that there is no place for a dilution claim in a counterfeiting case since the "poor-quality" issue is already remedied by the Lanham Act.[194]

Starting in 1947, various states enacted anti-dilution statutes as a means of protecting locally famous marks.[195] In 1996, the first federal anti-dilution law was passed as a result of increasing pressure from well-known brand holders to be able to protect themselves against others who, although not competing directly in the same types of goods or services, nonetheless were using a famous mark for their own commercial advantage. Some have referred to this type of activity as "commercial hitch-hiking," or "free-riding" on the fame of a brand for commercial gain.[196] Under this newer form of infringement, at least one critic has likened the legal claim to simply another form of the common law tort of unjust enrichment. One is getting the benefit of the use of the mark without having to have worked to establish its goodwill and value.[197] The Federal

---

[192] See requirement under 15 U.S.C. § 1116(d)(1)(B)(i).

[193] See Diane Von Furstenberg Studio v. Snyder, 2007 WL 2688184 at *1 (E.D. Va. September 10, 2007).

[194] See Burstein, "Dilution By Tarnishment: The New Cause of Action," 98 Trademark Rep., No. 5, p. 1238 (2008).

[195] McCarthy, "Dilution of a Trademark: European and United States Law Compared," 96 Trademark Rep. No. 6, p. 1166 (November-December 2004), available at https://www.inta.org/wp-content/uploads/member-only/resources/the-trademark-reporter/vol94_no6_a1.pdf (accessed March 05, 2021).

[196] Ty Inc. v. Perryman, 306 F.3d 509 (7th Cir. 2002); Landes and Posner, *The Economic Structure of Intellectual Property Law*, pp. 207–208 (2003).

[197] See Dogan, "What Is Dilution, Anyway?" 105 *Mich. L. Rev. First Impressions* 103 (2006).

Trademark Anti-Dilution Act of 1996 ("FTDA")[198] and the substantial revisions under the Trademark Dilution Revision Act of 2006 ("TDRA") provided victims of what looked like counterfeiting and, in many cases infringement, with a powerful additional tool for protection. Congress revised the FTDA as follows:

"The TDRA revised the FTDA in three significant ways: (I) a *likelihood of dilution*, rather than *actual dilution*, is now a prerequisite to establishing a dilution claim; (II) Courts may apply four factors to determine whether a mark is famous and protection denied to marks that are famous in only 'niche' markets; and (III) Courts may apply six factors to determine whether there is a likelihood of dilution."[199]

The most significant change was that the *defendant* must be making a trademark use of the term. In passing the FTDA and TDRA, Congress was moving away from a consumer-focused form of protection toward the establishment of a fixed property right in a trademark.

Trademark dilution has been characterized as "the legal theory that seeks to protect a trademark owner directly against the diminution of a trademark's 'commercial magnetism' of selling power by unauthorized junior use of the same or substantially similar mark.[200] The two means of diluting a trademark are "blurring" and "tarnishment." Blurring "seeks to protect the uniqueness and distinctiveness of a mark."[201] Tarnishment "occurs when a defendant uses the same or similar marks in a way that creates an undesirable, unwholesome, or unsavory mental association with the plaintiff's mark."[202] The "tarnishment" cause of dilution received

---

[198] Moseley v. V Secret Catalogue, Inc., 537 U.S. 418, 123 S.Ct. 1115, 155 L.Ed.2d 1 (2003) (discussing the FTDA).

[199] Century 21 Real Estate LLC v. Century Surety Co., 2007 U.S. LEXIS 8434 at **3–4 (D. Ariz. February 05, 2007). (Emphasis in original.)

[200] Staffin. 1995. "The Dilution Doctrine: Towards a Reconciliation with the Lanham Act," *Fordham Int. Prop. Media & E. L.J* 6, 105–107.

[201] *Id.* at 131 (citing *McCarthy on Trademarks and Unfair Competition*, § 24.12(1) (A)(II) (3d ed. 1995)).

[202] "Original Appalachian Artworks" *Inc. v. Topps Chewing Gum*, Inc., 642 F. Supp. 1031, 1039 (N.D. Ga. 1986).

attention in a well-publicized case[203] reviewed by the U.S. Supreme Court. In this case, a lingerie retailer sued the proprietors of an adult novelty store for dilution based on blurring (linking the store with the lingerie retail chain) and tarnishment (association with sex toys). Judicial opinions upholding claims of trademark dilution have sometimes been viewed with skepticism and as damaging to the basic ability of businesses to compete. Critics claim courts have gone too far by viewing the non-competitive use of a famous mark as "dilutive," that the courts are basically giving the rights holder a form of "patent" on the mark with the ability to exclude all others who would use it no matter what the nature of the use happened to be. This seems to have moved the legal claims of unfair competition far beyond harm to the consumer resulting from a likelihood of confusion.

"Traditional trademark law rests primarily on policy of protection of customers from mistake and deception, while anti-dilution law more closely resembles an absolute property right in a trademark."[204] By creating two forms of dilution, "dilution by blurring" and "dilution by tarnishment," the application of the TDRA, if broadly applied by the courts, could encompass almost all noncompetitive uses of a famous mark. For famous and distinctive brand holders who are the targets of counterfeiters and commercial hitchhikers, the expanded use of anti-dilution laws has become a welcome enforcement tool. However, there have been some well-known instances in which the courts have refused to find that dilution has taken place. For example, famous brands have tried to use the anti-dilution statutes against cybersquatters or registrants of upper-level domain addresses incorporating the famous marks. Some courts have rejected the dilution claims, holding that the FTDA has made dilution claims against cybersquatters untenable.[205] Under the TRDA, a mark must be well-known nationally, not just in a "niche" community or among the "relevant consuming public," as in trademark infringement

---

[203] Moseley v. V Secret Catalog, Inc. 537 U.S. 418, 424, 123 S.Ct. 1115, 155 L.Ed.2d 1 (2003).

[204] *McCarthy on Trademarks and Unfair Competition*, § 24.72 (4th ed. 2009).

[205] See Porsche Cars North America, Inc. v. Porsche.net, 302 F.3d 248, 64 U.S.P.Q. 2d 1248 (4th Cir. 2002).

cases.[206] In addition, the mark must have attained the national fame prior to the defendant commencing use.[207] Moreover, under the more recent TDRA, a plaintiff's mark must be "distinctive, inherently or through acquired distinctiveness."[208]

Under the TDRA's tarnishment prong, there was a shift in focus from the defendant's use of plaintiff's mark to defendant's own mark or trade name. In any event, the term had to be used as a mark or trade name. The defendant's use must indicate the source of its goods or services and, further, the use must be "in commerce."[209] There are additional differences between the two types of dilution. Dilution by blurring does not require actual tarnishment, but query whether it is a likelihood standard or an "actual" standard. Paragraph 1 sets forth the definition as an "association," and thereafter states: "In determining whether a mark or trade name is *likely to cause dilution* by blurring ... ."[210] Although there may be a question of the standard to be applied, the statute makes it somewhat clear that one "shall be entitled to an injunction against another person who ... commences use of a mark or trade name in commerce that is likely to cause dilution by blurring or dilution by tarnishment of the famous mark. ..."[211]

Nature of the Tarnishment

Under the TDRA, the courts have faced various factual scenarios involving a claim of likely damage to reputation. In one case, the world's largest luxury goods company sued a plush toy marketer that sells pet toys and beds with names that refer to famous luxury brands.[212] Plaintiff alleged that one of these names had "associate[d] 'inferior products' with the [plaintiff's] name." Unfortunately for the company plaintiff, the court

---

[206] Vista India v. Raaga, LLC, 401 F. Supp.2d 695, 623–624 (D.N.J. 2007).

[207] 15 U.S.C. § 1125(c)(1).

[208] 15 U.S.C. § 1125(c)(2)(A).

[209] 15 U.S.C. § 1125(c)(1).

[210] 15 U.S.C. § 1125(c)(2)(B). (Emphasis added.)

[211] 15 U.S.C. § 1125(c)(1).

[212] Louis Vuitton Malletier S.A. v. Haute Diggity Dog, LLC, 464 F. Supp.2d 495 (E.D. Va. 2006), *aff'd* 507 F.3d 252 (4th Cir. 2007).

found that "when the association is made through harmless or clean puns and parodies … tarnishment is unlikely."[213] The defendant prevailed on summary judgment, including dilution by tarnishment. The plaintiff had argued in court that a pet might in the future choke on one of the defendant's toys and cause a consumer to become angry at the plaintiff.[214] However, the court found this "possibility" to be a flimsy basis to find liability.

A well-publicized Supreme Court case, in which the Supreme Court remanded the case back to the trial court, was decided under the older FTDA. However, since the commencement of the case, the TDRA came into effect and the trial court decided that the newer law should be applied.[215] Here the court found that, although there was no evidence of dilution by blurring, there was a likelihood that the plaintiff's mark would be diluted by tarnishment for the offering of "unwholesome, tawdry merchandise."[216]

Defenses to Dilution Under the TDRA

In addition to not meeting the requirements discussed earlier, there are proscribed statutory exceptions to the provisions of the TDRA. These include: (a) fair use, including advertising and promotion, parody, criticism, and commentary upon the famous mark or owner of the famous mark; (b) all forms of news reporting and news commentary; and (c) any noncommercial use of a mark. Of importance is the requirement that the use be of a "famous mark … other than as a designation of source for the defendants' own goods or services."[217]

Use has become a statutorily prescribed defense to dilution. The Ninth Circuit has held that, "[a] defendant's use is nominative where

---

[213] *Id.*

[214] *Id.*

[215] V Secret Catalogue, Inc. v. Moseley, 2008 WL 2152189 (W.D. Ky. May 21, 2008).

[216] *Id.*

[217] 15 U.S.C. § 1125(c)(3)(A).

he or she used the plaintiff's dress to describe or identify the plaintiff's product, even if the defendant's ultimate goal is to describe or identify his or her own product."[218] The court has stated that nominative fair use may be for purposes of comparison, criticism, or point of reference such as in comparative advertising. The Ninth Circuit laid out a test that required the defendant to show (1) that defendant's product or service must be one not readily identifiable without the use of the trademark; (2) that it only used as much of the mark as necessary to identify defendant's product or service; and (3) that it made no use of the mark to indicate sponsorship or endorsement by the trademark holder.[219] Other circuit courts have adopted different tests, or have not adopted the nominative fair use defense at all. The parody exemption only applies where the famous mark is the subject of the parody. Again, the exemption should not apply where the defendant uses the parody as its own designation of source, that is as a trademark.[220] News reporting and news commentary seem to be the clearest of the exempted areas to the dilution statute; and, although "non-commercial" use would also be exempted, courts have not given clear direction as to what is to be considered "non-commercial."

Impact of New Technology on Trademark Protection: Three-Dimensional Printing

Although three-dimensional (3D) printing may have seemed like a technology still in its infancy, retail consumers are now able to buy such printers at their big-box hardware and office supply stores. 3D printing of consumer goods from jewelry and toys to smartphone cases and auto accessories is a present-day reality. It may not be an economical means of engaging in large-scale counterfeiting at this time, but that circumstance

---

[218] See Playboy Enterprises, Inc. v. Welles, 279 F.3d 796, 805 (9th Cir. 2002).

[219] Mattel, Inc. v. Walking Mountain Productions, 353 F.3d 792, pp. 809–810 (9th Cir. 2003).

[220] See Louis Vuitton Malletier S.A. v. Haute Diggity Dog, LLC, 507 F.3d 252, 269 (4th Cir. 2007).

may not be far off. Companies such as Shapeways and Thingiverse provide CAD files that may allow one to reproduce a trademarked consumer product such as Nokia smartphone cases or Mercedes-Benz-branded cufflinks.[221]

It has been argued that the proliferation of 3D products in commerce may undermine the ability of a brand to protect the goodwill associated with its trademark. The control that a brand maintains over the quality of the products bearing its mark or marks will be undermined if individuals can recreate branded products with a CAD file and a 3D printer.[222] If someone can print a trademark on a product that is not sold, but through gifting or otherwise enters into public use, does this not diminish the ability of a trademark to serve its traditional role as a "source identifier?" At the very least, the proliferation of 3D-printed products bearing trademarks will likely dilute the distinctiveness of the mark and diminish its value.

Upcycling of Trademarked Goods: Recycling for Sustainability or Upcycling for Profit

Many companies, particularly in the apparel and luxury goods industries, are looking for ways to reduce any adverse environmental footprint. It is with this objective in mind that consumers and industry have been looking at repurposing and recycling trademark goods. Upcycling of products bearing famous trademarks has become a popular phenomenon and, depending on the circumstances, may also have an adverse impact on a brand's equity. Upcycling can be defined as the modification or augmentation of a product bearing a trademark for the purpose of resale. The harm is caused by material differences in the resulting upcycled product, lack of quality control, alterations to a product not known to a consumer, as well as simply the creation of a counterfeit. Under the Lanham Act, upcyclers have defended their use by arguing that the product was one that had already been sold and is therefore protected by the first sale doctrine.

---

[221] Thingiverse.com, search "Nokia"; Shapeways.com, search "Auto."
[222] Grace, "The End of Post-Sale Confusion: How Consumer 3D Printing will Diminish the Function of Trademarks." 28 Harv. J. L. & Tech. 263 (Fall 2014).

The first sale doctrine does not exist under the Lanham Act and is not a defense to trademark infringement. In other instances, disclaimers as to the source of the upcycled product may be found to eliminate instances of confusion, particularly postsale confusion, where the consumer may have believed the upcycled product was approved or authorized by the owner of the trademark on the original product.

CHAPTER 7

International Trade Commission and U.S. Customs and Border Protection, the Lanham Act, and the Tariff Act

The International Trade Commission (ITC) and the Department of Homeland Security (DHS) are two U.S. government institutions that can provide significant assistance to rights holders who are the targets of foreign counterfeiting enterprises or significant infringers. Immigration and Customs Enforcement (ICE) is an agency of DHS. The ITC and DHS are playing increasingly significant roles in controlling the importation of counterfeit and infringing goods into the United States.

The International Trade Commission

The ITC is the U.S. government agency that investigates violations of Section 337 of the Tariff Act of 1930. Section 337 was intended by Congress as a redress for acts of unfair competition and unfair acts against U.S. industries.[1] Under the statute, the ITC has the power to protect U.S. industries from unfair competition by ordering the exclusion of and, in effect, banning the importation of certain infringing goods.

The ITC was actually formed prior to the enactment of Section 337. It was formed in 1916 and known as the United States Tariff Commission.

---

[1] 19 U.S.C. § 1337 (a)(1)(B)-(D).

Its duties included handling the tariffs administered by the United States as well as studying the impact of the U.S. Customs laws.

It was not until 1974 that the Tariff Act underwent significant changes. These changes made use of the ITC review and enforcement process more user-friendly and, therefore, more attractive to rights holders seeking to protect their industries. In addition, the proceedings were fairly "quick-paced," with determinations made in a period from 12 to 18 months. Rules related to the proceedings were also established, which allowed all participants to act on a more level playing field.

Despite the changes in 1974, the volume of ITC cases has remained fairly small, given the effectiveness of the remedies the ITC process provides. Nevertheless, since 2019, Section 337 complaints have focused on a wide range of goods, including wireless communication devices, toner cartridges, seafood, electric candles, mattresses, table computers, artificial eyelash extensions, chocolate milk powder, batteries, fitness devices, and robotic floor cleaning devices, among others.[2] Cases mainly involved low-tech items and many of the participants were individual patent holders and small companies.[3]

As a result of the passage of the Omnibus Trade and Competitiveness Act of 1988,[4] several important changes were made to the process under Section 337. For registered intellectual property rights holders, proof of injury was not a requirement. In addition, the amendments expanded the notion of what a domestic industry was. Patent cases continue to be in the majority. However, trademark counterfeiting cases have found their way to the ITC and, because of the high percentage of counterfeit goods that enter the United States from Asia each year, goods made in Asia account for 70 percent of the infringement matters before the ITC.[5] China and Hong Kong accounted for 85 percent of the value and 87 percent of the

---

[2] 337 Complaints US ITC. See , website of the ITC.

[3] *A Lawyer's Guide to Section 337 Investigations Before the U.S. International Trade Commission*, p.4 (Schaumberg ed., 2010).

[4] Pub. L. No. 100-418, 102 Stat. 1107 (August 23, 1988).

[5] See http://www.usitc.gov.

volume of counterfeit or pirate goods seized by U.S. Customs and Border Protection in 2018.[6]

Advantages of Using the ITC

Some of the general aspects of the ITC Section 337 action make it an important tool for enforcement of IP rights in the United States.

The ITC is an independent, quasi-judicial federal agency without political party affiliation, and, therefore, influence. It protects domestic industries against foreign actors who engage in significant unfair trade practices. ITC actions have become an important defensive mechanism in what are trade wars involving abuses of IP rights.

In light of the current overwhelming case load handled by the Federal Courts, one of the most attractive aspects of an ITC investigation is that the investigation usually only takes between 12 and 18 months to complete. Similar cases in a Federal District Court will likely take two to three years.[7] The speed of a 337 investigation allows the rights holder to better plan use of resources, including being able to budget the expense of such a proceeding. The relatively short duration of the ITC investigation results, in part, not only from a statutory requirement[8] to handle the matters expeditiously but also because the administrative law judges have a depth of experience in handling such specialized matters and there is no extensive "learning curve" with respect to the procedures and available remedies. Additionally, rights holders have a great advantage because they can basically choose when to file a complaint, so that prior to doing so the rights holder will have gathered the data to support its claim and prepared all of its discovery requests. The infringing party or respondent has very little time to mount a defense: it must respond to the complaint within 20 days and respond to discovery within 10 days.

The advantage of a speedier remedy becomes a greater possibility because of the ITC's new pilot program for interim initial determinations

---

[6] https://ustr.gov/issue-areas/intellectual-property.

[7] Adduci II and Sjoberf, "Everybody Comes to the ITC," *Legal Times* (July 11, 2005).

[8] 19 U.S.C. § 1337(e)(2).

(ID's) of key issues in a 337 investigation.[9] The presiding Administrative Law Judge will be able to hold evidentiary hearings and receive briefings on key issues prior to the main evidentiary issues. According to the ITC program, these issues could include infringement, patent invalidity and eligibility, standing, and meeting the requirement of harm to a domestic industry. The findings will oftentimes be dispositive of the entire case and are to be issued no later than 45 days prior to the scheduled main evidentiary hearing. The ID's will then be sent to the full Commission for review. This will likely save the parties greater expense and could potentially result in a quick resolution. The pilot program will apply to all investigations commencing after May 12, 2021.

Another advantage to the ITC proceeding is immediate relief, if it appears that the importation of goods will cause significant immediate harm to the rights holder. This is known as a temporary exclusion order (TEO). The requirements are similar to those for obtaining a temporary restraining order (TRO) or preliminary injunction, so the standards for obtaining one are high.

It is also important to note that the ITC exercises in rem jurisdiction over the merchandise or chattels as well as *in personam* jurisdiction.[10] Whether or not the ITC has jurisdiction over the parties who are often outside the country, it can focus on limiting the importation of infringing products coming from multiple foreign sources into various ports throughout the United States. If one were to try to do the same within the U.S. federal court system, it might be necessary to file in a number of jurisdictions in which the goods were being imported. In addition, an ITC investigation can tackle those situations in which multiple counterfeiters are flooding the U.S. market with counterfeit or infringing goods. All of the importers and sources can be named as respondents in one action, thereby saving both the rights holder and the government from expending enormous resources to check the acts of unfair competition.

---

[9] See ITC press release: www.usitc.gov/press_room/featured_news/337 pilotprogram.htm (accessed May 22, 2021).

[10] 19 U.S.C. § 1337(d)(2).

An additional advantage over use of the federal court system is the ability of the rights holder in an ITC proceeding to obtain discovery from foreign players without having to go through the burdensome process of service requirements. Discovery commences immediately upon publication of the notice of investigation in the Federal Register.[11] Although the Commission cannot issue subpoenas to foreign entities, it can hold them in contempt and award the rights holders significant monetary sanctions. These sanctions can be burdensome.[12]

If a rights holder is also seeking to recover monetary damages it is fairly routine for the rights holder to file a federal district court action seeking monetary remedies. The court action may be stayed pursuant to a motion from a respondent. However, by filing in the Federal Court as well as the ITC, a rights holder may prevent a potential respondent from forum shopping and filing a declaratory relief action in a less advantageous or less convenient federal district.

In a classic example,[13] the world's largest luxury goods company used the ITC and its exclusionary powers to fight a multitude of importers and purveyors of counterfeit and infringing handbags that were having a significant impact on the rights holder's sales of genuine products in the United States.

Disadvantage of Using the ITC Versus a Federal Lanham Act Action

An ITC investigation is not necessarily the sole appropriate route for a victim of counterfeiting or infringement. Remedies in an ITC action are prospective in nature. There are no remedies for prior acts of unfair competition. Indeed, where there is an urgent need to stop ongoing counterfeiting and infringement the remedy is a TEO. However, such an order

---

[11] "Actions at the ITC: A Primer on Intellectual Property Issues and Procedures at the U.S. International Trade Commission." 5 U. Balt. Int. Prop. L.J. 103, 113 (1997).

[12] "Certain Composite Wear Components and Products Containing Same (ITC Inv. No. 337-TA-644)". (awarding sanctions in the amount of $119,000).

[13] International Trade Commission: In Re Handbags, Luggage, Accessories and Packaging Thereof, ITC Inv. No. 337-TA-754 (June 13, 2012).

typically cannot be obtained as quickly as a TRO in Federal Court. With the need for the rights holder to work with the ITC staff prior to filing, the Federal Court is the better venue for immediate injunctive relief, particularly with the ex parte remedy available under Title 15, Section 1116 of the United States Code.

The realities of counterfeiting as recognized by Congress in providing for the seizure of records and documents acknowledges that obtaining the monetary proceeds of the illegal acts is often very difficult. With the ease of monetary transfers on the Internet and the use of nontraditional methods of moving illegal proceeds outside of traditional banking systems, the victim of counterfeiting cannot be assured that it will recover damages in the way of lost profits, profits of the counterfeiting activity, investigative costs, or attorney fees. As a result, obtaining exclusionary relief may be the most realistic and beneficial outcome to taking action against a counterfeiting operation.

Another issue to consider is that an ITC action takes place before an administrative judge and in a venue located in Washington, DC. This should not stand as a barrier in the case of a significant counterfeiting case, but there may be the need to hire additional counsel in Washington, DC, or the east coast of the United States, with specific expertise in organizing and litigating the matter before the Commission. This will often involve additional expense as well as the education of ITC counsel about the rights holder, its products, and the counterfeiting enterprise. The nature of the counterfeiting situation, however, may require that such an investment of company employee time and money be made in order to protect a company's valuable assets.

Complaint Before the ITC

A Section 337 action is an adversarial investigation involving the rights holder (complainant), the alleged infringers (respondents), and, unlike a federal court proceeding, the ITC staff. The objective of the investigation is to determine whether acts of unfair competition and resulting damage have occurred.

In commencing a Section 337 action, the rights holder will typically spend considerable time gathering facts so that it may prepare a complaint. However, the ITC on its own may also file a complaint.[14] The complaint is typically prepared well ahead of a prospective filing date and it must include the factual showing prescribed under Title 19, Section 210.12 of the Code of Federal Regulations, including the importation of the accused products, facts supporting the infringement (including a chart outlining claims) and factual support for the existence of a "domestic industry."

It is typical for the attorneys working in the Office of Unfair Import Investigations (OUII) to review the complaint and to provide comments with regard to the sufficiency of the information and the claims to the complainant. Any information provided to the OUII attorneys in this preliminary stage is treated as confidential and will not be disclosed.

After the complaint has been filed, the OUII conducts an investigation of the allegations and will even consult with the claimant and respondent. After concluding their investigation, the OUII will make a recommendation to the ITC as to whether a formal Section 337 investigation should be commenced. If the 337 investigation proceeds, a staff attorney from OUII will actively participate in the proceedings. The participation of the OUII attorney adds another layer of logistical issues and expense to these proceedings since the OUII attorney can conduct discovery, file motions, and examine witnesses at depositions, as if the OUII were a party in the action. The views of the OUII staff attorney are considered important when looking at the public interest aspect of the 337 investigation, given his or her role to insure that all actions in the matter protect the public's interest.

Of note is the increased number of filings of foreign-based intellectual property rights holders who have U.S. rights and sufficient business activity in the United States to satisfy the statutory requirements.[15]

Whether the complainant is U.S.-based or foreign-based, it is imperative the complainant prove that there is an established domestic industry in the United States, where the trademarks or copyrights are concerned

---

[14] 19 U.S.C. § 1337(b)(1).

[15] G.M. Hnath. 2006. "Protecting Your American Intellectual Property Rights: How Foreign Companies Can Utilize the U.S. International Trade Commission and Section 337 Investigations." *NCCU Int. Prop. Rev.*

or that there is an industry related to these rights that is actively being established.[16] A complainant can satisfy the statutory requirements if it can show that it has made a significant investment in facilities and equipment, employs a large number of people, and has invested substantial capital in the United States, or has spent considerable resources in exploiting the particular intellectual property right, such as research and development or licensing.[17]

Responding to a Complaint

Respondents are situated as they would be in a federal court action, with certain notable exceptions. Respondents must raise affirmative defenses that they must prove. However, they cannot file counterclaims in the ITC proceeding. Counterclaims must be brought in a federal court action, thereby increasing the burden and expense on respondents. Complainants must name all downstream parties they wish to bring under an exclusion order in their complaint. Should they choose to add additional parties, they will need to make a motion to amend before the Commission.[18]

In addition, third parties who may be affected by a possible exclusion order may intervene in the action under Title 19, Section 210.19 of the Code of Federal Regulations. It may, however, be just as effective, and consume fewer resources, for an interested party simply to submit to the Commission briefing that solicits input from the public, interested parties, and government agencies.[19]

Prima Facie Case

Unfair Acts

As noted earlier, the objective of Section 337 investigations is to prevent or ameliorate, on the basis of statutorily registered intellectual property rights or common law rights, acts of unfair competition affecting U.S.

---

[16] 19 U.S.C. §§ 1337(a)(2)–(3).

[17] 19 U.S.C. § 1337(a)(3).

[18] 19 C.F.R. § 210.14(b).

[19] 19 C.F.R. § 210.50(a)(4).

industries.[20] The same standards of proof by the complainant and the same affirmative defenses asserted by the respondents as found in a U.S. district court case are applicable here.[21]

There is a difference in the showing required for a complaint based on statutorily registered rights, such as a registered trademark or copyright, and for a complaint based on a common-law infringement, such as common law unfair competition, common law trademark infringement, false designation of origin, or violation of the Digital Millennium Copyright Act.[22] In the latter instance, the complainant must not only establish infringement, as well as importation and the domestic industry, but it must also establish that the unfair act will cause injury to the domestic industry.[23]

Importation

The definition of "importation" is the same as used by Customs, that is, "bringing of goods within the jurisdictional limits of the United States with the intention to unlade them."[24] Goods brought into a foreign trade zone or bonded warehouse, with no movement into the United States for consumption, are not included in the definition. However, those involved in pre- and post-importation activities of the goods are brought under the ambit of the statute. As a result, U.S. wholesalers, such as the "big box" chains, as well as small retailers that are down the distribution chain from the actual act of importation may be found in violation of the prohibited acts. Further, a 337 action may also apply to future acts of importation

---

[20] 19 U.S.C. § 1337(a)(1).

[21] See § 10.01 *supra*.

[22] Pub. L. No. 105-304, 112 Stat. 2860 (October 28, 1998).

[23] TianRui Group Co. v. ITC, No. 2010-1395 (Fed. Cir. October 11, 2011) (2-1 decision) (in common-law infringement cases, such as unfair competition, the injury to the domestic industry must be more extensive).

[24] Headquarters Ruling 115311 (May 10, 2001) (quoting Hollander Co. v. U.S., 22 C.C.P.A. 645, 648 (1935), and U.S. v. Field & Co., 14 Cust. App. 406 (1927)).

of the goods, even if the goods are no longer being imported at the time of the action.[25]

Domestic Market

In cases involving statutory IP such as registered trademarks and copyrights, the existence of a domestic market is established through a two prong analysis. The first prong is the "economic" prong, in which the complainant establishes that there are significant operations in the United States. The second prong is the "technical" prong, which requires a showing that the complainant's activities in the United States are related to the intellectual property rights that are the subject of the complaint.

The economic prong is deemed to exist in connection with statutory IP if there is in the United States, with respect to the articles protected by the patent, copyright, trademark, or mask work concerned:

- "Significant investment in plant and equipment;
- Significant employment of labor or capital; or
- Substantial investment in its exploitation, including engineering, research and development, or licensing."

Nonstatutory claims, however, will only be able to rely on the first two factors.[26]

The "technical prong" requires a complainant to show that the complainant's products are those covered by the statutory rights.[27]

Substantial Injury

As noted earlier, the 1988 amendments to Section 337 eliminated the need to show injury in cases of violations of statutory intellectual

---

[25] "Certain Steel Toy Vehicles," USITC Pub.880, Inc. No. 337-TA-031, Comm'n Op., at 4 (April 1978).

[26] 19 U.S.C. § 1337(a)(3); H.R. Rep. No. 100-40 at 17, 100th Cong., 1st Sess. (1987) (concerning § 1337(a)(3)(A)-(C)).

[27] See "Certain Agricultural Tractors Under 50 Power Take-Off Horsepower," Inv. No. 337-TA-380, Order No. 39 (pub. Version), at 5 (August 08, 1996).

property rights.[28] The common law and nonstatutory acts of unfair competition still require that the complainant show that the importation will "destroy or substantially injure an industry in the United States."[29] The complainant must show that the unfair acts cause the resulting injury to the domestic industry.[30] The injury may be prospective as well as actual.

In determining whether there has been substantial injury, the ITC has looked at numerous factors on a case-by-case basis. Unfortunately, there does not appear to be a simple formula. Factors that have been evaluated in these investigations have included:

- Increased lost sales from displacement of complainant's products;[31]
- Importation and sales of infringing articles;[32]
- Claimants decreasing profits from the sale of the imported article;[33]
- Sales of the imported article at lower prices than the complainant's prices;[34]
- Declining employment and productivity in the domestic industry;[35]

---

[28] See § 10.01 *supra*.

[29] 19 U.S.C. § 1337(a)(1)(A).

[30] See "Certain Digital Multimeters, and Products with Multimeter Functionality," Inv. No. 337-TA-558, Initial Determination (Pub. Version), at 18 (January 14, 2008).

[31] "Certain Inclined-Field Acceleration Tubes & Components Thereof," *USITC Pub.* 1119, Inv. No. 337-TA-67, Comm'n Op., at 20 (December 1980).

[32] "Certain Multicellular Plastic Film," *USITC Pub.* 987, Inc. No. 337-TA-54, Comm'n Op., at 21–22 (June 1979).

[33] "Certain Thermometer Sheath Packages," *USITC Pub.* 992, Inv. No. 337-TA-56, Comm'n Op., at 25–27 (July 1979).

[34] "Certain Molded-In Sandwich Panel Inserts & Methods for Their Installation," *USITC Pub.* 1246, Inv. No. 337-TA-99, Comm'n Op., at 9–10 (May 1982).

[35] "Vacuum Bottles," *USITC Pub.* 1305, Inv. No. 337-TA-108, Comm'n Op., at 29–30 (November 1982).

- Loss of royalties or income from licensees due to sales of the infringing product;[36]
- Significant market presence by infringing product;[37] and
- Harm to goodwill and reputation.[38]

Substantial injury may also be inferred with regard to future injury, based on an assessment of the market when the infringing product is present. In addition, the Commission will look at foreign cost and production advantages; ability to undersell complainant's product; or substantial foreign manufacturing capacity and ability to gain market share in the United States.[39]

As in most IP infringement cases, myriad specific facts regarding the industry, the rights holder, the respondent, and the marketplace will play a crucial role in determining the outcome of the investigation.

The Proceedings

One of the advantages of using a 337 investigation is the relatively fast and certain timetable in which the process takes place.[40] All of the procedural rules, including those set out by the administrative law judge, are used to keep the process moving along toward a timely resolution. For this reason, there is an enormous amount of preparatory work that must be done by the rights holder. The rights holder must put together the strongest presentation of the facts underlying the claims prior to commencing the process, even without the benefit of discovery, because the discovery process will move very quickly.

---

[36] "Certain Limited-Charge Cell Culture Microcarriers." *Inv.* No. 337-TA-129, Initial Determination, at 264 (June 06, 1983).

[37] "Certain Combination Locks," USITC Pub. 945, Inv. No. 337-TA-45, Comm'n Op., at 9–12 (February 1979).

[38] "Certain Digital Multimeters, and Products with Multimeter Functionality." *Inv.* No. 337-TA-558, Initial Determination (Pub. Version), at 18 (January 14, 2008).

[39] *Id.*

[40] See § 10.02 *supra.*

The rights holder should submit a draft complaint for evaluation by the OUII to determine if the facts known to the rights holder at the time are sufficient to support the claims or if there is a need for further fact-gathering by the complainant prior to the formal filing. In addition, it is considered good practice for the rights holder to have its initial round of fact discovery ready to be propounded to the respondent, since discovery opens once notice of the investigation is published.

A protective order is almost pro forma in these proceedings since there is likely to be confidential or proprietary information requested and disclosed by the rights holder or respondent. The protective orders govern access to this confidential information by experts and any other third parties involved in the proceedings.

The Administrative Law Judge (ALJ) will issue orders that govern the entire schedule of the proceedings as well as numerous other issues, including discovery, motion practice, settlement conferences, and so on. Each ALJ has his or her own rules. The ALJ's rules will be crafted to adhere to the Commission's Rules of Practice and Procedure, which, among other requirements, set the time frame in which an investigation must be completed.[41] The proceeding schedule will have a clear timetable for the various deadlines and elements in the case, similar to a scheduling order in federal court litigation. The parties can seek to modify the procedural order through motion practice or stipulation.

In certain instances, particularly where there is a pending concurrent federal district court case, one or both parties will seek to stay the ITC proceeding. Depending on the strategy of the parties, a stay may relieve them of spending significant resources in concurrent litigation matters. Alternatively, a district court must stay its own proceedings pending the investigation before the ITC if requested by one of the parties to the ITC investigation.[42] In such a case, the ITC record may be used in the district court litigation.[43] Although applicable mainly to patent-related cases,

---

[41] 19 C.F.R § 210.51(a).

[42] 28 U.S.C. § 1659(a).

[43] 28 U.S.C. § 1659(b).

a party may seek a stay of the ITC proceeding if there is a concurrent USPTO proceeding that is relevant to the 337 investigation.[44]

Though rarely granted, a TEO or cease and desist order may be sought by a complainant. As with federal court applications for TROs and preliminary injunctions, the complainant must make a very strong case that it will suffer immediate and substantial harm from the importation of goods without such extraordinary protection from the ITC.[45] Working against an application for a TEO or cease and desist order is the fact that the 337 investigation is premised on a relatively speedy determination, thereby requiring an applicant for such extraordinary relief to show that it will suffer enormous immediate injury without such relief from the ITC. There are rules that govern the procedure for temporary relief.[46] In any event, however, a TRO request must be acted upon within 90 days after the notice of application is published.[47] Again, the purpose of all these rules is to maintain the advantage of a speedy resolution to the investigation.

Prehearing

There is usually a 30-to-60-day window between the close of discovery and the hearing. As with federal court litigation, the ALJ requires that the parties submit a prehearing statement. The statement is to provide the ALJ and respondents with the basic elements of their case. This would include providing a list of witnesses, the nature of their testimony, and the time needed for such. The ALJ may determine that a witness's testimony may be introduced through a deposition transcript in order to keep the proceedings moving on schedule. The statement will include a list of exhibits. Stipulations between the parties help to narrow issues and again move the proceedings along. "The statement most importantly must contain a statement of the issues to be decided by the ALJ and the arguments in support thereof. ... Any contentions not expressed in the prehearing

---

[44] 35 U.S.C. § 302.

[45] 19 U.S.C. §§ 1337(e)(1) and (f)(1).

[46] Generally, 19 C.F.R. §§ 210.50-210.59.

[47] 19 C.F.R. § 210.51(b).

statement may be deemed abandoned or waived."[48] In addition, the pre-hearing statement must outline the issues of contention to be argued by the parties. The OUII also submits a prehearing statement. This is important because it discloses where the OUII stands on the claims in the investigation. It may support the rights holder or it may not believe that the claims have merit. Motions in limine are also filed. However, unlike motions in limine in Federal Court, the motions in an administrative hearing are not governed by the Federal Rules of Evidence but by the Commission Rule 210.37, which is broader in allowing "relevant, mate-rial, and reliable evidence."

Hearing

The 337 hearing is not conducted in accordance with the Federal Rules of Civil Procedure or the Federal Rules of Evidence; rather, it is governed by the Administrative Procedure Act.[49] It should be remembered that there are three parties presenting at the hearing. As a result, the ALJ may seek to have much of the testimony introduced through deposition transcripts. As for a determination, the ALJ may have up to two months to make a determination after reading post-hearing briefing. Post-hearing briefing is common and is the last opportunity for the parties to convince the ALJ of the merits of their positions. Closing arguments are typically not presented.

After considering all of the post-hearing briefing, the ALJ will render an opinion regarding the claims. The ALJ will also issue an order regard-ing the appropriate remedies for rights holders.

This is termed an Initial Determination (ID). The ID usually becomes the opinion of the Commission unless the Commission decides to review the decision within 60 days. The ALJ will also make a recommendation as to the range of appropriate remedies.

---

[48] A Lawyer's Guide to Section 337 Investigations Before the U.S. International Trade Commission, p.148 (Schaumberg ed., 2010).

[49] 5 U.S.C. §§ 554–556.

Appeals

There are a number of reviews and appeal proceedings involved with a Section 337 investigation determination.

Commission Rule 210.43(b) allows a party to appeal a determination of the ALJ to the full Commission for review. Once the Commission makes its determination that a respondent has violated Section 337, the decision is published in the Federal Register and at the same time is sent to the President of the United States for review. Until approved by the President, the determination does not become final.[50]

In addition to these appeals, at the end of the investigation inter-locutory appeals are available, based on decisions regarding motions. A motion for reconsideration of the ID is also available.

Remedies

The remedies available under Section 337 are prospective in nature and are nonmonetary.[51]

A limited exclusion order will bar the entry of counterfeit or infringing products against certain specified respondents.[52] A general exclusion order is appropriate if the Commission determines that "a general exclusion order from entry of articles is necessary to prevent circumvention of an exclusion order limited to products of named persons," or "there is a pattern of violation of this section and it is difficult to identify the source of infringing products."[53] As noted earlier, the TEO is very similar to a TRO.[54]

A cease and desist order is primarily directed at goods already imported into the United States as well as "prohibiting using, selling, marketing, distributing, transferring (except for exportation) or advertising the covered

---

[50] 19 U.S.C. § 1337(j); 19 C.F.R. § 210.49.

[51] See § 10.02 *supra*.

[52] 19 U.S.C. § 1337(d)(2). See also, In Re Handbags, Luggage, Accessories and Packaging Thereof, ITC Inv. No. 337-TA-754 (2012).

[53] "In the Matter of Certain Energy Drinks," *ITC Inv. No.* 337-TA-678, at 39 (2010).

[54] 19 U.S.C. § 1337(e)(3). See § 10.02 *supra*.

infringing products and aiding or abetting others to do the same." The cease and desist order may require respondents to report their sales of all products covered by the order, as well as keep records of the inventory of products under their control. As opposed to exclusion orders that are enforced by U.S. Customs, cease and desist orders are enforced by the ITC itself. Failure to comply may result in the levying of civil penalties, including statutory sanctions of up to $100,000 per day. Not only can the Commission bring a civil action in U.S. Federal Court to recover the fines but it can also order the seizure and forfeiture of the products.[55]

U.S. Customs and Border Protection ("Customs") Standards

One of the mandates of U.S. Customs and Border Protection ("Customs") is to restrict the entry of goods bearing counterfeit or "restricted" marks, which may damage the goodwill of a registered U.S. trademark. A "restricted" mark is one that "is similar to the genuine trademark such that it is likely to cause confusion as to source or sponsorship."[56] According to Customs regulations, "a 'copying or simulating' trademark or trade name is one which may so resemble a recorded mark or name as to be likely to cause the public to associate the copying or simulating mark or name with the recorded mark or name."[57] This definition is equivalent to the "likelihood of confusion" test for trademark infringement.[58]

Pursuant to the Tariff Act of 1930, Customs may seize or detain goods bearing marks that are confusingly similar to recorded trademarks.[59] The Tariff Act prohibits the importation of merchandise bearing a registered trademark without the permission of the owner of the trademark.[60] Subsection (e) of the Tariff Act actually incorporates two other statutes, Title

---

[55] 19 U.S.C. § 1337(f)(2).

[56] Customs Directive 2310-08, at 5.

[57] 19 C.F.R. § 133.22(a) (2004).

[58] See Ross Cosmetics Distribution Centers, Inc. v. U.S., 17 C.I.T. 814, 817-818 (1993) (equating "copy or simulate" with the "likelihood of confusion" test).

[59] 19 U.S.C. § 1595a(c) (2016).

[60] 19 U.S.C. § 1526(a) (1996).

15, Section 1127 and Section 1124 of the United States Code, both of which are part of the Trademark Act of 1946, otherwise known as the Lanham Act. The Tariff Act incorporates the definition of the term "counterfeit" from Section 1127,[61] and incorporates from Section 1124 the requirement that offending merchandise "copy or simulate" a registered U.S. trademark.[62] As discussed previously,[63] Section 42 of the Lanham Act protects against consumer deception or confusion about an article's origin or sponsorship by restricting the importation of trademarked goods.[64]

If Customs has a reasonable suspicion that goods entering the United States may bear one or more marks that infringe on a U.S. mark, it may detain the goods for 30 days from the date on which the merchandise is presented for Customs examination.[65] Release of detained goods may be obtained by establishing that one of the following Customs regulations exceptions applies.[66] An importer may secure release by: (1) removal or obliteration of the offensive marking on the good; (2) establishing that it has the authority of the trademark recordant to use the mark on the detained product; (3) showing that the foreign and U.S. marks are under common ownership or control; or (4) establishing that the U.S. recordant has given written consent.[67] If an importer cannot lay claim to any of the above conditions, then the goods can be seized by Customs 30 days after detention.

Recordation of Mark/Name With Customs

The restrictions on suspected infringing goods entering the United States only apply to goods bearing marks that have been recorded with Customs.[68] A Customs "recordation" is different from registration with the

---

[61] See § 10.12 *infra*.

[62] U.S. v. Able Time, Inc., 545 F.3d 824, 830 (9th Cir. 2008).

[63] For further discussion, see Chs. 5 and 6 *supra*.

[64] 15 U.S.C. § 1124 (1999).

[65] 19 C.F.R. § 133.25 (2015).

[66] 19 C.F.R. § 133.25(b) (2007).

[67] "Stuhlbarg International Sales Co." Inc. v. John D. Brush & Co., Inc., 240 F.3d 832, 838 (9th Cir. 2001).

[68] See § 10.09 *supra*.

U.S. Patent and Trademark Office (PTO) because a Customs "recordation" places information about a particular mark on file with Customs in order for Customs to identify, detain, and/or seize infringing merchandise. A trademark owner must make a separate recordation with Customs after receiving registration from the PTO in order to receive the benefit of the restrictions.[69]

Specifically, when an owner of a U.S. trademark makes a "recordation," it gives Customs information about the product, its appearance, its characteristics, its source (i.e., authorized manufacturers), and, in some cases, its authorized importers. Recording the mark with Customs along with logging product descriptions, photographs, and the names of authorized manufacturers and importers is instrumental in allowing Customs to correctly identify, detain, or seize infringing goods. According to Customs policy, if a federally registered trademark is not recorded with Customs, Customs will neither detain nor seize goods bearing marks that are confusingly similar to the federally registered trademark.[70]

Recordation provides a trademark owner with numerous benefits, one of which being that once counterfeit goods are seized, trademark owners must be notified of the following within 30 days of notice of seizure being issued to the importer:

1. "The date of importation;
2. The port of entry;
3. A description of the merchandise;
4. The quantity involved;
5. The name and address of the manufacturer;
6. The country of origin of the merchandise;
7. The name and address of the exporter; and
8. The name and address of the importer."[71]

---

[69] 19 C.F.R. § 133.1 (2012) (Trademarks registered by the PTO may be recorded with Customs if the registration is current).

[70] However, if a good bears a counterfeit mark, Customs may nevertheless engage in civil seizure pursuant to 19 U.S.C. § 1595a(c) for a violation of 18 U.S.C. § 2320.

[71] 19 C.F.R. § 133.21(c) (2007).

More information is disclosed with respect to seized counterfeit goods than with respect to detained confusingly similar goods. Customs regulations on counterfeits also permit the release of a specimen of the counterfeit goods to the trademark owners for "examination, testing, or other use in pursuit of a related private civil remedy for trademark infringement."[72]

Recording Assignment and/or Renewal of a Mark With Customs

After recordation, if ownership in a mark has changed, this must be reflected through recordation with the Customs Service. With regard to marks, where there is a change of ownership or a change of name with respect to the PTO registration, the new owner of the mark must file a certified status copy of the certificate of registration with the Commissioner of Customs and pay a fee in order to continue the Customs recordation.[73]

In order to renew Customs protection, a registered trademark owner must submit a written application to renew Customs recordation not later than three months after the date of expiration of the current 10-year registration issued by the PTO.[74] Additionally, the trademark owner must submit a status copy of the certificate of PTO registration showing renewal of the mark, a statement describing any change of ownership or in the name of the owner of the mark, and a fee for each trademark recordation renewal.[75]

As the term of recordation with Customs is concurrent with the term of PTO registration,[76] if a registration with the PTO is canceled, the Customs recordation will also be canceled.[77]

---

[72] 19 C.F.R. § 133.21(d) (2007).

[73] 19 C.F.R. §§ 133.5, 133.6 (2007).

[74] 19 C.F.R. § 133.7 (2007).

[75] Id.

[76] 19 C.F.R. § 133.4 (2007).

[77] Id.

Counterfeit Versus Grey Market

As discussed in earlier chapters, grey market goods are articles that are genuine but are not authorized for importation by the U.S. trademark holder. In contrast, counterfeit goods are not authorized for importation at all. A counterfeit mark is "a spurious trademark that is identical to, or substantially indistinguishable from, a registered trademark."[78] The difference between a restricted, confusingly similar mark and a counterfeit mark is that the former is simply confusing while the latter is identical to the actual, registered mark. A "substantially indistinguishable" mark is one that has only de minimis alterations from the original mark.[79] According to Customs, both an identical mark and a substantially indistinguishable mark are considered counterfeit; a mark need not be an exact replica of a registered mark in order to be deemed counterfeit.[80] If a mark needed to be absolutely identical to a U.S. registered mark to be deemed counterfeit, then counterfeiters could escape liability by making trivial changes to trademarks.[81] In order for a mark not to be deemed a counterfeit of a registered U.S. mark, it must possess pronounced differences from the actual, legitimate mark.[82]

Counterfeits of unrecorded marks are subject to seizure under the federal code related to criminal trafficking,[83] while counterfeits of recorded marks are subject to specific seizure authority under Customs laws and regulations. According to Customs regulations, "[a]ny article of domestic or foreign manufacture imported into the U.S. bearing a counterfeit trademark shall be seized and, in the absence of the written consent of the

---

[78] 19 C.F.R. § 133.21(a) (2015); 18 U.S.C.A. § 2320 (2016). See *Blacks Law Dictionary*, 1533 (9th ed. 2009) (defining "spurious" as "identical with, or substantially indistinguishable from" a registered trademark). See also, *American Heritage Dictionary*, 893, 1727 (4th ed. 2006) (defining "substantial" as "[c]onsiderable in importance, value, degree, amount, or extent," and defining "indistinguishable" as "[i]mpossible to differentiate or tell apart").

[79] 15 U.S.C. § 1127 (2006).

[80] 18 U.S.C.A. § 2320 (2016).

[81] U.S. v. Guerra, 293 F.3d 1279 (11th Cir. 2002).

[82] U.S. v. Lam, 677 F.3d 190, 199 (4th Cir. 2012).

[83] 19 U.S.C. § 1595a(c)(2) (2016); 18 U.S.C. § 2320 (2016).

trademark owner, forfeited for violation of the customs laws."[84] Compared to likely confusing, "restricted" marks, there is no applicable detention period for goods bearing counterfeit marks; once Customs determines that a good bears a counterfeit mark, the mark is seized immediately.

In addition to seizing the counterfeit items, Customs may issue a civil penalty even if Customs does not retain possession of the offending merchandise or obtain forfeiture of the merchandise.[85] Also, Customs may even impose a civil penalty on an importer of goods bearing an offending mark if the owner of the valid registered mark does not make the same goods as those bearing the counterfeit mark.[86]

In determining whether a good is counterfeit, Customs may compare the registered mark on actual merchandise with the allegedly counterfeit mark on the detained merchandise.[87] In certain cases, Customs may see fit to compare the offending mark to the U.S. mark's registration certificate.[88]

Sometimes the determination of whether a product bearing a mark is restricted or counterfeit is not clear-cut. In one case, the Second Circuit grappled with the question of whether certain imported watch bracelets, which looked similar to genuine Rolex watch bracelets, were counterfeit.[89] Initially, Customs determined that because an expert could easily distinguish between the marks on the domestic and foreign products, the foreign products should be allowed entry, provided the marks were obliterated or removed. However, plaintiff argued that the foreign products were counterfeit and should be seized or barred from importation, or both. In order to determine whether the confusing marks on the defendant's goods were counterfeit, the Second Circuit held that a court should

---

[84]   19 C.F.R. § 133.21(b) (2015).

[85]   19 U.S.C. § 1526(f) (1996).

[86]   See "United States v. Able Time." *Inc.*, 545 F.3d 824, 836 (9th Cir. 2008).

[87]   See Montres Rolex, S.A. v. Snyder, 718 F.2d 524, 532 (2d Cir. 1983) (district court did not err in comparing the registered and allegedly counterfeit marks as they appeared on actual merchandise).

[88]   See *United States v. Able Time, Inc.*, N. 9 *supra*, 545 F.3d at 836 (although courts may compare marks as they appear on actual merchandise, a court may also make do with comparing an alleged counterfeit mark to a domestic mark's registration certificate).

[89]   *Montres Rolex, S.A. v. Snyder*, N. 10 *supra*.

take the perspective of an average purchaser viewing the item and not an expert. Moreover, the court held that adopting a stringent standard of an expert's analysis would frustrate the central purpose of Section 1526(e) to provide an "effective sanction" against merchandise that "simulates or copies a registered trademark."[90]

Exceptions to the Restricted Mark Standard

Authorized Use and Common Control or Ownership

Before the United States Supreme Court's ruling in *K Mart Corp. v. Cartier*, there existed two exceptions to restricted marks: the authorized use exception and the common control or ownership exception.[91] The "common-control" exception permitted the entry of grey market goods made abroad by the U.S. trademark owner or an affiliate of the U.S. trademark owner, while the "authorized use" exception permitted the importation of grey market goods where foreign goods bore a recorded mark "applied under the authorization of the U.S. owner."[92] Since the Court's ruling, the authorized use exception is no longer valid, but the common control or ownership exception still applies.[93] In *K-Mart Corp.*, respondents collectively sought a declaration that Title 19, Sections 133.21(c)(1)–(3) of the Code of Federal Regulations were invalid and an injunction to bar their enforcement.[94] Respondents alleged that the common-control and authorized-use exceptions were inconsistent with Section 526 of the 1930 Tariff Act.[95]

The Supreme Court ultimately held that the common control exception of Customs Service regulation[96] was consistent with Section 526 of the 1930 Tariff Act. The Court found that the exception was consistent

---

[90] *Id.*, 718 F.2d at 531.

[91] K Mart Corp. v. Cartier, Inc., 486 U.S. 281, 108 S.Ct. 1811, 100 L.Ed.2d 313 (1988).

[92] *Id.*, 486 U.S. at 290.

[93] *Id.*, 486 U.S. at 281.

[94] *Id.*

[95] *Id.*, 486 U.S. at 290.

[96] *Id.*, 486 U.S. at 282.

insofar as it exempts the importation ban on goods that are manufactured abroad by the "same person" who holds the U.S. trademark or by a person who is "subject to common … control" with the U.S. trademark holder.[97]

However, the Court held that the authorized use exception could not stand because it denied a domestic U.S. trademark holder the power to prohibit the importation of goods made by an independent foreign manufacturer where the domestic trademark holder has authorized the foreign manufacturer to use the trademark. The Court found the subsection detailing the authorized use exception to be severable and that its invalidation would not impair the function of the statute as a whole.[98]

Exception to the Exception: Physical and Nonphysical Material Difference Between the Authorized Product and the Unauthorized Product

Although the "common-control" exception is still operative, if a material difference exists between the domestic product and the foreign product, then Customs may bar entry of the foreign product. In *Lever Brothers Co. v. United States*, plaintiff Lever Brothers Co. ("Lever U.S."), an American company, and defendant Lever Brothers Limited ("Lever UK"), a British affiliate, both manufactured deodorant soap under the "Shield" trademark and hand dishwashing liquid under the "Sunlight" trademark.[99] Both trademarks were registered in each country and both products were manufactured with differing attributes to suit local tastes in the United States and the United Kingdom. Importers eventually brought Lever UK products into the United States and in response Lever U.S. alleged that the unauthorized influx of such foreign products created substantial consumer confusion. However, in light of common ownership or control of the domestic and foreign trademarks between the parties, Customs allowed importation of the Lever UK goods.[100]

---

[97] K Mart Corp. v. Cartier, Inc., 486 U.S 281, 294, 108 S.Ct. 1811, 100 L.Ed.2d 313 (1988).

[98] *Id.*

[99] Lever Brothers Co. v. U.S., 981 F.2d 1330 (D.C. Cir. 1993).

[100] *Id.*, 981 F.2d at 1331–1332.

In response, the D.C. Circuit held that the "affiliate exception" or "common control" exception of Title 19, Section 133.21(c)(2) of the Code of Federal Regulations was inconsistent with Section 42 of the Lanham Act, which prohibits the importation of goods that copy or simulate the mark of a domestic manufacturer, with respect to materially different goods.[101] The court refused to recognize that trademarks applied to physically different goods were genuine from an American consumer's standpoint.[102] Further, the court held that "[S]ection 42 of the Lanham Act precludes the application of Customs' affiliate [or common-control] exception with respect to physically, materially different goods."[103]

In light of the D.C. Circuit's decision in *Lever*, Customs published a final rule to amend Customs regulations, which restricts, upon the application of a U.S. trademark owner, grey market goods that create a likelihood of consumer confusion because they are physically and materially different from goods bearing the U.S. trademark.[104] The restriction applies notwithstanding that the U.S. and foreign trademark owners are the same business entities, affiliates, or are otherwise subject to "common ownership or control."[105]

Before the change in Customs regulations, several circuit courts refused to exclude certain grey market goods in light of the common control or ownership exception.[106]

---

[101] *Id.*, 981 F.2d at 1338.

[102] *Id.*

[103] *Id.*

[104] Gray Market Imports and other Trade Market Goods, 63 Fed. Reg. 9058 (February 24, 1999) (modified at 19 C.F.R. §§ 133.2(e), (f), 133.21-27).

[105] *Id.* at 9058; see 19 C.F.R. § 133.23(b) (2012).

[106] See, e.g.:

Third Circuit: Ceramics & Glass, Inc. v. Dash, 878 F.2d 659 (3d Cir. 1989) (finding that the U.S. trademark "Lladro" was not infringed by the importation and sale of genuine "Lladro" figurines by one other than the trademark holder because the goods were identical and the foreign manufacturer and the U.S. trademark holder were related companies).

Ninth Circuit: NEC Electronics v. CAL Circuit Abco, 810 F.2d 1506 (9th Cir. 1987) (holding that the importation of genuine NEC computer chips by the defendant, an entity unrelated to any NEC company, did not constitute infringement of the U.S. "NEC" trademark because where the companies are commonly controlled, there is a reasonable assurance of similar quality).

Since the *Lever* decision, circuit courts have had to determine on a case-by-case basis what constitutes a material difference between a domestic product and a foreign product bearing the same mark when the holders of the domestic and the foreign trademarks are related companies, because the *Lever* court failed to detail what actually constitutes a material difference. Courts have found differences in packaging of authorized and unauthorized merchandise to be material.[107] Additionally, the removal of certain anti-counterfeiting measures placed on a product can invalidate the importation of a grey market good.[108] Also, a difference in warranty protections between an authorized and an unauthorized product can constitute a potential material difference.[109]

The First Circuit has held that a foreign owner of a U.S. mark can prevent the importation of a foreign food product bearing a similar mark when the foreign product is materially different in terms of ingredients.[110] Some courts have found material differences in situations where

---

[107] See Davidoff & CIE, S.A. v. PLD International Corp., 263 F.3d 1297, 1299 (11th Cir. 2001) (holding that the defendant sold materially different bottles of plaintiff's fragrance where defendant used an etching tool to remove batch codes from authentic fragrance bottles).

[108] See Zino Davidoff S.A. v. CVS Corp., 571 F.3d 238, 244-246 (2d Cir. 2009) (finding that plaintiff's affixation of a unique production label to its products and defendant's subsequent sale of plaintiff's products with the production labels removed or altered constituted a material difference because the production labels enabled plaintiff to more easily detect counterfeiting and plaintiff actually abided by its anti-counterfeiting measures).

[109] See Swatch S.A. v. New City, Inc., 454 F. Supp.2d 1245, 1251 (S.D. Fla. 2006) (finding that although warranties accompanied both authorized and unauthorized sales of plaintiffs' watches, warranties accompanying watches sold by defendant were void because they were only valid when accompanying products sold by a dealer authorized by plaintiff, which led the court to send to the jury the question of whether such an intangible difference such as warranty protection was material). See also, Bose Corp. v. Silonsonnic Corp., 413 F. Supp.2d 339 (S.D.N.Y. 2006) (holding that the lack of a warranty accompanying the unauthorized sale of plaintiff's products by defendant could be a material difference).

[110] See Societe Des Produits Nestlé v. Casa Helvetia, Inc., 982 F.2d 633 (1st Cir. 1992) (holding that the differences in terms of ingredients and quality control between the Italian and the Venezuelan versions of a certain brand of chocolate were material, to bar importation).

the domestic and the foreign products have different colors or shapes.[111] Additionally, courts have found differences in labeling and other written materials accompanying domestic and foreign products to be material.[112]

The definition of a "material difference" between foreign and domestic products can encompass quality control procedures. The Second Circuit has established two theories with respect to whether an owner's right to control the quality of its goods is a material difference as compared to the sale of identical, foreign goods. In one case, the Second Circuit held that the defendant infringed on plaintiff's mark on certain shoe products because the defendant sold those products without "certificates of inspection" from the plaintiff.[113] The court held that the inspections were integral to quality control and thus the products sold by the defendant were not genuine, which could lead to consumer confusion. However, the court cautioned that, in order to succeed on this theory, a trademark holder must show that it actually follows through on such quality control procedures.[114]

---

[111] See Martin's Herend Imports, Inc. v. Diamond & Gem Trading USA, Co., 112 F.3d 1296 (5th Cir. 1997) (finding that the foreign owner of a U.S. trademark could prevent the importation of authentic porcelain bearing the mark because it was materially different in color, pattern, and shape from the porcelain sold in the United States).

[112] See Pepsico v. Nostalgia Products Corp., 18 U.S.P.Q.2d 1404, 1405 (N.D. Ill. 1990) (finding material differences based on the fact that the Mexican "Pepsi" labels were in Spanish and did not contain a list of ingredients). See also: Original Appalachian Artworks v. Granada Electronics, 816 F.2d 68 (2d Cir. 1987) (holding that the U.S. owner of the "Cabbage Patch" mark could prevent the importation of "Cabbage Patch" dolls that were made and sold abroad under a license from the U.S. owner of the mark on the grounds that the dolls sold abroad were materially different from the dolls authorized for sale in the United States because the adoption papers and instructions were in Spanish); Osawa & Co. v. B & H Photo, 589 F. Supp. 1163, 1169 (S.D.N.Y. 1984) (finding material differences as to domestic and foreign yet identical camera equipment because the instruction manuals were in different languages).

[113] El Greco Leather Products Co., Inc. v. Shoe World, Inc., 806 F.2d 392, 395 (2d Cir. 1986).

[114] See Polymer Technology Corp. v. Mimran, 37 F.3d 74, 78–79 (2d Cir. 1994) (finding that because plaintiff did not carefully monitor its quality control procedures, defendant's unauthorized distribution of plaintiff's products was not a violation of plaintiff's quality control standards).

The Second Circuit refined what constitutes a material difference in terms of quality control in a later case.[115] In that case, the Second Circuit set out a three-prong test that a trademark holder must satisfy in order to establish the existence of a material difference on quality control grounds.[116] A U.S. trademark holder must demonstrate that: "(i) it has established legitimate, substantial and nonpretextual quality control procedures, (ii) it abides by these procedures, and (iii) the non-conforming sales will diminish the value of the mark."[117] This test refines the earlier standard set out by the Second Circuit by noting that "[e]ven if some non-conforming products survive a mark holder's quality control procedures and enter the marketplace, the sale of additional non-conforming products [by an unauthorized dealer] could further devalue the trademark," which would then still give rise to a Lanham Act claim.[118]

In a grey market infringement case, the trademark owner must establish that all or substantially all of its sales are accompanied by the alleged material difference in order to show that its goods are materially different from unauthorized goods.[119] The Federal Circuit has supported such a requirement because, "[i]f less than all or substantially all of a trademark owner's products possess the material difference, then the trademark owner has placed into the stream of commerce a substantial quantity of goods that are or may be the same or similar to those of the importer, and then there is no material difference."[120]

Overall, courts have set a low bar for materiality, "requiring no more than showing that consumers would be likely to consider the differences between the foreign and domestic products to be significant when purchasing the product, for such differences would suffice to erode the

---

[115] Warner-Lambert Co. v. Northside Development Corp., 86 F.3d 3 (2d Cir. 1996).

[116] *Id.*, 86 F.3d at 6.

[117] *Id.*

[118] *Id.*, 86 F.3d at 7.

[119] SKF USA, Inc. v. International Trade Commission, 423 F.3d 1307, 1315 (Fed. Cir. 2005).

[120] *Id.*

goodwill of the domestic source."[121] Differences that may be readily apparent to consumers may still be material. For instance, the Federal Circuit held that the U.S. ITC was right to find that no factual basis existed for assuming, as the plaintiff proposed, that a domestic purchaser of a foreign manufactured tractor should be aware that replacement parts would not be available for its product from domestic service centers because the foreign manufactured product had Japanese labels.[122]

With regard to the Lanham Act, a product need not be of foreign manufacture to violate a registered mark owner's importation right. In a case in which the Federal Circuit dealt with a product made in the United States for sale abroad and subsequently reimported into the U.S. without the trademark owner's permission,[123] the court found that Chapter 19, Section 1337 of the United States Code Annotated (unfair practices in import trade) makes no mention of the term "grey market." Moreover, the Federal Circuit held that grey market law is not concerned with where a good is manufactured, but rather with whether a trademark owner has authorized the use of its trademark on a particular product in the United States and whether the trademark owner has control over such a product associated with its mark in the United States. Thus, the court held that "importation and sale of a trademarked good of domestic manufacture, produced solely for sale abroad and not authorized by the owner of the trademark for sale in the United States, may violate Section 1337 if the imported good is materially different from all or substantially all of those goods bearing the same trademark that are authorized for sale in the United States."[124]

---

[121] "Gamut Trading Co. v. U.S. International Trade Commission," 200 F.3d 775, 779 (Fed. Cir. 1999). See also, Hokto Kinoko Co. v. Concord Farms, Inc., 738 F.3d 1085, 1092 (9th Cir. 2013).

[122] *Id.*

[123] "Bourdeau Brothers, Inc. v. International Trade Commission." 444 F.3d 1317, 1322 (Fed. Cir. 2006).

[124] *Id.*, 444 F.3d at 1323.

Obtaining Lever Protection From Customs

In order to receive *Lever* rule protection, a trademark owner must submit to Customs a detailed explanation for the basis of its eligibility and a detailed explanation of the physical and material differences in the products.[125] In determining whether trademarks are entitled to *Lever* protection, Customs considers the following attributes:

1. "The specific composition of both the authorized and grey market product(s) (including chemical composition);
2. Formulation, product construction, structure, or composite product components, of both the authorized and grey market product;
3. Performance and/or operational characteristics of both the authorized and grey market product;
4. Differences resulting from legal or regulatory requirements, certification, etc.;
5. Other distinguishing and explicitly defined factors that would result in, as prescribed under applicable law, consumer deception or confusion ..."[126]

Customs requires that claims for physical and material differences be stated with particularity.[127] If *Lever* protection is granted, Customs will publish in the Customs Bulletin a notice that the mark will receive trademark protection and that any subsequent importation of physically and materially different products will be denied.[128]

Gaining Entry Despite the Existence of a Material Difference Between a Grey Market Product and a Domestic Product

Even if a material difference exists to bar entry of an unauthorized product, an importer could potentially still gain entry of the merchandise through

---

[125] 19 C.F.R. § 133.2(e) (2007) (Trademark owners must provide "summaries of physical and material difference for publication").

[126] 19 C.F.R. § 133.2(e)(1)-(5) (2007).

[127] Gray Market Imports, 63 Fed. Reg. at 14,664.

[128] 19 C.F.R. § 133.2(f) (2007); 19 C.F.R. § 133.23(a)(3), (c) (2012).

conspicuous labeling. According to Customs, an informative label appearing prominently on trademarked grey market goods constitutes a "specially differentiating feature" that prevents consumer confusion. Moreover, even if a grey market good is unauthorized and is materially different, if a label noting that the grey market good is different from the product authorized by the U.S. trademark owner for importation is affixed to the good, then harm is prevented.[129] In such cases, Customs will find that the trademark will not "copy or simulate" the U.S. mark. This amended regulation applies only to Section 42 of the Lanham Act and no other provisions. There is no specific regulatory requirement for such labeling, but the labeling provision was intended to ensure that such labels would be sufficiently conspicuous and legible in order to eliminate confusion or incorrect inferences by consumers.[130]

[129] Gray Market Imports, 63 Fed. Reg. at 14,663.
[130] 19 C.F.R. § 133.23(b) (2012).

CHAPTER 8

Issues Relating to Websites

From the earliest days at Apple, I realized that we thrived when we created intellectual property. If people copied or stole our software, we'd be out of business. If it weren't protected, there'd be no incentive for us to make new software, or product designs. If protection of intellectual property begins to disappear, creative companies will disappear or never get started. But there's a simpler reason: It's wrong to steal. It hurts other people. And it hurts your own character.

—Steve Jobs (1955–2011)

Overview

Since its birth as the Advanced Research Projects Agency network (ARPAnet) (the world's first multiple-site computer network created in 1969), the Internet (as it has been known since 1982)[1] has been an extraordinarily powerful medium for publishing, distributing, and reproducing all kinds of information, and bringing it to millions of people. The Internet opened a global marketplace where consumers can find anything they are looking for and compare prices no matter where they live. For businesses, it is a marketplace with an enormous pool of potential customers and without any barriers for market entry. Online commerce makes it easy for individuals and businesses alike to offer the widest range of goods and services.

Along with the success of legitimate online commerce, this proliferation has also given rise to unprecedented opportunities for grey marketers.

---

[1] T.L. Opfer 1999. "Running Head: The History of the Internet According to Itself." *Norfolk Univ.* Available at http://nebula.wsimg.com/c3d7154f7c82a460b b7da28c5dfdeaa7?AccessKeyId=A49B64B46F0719FB4B2E&disposition=0&all oworigin=1 (accessed March 02, 2021).

"Although e-commerce provides consumers with a larger distribution of goods and lower prices, product manufacturers in developed countries, such as the United States and United Kingdom, are concerned about their products being sold on the burgeoning grey market via the Internet because grey marketers undercut manufacturers' prices on their own products ..."[2] When it comes to IP, the Internet promises greater quantity and easier access; however, it can also be an instrument for diminishing the rewards to creators and other intellectual property rights holders.

"Innovation protected by IP rights is key to creating new jobs and growing exports. Innovation has a positive pervasive effect on the entire economy, and its benefits flow both upstream and downstream to every sector of the U.S. economy. Intellectual property is not just the final product of workers and companies—every job in some way, produces, supplies, consumes, or relies on innovation, creativity, and commercial distinctiveness. Protecting our ideas and IP promotes innovative, open, and competitive markets, and helps ensure that the U.S. private sector remains America's innovation engine. ..."[3]

In hard numbers, this translates to "more than $7.7 trillion" and "more than 19 million" jobs.[4] Protecting American intellectual property from

---

[2] A.G. Galstian. 2000. "Protecting Against the Gray Market in the New Economy." *Loyola U.L.A. Int. & Comp. L. Rev.* 22, p. 509.

[3] Economics and Statistics Administration and the United States Patent and Trademark Office. March 2012. "Intellectual Property and the U.S. Economy: Industries in Focus." report, U.S. Department of Commerce." Available at www.uspto.gov/news/publications/IP_Report_March_2012.pdf (accessed March 02, 2021).

[4] Pham. January 2011. "Employment and Gross Output of Intellectual Property Companies in the United States." NDP Consulting Research Paper, at 2. Available at http://static.squarespace.com/static/52850a5ce4b068394a270176/t/52d85c82e4b08a516dd4de4f/1389911170146/employment__gross_output_of_ip_companies_in_the_us_-_jan_2011_low_res.pdf (accessed March 09, 2021). See also: Oversight of the Office of the Intellectual Property Enforcement Coordinator Before the U.S. Senate Committee on the Judiciary, S. Hrg. 111th Cong. 2 (2010) (written statement of Hirschmann, President and CEO, Global Intellectual Property Center, U.S. Chamber of Commerce) at 4; Targeting Websites Dedicated to Stealing American Intellectual Property Before the U.S. Senate Committee on the Judiciary, S. Hrg. 112th Cong. 1 (2011) (written statement

theft is therefore critical to U.S. prosperity, welfare, and job creation.[5] The theft of American IP threatens that prosperity.[6] Although estimates of the harm caused to the American economy by counterfeit products and the theft of copyrighted works differ and are difficult to confirm, according to the U.S. Senate Committee on the Judiciary, copyright piracy and the sale of counterfeit goods are reported to cost American creators and producers billions of dollars per year.[7] Intellectual property theft also

---

of Adams, CEO, Rosetta Stone Inc.) at 1 ("Intellectual property industries are a cornerstone of the U.S. economy, employing more than 19 million people and accounting for 60 percent of our exports"); Oversight of the Office of the Intellectual Property Enforcement Coordinator Before the U.S. Senate Committee on the Judiciary, S. Hrg. 111th Cong. 2 (2010) (written statement of Almeida, President, Department for Professional Employees, AFL–CIO) at 2, 4.

[5] "Strong intellectual property enforcement saves American jobs, it creates American jobs, it protects American ideas and it invigorates our economy." Oversight of the Office of the Intellectual Property Enforcement Coordinator before the U.S. Senate Committee on the Judiciary, S. Hrg. 111th Cong. 2 (2010) (written statement of Espinel, Intellectual Property Enforcement Coordinator, Office of Management and Budget) at 2.

[6] "The revenue lost to American businesses from intellectual property theft carries with it lost funding for public services to compound the harm caused to our economy." *Id.* at 2.

[7] See: Targeting Websites Dedicated to Stealing American Intellectual Property Before the U.S. Senate Committee on the Judiciary, S. Hrg. 112th Cong. 1 (2011) (written statement of Adams, CEO, Rosetta Stone Inc.) at 2 ("The global sales of counterfeit goods via the Internet from illegitimate retailers reached $135 billion in 2010. As a consequence of global and U.S.-based piracy of copyright products, the U.S. economy lost $58.0 billion in total output in 2007"); Press Release, FBI, The Federal Bureau of Investigation and the U.S. Customs Service today announced the National Intellectual Property Rights Coordination Center's first conference for members of Congress and the industry in Washington (July 16, 2002), Available at www.fbi.gov/news/pressrel/press-releases/the-federal-bureau-of-investigation-and-the-u.s.-customs-service-today-announced-the-national-intellectual-property-rights-coordination-centers-first-conference-for-members-of-congress-and-industry-in-washington (accessed March 09, 2021) ("Losses to counterfeiting are estimated at $200-250 billion a year in U.S. business losses"); Press Release, U.S. Customs and Border Protection section of the Department of Homeland Security, U.S. Customs Announces International Counterfeit Case Involving Caterpillar Heavy

reportedly results in hundreds of thousands of lost jobs annually, and severely reduces the income of those who are employed.[8]

According to a U.S. Commerce Department study released in 2012, the innovative and creative industries in the United States support roughly $775 billion in exports annually and 40 million U.S.-based jobs. The online retail and distribution of pirated and counterfeit goods diminishes the value and salability of the work and threatens jobs in these industries.[9]

With more and more information being stored and transported in digital format, in the form of peer-to-peer networks, cyberlockers, streaming sites, or one-click hosting services, copyright infringement in particular has grown rampant on the Internet and crosses virtually unlimited geographic markets. The U.S. Government Accountability Office reports that:

Equipment (May 29, 2002), available at www.gpo.gov/fdsys/pkg/CRPT-111srpt373/html/CRPT-111srpt373.htm (accessed March 09, 2021) ("Customs estimates that businesses and industries lose about $200 billion a year in revenue … due to the counterfeiting of merchandise"); Siwek, "The True Cost of Copyright Industry Piracy to the U.S. Economy," Institute for Policy Innovation, IPI Policy Report No. 189, at 1 (October 03, 2007), available at www.ipi.org/ipi_issues/detail/the-true-cost-of-copyright-industry-piracy-to-the-us-economy (accessed March 09, 2021) ("[E]ach year, copyright piracy from motion pictures, sound recordings, business and entertainment software and video games costs the U.S. economy $58 billion in total output, costs American workers 375,375 jobs and $16.3 billion in earnings, and costs Federal, State, and local governments $2.6 billion in tax revenue").

[8] Preventing Real Online Threats to Economic Creativity and Theft of Intellectual Property Act of 2011, July 22, 2011, "Mr. LEAHY, from the Committee on the Judiciary, submitted the report [To accompany S. 968]. The Committee on the Judiciary, to which was referred the bill (S. 968), to prevent online threats to economic creativity and theft of intellectual property, and for other purposes, having considered the same, reports favorably thereon, with an amendment in the nature of a substitute, and recommends that the bill, as amended, do pass." www.gpo.gov/fdsys/pkg/CRPT-112srpt39/pdf/CRPT-112srpt39.pdf (accessed March 09, 2021).

[9] https://ustr.gov/about-us/policy-offices/press-office/press-releases/2014/February/Notorious-markets-list-focuses-fight-against-global-piracy-and-counterfeiting (accessed March 09, 2021).

Sectors facing threats from digital piracy include the music, motion picture, television, publishing, and software industries ... but piracy impacts virtually any online industry that relies on copyright protection ... The sellers of counterfeit goods via Internet sites ... can quickly deliver items in sophisticated packaging .... In many cases, these Internet sites are able to conceal the inauthentic nature and low quality of the product being purchased ... therefore, preventing counterfeit sales is not only important to our economy and job creation, but it protects unsuspecting consumers from inferior and often dangerous products ... .[10]

"[T]he online theft of ... intellectual property is a growing criminal enterprise both because of the ease by which it can be done online and the ability of the sellers and distributors to remain anonymous, operate from overseas, and avoid traditional methods for protection ... ."[11] Operators of rogue Internet sites, which do nothing but traffic in infringing goods, can act with impunity from abroad.[12] The rogue Internet sites that operate as virtual stores for the infringing products are well designed and give the appearance of legitimacy.[13] These rogue sites are easily accessed by entering or browsing domain names that sound legitimate and that often

---

[10] See "Report on Economic Effects of Counterfeit and Pirated Goods," available at https://iccwbo.org/publication/economic-impacts-counterfeiting-piracy-report-prepared-bascap-inta/#:~:text=This%20report%20shows%20that%20the,vital%20public%20services%2C%20forces%20higher (accessed March 09, 2021).

[11] *Id.* at 8–9.

[12] The Council of Europe Convention on Cybercrime, to which the United States is a signatory, requires signatories to have in place criminal copyright laws that apply to copyright infringement on the Internet. See Convention on Cybercrime, November 23, 2001, TIAS 13174, Available at www.europarl.europa.eu/meetdocs/2014_2019/documents/libe/dv/7_conv_budapest_/7_conv_budapest_en.pdf (accessed March 09, 2021). This Act provides an additional mechanism in the fight against online infringement occurring overseas.

[13] For an example of the unfortunate ease with which operators of rogue Internet sites can clone legitimate Internet sites to trick consumers, see Peachey, "Fake website' takes seconds' to set up" (September 20, 2010), available at www.bbc.co.uk/news/business-11372689 (accessed March 09, 2021).

accept payment through well-respected credit card companies; use "e-wallet" or alternative payment methods such as PayPal, AsiaPay, plug'npay, Moneybrokers, Western Union, AlertPay, and Gate2Shop to allow for the receipt of payment from the public; use advertising by legitimate companies; and include reward programs for frequent purchasers. All of this creates a feeling of legitimacy even though the products being sold are illegal, often inferior, or even dangerous. While completing purchases, consumers may unwittingly be giving their credit card information to overseas organized crime syndicates that own these rogue Internet sites.[14]

---

[14] Holder, Attorney General of the United States, remarks at the Rio De Janeiro Prosecutor General's Office (February 14, 2010) ("Unfortunately, the success of this worldwide, digital marketplace has also attracted criminals who seek to exploit and misappropriate the intellectual property of others. The same technologies that have created unprecedented opportunities for growth in legitimate economies have also created global criminal organizations that are eager to steal the creativity and profits from our domestic industries and workers … These groups, who do not respect international boundaries or borders, have developed sophisticated, efficient and diverse methods for committing almost every type of intellectual property offense imaginable, including: widespread online piracy of music, movies, video games, business software and other copyrighted works; well-funded corporate espionage; sales of counterfeit luxury goods, clothing and electronics, both on street corners and through Internet auction sites; and increased international trade in counterfeit pharmaceuticals and other goods that pose a substantial risk to the health and safety of our consumers"). See also: Protecting Intellectual Property Rights in a Global Economy: Current Trends and Future Challenges Before the Subcommittee on Government Management, Organization, and Procurement of the H. Committee on Oversight and Government Reform, 111th Cong. 1 (2009) (written statement of Weinstein, Deputy Assistant Attorney General, Criminal Division, U.S. Department of Justice) at 5 ("Because intellectual property crime is perceived as a low-risk criminal enterprise with the potential for high profit margins, it is not surprising that the sale of counterfeit and pirated goods is also becoming an attractive revenue source for traditional organized crime groups"); Jones, National Security Advisor to the President of the United States, Remarks at the Sochi Security Council Gathering, Sochi Russia (October 05, 2010), available at www.whitehouse.gov/the-press-office/2010/10/05/remarks-gen-james-l-jones-national-security-advisor-sochi-security-counc (accessed March 09, 2021) (Criminal syndicates "generate … trillions of dollars annually from illicit activities such as money laundering,

If these sites operated in the physical world, rather than online, the perpetrators would be the subject of civil lawsuits and criminal penalties.[15] "Because this theft is veiled by the complexities of the online world and many of the perpetrators are located overseas, the task of enforcing U.S. intellectual property laws on the Internet is a difficult one. Too often our government, as well as the businesses and consumers who are harmed by online infringement, are forced to sit idly by while this theft continues undeterred ..."[16]

In summary, IP theft committed by rogue Internet sites is harmful in number of ways:

1. Online infringement harms content, copyright, and trademark owners through lost revenues, lost brand value, or increased costs invested in protecting their IPR. Even worse, it decreases incentives for IPR owners to invest in innovation, research, and development.

2. Online infringement harms consumers who receive poor quality products, and, in a worst-case scenario, products that may cause physical harm.

3. Online infringement harms federal, state, and municipal governments in the form of lost tax revenues, increased law enforcement costs, and the direct harm caused by the counterfeit products purchased by governments themselves.

---

trafficking, counterfeiting, environmental crime, and financial fraud ... many of these criminal syndicates operate globally; they [comprise] loose networks that cooperate intermittently but maintain their independence; and they employ sophisticated technology and financial savvy").

[15] See, e.g.: 17 U.S.C. § 506; 18 U.S.C. § 2319; 18 U.S.C. § 2320.

[16] In a hearing before the Senate Committee on the Judiciary, a U.S. Intellectual Property Enforcement Coordinator stated that "legislative action may be required in order to fulfill our goals" of effective intellectual property protection. Oversight of the Office of the Intellectual Property Enforcement Coordinator Before the U.S. Senate Committee on the Judiciary, 111th Cong. 2 (2010) (written statement of Espinel, Intellectual Property Enforcement Coordinator, Office of Management and Budget).

4. Online infringement harms international trade—the countries with developed IP enforcement regimes have less interest in partnering with countries that have weaker IP enforcement regimes.[17]

5. Online infringement reduces the incentives to create and disseminate ideas, which, as the U.S. Supreme Court has recognized, harms the free expression principles of the First Amendment.

6. "Online infringement supports international organized crime syndicates, which pose risks to our national security ... ."[18]

In February 2014, the Office of U.S. Trade Representative published a Special 301 Out-of-Cycle Review of Notorious Markets for 2013, identifying both online and physical marketplaces around the world that cause harm to American businesses globally and infringe on intellectual property rights. The report notes that in 2013, activities of several online markets from the 2012 list were disrupted as a result of enforcement efforts, for example:

> Canada-based IsoHunt.com, one of the largest BitTorrent indexes in the world, agreed to shut down the site and pay $110 million to the plaintiff as part of a litigation settlement agreement reached in United States Federal court. In some instances, in an effort to legitimize their overall business, companies made the decision to close down problematic aspects of their operations, as China's Xunlei.com did with its multi-platform site GouGou.com; or to cooperate with authorities to address unauthorized conduct on

---

[17] Copyright Clause, U.S. Const., Art. I, § 8, and the United Nations' Universal Declaration of Human Rights, which has become a model for treaties and constitutions around the world, proclaimed the "right of authors" as inalienable. Universal Declaration f Human Rights, G.A. Res. 217 (III) A, U.N. Doc A/810 at Art. 27 ¶ 2 (December 10, 1948).

[18] Oversight of the Office of the Intellectual Property Enforcement Coordinator Before the U.S. Senate Committee on the Judiciary, S. Hrg. 111th Cong. 2 (2010) (written statement of Espinel, Intellectual Property Enforcement Coordinator, Office of Management and Budget) at 2. See also, N. 12 *supra*.

the site, as in the case of Warez-bb.org. These markets have been removed from the List ...[19]

"The Report" chronicles websites and physical marketplaces that have been the subject of enforcement actions in many countries and exemplify concerns about IP counterfeiting and piracy.[20]

Increase in Online Infringement

On August 5, 2013, the European Commission published 2012 statistics showing almost 90,000 Customs detention cases, which is approximately the same as in 2011 and an increase from 60,000 in 2010. The large number of detentions in 2011 and 2012 is mostly attributed to an increase in shipments of small parcels, likely as a result of Internet sales. The 40 million detained articles (down from almost 120 million in 2011 and 103 million in 2010) are estimated to be valued at just below 1 billion euro.[21] The official Chinese news agency Xinhua said that in 2014 "more than 40 percent of goods sold online in China ... were either counterfeits or of bad quality ... ."[22]

As a result of this growth in the market for counterfeit goods, there has also been a significant increase in enforcement directed toward spam, Internet auctions, retail sites, and other Internet activities that sell or distribute counterfeit and pirated items. According to Net-Security, a computer forensics and security consulting company:

---

[19] United States Trade Representative, 2013 Out-of-Cycle Review of Notorious Markets (February 12, 2014), available at www.ustr.gov/sites/default/files/FINAL-PUBLISHED%202013_Notorious_Markets_List-02122014.pdf (accessed March 09, 2021).

[20] Id.

[21] http://ec.europa.eu/taxation_customs/customs/customs_controls/counterfeit_piracy/statistics/index_en.htm (accessed March 09, 2021).

[22] Reuters. November 02, 2015. "Over 40 percent of China's Online Sales Counterfeit, Shoddy: Xinhua." Available at www.reuters.com/article/us-china-counterfeits-idUSKCN0SS02820151103 (accessed March 09, 2021).

For more than two years, online auction fraud has been the number one complaint of New York state residents to government organizations that keep track. The WebWatch survey shows that 27 percent of state residents who have ever used an online auction Web site, such as eBay or Amazon, have experienced a scam or deceptive practice—32 percent of eBay users were scammed ... 11 percent of online auction site users reported they never received the goods they bid on, the most common complaint. In addition, 7 percent of survey respondents who received their goods said they were not in the condition they expected ... .[23]

The problem does not stop with hard goods sold through websites and online auctions. "Almost a quarter of New York Internet users have encountered a badware problem over the past year, often slowing their computers and prompting them to run software to fix the problem ... ."[24] Badware (also known as spyware or malware) from infected websites, memory devices such as flash drives (memory sticks), and even digital picture frames can maliciously infect computers. It can range from "benign" and more annoying than dangerous (pop-up advertisements on a monitor) to "malignant" and very dangerous (uploading programs that take control of a computer, sending private data to third parties). "[B]adware can even link your computer to worldwide organized crime networks which, in turn, use it to attack financial and government institutions ..."[25]

Peer-to-Peer (P2P) services such as eDonkey and BitTorrent play a significant role in copyright infringement because they distribute music, films, software, and books for free or at very low costs.

Besides online auctions and P2P sites, there are rogue sites that exist solely to distribute stolen and counterfeited goods and IP of others. These rogue sites are unfortunately often assisted by legitimate businesses whose brokers use the sites to place ads, or by financial services that provide

---

[23] "Problems with Online Auctions, Badware, Protecting Personal Data." *Help Net Security*, December 18, 2008. Available at www.net-security.org/secworld. php?id=6866 (accessed March 09, 2021).

[24] *Id.*

[25] *Id.*

funding. In June 2010, the U.S. Intellectual Property Enforcement Coordinator reported to Congress that "the Internet and other technological innovations have revolutionized society and the way we obtain information and purchase products ... . These innovations have also facilitated piracy and counterfeiting on a global scale ... [which] unfairly devalue America's contribution, hinder our ability to grow our economy, compromise good, high-wage jobs for Americans and endanger strong and prosperous communities ... ."[26] According to the Motion Picture Association of America, "some of the most pernicious forms of digital theft occur through the use of websites. The sites, whose content is hosted and whose operators are located throughout the world[,] take many forms, but have in common the simple fact that all materially contribute to, facilitate, and/or induce the distribution of copyrighted works, such as movies and television programming ... ."[27] The theft of copyrighted movies by rogue websites can occur via unauthorized copying, streaming, and downloading; streaming or downloading by linking to a torrent or to other metadata files; linking to other unauthorized sites offering unauthorized copies; and by hosting unauthorized copies. These rogue websites often share the same attributes as legitimate websites. Moreover, some rogue sites "mirror" the legitimate websites.

"More than 2.4 million people work in the motion picture and television industry alone, in states all across the nation, earning over 41 billion US dollars in wages. These are creative, good-paying jobs—including costume designers, truck drivers, stage crews, actors, architects, directors and accountants, who face a relentless challenge to their livelihoods from intellectual property theft."[28]

---

[26] "U.S. Joint Strategic Plan on Intellectual Property Enforcement Announced." December 12, 2016, Available at www.uspto.gov/about-us/news-updates/us-joint-strategic-plan-intellectual-property-enforcement-announced(accessed March 09, 2021).

[27] See www.csbj.com/2011/05/06/major-opportunities-in-the-movie-world/ (accessed March 09, 2021).

[28] www.smh.com.au/technology/us-unveils-strategy-to-fight-piracy-of-intellectual-property-20100622-yw4n.html (accessed March 09, 2021).

A major *Wall Street Journal* investigation recently revealed that Amazon has listed "thousands of banned, unsafe, or mislabeled products," from dangerous children's products to electronics with fake certifications. The Verge reported that even Amazon's listings for its own line of goods are "getting hijacked by impostor sellers." CNBC found that Amazon has shipped expired foods—including baby formula—to customers, pointing to an inability to monitor something as basic as an expiration date.[29] Because of the proliferation of counterfeits and what Birkenstock describes as Amazon's unwillingness to help it fight them, Birkenstock won't sell on Amazon anymore. Nike announced that it is also pulling out of Amazon. "Many consumers are … unaware of the significant probabilities they face of being defrauded by counterfeiters when they shop on e-commerce platforms," reads a January 2020 Department of Homeland Security report (PDF) recommending measures that would force e-retailers to take counterfeits even more seriously. "These probabilities are unacceptably high and appear to be rising."

Over several months of research, we were able to purchase items through Amazon Prime that were either confirmed counterfeits, lookalikes unsafe for use, or otherwise misrepresented. We talked with many brands about the rise of fakery and their efforts to combat it. And we tried to understand the new landscape of counterfeits and how to navigate it, so that you can as well.

Amazon, too, is clearly aware of the problem and is taking plenty of measures to combat counterfeits on its site. But critics say its efforts are not nearly enough. (Read more about Amazon's efforts to fight counterfeits).[30]

Internet Monitoring

Some auction sites have programs providing rights holders with opportunities to initiate removal of goods that infringe their IP. For example, eBay

---

[29] NY Times (Wirecutter). February 11, 2020. "Welcome to the Era of Fake Products." www.nytimes.com/wirecutter/blog/amazon-counterfeit-fake-products/ (accessed March 09, 2021)

[30] *Id.*

developed the Verified Rights Owner (VeRO) Program to help protect not only IP but also consumers. Highlights of the program include: (i) expeditious removal of auction listings reported to eBay by IP rights owners; (ii) proactive monitoring and removal of auction listings that violate eBay policies; (iii) suspension of repeat offenders; and (iv) provision of information (including personal information) about alleged infringers to rights holders. Because eBay is not an expert in other rights holders' IP, eBay requires that rights holders identify infringing listings before submitting the request for removal to eBay.[31]

Another example is MercadoLibre, which operates in Latin American countries, including Argentina, Brazil (as MercadoLivre), Chile, Colombia, Costa Rica, the Dominican Republic, Ecuador, Mexico, Panama, Peru, Portugal, Uruguay, Venezuela, and in the United States (where it is redirected to eBay, which has a strategic alliance with MercadoLibre).[32] Latin American trademark owners find it difficult to enforce their rights on the Internet because most of their countries lack a legal framework for such protection—in particular, on online auction platforms. Because of the growing presence of counterfeits in online auctions, MercadoLibre developed an Intellectual Property Protection Program (IPPP) that requires sellers using the auction platform to sell only authentic goods and requires the auction site operator to remove any goods that infringe registered trademarks.

Since, in some countries, obtaining a warrant from the courts to remove counterfeit goods from an online auction site can take weeks or even months, the IPPP provides a solution that speeds up this process. Rights holders have the opportunity to register their intellectual property with the IPPP (the IPPP does not require rights holders' intellectual property to be legalized with an apostille[33] as the IPPP is based on trust) and enter into a cooperation agreement with the auction site operator (since they vary per country), who will then remove any counterfeit goods

---

[31] "Reporting Intellectual Property Infringements (VeRO)." Available at http://pages.ebay.com/help/tp/vero-rights-owner.html (accessed March 09, 2021).

[32] See www.mercadolibre.com (accessed March 09, 2021).

[33] See the Hague Convention Abolishing the Requirement for Legalization for Foreign Public Documents, October 05, 1961, 33 U.S.T. 883, 527 U.N.T.S. 189.

from auction. In order to remove counterfeit goods from the auction site, rights holders participating in the IPPP must monitor auctions and detect counterfeit goods themselves. Once counterfeits have been detected, the rights holder must send a letter to the administrator of the IPPP, providing detailed specifics of the auctions that violate the rules of the MercadoLibre by offering infringing goods. Within a few hours of receiving the report, the administrator will remove the suspected goods. The infringing seller will not be able to recover the auction fees.

Recognizing that most copyright holders have their own international distribution channels or authorized resellers, and since many online auction listings in the past have proven to infringe the IP rights Alibaba.com has a takedown policy to remove allegedly infringing listings reported by intellectual property rights holders in complaints supported by valid IP proofs. Any product listing on www.alibaba.com, www.aliexpress.com, www.1688.com, www.TaoBao.com, www.Tmall.com, and latest www.lazada.com allegedly infringing any intellectual property rights can be submitted by the appropriate rights holder to the Alibaba Intellectual Property Platform (IPP) online reporting system for intellectual property infringement claims.[34]

Because of the complexity and global nature of e-commerce, there has really been no legal framework written that would effectively protect rights holders and consumers. Fortunately, there are a few things consumers can do that can help them avoid being taken advantage of. Consumers should always take the time to learn more about a seller before buying from the seller, and should investigate the seller's reputation on online auction sites such as eBay and check the feedback on the sites.

Before rights holders can enforce their rights in online space, however, there is the critical matter of collecting relevant intelligence. Many rights holders still use the traditional ways of monitoring the online presence of their IP—for example, a tedious and time-consuming process of web crawling—manually or leveraging some of the web crawling services. Using the common search engines to monitor ecommerce sites may yield huge amounts of unorganized and unformatted data that first must be

---

[34] https://ipp.alibabagroup.com/register.htm (accessed March 09, 2021).

cleaned in order to properly identify and analyze potential infringements and select actionable targets.

The key to making monitoring efficient is to leverage technologies that drive benefits from implementing a cloud-based technology designed to help manage the tremendous amounts of data linked directly to the brand protection initiatives. Technology not only breaks the barriers between distributed teams (often using Excel spreadsheets, e-mail, and various siloed systems) and external sources but it also adds process efficiencies that can have a material impact on the overall effectiveness of the team. Some of the benefits of implementing a cloud-based technology in brand protection include:

- Centralizing information in the cloud (a secure, anytime, anywhere access to critical information; centralized knowledge management repository that ensures transparency and accountability across various teams; no more silos).
- Insights/Visibility (connecting the dots across all data; identify, prioritize, and track infringements and infringers; visual dashboards provide a real-time view of progress against goals and revenue recovered).
- Team productivity/Process efficiencies (no more messy spreadsheets and disjointed e-mail threads; streamlining complex processes and tasks; centralized communications within a secure, always-connected platform; balance team workloads; track third-party resources/control costs.

Raising Awareness About Online Counterfeit Trade

The best method to prevent counterfeit trade is to provide the public with the best information possible. As in the case of infectious diseases, where providing timely communication and education can play an essential role in the successful containment of a potential outbreak, it is crucial to educate and inform the public about the perils associated with grey market, counterfeit, pirated, and other infringing goods.

The basic education needs to take place long before any such infringement occurs. Like basic rules of health and safety—washing hands, brushing teeth, and "not talking to strangers"—that are taught in childhood, some basic safety rules should be taught about counterfeiting, fraud, and safe use of the Internet (IM, social media, etc.)—do not open spam, do run an antivirus check, do not buy from "strangers," do not share private information over the Internet, make sure that downloaded data are legitimate, and so on. Some people learn from bad experiences and word of mouth, but for the most part, it is up to the rights holders, governments, and law enforcement to drive the education and prevention efforts.

Many rights holders have already put significant efforts into education, issuing product bulletins that warn consumers about dangers related to counterfeits of specific products, and providing online tools for product verification by serial numbers, software key-codes, or other unique product identifiers.

For example, the Coach[35] and UGG Australia[36] websites provide general information about counterfeiting, as well as information specific to their products, including counterfeit hotline or e-mail addresses, or both. UL, the global independent safety science company, sponsors an anti-counterfeiting program.

For almost 15 years, UL has taken an aggressive stance against counterfeiting through a comprehensive program that involves law enforcement agencies from around the world. UL works closely with U.S. Customs and Border Protection, U.S. Immigration and Customs Enforcement, the Federal Bureau of Investigation (FBI), the RCMP, INTERPOL, and other law enforcement agencies around the world to provide them with the information necessary to distinguish between authentic and counterfeit UL Marks.[37]

The vice-president and country manager Europe for Philips Intellectual Property and Standards offers this advice:

---

[35] See https://singapore.coach.com/brand-protection.html (accessed March 09, 2021).

[36] See www.ugg.com/counterfeit.html (accessed March 09, 2021).

[37] UL, "Brand Integrity." Available at www.ul.com/about/brand-integrity (accessed March 09, 2021).

"We've also found it very helpful to work with the authorities whenever we can. For example in China we support, with the so-called IP Academy, two universities in Beijing and one in Shanghai. We have people from the company who teach in their law departments and we fund scholarships and IP courses. We have also funded exchange programmes between professors in China and the European Union. Philips also believes strongly in the importance of giving the media information about the problem of counterfeiting so we have set up an IP Media Club that provides background about IP and aims to give journalists whatever information they need. It is vital to create an awareness of the value and role of intellectual property, as well as focusing on the problem of fakes … ."[38]

Philips' focus on China is quite understandable, since (and this is not a surprise) "most of fakes are manufactured in China … ;"[39] however, (and this may be surprising) China is also leading the world in Internet usage, followed by the United States and India.[40]

There are also industry platforms where IP rights holders, governments, and law enforcement come together to discuss and address problems related to intellectual property protection.[41]

On September 27, 2011, the International AntiCounterfeiting Coalition (IACC) announced that it had signed a deal with G2 Web Services, LLC, the leading provider of merchant compliance monitoring and risk management services, to develop a portal-based system designed to help brands put "rogue websites" selling counterfeit goods online out

---

[38] J. Vandekerckhove. May 01, 2010. "How Philips Tackles Fakes." *Managing Intellectual Property*. Available at www.managingip.com/Article/2476976/How-Philips-tackles-fakes.html (accessed March 09, 2021).

[39] Dickler. February 09, 2012. "Top Counterfeit Goods." *CNN Money.com* Available at https://money.cnn.com/galleries/2012/pf/1202/gallery.counterfeit-goods/index.html (accessed March 09, 2021).

[40] Internet World Stats, available at www.internetworldstats.com/top20.htm (accessed March 09, 2021).

[41] For example, the World Customs Organization initiated and is responsible for Interface Public-Members, a platform for intellectual property rights holders and Customs administrators to exchange information about efforts to combat counterfeiting. See Ch. 14 *infra*. And see, § 12.05 *infra*.

of business. According to the IACC, the system is emblematic of a fresh strategy in online intellectual property enforcement: hitting counterfeiters in the wallet by working with financial institutions to shut down their ability to process payments. "[T]he ... program represents a historic collaboration between members of the financial industry and rights holders ... . The groundbreaking technology from G2 Web Services and unprecedented cooperation from the payment processors will deliver a serious blow to the online counterfeiting schemes that dupe consumers and cost the U.S. economy much needed jobs and hundreds of billions of dollars in revenue ..."[42]

According to Business Software Alliance (BSA), software piracy strains technology companies' ability to innovate and create jobs, harms local IT services firms, saps government tax revenues, and increases the risk of cybercrime and security problems. BSA works to expand legal software markets on a global scale, with special attention to the world's top emerging markets. One of the most effective ways that BSA prevents software piracy and the associated risks to society is by raising awareness of the negative impacts, which it does through the news media, schools, and direct outreach to affected communities.[43] BSA also provides consumers and businesses with the opportunity to report instances of piracy at their "Report Piracy" portal.[44]

The Alliance for Gray Market and Counterfeit Abatement (AGMA) focuses on scrutinizing all potential areas of counterfeiting and cooperating to help address the problem and offer best practices for technology-intensive businesses to fight the grey and black markets. AGMA members meetings provide a forum for discussing industry grey

---

[42] PR Newswire, "The International AntiCounterfeiting Coalition Developing New Online Tools to Choke Off Money to Rogue Websites" United Business Media (September 27, 2011). Available at www.prnewswire.com/news-releases/ the-international-anticounterfeiting-coalition-developing-new-online-tools-to-choke-off-money-to-rogue-websites-130625473.html (accessed March 09, 2021).

[43] See www.bsa.org/about-bsa?sc_lang=en-GB (accessed March 09, 2021).

[44] See https://reporting.bsa.org/r/report/add.aspx?src=us&ln=en-us (accessed March 09, 2021).

market and counterfeit issues and an opportunity for members to work together to identify solutions and tackle new challenges[45]

Enforcement Against Online Infringers

The U.S. Department of Justice (DoJ) Computer Crime and Intellectual Property Section (CCIPS) is responsible for execution of the DoJ's strategy for "combating computer and intellectual property crimes worldwide ..."[46] CCIPS's mandate is to "prevent, investigate, and prosecute computer crimes in collaboration with other government agencies, the private sector, academic institutions, and foreign counterparts ..."[47] DoJ recognizes that:

> Intellectual Property (IP) has become one of the principal U.S. economic engines, and the nation is a target of choice for thieves of material protected by copyright, trademark, or trade-secret designation ... [therefore] CCIPS attorneys regularly run complex investigations, resolve unique legal and investigative issues raised by emerging computer and telecommunications technologies; litigate cases; provide litigation support to other prosecutors; train federal, state, and local law enforcement personnel; comment on and propose legislation; and initiate and participate in international efforts to combat computer and intellectual property crime.[48]

The U.S. Internet Crime Complaint Center ("IC3"), formerly known as the Internet Fraud Complaint Center, was established as a partnership between the FBI and the National White Collar Crime Center to

---

[45] AGMA. December 16, 2020. "New Study Examines Evolving Challenges Posed by Counterfeit and Illicit Trade." Available at www.globenewswire.com/news-release/2020/12/16/2146435/0/en/New-Study-Examines-Evolving-Challenges-Posed-by-Counterfeit-and-Illicit-Trade.html (accessed March 09, 2021).
[46] Department of Justice, About CCIPS. Available at www.justice.gov/criminal/cybercrime/about/ (accessed March 09, 2021).
[47] *Id.*
[48] *Id.*

provide means of reporting Internet-related criminal complaints. IC3 can refer the criminal complaints to federal, state, local, or international law enforcement and regulatory agencies for any investigation they deem to be appropriate. The IC3 assists federal, as well as state, local, and international agencies combating Internet crime.

Since its inception, the IC3 has received complaints including online fraud, computer intrusions (hacking), economic espionage (theft of trade secrets), online extortion, international money laundering, identity theft, and other Internet-related crimes.[49]

Current laws already provide rights holders with means to pursue infringements of their intellectual properties in courts; however, it is not practical or possible to address all infringements everywhere. Rights holders need to decide where they can make the biggest impact; they need to evaluate damages caused and prioritize enforcement targets and follow up with investigation. Results of the investigation can lead to a number of activities, including sending cease and desist letters, product or website takedowns, civil or criminal litigation, and cooperation with government in criminal enforcement actions.

Megaupload, a file-sharing site, allowed for the unauthorized distribution of protected content through subscriptions and rewards for uploading. It was shut down by the FBI on January 19, 2012. Megaupload Ltd., based in Hong Kong, and related websites "generated more than $175 million in criminal proceeds and caused more than half a billion dollars in harm to copyright owners."[50] "[S]ites such as Megaupload, known as cyberlockers, have grown in popularity and shifted the technology and business of stealing content. Cyberlockers—so called because they offer virtual storage homes for files that can be accessed from any device ... are

---

[49] See www.ic3.gov/ (accessed March 09, 2021).

[50] See www.justice.gov/opa/pr/2012/January/12-crm-074.html (accessed March 03, 2021). Megaupload Limited and Vestor Limited—were indicted by a grand jury in the Eastern District of Virginia on January 05, 2012, and charged with engaging in a racketeering conspiracy, conspiring to commit copyright infringement, conspiring to commit money laundering and two substantive counts of criminal copyright infringement. *Megaupload Ltd.* 1:12-cr-00003-LO (E.D. Va., *filed January* 05, 2012).

often foreign sites that offer a smorgasbord of pirated movies, TV shows, music, and e-books that people can download with a few clicks ... and now account for about half of all online pirate activity ... ."[51]

"Before its shutdown, the file-sharing site Megaupload was, at its peak, the 13th most frequently visited site on the Internet, according to the Justice Department. The site itself claimed 50 million active users per day, 180 million registered users and nearly 800 file transfers a day." [52]

What Is Cybersquatting and How Does It Affect Business?

Just as choosing the best location on Main Street can be critical for brick-and-mortar stores looking to bring in customers, choosing the Internet address that will best lead customers to a brand is vital. When an individual or entity seeks to capitalize on another's brand by sweeping up the domain names potentially associated with that brand before the rightful owner can register them, the process is called cybersquatting. When consumers navigate to a website with the brand owner's name and find advertisements, inappropriate content, or simply an empty page, the result may be a loss of goodwill for the rights holder. Fortunately, Congress and the international community have passed measures designed to combat cybersquatting practices.[53]

This chapter will examine the practice of cybersquatting, state and federal legislation designed to combat the practice, how owners protect their domain names, and other issues in this area, such as Facebook usernames and the release of new gTLD names.

---

[51] See www.wsj.com/articles/SB1000142405297020461650457717106061194 8408 (accessed March 03, 2021).

[52] T. Hayley. January 20, 2012. "FAQ: What is Megaupload?" *Washington Post*. Available at www.washingtonpost.com/business/technology/faq-what-is-megaupload/2012/01/20/gIQAIiqFEQ_story.html (accessed March 03, 2021).

[53] Anticybersquatting Consumer Protection Act (ACPA), 15 U.S.C. § 1125(d).

What Is Cybersquatting and How Does It Affect Business?

When someone goes online, searching for a famous brand, perhaps a luxury brand purse, there will likely be thousands of results. Yet, it can be hard to tell which sites are authorized retailers of the name brand product. Dealers of counterfeit goods take advantage of this online consumer confusion to market their products.[54] By registering domain names that include the verbatim brand name or a slightly misspelled version, these illicit dealers mislead customers into believing that the dealers are offering the brand owners' products. The registrant may even attempt to profit from the site by either offering to sell it to the legitimate brand owner for a high price or by selling advertising on the site and profiting when consumers accidentally navigate to the page.

As of March 2015, more than 290 million top-level domain names had been registered, which marked an increase of 17.8 million domain names, or 6.5 percent, year over year.[55] Disputes over these domain names arise primarily in two contexts: cybersquatting and typosquatting. Cybersquatting is the act of reserving a domain name on the Internet, and then seeking to profit by selling or licensing the name to a company that has an interest in being identified with the domain name.[56]

Typosquatting occurs when an individual or entity registers a domain name that is a slight misspelling of a brand name.[57] This practice can result in requiring the registrant to transfer the misspelled domain name to the brand owner when the domain name is confusingly similar to the owner's mark and the registration was done in bad faith.[58]

---

[54] Chen. November 16, 2010. "Tis the Season to Shop and Counterfeiters Know that." *The Mark Monitor Blog*. Available at www.markmonitor.com/mmblog/tis-the-season-to-shop-and-the-counterfeiters-know-that/ (accessed March 09, 2021).

[55] "The Domain Name Industry Brief," 12 Verisign, Issue 2, p. 2 (June 2015).

[56] *Black's Law Dictionary* (9th ed. 2009).

[57] See ESPN, Inc. v. XC2, WIPO Case No. D2005-0444 (June 28, 2005). Available at www.wipo.int/amc/en/domains/decisions/html/2005/d2005-0444.html (accessed March 09, 2021).

[58] See: 24 Hour Fitness USA, Inc. v. Stanley Pace, Claim No. FA1003001315664 (National Arbitration Forum May 10, 2010), Available at www.adrforum.com/domaindecisions/1315664.htm (accessed March 09, 2021) (holding that domain

Because so much business is conducted on the Internet, it is crucial for a brand owner to keep track of both owned and unowned but potentially relevant domain names. These names allow potential consumers to easily find, communicate with, and ultimately purchase from the brand owner. When others improperly register and post information on a site with a domain name that a consumer would expect to be associated with the brand owner, it can blur or damage the brand owner's identity. For example, the registrant may sell counterfeit goods, post information that may harm the brand, or direct users to sites or content that may transfer viruses or malware to their computers.

Additionally, the prevalence of social networks creates a unique battle over the pages for brands or famous individuals. When these networks allow the creation of a "fan" page or dedicated URL, it falls to the brand owner to police the pages, to ensure that no one illicitly registers a page using the brand owner's trademark.[59]

For background, a domain name is created when the sequence of letters is registered with a registry operator.[60] The registry operator maintains the database that associates domain names with the Internet protocol numbers for the domain name servers.[61] Companies serve as registrars to

---

name 24houfitness.com was confusingly similar to Complainant's mark 24 HOUR FITNESS because removing the "r" was not enough to consider the domain name distinct from the trademark and pay-per-click links to Complainant's competitors was not bona fide offering of goods or services, and ordering transfer of the domain name to Complainant); Morgan Stanley v. Domain Admin c/o Taranga Services Pty Ltd., Claim No. FA1002001306534 (National Arbitration Forum April 01, 2010). Available at www.adrforum.com/domaindecisions/1306534.htm (accessed August 29, 2016) (holding Respondent's morganstanley.com was confusingly similar to Complainant's MORGAN STANLEY mark, the registration was made in bad faith because the domain name directed to a web page with Respondent's services and those of Complainant's competitors, and transferring the domain name to Complainant).

[59] For example, Facebook allows personalized usernames to appear at the end of the facebook.com address, that is, facebook.com/globalbranding.

[60] Coalition for ICANN Transparency, Inc. v. Verisign, Inc., 611 F.3d 495 (9th Cir. 2010).

[61] *Id.*

connect the servers and available domain names.[62] Finally, a registrant is the individual or entity who registers, or claims, a domain name for a fee through the registrar.

Overall, protecting brand identity online can be incredibly important because of the anonymity of the web and the inability to personally verify information. It is critical for brand owners to monitor domain name registrations as new domains open or new products are released, and to maintain the registrations for those sites. When cybersquatters do strike, avenues such as WIPO arbitration[63] allow quick and less expensive means for getting domain names back, while litigation in U.S. courts is longer and more expensive but provides more comprehensive remedies.[64] Finally, brand owners must stay current with the latest social network offerings and ensure that the only persona tied to the company is the official persona monitored by the owner.[65]

Responding to Cybersquatting

In the mid-1990s, as the Internet expanded and the practice of cybersquatting grew, the problems of brand ownership and trademark infringement became an issue that needed a forum for resolution and remedy.

Arbitration for Domain Name Disputes

The International Corporation of Assigned Names and Numbers (ICANN) was created in 1998 to oversee domain names and other identifying systems on the Internet.[66] In 1999, ICANN appointed the National Arbitration Forum ("Forum") to resolve domain name disputes around the world.[67] ICANN also instituted the Uniform Domain Name Dispute

---

[62] *Id.*

[63] See § 13.02[1] *infra.*

[64] See § 13.02[2]-[4] *infra.*

[65] See § 13.05 *infra.*

[66] ICANN, "What Does ICANN Do?" Available at www.icann.org/resources/pages/what-2012-02-25-en (accessed March 09, 2021).

[67] ICANN. 2021. "Timeline for the Formulation and Implementation of the Uniform Domain-Name Dispute-Resolution Policy." p. 1, Available at www.icann.org/resources/pages/what-2012-02-25-en (accessed March 09, 2021).

Resolution Policy (UDRP) to govern all accredited registrars, and it applies to transactions between the registrar and the customer or registrant of the domain name.[68] The UDRP governs most Forum disputes.[69] Today, the Forum provides limited relief at low cost for individuals and entities engaged in domain name disputes.[70] However, the UDRP only applies to trademark infringement in domain names, not to anything after the top-level domain (i.e., anything after ".com," ".net").[71]

Internationally, the World Intellectual Property Organization (WIPO) runs the WIPO Arbitration and Mediation Center for resolving domain name disputes outside of the United States.[72] The fast-track process offered by WIPO has allowed many famous individuals to take back domain names that use their personal names, including John Galliano, fired designer at the Christian Dior fashion house, Tom Cruise, and Julia Roberts.[73] Despite a brief lull around 2003, the prevalence of WIPO proceedings has grown each year since, as the number of domain names increases.[74]

---

[68] ICANN. October 24, 1999. "Uniform Domain Name Dispute Resolution Policy." Available at www.icann.org/resources/pages/help/dndr/udrp-en (accessed March 09, 2021).

[69] www.adrforum.com/domain-dispute (accessed March 09, 2021).

[70] ICANN. "Rules for Eligibility Requirements Dispute Resolution Policy." Available at www.icann.org/resources/pages/rules-c0-2012-02-25-en (accessed March 09, 2021).

[71] Romantic Tours, Inc. v. LiquidNet US LLC, Claim No. FA1003001316585 (National Arbitration Forum May 27, 2010), available at www.adrforum.com/domaindecisions/1316585.htm (accessed March 09, 2021) (holding the Claimant failed to establish the UDRP elements against Respondent's agencyscams.com/why/hotrussianbrides in part because "UDRP does not apply to trademark infringement in post-domains").

[72] WIPO, www.wipo.int/amc/en/domains/ (accessed March 09, 2021).

[73] "Galliano Wins Cybersquatting Case at U.N. Agency." *Reuters*. March 02, 2011. Available at http://mobile.reuters.com/article/idUSTRE7216UR20110302?ca=rdt (accessed March 09, 2021).

[74] "Cybersquatting hits record level, WIPO Center Rolls out New Services," WIPO (March 31, 2011), available at www.wipo.int/pressroom/en/articles/2011/article_0010.html (accessed March 09, 2021).

The UDRP proceedings by either the Forum or WIPO are not precedential for U.S. courts and the standards used by arbitration panels are different from those courts use to consider claims under the Lanham Act.[75]

U.S. Anti-Cybersquatting Legislation

In the United States, early cases of cybersquatting were addressed under federal dilution law.[76] But dilution law failed to provide a sufficient redress for the virtual land grab that was occurring as individuals scooped up famous domain names with the intent to sell them for large sums of money.[77] In 1999, the U.S. Congress passed the Anti-Cybersquatting Consumer Protection Act (ACPA)[78] and courts have relied on this legislation to address claims against registration of or trafficking in a domain name.[79] The ACPA provides two methods for going after cybersquatters. If the individual cybersquatter is known or can be found and is subject to personal jurisdiction, the trademark owner can sue the cybersquatter directly. However, if the cybersquatter is not subject to personal jurisdiction, a trademark owner can institute an in rem action against the domain name itself, but remedies are limited simply to the transfer of the domain name to the trademark owner.[80]

---

[75] *First Circuit:* Sallen v. Corinthians Licenciamentos LTDA, 273 F.3d 14, 28 (1st Cir. 2001).

Fourth Circuit: Barcelona.com, Inc. v. Excelentisimo Ayuntamiento De Barcelona, 330 F.3d 617, 626 (4th Cir. 2003).

[76] Panavision, International v. Toeppen, 945 F. Supp. 1296, 1303 (C.D. Cal. 1996), *aff'd* 141 F.3d 1316 (9th Cir. 1998) (holding defendant Toeppen's registration of Panavision.com diluted plaintiff's mark under Federal Dilution law 15 U.S.C. § 1125(a)-(c) because Panavision's mark was famous and the defendant was engaging in commercial use because his business was to register domain names and charge the mark holder a fee to gain control).

[77] "Lucas Nursery & Landscaping." Inc. v. Grosse, 359 F.3d 806, 808–809 (6th Cir. 2004).

[78] 15 U.S.C. § 1125(d) (Lanham Act § 43(d) cyberpiracy prevention).

[79] See Ford Motor Co. v. Greatdomains.com, Inc., 177 F. Supp.2d 635, 648 (E.D. Mich. 2001) ("Such acts must be challenged, if at all, under the ACPA").

[80] 15 U.S.C. § 1125(d)(2).

Personal Jurisdiction With ACPA Claim

The in personam action requires the following: (1) a distinctive or famous mark entitled to protection under the ACPA,[81] (2) a domain name that is identical or confusingly similar to the mark,[82] and (3) a registrant with a bad faith intent to profit from the mark.[83] Additionally, the ACPA expressly provides protection for personal names.[84]

The first two factors are familiar considerations in trademark law analysis—distinctiveness and likelihood of confusion analyses are the same as in cases arising under other areas of the statutory scheme. Because the ACPA was intended to curb illicit profiting from another's mark online,[85] much of the case law relies on whether the defendant/registrant had a bad faith intent to profit. The ACPA sets out a list of nine factors for courts to consider:

I. "The trademark or other intellectual property rights of the person, if any, in the domain name;

II. The extent to which the domain name consists of the legal name of the person or a name that is otherwise commonly used to identify that person;

III. The person's prior use, if any, of the domain name in connection with the bona fide offering of any goods or services;

IV. The person's bona fide non-commercial or fair use of the mark in a site accessible under the domain name;

V. The person's intent to divert consumers from the mark owner's online location to a site accessible under the domain name that could harm the goodwill represented by the mark, either for commercial gain or with the intent to tarnish or disparage the mark, by creating a likelihood of confusion as to the source, sponsorship, affiliation, or endorsement of the site;

---

[81] 15 U.S.C. § 1125(d)(1)(A)(iii).

[82] *Id.*

[83] 15 U.S.C. § 1125(d)(1)(A)(i).

[84] 15 U.S.C. § 1125(d)(1)(A)(ii)(III).

[85] H.R. Rep. 106-412 at *5 (October 25, 1999).

VI.   The person's offer to transfer, sell, or otherwise assign the domain name to the mark owner or any third party for financial gain without having used, or having an intent to use, the domain name in the bona fide offering of any goods or services, or the person's prior conduct indicating a pattern of such conduct;

VII. The person's provision of material and misleading false contact information when applying for the registration of the domain name, the person's intentional failure to maintain accurate contact information, or the person's prior conduct indicating a pattern of such conduct;

VIII. The person's registration or acquisition of multiple domain names which the person knows are identical or confusingly similar to marks of others that are distinctive at the time of registration of such domain names, or dilutive of famous marks of others that are famous at the time of registration of such domain names, without regard to the goods or services of the parties; and

IX.   The extent to which the mark incorporated in the person's domain name registration is or is not distinctive and famous within the meaning of [15 U.S.C. 1125] subsection (c) of this section."[86]

A registrant's statements to the media that he wants the mark holder to settle with him or make him an offer weighs toward a finding of bad faith.[87] In one case, the Fourth Circuit affirmed a district court's ruling finding the defendant's bad faith registration of peta.org in violation of ACPA when (1) the defendant had no intellectual property right in the domain name, (2) peta.org was not the defendant's name, (3) the defendant had not used the domain name to offer goods or services, (4) the defendant had used the name in a commercial manner, (5) the defendant intended to confuse customers looking for People for the Ethical Treatment of Animal's (PETA's) website, (6) the defendant made statements to the media, (7) the defendant used false information in

---

[86] 15 U.S.C. § 1125(d)(1)(B)(i).

[87] "People for the Ethical Treatment of Animals v. Doughney." 263 F.3d 359, 368 (4th Cir. 2001).

registering the domain, and (8) the defendant registered other marks of famous people and organizations.[88]

Bad faith was also found where defendants' income resulted from visitors clicking on links on the domain name website, sometimes leading to the plaintiff's competitors.[89] Generally, requests for money in exchange for transferring the domain name weigh strongly in favor of bad faith.[90] When a registrant has previously been punished by courts for registering several domain names of other mark holders, courts also find bad faith.[91] When a serial registrant registered drinkcoke.org, mycoca-cola. com, mymcdonalds.com, mypepsi.org, and my-washingtonpost.com, among other names, and offered to stop registering in exchange for space on the Washington Post's editorial page, the court found he was using the famous marks to mislead Internet users into thinking they were visiting the plaintiffs' websites.[92]

The bad faith factors do not all need to be met, if the court finds that the overall conduct was motivated by a bad faith intent to profit.[93] The unique circumstances of a case, even if they do not fit squarely into the nine statutory factors, have led to a finding of bad faith where evidence showed the registrant intended to enter into direct competition with the mark holder and the excuses given for registering the particular domain name were "more amusing than credible."[94]

---

[88] *Id.*, 263 F.3d at 369.

[89] Lahoti v. VeriCheck, Inc., 586 F.3d 1190, 1202–1203 (9th Cir. 2009).

[90] Ford Motor Co. v. Catalanotte, 342 F.3d 543, 549 (6th Cir. 2003).

[91] Lahoti v. VeriCheck, Inc., N. 24 *supra*.

[92] Coca-Cola v. Purdy, 382 F.3d 774 (8th Cir. 2004).

[93] *"Fourth Circuit:* Virtual Works." Inc. v. Volkswagen of America, Inc., 238 F.3d 264, 269 (4th Cir. 2001).

Fifth Circuit: The Southern Co. v. Dauben, Inc., 324 Fed. Appx. 309 (5th Cir. 2009).

Sixth Circuit: Lucas Nursery & Landscaping, Inc. v. Grosse, 359 F.3d 806, 811 (6th Cir. 2004).

[94] "Sporty's Farm LLC v. Sportsman's Market." Inc., 202 F.3d 489, 499 (2d Cir. 2000). But see, Southern Grouts & Mortars, Inc. v. 3M Co., 575 F.3d 1235, 1245–1246 (11th Cir. 2009) (when the unique circumstances lacked evidence of a bad faith intent to profit).

As a threshold matter, some courts have recognized a commercial use requirement—meaning the registrant must be using the domain name for a commercial purpose in order to be liable under the ACPA.[95] For example, registering a website to complain about medical services received would not trigger liability under ACPA.[96] Creating a parody website to criticize a famous reverend's views was also shielded from liability.[97]

Remedies for violation of the ACPA are more extensive than what is available under the UDRP arbitration. While forfeiture, cancellation and transfer of a domain name to the mark owner remain available,[98] mark owners may also recover either (a) defendant's profits, plaintiff's damages and costs,[99] or (b) statutory damages.[100] Statutory damages range from $1,000 to $100,000 per domain name. One repeat cybersquatter was once required to pay $100,000 per infringing domain name, for a total of $500,000.[101]

In Rem Jurisdiction for ACPA Claim

If the registrant of an infringing domain name is in another country, jurisdictional problems make it difficult for brand owners in the United States to reach the cybersquatter. When the registrant cannot be found after due diligence, a mark owner may file an in rem action against the

---

[95] Utah Lighthouse Ministry v. Foundation for Apologetic Information & Research, 527 F.3d 1045 (10th Cir. 2008).

[96] Bosley Medical Institute v. Kremer, 403 F.3d 672 (9th Cir. 2005).

[97] Lamparello v. Falwell, 420 F.3d 309 (4th Cir. 2005).

[98] 15 U.S.C. § 1125(d)(1)(C).

[99] 15 U.S.C. § 1117(a).

[100] 15 U.S.C. § 1117(d).

[101] "Electric Boutique Holdings Corp. v. Zuccarini." 2000 U.S. Dist. LEXIS 15719 (E.D. Pa. October 30, 2000) (after Zuccarini was enjoined from registering domain name misspellings, assessed damages of $10,000 per domain name, and required to pay attorney fees, Zuccarini continued to register misspellings that resulted in the present litigation, and the court imposed the damages because "Mr. Zuccarini boldly thumbs his nose at the rulings of this court and the laws of our country.").

domain name itself.[102] However, the only remedies available are forfeiture or cancelation of the domain name, or the transfer of the domain name to the owner.[103]

The in rem arm of the statute has been criticized for making U.S. law the trademark law of the Internet[104] and for running afoul of the Due Process clause of the Constitution.[105] In a Fourth Circuit case, the court looked to a Supreme Court case to determine that when claims to property itself are the source of the underlying controversy, then the presence of the property in the jurisdiction justifies the exercise of in rem jurisdiction.[106]

However, even disputes that seem as though they would not affect the United States, such as a dispute between an Italian airline and a foreign registrant who purchased the domain name casinoalitalia.com, have also been litigated in our courts.[107] The Eastern District of Virginia found personal jurisdiction in the forum because Virginia residents could view the website, business was conducted over the Internet and Virginia residents could interact with the website, and the record indicated five people had used the website and provided Virginia billing addresses.[108]

The Fourth Circuit court also determined that the in rem provision provides for jurisdiction under not only bad faith registration with intent

---

[102] 15 U.S.C. § 1125(d)(2)(A).

[103] 15 U.S.C. § 1125(d)(2)(D).

[104] Coran, S.J. 2001. "The Anticybersquatting Consumer Protection Act's In Rem Provision: Making American Trademark Law the Law of the Internet?" *Hofstra L. Rev* 30, pp. 169–188; Hwang, J. Summer 2004. Note "Is the ACPA a Safe Haven for Trademark Infringers?–Rethinking the Unilateral Application of the Lanham Act." *J. Marshall J. Computer & Info. L* 22. pp. 655–656.

[105] M.P. Allen. Winter 2002. "In Rem Jurisdiction from Pennoyer to Shaffer to the Anticybersquatting Consumer Protection Act." *Geo. Mason L. Rev* 11, pp. 243–266.

[106] "Harrods Ltd. v. Sixty Internet Domain Names." 302 F.3d 214, 225 (4th Cir. 2002) (construing *Shaffer v. Heitner, 433 U.S. 186,* 97 S.Ct. 2569, 53 *L.Ed.*2d 683 (1977).

[107] "Alitalia-Linee Aeree Italiane S.p.A. v. Casinoalitalia.Com." 128 F. Supp.2d 340 (E.D. Va. 2001).

[108] *Id.*, 128 F. Supp.2d at 350.

to profit but also the infringement and dilution causes of Title 15, Section 1125(a) and (c) of the United States Code.[109]

To that end, ACPA's in rem jurisdictional grant includes exclusively the judicial district in which the registrar or domain-name authority is located.[110] The plaintiff must initiate the action only in that district.

State Anti-Cybersquatting Legislation

Some states have instituted their own anti-cybersquatting legislation. In California, the Political Cyberfraud Abatement Act attempts to prevent confusion, which visitors may experience when viewing political websites.[111] New York protects individuals' names from being registered as domain names without their consent.[112]

Meanwhile, Utah's statute nearly mirrors the federal legislation, and allows a plaintiff to recover court costs, attorney fees, and statutory damages, in addition to giving its court jurisdiction to transfer domain names that are only protected in Utah, even if the cybersquatter is outside of Utah.[113] Similarly, Hawaii also forbids bad faith registration of a domain name that is identical or confusingly similar to a mark registered and used in Hawaii.[114] In addition to equitable relief, damages, costs, and attorney fees, Hawaii provides for punitive damages.[115]

Protecting Your Domain Name

Of course, most brand owners prefer protecting brand names before they are scooped up by squatters and without resorting to litigation. Many times the issue is not that a registrant has an infringing domain name, but rather that the registrant simply owns a domain name the brand owner desires. Domain names are frequently bought and sold overtly or

---

[109] *Id.*

[110] Mattel, Inc. v. Barbie-Club.com, 310 F.3d 293 (2d Cir. 2002).

[111] Cal. Corp. Code §§ 18320–18323.

[112] N.Y. GBS. L. §§ 148–149.

[113] Utah Code Ann. § 70-3a-309.

[114] Haw. Rev. Stat. § 481B-22.

[115] *Id.* at § 481B-25.

covertly.[116] The exchange can mean big money for the sellers. For example, in 2010, Sex.com sold for $13 million.[117] Facebook acquired fb.com from American Farm Bureau Federation for $8.5 million the same year.[118]

Renewing domain name registrations each year, or each period assigned by the registrar, is critical to most if not all businesses. When the Dallas Cowboys forgot to renew the registration for its domain name, the team's website went down and showed an ad for the company Network Solutions.[119] Fans were confused, especially as the time coincided with big news from the team.[120]

Keeping close track of the website and content housed on it can also be important. A New Jersey man pled guilty to what is considered the first conviction of theft of a domain name.[121] He accessed the P2P.com GoDaddy account and transferred the domain name to his own personal account. The man then put the website up for sale on eBay, where it was purchased by a NBA Los Angeles Clippers player for more than

---

[116] Major corporations frequently use agents, posing as potential buyers, to interact with domain name owners in order to avoid the markup the owners would certainly charge if they knew which company was interested in buying the domains.

[117] Domain Name Journal's 2010 Top 100 Sales Chart, available at www.dnjournal.com/archive/domainsales/2010/2010-final-ytd-sales-charts.htm (accessed March 09, 2021).

[118] "Farm Bureau finds wealthy friend in Facebook." *Reuters.* January 11, 2011. Available at http://blogs.reuters.com/mediafile/2011/01/11/farm-bureau-finds-wealthy-friend-in-facebook/ (accessed March 09, 2021) (the terms of the deal were not disclosed, but Farm Bureau officials told investors that the organization made $8.5 million selling a couple of domain names).

[119] "Report: Cowboys website goes down," ESPNDallas.com. November 09, 2010. Available at http://sports.espn.go.com/dallas/nfl/news/story?id=5783730 (accessed March 09, 2021).

[120] *Id.*

[121] DN Journal. July 22, 2011. "It's Official - Domain Thief Daniel Goncalves Sentenced to 5 Years in Prison in Precedent Setting Case." Available at www.dnjournal.com/archive/lowdown/2011/dailyposts/20110722.htm (accessed March 09, 2021).

$100,000.[122] The domain name owners did not notice until a visitor complained about some changed content on the site.[123]

Further, staying on top of newly released TLDs may also allow expanded branding opportunities. Top-level domains are the portion of the domain name appearing after the period, such as .com, .net or .org. Country abbreviations have been periodically released, although some require application processes and proof of intent to do business or some significant tie to the country.[124]

ICANN's release of generic top-level domains (gTLDs) allows companies to register domains closer to their brand. For instance, Ford may register ford.car. Businesses have objected to the implementation, the negative impact that may occur for large brands, and the high cost of defending brands from infringement.

Beyond Traditional Domain Names: Social Media Usernames

As users gravitate to social media, the opportunity to have a personal web page through services such as Facebook and Twitter has resulted in confusing registrations. In 2009, Facebook began its "username" feature, allowing brand owners and individuals to add a specialized username after the .com and pass this customized URL along to friends or customers.[125]

In the first five days of Facebook's customized addresses, 9.5 million people created their own usernames. Like the domain name debate, this was another chance for brand owners to create specialized pages to pull in consumers, and a chance for squatters to capitalize on the opportunity. Initially, Facebook gave trademark owners the opportunity to submit

---

[122] *Id.*

[123] *Id.*

[124] Gross. March 24, 2010. "Go Daddy to Stop Registering .CN Domain Names." *ComputerWorld,* Available at www.computerworld.com/s/article/9174058/ Go_Daddy_to_stop_registering_.cn_domain_names (accessed March 09, 2021) (China requires the registrar to provide photo identification, business identification, and physically signed registration for all domains).

[125] B. Stone June 17, 2009. "Keeping a True Identity Becomes a Battle Online." *The New York Times.* Available at www.nytimes.com/2009/06/18/technology/ internet/18name.html?_r=1 (accessed March 09, 2021).

their trademarks, and the website blocked any unauthorized requests to use those particular names. However, this process has since closed and the only opportunity for redress is through the form objection. Facebook does allow trademark owners to report an infringing username with a form accessed through the website's Help Center.[126] The value of the usernames themselves is questionable, because Facebook does not allow transfer of usernames from one account to another. Yet, nothing stops a user from handing over an account login and password to an entity willing to pay for it.

For a period of time, Twitter also allowed individuals and entities to verify their accounts, so users could tell the Tweets were actually coming from a legitimate source.[127] Without this process, it can be easy for an individual to snag a famous person's name and begin Tweeting through that person's persona. For example, the city of Chicago watched as the 2010 mayoral election heated up and an individual Tweeting @MayorEmanuel offered daily thoughts, expletives, and outbursts.[128] The problem was that the communications were not those of the eventually elected mayor, Rahm Emanuel. Then-candidate Emanuel drew the responsible culprit out from anonymity by offering a charitable award in exchange for the person revealing himself.

---

[126] Facebook, www.facebook.com/help/contact/208282075858952 (accessed March 09, 2021).

[127] Twitter. http://support.twitter.com/groups/31-twitter-basics/topics/111-features/articles/119135-about-verified-accounts (accessed March 09, 2021).

[128] M. Caro. February 28, 2011. "'Mayor Emanuel' Tweeter Revealed." *Chicago Tribune.* Available at http://articles.chicagotribune.com/2011-02-28/news/ct-met-mayor-emanuel-0301-20110228_1_mayoremanuel-twitterer-dan-sinker (accessed March 09, 2021).

CHAPTER 9

New Technologies and Alternative Methods to Combat Counterfeiting and Grey Market

Expanding global trade has brought about more complexity in supply chain management. Ever-increasing numbers of suppliers, products, raw materials, and components coming from different parts of the world lengthened the overall supply chain resulting in "elongation" in every step of supply chains and provided yet another "infiltration" opportunity for counterfeiters.

The report commissioned by the International Trademark Association (INTA) and the International Chamber of Commerce (ICC) indicates that counterfeiting and piracy could reach a value of $3.2 trillion by 2022. The Organization for Economic Cooperation and Development (OECD) estimates that the global loss of jobs due to counterfeit goods will amount to 4.2 to 5.2 million by 2022.[1]

Using solely conventional techniques to combat counterfeiting and grey market is no longer sufficient. Inadequate supply chain management can lead to undesirable results: the examples of disruptions and undesirable outcomes can be found in all industries and some industries such as food, pharmaceutical or automotive, it also comes with tackling public health or consumer safety. For most industries, a lack of visibility of the entire supply chain process significantly increases the risks of waste,

---

[1] See https://iccwbo.org/publication/economic-impacts-counterfeiting-piracy-report-prepared-bascap-inta/#:~:text=We%20find%20significant%20effects%20on,to%205.4%20million%20by%202022 (accessed March 25, 2021)

losses (such as pilferage and product leaks), delays, and grey market which results in reputational risks to their businesses.

Fortunately, while counterfeiters and grey marketers are "inventing" new ways to undermine the rights holders and scam the unsuspecting consumers, some new technologies show promising results in combating such activity in new ways.

Artificial Intelligence

Many businesses look for assistance from IP law firms, investigators, and brand protection professionals to help reduce the financial losses they incur from the counterfeiting of their products. However, most traditional means of detecting and disrupting counterfeiting operations used today are time consuming, reactive, and slow in delivering the results. Taking down websites and shops selling counterfeit products are temporary fixes as many of these operations resurface under new names, websites, and shops.

The counterfeiters' "modus operandi" is constantly changing. Financial hardships brought about by increasing unemployment caused by the pandemic have created an incentive for illicit operators to take the risk of smuggling (yet again) larger shipments of cheaper counterfeit goods, this is a shift from the past where counterfeiters used smaller size shipments, direct mail, and courier services to avoid the detection by spreading the goods over multiple shipments and lowering the losses from detention of such smaller shipments versus from a single large container.

Good news is that advances in artificial intelligence (AI) and Machine Learning (ML) provide rights holders with the opportunities to analyze a large amount of data across the supply chains and predict suspect activities and shipments.

Typology and Analytics, KYC, and AML connection

Rights holders need to use better strategic research direction to ensure the current illicit players are fully investigated and their complete network is mapped out. They need to understand (i) who are the "ring leaders," the distributors, the production and marketing; (ii) how does the distribution work and who else is involved in it; (iii) how are the goods declared as and how are the channels working; (iv) the key individuals at the top of the counterfeiting network; (v) what other criminal activities the targets may be involved in to increase the scale of their penalties; and (vi) location of their assets to assist in seizures.

"Following the money" and using typology of a financial crime can be effective in disrupting counterfeiting networks. There are AI-enabled tools that can get the job done. For example, **RisikoTek**'s SaaS platform Amalia[2] provides an analysis of the networks related to the targeted companies and individuals. It provides initial review and looks for signs of criminal activity using data such as company and director data, adverse media, sanctions, and PEPs (politically exposed persons), producing a network of the targets (dynamic network diagram) and case findings report. Further, it can dive deeper into the actors' key networks, analyze trade data for suspicious trade patterns (tax/duty evasion) from import/export trade data and government data, and deliver a law enforcement (grade) case report.

How is it done? By studying the typologies for all known red flags to investigate (e.g., typologies for cigarette smuggling and counterfeiting, selection of typologies and patterns for investigation), connecting to key databases (e.g., global company data, global trade data, and global people risk data). Using algorithms it performs data ingestion, pattern investigation and analytics, data analytics, supplementary secondary research, and combinations and variations. Further, by analyzing all individuals involved (their social networks, past criminal convictions, linked people and their activities), RisikoTek can establish how much tax has likely been evaded, helps to understand the goods movements for volume, understand the patterns of movement, and aim to forecast seizures. It also helps to understand how the money laundering is likely working, targets company structures and understands the people involved, builds out the full network of production, distribution, marketing and sales, understands the geographies in operation and the industry declaration, and continuously monitor new company opening and new people involved.

---

[2] www.risikotek.com/solutions.html (accessed March 29, 2021).

Gray Falkon's Horus[3] is a proprietary AI and automation technology protecting brand owners from rogue sellers. Horus can eliminate 86 percent of illegitimate sellers by simultaneously pursuing two channels that are critical to eradicating unauthorized product transactions: the marketplace and the seller. By developing detailed profiles of each illegitimate seller and studying them, Horus learns the habits of each illegitimate seller and sends direct tailored messages to coerce them to remove their listings. It can predict the sellers' behavior in order to effectively respond to their rogue activity. As the unauthorized resale and digital market place landscapes change, Horus maneuvers through the complicated landscape of evolving policies and loopholes in these online spaces, learns the new terrain and changes its strategy to adapt to each unique challenge and engage in evicting illegitimate sellers.

Dangerous Goods, Undeclared/Misdeclared Goods

The International Cargo Handling Coordination Association has estimated that among all cargos that are declared, approximately 55 percent contain one or more deficiencies.[4] However, the deficiencies alone do not pose serious threats, unless they contain counterfeits including dangerous goods such as counterfeit drugs that can harm the consumer.

According to Drewry Shipping Consultants Ltd., the fines imposed on misdeclaration may lead to more carriers to follow the regulations, but while the threat of financial punishment might help to correct the behavior of the less negligent shippers, it is unlikely to change the attitude of any rogue shipper who will continuously attempt to evade the net.

This is where AI and ML can play a pivotal role. For example, Singapore based **Moaah Pte. Ltd.**[5] uses AI deep learning and ML to identify the dangerous goods by abstracting information from the International Maritimes Dangerous Goods (IMDG) code, United Nations Economic Commission for Europe (UNECE) list, and other relevant regulatory

---

[3] www.grayfalkon.com/horus (accessed April 26, 2021).
[4] See www.agcs.allianz.com/news-and-insights/expert-risk-articles/shipping-2020-loss-trends-misdeclared-cargo.html (accessed March 29, 2021).
[5] https://moaah.com/ (accessed March 29, 2021).

documents. Because shippers may deliberately provide misleading information, MOAAH includes searches for commonly used misdescription terms as well as analyzes the shippers' behavioral patterns with the dangerous substance alert list and provides customizable analytics to carriers, ports of authorities, and cargo facilities.

Goods Authenticity

Ensuring traceability and reducing waste are the major hurdles for an efficient export supply chain of perishable food. It is estimated that optimizing efficiency to reduce inventory by only half a day could lead to more than 40 percent reduction in food waste (*source* IMD).

With a unique combination of sensors and analytics companies like **Rubens Technologies**[6] can monitor quality and ensure proof of provenance of your crop and food. Rubens' molecular fingerprint provides data and intelligence about a food product without damaging it (if it's fresh) or opening it (if it's bottled or wrapped). Data is acquired directly from the product itself, not a label or a barcode, uniquely linking your product to its digital image. For instance, we can prove the authenticity of a bottle of wine capturing data from the wine itself measured through the bottle. The proprietary AI algorithms provide analytics and authenticity verification.

Veracity Protocol's[7] microstructure traceability SaaS solution is built on over 30 Computer Vision (CV)/ML methods and proprietary datasets with tens of millions of microstructure images designed to trace and secure a product's integrity, identity, and authenticity that can be verified and traced using only a smartphone. As every object has its own unique material structure and manufacturing characteristics, this noninvasive and tamper-proof solution enables any camera to capture these characteristics and create a digital asset—Physical Code—that links the physical object itself to client's business applications. Physical Code cannot be changed, manipulated, or tampered with because it is based on an item's unique material structure—unlike tags, chips, or invisible markers. It is resistant

---

[6] https://rubenstech.com/ (accessed March 31, 2021).

[7] www.veracityprotocol.org/ (accessed April 30, 2021).

to damages, different lighting, and camera variability, and it works on many materials with no special hardware devices with up to 99.99 percent accuracy. The solution can also be used for detecting compromised hardware, product tampering and anomalies, track and trace down to a product's component level, automating QA and visual inspection in manufacturing, verification of authenticity of ID documents, detection of tampered or altered ID documents, automating batch authentication, and so on. It securely links physical items to any database or blockchain allowing anyone to create an immutable digital twin of an item enabling reliable track and trace, provenance and ownership transfer.

Blockchain

Internet of Things (IoT) technologies, smarter supply chains, assisted by digital and physical infrastructures, where smart objects can communicate and collaborate directly without human intervention, are rapidly emerging. Entire systems can be interconnected—supply chains not only with other supply chains but also with transportation systems and financial markets. With built-in intelligence, rights holders abilities can shift from decision support to decision delegation and, ultimately, predictability. Next-generation "control towers" will be intelligent and data-driven. For example, **Portcast**[8] enables real-time dynamic supply chain visibility through ML and advanced datasets, accurately predicting container arrival and forecasting cargo demand.

Although operational activities, such as the tracing and tracking of goods, are already implemented in smart supply chains via various methods, a hype related to crypto and underlying technology—blockchain open the question of a potential use case within the supply chains. Overall, blockchain technology can be used to verify the authenticity and the quality of physical assets in a cost-efficient and simple manner, and create reliable end-to-end visibility, contributing to business success and customer satisfaction. Blockchain can deliver security, trust, transparency, and speed, which are desirable capabilities for the digital economy.

---

[8] https://portcast.io/ (accessed March 29, 2021).

Use in a Supply Chain

The trusted chain of custody, known ownership, title transfer, notarization, and time stamping of all cryptocurrency events is what a trusted supply chain could use, and together with the immutability of the encrypted Hyperledger containing all the events and transactions, adapting a blockchain platform for use in supply chain is "a no-brainer," although there is unlikely much use for blockchains in supply chains beyond the Hyperledger.

Year 2020 has shown that supply chains are both vital and very vulnerable, underscoring the need for trust and transparency. To meet that need, blockchain can play an increasingly prominent role and Hyperledger technologies can underpin most of the biggest and best-known networks, including FoodTrust and TradeLens. There are successful examples of Hyperledger technologies in action in the supply chain space.

Accenture: True Supplier Marketplace

Inaccurate supplier master data and incomplete risk assessments can cost businesses on average $15 million per year. Accenture used Hyperledger Fabric to develop a double-sided procurement marketplace to source, onboard, and maintain supplier relationships dropping onboarding from weeks to hours, while adherence to risk assessments improves. By giving suppliers ownership of their own data, the solution creates a shared source of truth between parties that improves risk compliance, speeds time to onboard, and removes the manual effort required to maintain siloed systems. Accenture's True Supplier Marketplace is live and available now.

DL Freight

Developed by DLT Labs,[9] DL Freight is the standard for freight invoice management for Walmart Canada and its national network of third-party transportation companies or carriers. The system tracks deliveries, verifies transactions, and automates invoices in real time across the network of

---

[9] www.dltlabs.com/ (accessed April 02, 2021).

up to 70 different carriers in Walmart's supply chain. DL Freight is built on Hyperledger Fabric, an open-source platform that allows Walmart to bring together the carriers within its multipartner freight operations, under one architecture, to automate and implement universal workflows across the network. At the same time, through Hyperledger Fabric's unique "channels" feature, the solution allows independent and protected relationships for each organization directly between itself and Walmart, and the information is not accessible to other members.

Within DL Freight, carriers are the peers, and the governance of the platform is controlled by the applicable contracts, as in any conventional business. The difference is that the freight, legal, and finance departments of Walmart, as well as all the carriers, have all agreed that the solution fairly and accurately represents those agreements so it processes them automatically. As a result, it has removed the guesswork and any real potential for dispute over the interpretation of agreements.

Telefónica's e2e Supply Chains

In the context of the ever-increasing complexity of supply chains, collaboration has become a key to streamlining operations. To manage this complexity, Telefónica[10] launched a project to transform the way it collaborates with third parties by blockchain-enabled e2e Supply Chain solutions to make it faster, simpler, and more efficient. Trust is at the heart of that collaboration, and, to build that trust, Telefónica selected Hyperledger Fabric as the underlying technology that serves as a secure and transparent single source of truth for all.[11] Telefónica started using the blockchain-based supply chain solution to support one of its core products—CPE (Customer Premise Equipment)—the routers, decos, and other devices that provide connectivity and services at home to their

---

[10] www.telefonica.com/en/ (accessed April 02, 2021).

[11] PRESS RELEASE: Telefónica Tech and Alastria launch a blockchain network based on Hyperledger Fabric for productive applications (February 05, 2021), https://iot.telefonica.com/en/whats-new/news/telef%C3%B3nica-tech-y-alastria-impulsan-una-red-blockchain-basada-en-hyperledger-fabric-para-aplicaciones-productivas/ (accessed April 02, 2021).

customers. The company manufactures over 15 million serialized devices a year that are then distributed and installed by a field force of over 30,000 technicians.

Telefónica put this blockchain platform for operations into production in 2019 in Brazil, where the program delivered ROI in less than six months. Telefónica is planning to extend the use of its blockchain-enabled e2e solution to the rest of its fixed operations and other products in the coming months.

Trust Your Supplier

Just named as the 2020 Winner of Blockchain Revolution's Innovative Entrepreneurship in Blockchain Award in the Supply Chain Applications category, Trust Your Supplier is an innovative solution developed in a partnership between IBM and Chainyard to address the inefficiencies and risks associated with supplier information management. During this time of a global pandemic, many buyers are procuring goods and services in the context of a supply-constrained situation. This has resulted in substantial challenges in vetting and onboarding new suppliers.

Built on Hyperledger Fabric, Trust Your Supplier provides both a cross-industry network and a blockchain-secured platform to speed onboarding and minimize risk. Blockchain provides cryptographic security that allows suppliers to control access to their single digital identity. Buyers are able to view profiles of their connected suppliers, as well as a timeline of all the various activities that have taken place with this supplier. Writing this information onto the blockchain allows for an immutable record of all the events that have taken place with this supplier and are fantastic for supporting auditing capabilities. Trust Your Supplier is bringing speed, accuracy, and most importantly trust, to supplier information management and the supply chain needs of today's world.[12]

---

[12] www.hyperledger.org/blog/2020/10/28/hyperledger-powered-supply-chain-solutions-in-action (accessed April 02, 2021).

Use in Brand Protection

There have been some well-publicized initiatives in the physical goods supply chain that has blockchain as the reinforcements of "protection," involving data entry at various points along the supply chain, with product transaction updates (blocks) input into the ledger history (chain) by a variety of methods. For example, special readers identifying the gemstones. However, each point of such supply chain would require these specialized devices to update the provenance of the item.

In more common use, barcodes are being used throughout the supply chain as the method of identifying goods and uploading the data to the shared blockchain ledger. Even here, there is still a natural limitation in using barcodes as they are disconnected between the product packaging, palettes, and containers, and decidedly nondigital. Barcodes are also easily replicated, which reduces the trust in mass barcode utilization using blockchain. Barcode-enabled physical product blockchain solutions, require the capability not to just read the barcode but also authenticate it as legitimate, and connect it to the digital records creating a closed loop of trust necessary for physical (nondigital) items. Linking serialized barcodes with static UPC codes can add a packaging link between the digital blockchain and the physical item; this, together with other authentication solutions such as covert/overt authentication labels, security inks, and taggants, can establish a trusted link between the physical and the digital. These solutions designed to reduce the risk of counterfeits connecting to the blockchain usually require physical application to the packaging; this is adding significant cost and complexity to the pack-out or manufacturing process and in some cases taking up valuable product or packaging real estate and, unfortunately, can still be replicated by sophisticated counterfeiters. However, the barcodes still have the untapped potential to be the critical link of the physical product to the digital world, and closing the blockchain loop. However, the printing process is not perfect. Manufacturing and environmental conditions such as line speed, air quality, humidity, ink level, and substrate variances introduce microdifferentiations in the printing process. Millions of the same UPC codes are printed daily, yet they are inherently unique and could be leveraged to create a distinctive identifier for each individual item.

Increasing interest in the sustainability and ethical sourcing of food as well as apparel by consumers drives a need to prove the origins of sourced food, ingredients, and textiles. While the basic tracking can be handled by existing supply chain process, blockchain is being implemented as a solution because it can also handle the tracking and tracing of the related product metadata (e.g., farm, harvesting, and processing dates, locations, and so on, and as a result adding to the authenticity of the produce).

For blockchain to provide credible safety and brand protection in the supply chain, it needs to provide not just the assurance of item authenticity but also a seamless product data connectivity path. With encryption, immutability and peer-to-peer visibility, blockchain can deliver a strong system to create and manage a product's digital identity and provide a viable resource for brand protection.

The dynamics and requirements of the supply chain make blockchain something that leaders must investigate. Closing the loop of physical world to digital world is a critical issue when evaluating blockchain for supply chain use. The ability to connect the once nonconnected to ensure authenticity is a critical step to achieving ultimate product safety, brand protection, and consumer satisfaction.

Robotics

Why are we talking about robotics and what does robotics have to do with brand protection? The answer is quite simple. The pandemic created a need for "touchless" and monitored end-to-end process from the vendors all the way to a consumer ensuring no disruption to the consistency of such supply chain, with no interjection points (for counterfeiters or fraudsters).

Storage and Securing a Supply Chain

The requirements for new technologies within the traditional warehousing market are prompting a rethink of fulfillment and ensuring the authenticity of the goods. Today the vast majority of e-commerce fulfillment is done using very traditional (human) warehousing, picking/packaging, and shipping methodologies. These are labor intensive, real estate intensive, extremely complicated, and difficult to scale. Moreover, they provide the opportunity for illicit goods to enter the supply chain.

Attabotics,[13] a Calgary, AB-based company offers 3D robotic goods-to-person storage, retrieval, and real-time order fulfillment that can secure the end-to-end supply chain. Attabotics is reinventing a more efficient, agile, and simple supply chain world. Their robotics technology is a disruptive change to goods-to-person fulfillment, and the vision is to change the face of today's supply chain. Besides reducing the real estate by implementing 3D storage solution, use of proprietary storage bins with sensors and monitoring devices that allow product to seamlessly flow between the originator (supplier) through 3PL to seller and end user , 3D storage real-time monitoring, provides solution not just the authentication but information on the source, and status of the goods. This is without having to rely on blockchain applications as a tool to provide the two-source authentication.

Security and Monitoring

While Attabotics' solution enables end-to-end monitoring and security, there are many other solutions and attempts focusing on securing the last mile security. The most prevalent technology to enable the end-to-end and the last mile tracking is the use of IoT tracking devices. 5G technology enables wider use of such devices, though one has to query how all these solutions address the cybersecurity of all solutions that are always online, connected to the Internet and communication networks.

Traceability and Authentication Technologies

An estimated 10 percent of all retail products are counterfeit, adulterated, or not from declared sources. To prevent counterfeiting and to track your raw materials back to their origins, there are several technologies in development none of which however have been widely adapted. These include biomarkers/molecular fingerprint, DNA sequencing,

---

[13] www.attabotics.com/ (accessed April 09, 2021).

DNA barcoding, isotope ratio mass spectrometer (IRMS), molecular fingerprint, and rare earths.

DNA Sequencing/Barcoding

Companies such as **NaturalTrace** can provide batch-level traceability, very high accuracy, and 100 percent clean (fully vegan, halal, kosher, allergen, and GMO-free) labels. Partnering with state-of-the art DNA sequencing device manufacturers for cost competitive, fast, and robust field applications, each batch has a different combination of markers (mixtures of proprietary plants with unique sequences). The technology will support a virtually unlimited number of unique codes. Each marker code has a unique block chain number. Markers are shelf stable and tamper proof and their primary use is in high value food and fragrance ingredient industry.

Isotope Ratio Mass Spectrometer (IRMS)

Technologies such as IRMS and multicollector inductively coupled plasma mass spectrometry (MC–ICP–MS) can provide forensic evidence and can be used for the detection of counterfeit pharmaceuticals.

"An extensive study for the antiviral drug Heptodin™ has been performed for several isotopic ratios combining MC-ICP-MS and an elemental analyser EA-IRMS for stable isotope amount ratio measurements. The study has been carried out for 139 batches of the antiviral drug and analyses have been performed for C, S, N, and Mg isotope ratios. Authenticity ranges have been obtained for each isotopic system and combined to generate a unique multi-isotopic pattern only present in the genuine tablets. Counterfeit tablets have then been identified as those tablets with an isotopic fingerprint outside the genuine isotopic range.

The combination of those two techniques has therefore great potential for pharmaceutical counterfeit detection. A much greater power of discrimination is obtained when at least three isotopic systems are combined. The data from these studies could be presented as evidence in court and therefore methods need to be validated to support their credibility. It is also crucial to be able to produce uncertainty values associated to the isotope amount ratio measurements so that significant differences can be identified and the genuineness of a sample can be assessed."[14]

Molecular Fingerprint

Rubens Technologies'[15] molecular fingerprint provides data and intelligence about a food product without damaging it (if it's fresh) or opening it (if it's bottled or wrapped). Data is acquired directly from the product itself, not a packaging, label, or a barcode, using Rubens' own multispectral scanner.

Typical use cases include nondestructive product quality assessment (for instance, predicting how sweet a pineapple is going to be at different stages along the supply chain) for perishable items and authenticity of specific products.

About a third of the food produced every year in the world is wasted at some stage along the supply chain with an estimated value of about $1T, let alone the societal and environmental impact of the waste. At the same time, food frauds and food safety issues are on the rise. For instance, 1 in 10 people will get sick by food poisoning over the course of their life. WHO estimated that this amounts to 33 million years of healthy lives lost due unsafe food each year.

All of these issues are connected to different extents to the lack of transparency affecting supply chains. Products often have a long journey from producer to consumers, whereby the lack of trust and oversight has a negative impact on quality for the consumers, and causes loss of income for the producers.

Rubens' combination of sensors, analytics, and AI is uniquely linking products to their digital image and proving the authenticity being it a

---

[14] "Detection of counterfeit antiviral drug Heptodin™ and classification of counterfeits using isotope amount ratio measurements by multicollector inductively coupled plasma mass spectrometry (MC-ICPMS) and isotope ratio mass spectrometry (IRMS)" *Science & Justice* 49, no. 2, June 2009, Elsevier; www.sciencedirect.com/science/article/abs/pii/S1355030608001603 (accessed April 07, 2021).

[15] https://rubenstech.com/ (accessed April 07, 2021).

bottle of wine or whiskey—capturing data from the wine itself measured through the bottle, or fragrance, or packaged meat.

Alternative Approaches to Enforcement

Ovid said, "gutta cavat lapidem non vi sed saepe cadendo" (water hollows a stone not by force but persistence).[16] Sometimes this is exactly what rights holders have to do to protect their brand and reputation. Where the classical methods of enforcement do not deliver desired outcomes, alternate methods may succeed.

Taking Down "whack-a-moles"

Online listings takedowns are not effective (whack-a-mole effect—online listings taken down more often than not reappear again later (modified or unmodified) on the same seller store or new store that belongs to the original seller, or even under a new business that again is linked or owned by the initial seller), have significant reoccurring costs, and are often cost prohibitive to smaller rights holder/brands.

Unified Brands' The ANTICOUNTERFEITER (shown in Figure 9.1) is a service that can produce between $100,000 and $2 million (on average) for the brand holder, with no costs or long-term commitment, while stopping fake listings and deterring future activity.[17] How does it work?

---

[16] Pūblius Ovidius Nāsō, known in English as Ovid, was a Roman poet who lived during the reign of Augustus.

[17] www.unifiedbrands.us/ (accessed April 07, 2021).

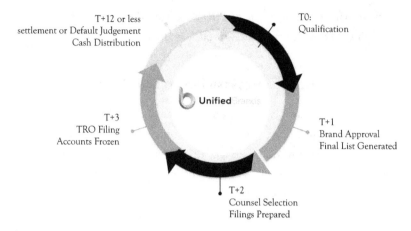

Figure 9.1 Unified brands' The anti-counterfeiter service

Protection your IP against NPE/Patent Trolls

Protecting Unified Patents is a 200+ international membership organization that seeks to improve patent quality and deter unsubstantiated or invalid patent assertions. Its actions are focused broadly in technology sectors with substantial assertions by standards essential patents (SEP) holders and/or nonpracticing entities (NPEs). These actions may include analytics, prior art, invalidity contests, patentability analysis, administrative patent review (PTAB), amicus briefs, economic surveys, and essentiality studies. Unified works independently of its members to achieve its deterrence goals. Small members join for free, while larger ones pay modest annual fees.[18]

---

[18] www.unifiedpatents.com/join (accessed April 07, 2021).

CHAPTER 10

International Remedies

Global business leaders make their important decisions after taking into consideration not only variable market factors such as customer preference and demand, competition, and local economic ecosystem, but also factors that can enable or disable, accelerate or decelerate, and protect or expose their intellectual property in local markets around the world. These include international treaties and trade agreements, laws, and governmental, intergovernmental, and other agencies that help to enforce intellectual property rights (IPR).[1] This chapter provides a brief overview of the most relevant U.S. trade agreements and global treaties for protection of intellectual property throughout the world, as well as the challenges and potential remedies.

---

[1] 2021 Trade Policy Agenda and 2020 Annual Report OF THE PRESIDENT OF THE UNITED STATES ON THE TRADE AGREEMENTS PROGRAM, published by the Office of the United States Trade Representative (USTR), is a survey of significant foreign barriers to U.S. exports throughout the world. It includes individual reports on various countries and information about what they are doing to eliminate these barriers. National Trade Estimate Report on Foreign Trade Barriers, Available at https://ustr.gov/sites/default/files/files/reports/2021/2021%20Trade%20Agenda/Online%20PDF%202021%20Trade%20Policy%20Agenda%20and%202020%20Annual%20Report.pdf (accessed March 18, 2021).

The Special 301 Report, detailing efforts to maintain adequate IPR protection and enforcement worldwide, includes identification of issues such as deterioration of protection in some countries and the continuing challenges of copyright piracy in others. Office of the United States Trade Representative, "Special 301 Report" (2019). Available at https://ustr.gov/sites/default/files/2019_Special_301_Report.pdf (accessed March 18, 2021).

World Customs Organization (WCO)

The WCO is an intergovernmental organization focused exclusively on Customs matters. It is recognized for its work in such areas as the development of global standards for Customs procedures, facilitation, and security of international trade, Customs compliance activities, anti-counterfeiting and piracy initiatives, and sustainable Customs capacity-building programs. "The WCO also maintains the international Harmonized System goods nomenclature, and administers the technical aspects of the WTO Agreements on Customs Valuation and Rules of Origin."[2]

The WCO introduced IPM (Interface Public-Members) to the world's senior Customs officials during the WCO Council Meeting in June 2010.[3] IPM is a secure, web-based communication platform for the exchange of information among rights holders and Customs administrations. It provides right holders with access to the WCO's tools, publications (e.g., compilations of national legislations on IPR, counterfeiting reports by sector or by project) and the genuine/fake database used by field Customs officers. The genuine/fake information is entered by rights holders and contains product information highlighting key features such as brand name and product appearance, packaging, and routes. It provides Customs officers with valuable information to help them identify suspect products. This database serves as a continuous training tool available to Customs officers in the field and accessible via Customs officers' intranet, and includes real-time updates by the rights holders.

IPM has been developed to be accessible to Customs field officers anywhere in the world, at any time, in their own language, via simple and secure user interfaces. Customs administrations across all continents have expressed an interest in using IPM, which will also be offered to all the

---

[2] World Customs Organization. Available at http://unstats.un.org/unsd/trade/globalforum/international-organizations.asp (accessed March 18, 2021).

[3] The Interface Public-Members (IPM) platform, the World Customs Organization's unique tool in the fight against counterfeiting, became operational in 2011 and has already seen many improvements since its conception, available at www.wcoomd.org/en/media/newsroom/2015/october/wco-launches-the-new-ipm-platform.aspx (accessed March 18, 2021).

national and international agencies involved in combating counterfeiting and piracy.[4]

International Treaties

The following is a discussion of the international treaties currently in effect that are applicable to U.S. rights holders concerned with the ability to protect and enforce their IPR in foreign markets.

Agreement on Trade-Related Aspects of Intellectual Property Rights (TRIPS)

The TRIPS Agreement[5] is Annex 1C of the Marrakesh Agreement, the establishing agreement of the World Trade Organization, signed in Marrakesh, Morocco, on April 15, 1994, and was negotiated at the end of the Uruguay Round of the General Agreement on Tariffs and Trade (GATT).[6]

The TRIPS Agreement pioneered intellectual property law in international trade. TRIPS (Part II: Standards concerning the availability, scope, and use of Intellectual Property Rights) requires that a nations' laws must protect (1) copyright and other related rights, including the rights of performers and content producers such as those in music and movies; (2) trademarks; (3) geographical indications, including appellations of origin; (4) industrial designs; (5) patents; (6) layout designs (topographies) of integrated circuits; undisclosed information; and control of anticompetitive practices in contractual licenses.[7] TRIPS

---

[4] See https://ustr.gov/trade-agreements/free-trade-agreements/united-states-mexico-canada-agreement/fact-sheets/modernizing (accessed March 18, 2021).

[5] See www.wto.org/english/tratop_e/trips_e/trips_e.htm#:~:text=The%20 WTO%20Agreement%20on%20Trade,on%20intellectual%20property%20 (IP).&text=The%20Agreement%20is%20a%20legal,for%20a%20balanced%20IP%20system. (accessed March 18, 2021).

[6] See www.wto.org/english/docs_e/legal_e/legal_e.htm (accessed March 18, 2021).

[7] See www.wto.org/english/thewto_e/whatis_e/tif_e/agrm7_e.htm (accessed March 18, 2021).

(Part III: Enforcement of Intellectual Property Rights) also details (1) general obligations; (2) civil and administrative procedures and remedies; (3) provisional measures; (4) special requirements related to border measures; and (5) criminal procedures.[8]

World Intellectual Property Organization Copyright Treaty ("WIPO Copyright Treaty")

The WIPO Copyright Treaty is an international treaty on copyright law adopted in 1996 by the member states of the World Intellectual Property Organization (WIPO); the Treaty entered into force on March 6, 2002.[9] Parties to this Treaty must adhere to the provisions of the Berne Convention for the Protection of Literary and Artistic Works and observe additional protections for computer programs[10] and for the arrangement and selection of database material.[11]

The Treaty gives authors the right to control rental and distribution of their works.[12] It requires adequate legislative and legal support of

---

[8] See www.wto.org/english/thewto_e/whatis_e/tif_e/agrm7_e.htm (accessed March 18, 2021).

[9] See www.wipo.int/treaties/en/ip/wct/summary_wct.html (accessed March 18, 2021).

[10] WIPO Copyright Treaty, Art. 4, Available at https://wipolex.wipo.int/en/text/295157 (accessed March 18, 2021). The scope of protection for computer programs under Article 4 of this Treaty is consistent with Article 2 of the Berne Convention and on a par with the relevant provisions of the TRIPS Agreement.

[11] *Id.,* Art. 5 "Compilations of data or other material, in any form, which by reason of the selection or arrangement of their contents constitute intellectual creations, are protected as such. This protection does not extend to the data or the material itself and is without prejudice to any copyright subsisting in the data or material contained in the compilation." The scope of protection for compilations of data (databases) under Article 5 of this Treaty is consistent with Article 2 of the Berne Convention and on a par with the relevant provisions of the TRIPS Agreement.

[12] *Id.,* Art. 6: "(1) Authors of literary and artistic works shall enjoy the exclusive right of authorizing the making available to the public of the original and copies of their works through sale or other transfer of ownership; (2) Nothing in this Treaty shall affect the freedom of Contracting Parties to determine the conditions,

technological measures for the protection of works[13] and effective legal remedies against unauthorized modification of rights management information contained in works.[14]

---

if any, under which the exhaustion of the right in paragraph (1) applies after the first sale or other transfer of ownership of the original or a copy of the work with the authorization of the author."

Art. 8: "Without prejudice to the provisions of Articles 11(1)(ii), 11bis(1)(i) and (ii), 11ter(1)(ii), 14(1)(ii) and 14bis(1) of the Berne Convention, authors of literary and artistic works shall enjoy the exclusive right of authorizing any communication to the public of their works, by wire or wireless means, including the making available to the public of their works in such a way that members of the public may access these works from a place and at a time individually chosen by them." "It is understood that the mere provision of physical facilities for enabling or making a communication does not in itself amount to communication within the meaning of this Treaty or the Berne Convention. It is further understood that nothing in Article 8 precludes a Contracting Party from applying Article 11bis(2)."

[13] *Id.*, Art. 11: "Contracting Parties shall provide adequate legal protection and effective legal remedies against the circumvention of effective technological measures that are used by authors in connection with the exercise of their rights under this Treaty or the Berne Convention and that restrict acts, in respect of their works, which are not authorized by the authors concerned or permitted by law."

[14] *Id.*, Art. 12: "(1) Contracting Parties shall provide adequate and effective legal remedies against any person knowingly performing any of the following acts knowing, or with respect to civil remedies having reasonable grounds to know, that it will induce, enable, facilitate or conceal an infringement of any right covered by this Treaty or the Berne Convention: (i) to remove or alter any electronic rights management information without authority; (ii) to distribute, import for distribution, broadcast or communicate to the public, without authority, works or copies of works knowing that electronic rights management information has been removed or altered without authority.

"(2) As used in this Article, 'rights management information' means information which identifies the work, the author of the work, the owner of any right in the work, or information about the terms and conditions of use of the work, and any numbers or codes that represent such information, when any of these items of information is attached to a copy of a work or appears in connection with the communication of a work to the public." (It is understood that the reference to "infringement of any right covered by this Treaty or the Berne Convention" includes both exclusive rights and rights of remuneration.)

The WIPO Copyright Treaty is implemented in United States law by the Digital Millennium Copyright Act.[15] The European Union approved the Treaty in March 2000.[16]

Patent Law Treaty (PLT)

The PLT is a WIPO accord adopted on June 1, 2000, in Geneva, Switzerland,[17] by 53 states. The PLT is designed to simplify and harmonize administrative practices among national and regional intellectual property offices (IPOs). The Treaty aims to encourage the use of intellectual property systems, stimulate innovation, and facilitate access among various IPOs.

Convention on Cybercrime

The (Budapest) Convention on Cybercrime is the only binding international treaty addressing computer and Internet crimes by harmonizing national laws, improving investigative techniques, and increasing cooperation among nations.[18] It was drawn up by the Council of Europe in Strasbourg, opened for signature in Budapest on November 23, 2001, and entered into force on July 1, 2004. It serves as a guideline for any country developing comprehensive national legislation against cybercrime and as a framework for international cooperation among parties to the treaty.[19]

---

[15] Pub. L. No. 105-304, 112 Stat. 2860 (October 28, 1998); 17 U.S.C. §§ 1201 *et seq.*

[16] Decision 2000/278/EC of 16 March 2000. European Union Directives that largely cover the subject matter of the treaty are: Directive 91/250/EC creating copyright protection for software, Directive 96/9/EC on copyright protection for databases, and Directive 2001/29/EC prohibiting devices for circumventing "technical protection measures" such as digital rights management.

[17] See www.wipo.int/treaties/en/ip/plt/trtdocs_wo038.html (accessed March 18, 2021).

[18] See http://conventions.coe.int/Treaty/Commun/QueVoulezVous.asp?NT= 185&CM=8&DF=&CL=ENG (accessed March 18, 2021).

[19] For Information About Which States have Signed and Ratified the Convention, see http://conventions.coe.int/Treaty/Commun/ChercheSig.asp?NT=185 &CM=8&DF=28/10/2010&CL=ENG (accessed March 18, 2021).

Anti-Counterfeiting Trade Agreement (ACTA)

The idea of creating a plurilateral agreement on counterfeiting was developed by Japan and the United States in 2006, with Canada, the European Union, and Switzerland joining the preliminary talks throughout 2006 and 2007, and finally concluding negotiations in October 2010. ACTA, signed by the United States, Australia, Canada, South Korea, Japan, New Zealand, Morocco, and Singapore on October 1, 2011, in Tokyo, is establishing international standards on IPR enforcement and strengthening "[t]he international legal framework for effectively combating global proliferation of commercial-scale counterfeiting and piracy. In addition to calling for strong legal frameworks, the agreement also includes innovative provisions to deepen international cooperation and to promote strong intellectual property rights (IPR) enforcement practices ... ."[20]

U.S. trade agreements in effect in 2021 are Australian FTA, Bahrain FTA, CAFTA-DR (Dominican Republic–Central America FTA), Chile FTA, Colombia TPA, Israel FTA, Jordan FTA, KORUS FTA, Morocco FTA, Oman FTA, Panama TPA, Peru TPA, Singapore FTA, and United States–Mexico–Canada Agreement. All these agreements have sections dedicated to treatment and protection of intellectual property. Detailed information can be found at https://ustr.gov/trade-agreements/free-trade-agreements/colombia-tpa.

Europe and Middle East

European Union

"The European Union is a family of democratic European countries, committed to working together peacefully and cooperatively. Its Member States have set up common institutions to which they delegate some of their sovereignty so that decisions on specific matters of joint interest can be made democratically at a centralized European level ... . The EU's decision-making comes from the three main EU institutions, which produce policies and laws (in the form of directives, regulations and

---

[20] See www.ustr.gov/acta (accessed March 18, 2021).

decisions) … ."[21] These institutions are: (1) The Council of the European Union (which represents the governments of the Member States) serves as the EU's main legislative and decision-making body; (2) the European Parliament consists of representatives elected directly by the citizens of EU Member States; it supervises the Commission and shares authority for the EU budget with the Council; and (3) the European Commission is the centralized "executive body" of the European Union, which drafts new laws and proposes them to the European Parliament and the Council; the Commission represents the European Union on the international stage, for example, by negotiating agreements between the European Union and countries outside of the European Union.[22]

In January 2001, the EU Commission adopted a communiqué, "Creating a Safer Information Society by Improving the Security of Information Infrastructures and Combating Computer-related Crime," as a comprehensive policy program to fight cybercrime by adopting adequate, substantive, and procedural legislative provisions to deal with both domestic and transnational criminal activities, and by improving cooperation among consumers, industry, and law enforcement.

In October 2004, the Commission issued a communiqué on "Critical Infrastructure Protection in the Fight against Terrorism," summarizing the actions the EU Commission is taking to protect critical infrastructures, including information systems.

The EU Commission set out a European Agenda on Security for the period 2015 to 2020 "[t]o support Member States' cooperation in tackling security threats and step up our common efforts in the fight against terrorism, organised crime and cybercrime … ."[23] The European

---

[21] See https://europa.eu/european-union/about-eu/institutions-bodies_en (accessed March 18, 2021).

[22] *Id.*

[23] European Commission, "Anti cybercrime legislative proposals on Council Table." Available at http://europa.eu/rapid/press-release_IP-15-4865_en.htm (accessed March 18, 2021).

Commission's "TransAtlantic IPR portal" provides useful tips on best practices and case studies for enforcement of IPR and border protection.[24]

The European Union Intellectual Property Office (EUIPO)[25] hosted the International IP Enforcement Summit in London in June 2014. The Summit provided a forum for discussion of crucial international IP enforcement matters, increased engagement among national and international partners in combating counterfeiting and piracy, and interaction and sharing of successful examples of international best practice strategies.[26]

"On November 28, 2013, the European Commission introduced a proposal for a Directive of the European Parliament and of the Council on the Protection of Undisclosed Know-How and Business Information (Trade Secrets) Against Their Unlawful Acquisition, Use and Disclosure. This Directive would harmonize civil trade secret law throughout the EU ... ."[27]

REACT (the European Anti-Counterfeiting Network)

REACT is a nonprofit organization with more than 175 members and more than 20 years' experience fighting counterfeit trade in various industries. The organization has a large international network with offices around the world, allowing it to perform raids and take basic legal actions at local (lower) rates in most European and many non-European countries.

To increase its effectiveness working with members, REACT established the IPR Business Partnership,[28] which acts as a forum for public–private sector discussions and improvements in combating infringement of IPR. The IPR Business Partnership cooperates with various national

---

[24] See https://ec.europa.eu/growth/tools-databases/ipr_en (accessed March 18, 2021).

[25] See https://euipo.europa.eu/ohimportal/en/international-ip-enforcement-summit-2017 (accessed March 18, 2021).

[26] Id.

[27] See www.partiseapate.eu/wp-content/uploads/2013/04/com2013_0133en01.pdf (accessed March 18, 2021).

[28] See www.react.org/about-us (accessed March 18, 2021).

and international authorities such as WIPO and the United Nations Economic Commission for Europe.

Saudi Arabia

"In 2017, Saudi Arabia established the Saudi Authority for Intellectual Property (SAIP), which when fully operational will reportedly be responsible for all IP Policy-making Functions, including IP enforcement policy, as well as the registration of all copyrights, trademarks, industrial designs, and patents. While the United States commends the creation of SAIP, its impact on addressing outstanding IP concerns is unclear, particularly with respect to ongoing pharmaceutical and satellite piracy concerns and IP enforcement generally. There has been notable cooperation between SAIP and the U.S. Patent and Trademark Office including the signing of a Memorandum of Understanding in September 2018. In particular, the United States notes SAIP's efforts to increase transparency, join international treaties, improve stakeholder involvement in policy making, and continue legislative development. Efforts by the Saudi Arabia Customs Authority are aiming to significantly enhance its IP enforcement efforts and capacity, including partnering closely with trademark and copyright owners and to systematically notify right holders of suspected illicit shipments.

In recent years, the Saudi Arabia Food and Drug Authority (SFDA), under the Minister of Health, has authorized domestic companies to produce generic versions of pharmaceutical products that are under patent protection either in Saudi Arabia or the Gulf Cooperation Council (GCC), or that are still covered by Saudi Arabia's system for protecting against the unfair commercial use, as well as the unauthorized disclosure, of undisclosed test or other data generated to obtain marketing approval. After granting marketing approval in 2016 and 2017 to produce generic versions of two pharmaceutical products protected by Saudi Arabian or GCC IP rights, the SFDA again granted marketing approvals to produce generic versions of additional innovative pharmaceutical products this past year. These approvals reportedly relied on data from innovators that is subject to Saudi Arabia's system for protection against the unfair commercial use, as well as the unauthorized disclosure, of undisclosed test or other data generated to obtain marketing approval. Furthermore, in 2018, the National Unified Procurement Company for Medical Supplies, also overseen by the Minister of Health, reportedly awarded a national tender, in part, to a generic manufacturer while the innovative product covered by the tender was still under patent protection in the GCC.

Rampant satellite and online piracy is a rising concern in Saudi Arabia. BeoutQ, an illicit service for pirated content whose signal is reportedly carried by Saudi Arabia-based satellite provider Arabsat, continues to be widely available in Saudi Arabia and throughout the Middle East and Europe. BeoutQ's activities include satellite and online piracy, as well as support for devices and related services, such as apps and illicit streaming devices, that facilitate this piracy and allow access to unlicensed movies and television productions, including sports events. While Saudi officials have confirmed the illegal nature of BeoutQ's activities and claim to be addressing this issue by seizing BeoutQ set-top boxes, such devices nevertheless continue to be widely available and are generally unregulated in Saudi Arabia. Saudi Arabia also has not taken sufficient steps to address the purported role of Arabsat in facilitating BeoutQ's piracy activities. Additionally, there are ongoing concerns regarding IP enforcement, including difficulty for stakeholders to obtain information on the status of enforcement actions and investigations, the lack of seizure and destruction of counterfeit and pirated goods in markets, and limits on the ability to enter facilities suspected to be involved in the sale or manufacture of counterfeit goods, including facilities located in residential areas."[29]

Russia

"Challenges to intellectual property (IP) protection and enforcement in Russia include continued copyright infringement, trademark counterfeiting, and the existence of non-transparent procedures governing the operation of collective management organizations (CMO). In particular, stakeholders report that IP enforcement overall is down from where it was a decade ago, and that Russian enforcement agencies continue to lack

---

[29] See https://ustr.gov/sites/default/files/2019_Special_301_Report.pdf (accessed March 18, 2021).

sufficient staffing, expertise, and the political will to combat IP violations and criminal enterprises.

Russia took some positive steps in 2018, but the overall IP situation remains extremely challenging. The lack of robust enforcement of IP rights is a persistent problem, which has been compounded by long delays regarding criminal action and prosecutions. Additionally, burdensome procedural requirements continue to hinder right holders' ability to bring civil actions, which are exacerbated for foreign right holders by strict documentation requirements such as verification of their corporate status. Inadequate and ineffective protection of copyright, including with regard to online piracy, continues to be a significant problem, damaging both the market for legitimate content in Russia, as well as in other countries. While recent implementation of anti-piracy legislation holds some promise, Russia remains home to several sites that facilitate online piracy, as identified in the 2019 Notorious Markets List.[30] Stakeholders continue to report significant piracy of video games, music, movies, books, journal articles, and television programming. Mirror sites related to infringing websites are playing a role in the surge of the number of pirate websites in Russia. Russia needs to direct more action to rogue web platforms targeting audiences outside the country. Recently, right holders and Internet platforms in Russia signed an anti-piracy memorandum to facilitate the removal of links to infringing websites. However, this memorandum is set to expire in September 2019, and compliance is unlikely if legislation is not adopted by this deadline. Furthermore, Russia has enacted legislation that enables right holders to obtain court-ordered injunctions against pirate websites, but additional steps must be taken to target the root of the problem—namely, investigating and prosecuting the owners of the large commercial websites distributing pirated material, including software. Moreover, stakeholders report a 200 percent increase since 2015 in unauthorized camcords that often appear on the Internet within a few days of a movie's theatrical release. Stakeholders further report that these problems negatively affect, in particular, independent producers and distributors, the majority of which are small and medium-sized enterprises. Royalty

---

[30] See https://ustr.gov/sites/default/files/2019_Review_of_Notorious_Markets_for_Counterfeiting_and_Piracy.pdf (accessed March 18, 2021).

collection by CMOs in Russia continues to lack transparency and fails to meet international standards. The United States encourages CMOs to update and modernize their 60 procedures, including the full representation of right holders in CMO governing bodies, regardless of whether right holders are individuals or legal entities. Russia remains a thriving market for counterfeit goods sourced from China. Similarly, there is little enforcement against counterfeits trafficked online, including apparel, footwear, sporting goods, pharmaceutical products, and electronic devices. The United States is also concerned about Russia's implementation of its World Trade Organization commitments related to the protection against the unfair commercial use, as well as the unauthorized disclosure, of undisclosed test or other data generated to obtain marketing approval for pharmaceutical products. Stakeholders report that Russia is eroding protections for undisclosed data, and should adopt a system that meets international norms of transparency and fairness. Stakeholders are also concerned about recent regulatory initiatives that reportedly may inappropriately expand the use of compulsory licensing."[31]

Asia

Rapid economic growth in Asia presents significant intellectual property protection challenges—foreign and homegrown. Most Asian countries need to establish legal regimes and enforcement systems to better combat counterfeiting and piracy. The United States has led efforts to ensure effective implementation of IPR protection and enforcement initiatives, including the Asia-Pacific Economic Cooperation (APEC) Anti-Counterfeiting and Piracy Initiative and the APEC Cooperation Initiative on Patent Acquisition Procedures.[32] IPR enforcement in Asia varies from country to country.[33]

---

[31] See https://ustr.gov/sites/default/files/2019_Special_301_Report.pdf (accessed March 18, 2021)

[32] See www.wipo.int/edocs/mdocs/aspac/en/wipo_inn_tyo_10/wipo_inn_tyo_10_ref_theme01b_01.pdf (accessed March 18, 2021).

[33] The Office of the United States Trade Representative publishes an annual "Special 301 Report," a "review of the global state of intellectual property rights

China

"In 2015, China's leadership continued to affirm the importance of developing and protecting intellectual property and emphasized that stronger protection and enforcement of IPR are essential to achieving China's economic objectives. China expressly committed not to 'conduct or knowingly support misappropriation of intellectual property, including trade secrets and other confidential business information with the intent of providing competitive advantages to its companies or commercial sectors. China also committed not to require the transfer of intellectual property rights or technology as a condition of doing business. As part of its legal reform effort, China continued to develop draft measures on a wide range of subjects, including on copyright, patents, trade secrets, drug review and approvals, Anti-Monopoly Law enforcement as it relates to intellectual property, and regulations on inventor remuneration. Despite a broad government reorganization, including of intellectual property (IP) responsibilities among government agencies, and proposed revisions to IP laws and regulations, China failed to make fundamental structural changes to strengthen IP protection and enforcement, open China's market to foreign investment, allow the market a decisive role in allocating resources, and refrain from government interference in private sector technology transfer decisions. For U.S. persons who rely on IP protection in what is already a very difficult business environment, severe challenges persist because of gaps in the scope of IP protection, stalled legal reforms, and weak enforcement channels."[34]

"As China has become the largest e-commerce market in the world, widespread online piracy and counterfeiting in e-commerce markets represent critical concerns for U.S. right holders. According to published reports, online retail sales in China are expected to grow to $1.9 trillion in 2019.

OECD reports have noted that the growth of small parcels carrying counterfeit and pirated goods reflected the move from offline to online

---

(IPR) protection and enforcement." It is available at https://ustr.gov/sites/default/files/2019_Special_301_Report.pdf (accessed March 18, 2021). The Report contains a "Priority Watch List" of countries where persistent inadequacies present barriers to U.S. exports and investments.

[34] See https://ustr.gov/sites/default/files/USTR-2016-Special-301-Report.pdf (accessed March 18, 2021).

sales, and China together with Hong Kong have been the leading source of seized counterfeit goods shipped by mail or express couriers. Right holders report that online sellers of counterfeit goods often advertise that orders will be fulfilled via China Post's express mail service and exploit the high volume of packages to the United States to escape enforcement. Furthermore, although some leading online sales platforms have reportedly streamlined procedures to remove offerings of infringing articles and enhanced cooperation with stakeholders to improve criminal and civil enforcement of IP, right holders continue to express concerns about ineffective takedown procedures, slowness to respond to small and medium-sized enterprises (SMEs), and insufficient measures to deter repeat infringers. Other right holders report growing online piracy in the form of thousands of 'mini Video on Demand' (VOD) locations that show unauthorized audiovisual content and online platforms that disseminate unauthorized copies of scientific, technical, and medical journal articles and academic texts. A range of such concerns led to the re-listing of DHgate.com and Alibaba online sales platform Taobao as notorious markets in the 2018 Out-of-Cycle Review of Notorious Markets (Notorious Markets List), as well as the first-time listing of Pinduoduo.com.

The new E-Commerce Law took effect on January 1, 2019. Despite extensive U.S. engagement regarding drafts of the law, China failed to address major concerns regarding provisions that would impose burdensome requirements on right holders seeking to enforce their IP, while allowing infringing sellers to halt takedown procedures through submission of counter-notifications that lack sufficient information to ensure their validity and without penalties for submissions in bad faith. It is critical that the E-Commerce Law, as implemented, does not undermine the existing framework for Internet service provider notices of copyright infringement and cease-and-desist letters. A further negative signal was the issuance of a draft Tort Liability Chapter of the Civil Code that contained similar provisions to problematic portions of the E-Commerce Law. The final version of the Tort Liability Chapter should implement a predictable legal environment that promotes effect."[35]

---

[35] *Id.*

"China's 2017 amendment of the Anti-Unfair Competition Law (AUCL) went into effect on January 1, 2018. The amended AUCL represented a major missed opportunity to address critical concerns, including the overly narrow scope of covered actions and actors, the failure to address obstacles to injunctive relief, and the need to allow for evidentiary burden shifting in appropriate circumstances.

One particular area for continued monitoring is the availability of preliminary injunctions in trade secret and other IP disputes. A new judicial interpretation, titled the 'Provisions of the Supreme People's Court Regarding Certain Issues Concerning the Application of Law During the Examination of Act Preservation in Intellectual Property and Competition Disputes,' went into effect on January 1, 2019. It remains unclear whether, in practice, this judicial interpretation will enable right holders to obtain timely preliminary injunctions against all categories of trade secret misappropriation.

China should not only address these shortcomings, but also issue guiding court decisions to improve consistency in judicial decisions on trade secrets. Reforms also should prevent the disclosure of trade secrets and other confidential information submitted to government regulators, courts, and other authorities, and address obstacles to criminal enforcement."[36]

"With respect to changes in copyright laws, Chinese authorities have indicated that they made progress toward draft amendments of the Copyright Law, but no draft has been published. It is critical to address major deficiencies in China's copyright framework, such as the failure to provide deterrent-level remedies and penalties, protection against unauthorized transmission of sports and other live broadcasts, and effective criminal enforcement, including amendments to the Regulations on the Transfer of Alleged Criminal Cases by Administrative Enforcement Organs to adopt a 'reasonable suspicion' threshold for the transfer of administrative cases to criminal investigation and prosecution."[37]

"Since enacting its Cybersecurity Law (CSL) in 2017, China has taken multiple steps backward through its efforts to invoke cybersecurity as a

---

[36] *Id.*

[37] *Id.*

pretext to force U.S. IP-intensive industries to disclose sensitive IP to the government, transfer it to a Chinese entity, or both. Through draft and final measures, China has often applied the poorly-defined concept of 'secure and controllable' information communications technology (ICT) products and services and associated 'risk' factors as a putative justification for erecting barriers to sale and use in China.

On June 27, 2018, China released draft Cybersecurity Classified Protection Regulations (CCPR), which represent a continuation of the Multi-Level Protection Scheme requirements that, among other restrictions, limit procurement of software and other ICT products for purportedly sensitive systems to those containing indigenous Chinese IP. The CCPR imposed restrictions on networks operating within China, such as requiring that certain systems be connected with the Public Security Bureau system and that technical maintenance be performed within China. In September 2018, the Ministry of Public Security released the Internet Security Supervision and Inspection Provisions by Public Security Organs, which authorized public security authorities to enforce the CSL. As previously reported, pursuant to the CSL, China may require disclosure of critical source code and IP to government authorities, require IP rights be owned in China, require associated research and development be conducted in China, and curtail or prohibit cross border data flows in sectors such as cloud services.

Right holders continue to report strong concerns about other draft and final measures, particularly requirements for public disclosure of enterprise standards under the amended Standardization Law.

The draft standards published by the National Information Security Standardization Technical Committee (TC-260) would assign scores to ICT products based on inappropriate benchmarks (e.g., the extent to which a party discloses sensitive IP). The draft Encryption Law would impose severe restrictions on foreign businesses to keep them from competing in the commercial cryptography market.

U.S. right holders should not be forced to choose between protecting their IP against unwarranted disclosure and competing for sales in China. Going forward, China must not invoke security concerns in order to erect market access barriers, require the disclosure of critical IP, or discriminate against foreign-owned or -developed IP.

Other Concerns Stakeholders report considerable concern that China's rules and procedures limit parties' abilities to challenge geographic indications (GI's) via opposition, cancellation, invalidation, and other processes that would ensure GIs do not impose market access barriers to U.S. exports. In 2014 and 2015, the United States welcomed important Chinese commitments on rules and procedures concerning the registration of GIs under China's existing systems, as well as those registered pursuant to an international agreement. In late February 2019, China National Intellectual Property Administration (CNIPA) issued for comment draft revisions to the Measure on Protection of Foreign Geographical Indication Products. In detailed comments on the draft, the United States explained that it is critical that the final version of the revisions ensure full transparency and procedural fairness with respect to the protection of GIs, including safeguards for generic terms, respect for prior trademark rights, clear procedures to allow for opposition and cancellation, and fair market access for U.S. exports to China relying on trademarks or the use of generic terms.

The United States continues to urge all levels of the Chinese government, as well as state-owned enterprises (SOEs), to use only legitimate, licensed copies of software. Right holders report that government and SOE software legalization programs still are not implemented comprehensively and urge the use of external audits to ensure accountability. Though it reflects a slight decline from past years, the reported 66 percent rate of unlicensed software use in China represents $6.8 billion in lost commercial value, far above regional and global rates.

Finally, stakeholders have identified concerns relating to opposition examiners at the China Trademark Office, who face very large dockets and whose decisions on likelihood of confusion are often narrowly focused on goods or services in the same sub-class rather than also taking into account goods and services in other classes and other market realities. Stakeholders continue to report that trademark authorities do not give full consideration to co-existence agreements and letters of consent in registration processes, among other issues. Additional concerns include onerous documentation requirements for opposition, cancellation, and invalidation proceedings, lack of transparency in opposition proceedings, absence of default judgments against applicants who fail to appear, and legitimate right holders' difficulty in obtaining well-known trademark status. Moreover, changes to trademark opposition procedures eliminated appeals for opposers, which resulted in longer windows for bad-faith trademark registrants to use their marks—or blackmail the legitimate brand owner—before a decision is made in an invalidation proceeding."[38]

India

"India has yet to take steps to address long-standing patent issues that affect innovative industries. Companies across different sectors remain concerned about narrow patentability standards, the potential threat of compulsory licensing and patent revocations, as well as overly broad criteria for issuing such licenses and revocations under the India Patents Act. Furthermore, patent applicants face costly and time-consuming patent opposition hurdles, long timelines for receiving patents, and excessive reporting requirements."[39]

"In the pharmaceutical and agricultural chemical sectors, India continues to lack an effective system for protecting against the unfair commercial use, as well as the unauthorized disclosure, of undisclosed test or other data generated to obtain marketing approval for such products. In the pharmaceutical sector, Section 3(d) of the India Patents Act restricts patent-eligible subject matter in a way that fails to properly incentivize innovation that would lead to the development of improvements with benefits for Indian patients. India still lacks an effective system for notifying interested parties of marketing approvals for follow-on pharmaceuticals in a manner that would allow for the early resolution of potential patent disputes. Despite India's justifications of limiting IP protections as a way to promote access to technologies, India maintains extremely high customs duties directed to IP-intensive products, such as medical devices, pharmaceuticals, information communications technology (ICT) products, solar energy equipment, and capital goods. India still maintains the draft Ministry of Agriculture and Farmers Welfare's 'Licensing and Formats for Genetically-Modified Technology Agreement Guidelines,

---

[38] *Id.*

[39] See *id.*

2016' that contain overly prescriptive terms and imposes mandatory licensing requirements that, if implemented, would undermine market incentives critical to the agricultural biotechnology and other innovative sectors."[40]

India's overall IP enforcement remains inadequate, and the lack of uniform progress across the country threatens to undercut the positive steps that certain states have taken. A 2019 publication produced by the Organisation for Economic Co-operation and Development (OECD), "Trends in Trade in Counterfeit and Pirated Goods," finds that India is among the top five provenance economies for counterfeit goods. A 2017 report from the OECD and the European Union Intellectual Property Office, "Mapping the Real Routes of Trade in Fake Goods," revealed India to be a key producer and exporter of counterfeit foodstuffs, pharmaceuticals, perfumes and cosmetics, textiles, footwear, electronics and electrical equipment, toys, games, and sporting equipment. The 2017 report also found that 55 percent of global seizures of counterfeit pharmaceuticals, by total value, originated in India—making it by far the largest producer. The report noted that these counterfeit pharmaceuticals are shipped "around the globe, with a special focus on African economies, Europe, and the United States."[41]

Indonesia

"Right holders continue to face challenges in Indonesia with respect to adequate and effective intellectual property (IP) protection and enforcement, as well as fair and equitable market access.

Concerns include widespread piracy and counterfeiting and, in particular, the lack of enforcement against dangerous counterfeit products. To address these issues, Indonesia would need to develop and fully fund a robust and coordinated IP enforcement effort that includes deterrent-level penalties for IP infringement in physical markets and online. Indonesia's law concerning geographical indications (GIs) raises questions about the

---

[40] *Id.*, p. 40.
[41] See https://ustr.gov/sites/default/files/2019_Special_301_Report.pdf (accessed March 18, 2021).

effect of new GI registrations on preexisting trademark rights and the ability to use common food names. Indonesia's Patent Law continues to raise concerns, including with respect to the patentability criteria for incremental innovations, local manufacturing and use requirements, the grounds and procedures for issuing compulsory licenses, and disclosure requirements for inventions related to traditional knowledge and genetic resources. Indonesia also lacks an effective system for protecting against the unfair commercial use, as well as unauthorized disclosure, of undisclosed test or other data generated to obtain marketing approval for pharmaceutical and agricultural chemical products. In addition, the United States remains concerned about a range of market access barriers in Indonesia, including requirements for domestic manufacturing and technology transfer for pharmaceuticals and other sectors, as well as certain measures related to motion pictures.

In 2018, the Ministry of Law and Human Rights (MLHR) issued Regulation 15/2018, which provides welcome allowances for patent holders to request postponement of the Patent Law's problematic local working requirement, but the United States continues to encourage Indonesia to amend the 2016 Patent Law to eliminate this requirement entirely. In late 2018, MLHR issued, without an opportunity for public comment, Regulation 39/2018, which establishes procedures for compulsory licenses that raise serious concerns from the perspective of IP rights and trade policy, transparency and due process, and global innovation. Indonesia also has imposed excessive and inappropriate penalties upon patent holders as an incentive to collect patent maintenance fees. As Indonesia continues to develop implementing regulations for the Patent Law, the United States urges Indonesia to address these concerns and to provide affected stakeholders with meaningful opportunities for input. The United States welcomes Indonesia's agreement to a bilateral Intellectual Property Rights Work Plan under the U.S.-Indonesia Trade and Investment Framework Agreement and plans continued, intensified engagement with Indonesia to address these important issues."[42]

---

[42] See https://ustr.gov/sites/default/files/2019_Special_301_Report.pdf (accessed March 18, 2021).

Thailand

"Thailand continues to make progress to implement the 2016 Work Plan and address concerns raised as part of the bilateral U.S.-Thailand Trade and Investment Framework Agreement (TIFA), and a subcommittee on enforcement against intellectual property (IP) infringement, led by a Deputy Prime Minister, continues to convene.

This strong interest from the highest levels of the government has led to improved coordination among government entities, as well as enhanced and sustained enforcement efforts to combat counterfeit and pirated goods throughout the country. One particular focus of Thailand's enforcement efforts has been physical markets previously listed on the Office of the U.S. Trade Representative's Notorious Markets List. Thailand also continues to take steps to address backlogs for patent and trademark applications, including significantly increasing the number of examiners and preparing legislative amendments to streamline the patent registration process and reduce patent backlog and pendency. Thailand has been building capacity and awareness since joining the Madrid Protocol, making it easier for U.S. companies to apply for trademarks, and taking steps to address concerns regarding online piracy affecting the U.S. content industry. In addition, Thailand also is considering draft amendments to the Patent Act to help prepare for accession to the Hague Agreement. With respect to copyright legislation, Thailand amended the Copyright Act to accede to the Marrakesh Treaty and is in the process of further amending this act to prepare for accession to the World Intellectual Property Organization Internet Treaties. However, concerns remain regarding the availability of counterfeit and pirated goods, both in physical markets and online, and the United States urges Thailand to continue to improve on its provision of effective and deterrent enforcement measures. In addition, the United States remains concerned about a range of copyright-related issues. In particular, the United States urges Thailand to address through amendments to the 2014 Copyright Act concerns expressed by the United States and other foreign governments and stakeholders, including overly broad technological protection measure exceptions and procedural obstacles to enforcement against unauthorized camcording.

The United States urges Thailand to address these issues in upcoming amendments to its Copyright Act. Other U.S. concerns include a backlog in pending patent applications (particularly for pharmaceutical applications), widespread use of unlicensed software in both the public and private sectors, unauthorized collective management organizations, lengthy civil IP enforcement proceedings and low civil damages, and extensive cable and satellite signal theft. U.S. right holders have also expressed concerns regarding legislation that allows for content quota restrictions. The United States also continues to encourage Thailand to provide an effective system for protecting against the unfair commercial use, as well as unauthorized disclosure, of undisclosed test or other data generated to obtain marketing approval for pharmaceutical and agricultural chemical products. In addition, the United States urges Thailand to engage in a meaningful and transparent manner with all relevant stakeholders, including IP owners, as it considers ways to address the country's public health challenges while maintaining a patent system that promotes innovation. The United States looks forward to continuing to work with Thailand to address these and other issues through the TIFA and other bilateral engagement."[43]

Central and South America

Countries in Latin America represent increasingly attractive investment opportunities for many IP rights holders; however, counterfeiting and software piracy are serious and growing problems in many of these countries.[44] Free trade zones in Panama and Uruguay, for example, are aiding the transit of counterfeit merchandise, especially from China. The proliferation of illicit goods in Latin America negatively affects foreign

---

[43] *Id.*

[44] See https://ustr.gov/sites/default/files/2019_Special_301_Report.pdf (accessed March 18, 2021).

investment and contributes to tax evasion.[45] The Paraguayan city Ciudad del Este is the international epicenter for piracy and counterfeiting.[46]

Brazil

"National Council to Combat Piracy and Crimes Against Intellectual Property has approved a three-year National Plan to Combat Piracy and coordinated activities among multiple government and private sector organizations. The Brazil Film Agency established a Technical Working Group to Combat Piracy, which focused on educating the public and developing policies to address IP protection. Notable successes include a record level of seizures of counterfeit and pirated goods, as well as enforcement against illegal telecommunication products, set-top boxes, and piracy websites. The United States also commends the cooperation of Brazilian law enforcement with counterparts in its neighboring countries and in the United States. Nevertheless, levels of counterfeiting and piracy in Brazil, including online piracy, use of unlicensed software, and illicit camcording, remain unacceptably high. The dedication of additional resources at the federal, state, and local levels for IP enforcement, IP aware-ness campaigns, and stakeholder partnerships would help address these challenges, as would the enactment of legislation to increase deterrent penalties for IP crimes and to criminalize unauthorized camcording. The United States also recognizes positive developments at Brazil's National Institute of Industrial Property (INPI), which streamlined procedures for certain review processes and implemented measures to increase exam-iner productivity for patent and trademark decisions. The United States welcomes the next phase of INPI's Patent Prosecution Highway pilot program with the U.S. Patent and Trademark Office. The proposals to

---

[45] "Develop Your Enforcement Strategy in Latin America," Managing IP Maga-zine (March 01, 2008), available at www.managingip.com/Article/1886980/Develop-your-enforcement-strategy-in-Latin-America.html (accessed March 18, 2021).

[46] A.R. Sverdlick. 2005. "Research Note: Terrorists and Organized Crime Entre-preneurs in the 'Triple Frontier' Among Argentina, Brazil, and Paraguay." *Trends in Organized Crime* 9, no. 2, pp. 84–93.

allow INPI to retain patent and trademark filing fees would help address budgetary constraints. Despite this positive progress, the concerns remain about the long pendency of patent applications, as well as INPI's actions to invalidate or shorten the term of a significant number of 'mailbox' patents for pharmaceutical and agricultural chemical products.[47] The United States welcomes the agreement that limits the role of Brazil's National Sanitary Regulatory Agency (ANVISA) on issues relating to the patentability of new biopharmaceutical inventions, but continues to monitor the situation in light of long-standing concerns about duplicative reviews by ANVISA of pharmaceutical applications. Also, although Brazilian law and regulations provide for protection against unfair commercial use, as well as unauthorized disclosure, of undisclosed test and other data generated to obtain marketing approval for veterinary and agricultural chemical products, they do not provide similar protection for pharmaceutical products. Right holders are also concerned about the protection of patent rights during Brazil's process for establishing Productive Development Partnerships for pharmaceutical products.[48] The United States encourages Brazil to provide transparency and procedural fairness to all interested parties in connection with potential recognition or protection of geographical indications including in connection with trade agreement negotiations with other trading partners. Strong IP protection, available to both domestic and foreign right holders, provides a critical incentive for businesses to invest in future 79 innovation in Brazil, and the United States looks forward to engaging constructively with Brazil to build a strong IP environment and to address remaining concerns."[49]

Argentina

"Argentina made limited progress in IP protection and enforcement. Beset with economic challenges, Argentina's government agencies were strapped by a reduction of funding and a government-wide hiring freeze,

---

[47] See https://ustr.gov/sites/default/files/2019_Special_301_Report.pdf (accessed March 18, 2021).

[48] *Id.*

[49] *Id.*

and many of Argentina's IP-related initiatives that had gained momentum last year did not gain further traction due to a lack of resources. Despite these circumstances, the National Institute of Industrial Property (INPI) revamped its procedures and began accepting electronic filing of patent, trademark, and industrial designs applications as of October 1, 2018. Argentina also improved registration procedures for trademarks and industrial designs. On trademarks, the law now provides for a fast track option that reduces the time to register a trademark to four months. The United States continues to monitor this change as INPI works on the implementing regulation. For industrial designs, INPI now accepts multiple applications in a single filing, and applicants may substitute digital photographs for formal drawings. To further improve patent protection in Argentina, including for small and medium sized enterprises, the United States urges Argentina to ratify the Patent Cooperation Treaty.

Enforcement of IP rights in Argentina continues to be a challenge, and stakeholders report widespread unfair competition from sellers of counterfeit and pirated goods and services. La Salada in Buenos Aires remains the largest counterfeit market in Latin America. Argentine police generally do not take ex officio actions, prosecutions can stall and languish in excessive formalities, and, when a criminal case does reach final judgment, and criminal infringers rarely receive deterrent sentences. Hard goods counterfeiting and optical disc piracy is widespread, and online piracy continues to grow as criminal enforcement against online piracy is nearly nonexistent. As a result, IP enforcement online in Argentina consists mainly of right holders trying to convince cooperative Argentine Internet service providers (ISPs) to agree to take down specific infringing works, as well as attempting to seek injunctions in civil cases. Right holders also cite widespread use of unlicensed software by Argentine private enterprises and the government."[50]

When it comes to Customs and border enforcement, in addition to the WTO-coordinated IPM database,[51] some South American countries have unique systems and tools for use by Customs. For example, the

---

[50] See https://ustr.gov/sites/default/files/2019_Special_301_Report.pdf (accessed March 18, 2021).

[51] For a discussion of the IPM database, see § 14.01 *supra*.

Argentinean and Uruguayan "Sistema de Asientos de Alerta" is a system by which companies can register their trademarks with Customs in order to get e-mail notification by Customs every time a product bearing the recorded trademark is detained at Customs for verification.[52] The system also allows for determination of "safe" importers so that they can be excluded from inspections.

Colombia

"The Government of Colombia has made solid progress in the areas of internal coordination of enforcement agencies and training judges and law enforcement officials on IPR issues. However, this IPR progress was reversed in 2013 when the Colombian Constitutional Court invalidated on procedural grounds the law enacting many IPR-related commitments made under the United States-Colombia Trade Promotion Agreement (CTPA).[53] Persistently high levels of counterfeits as well as online piracy, particularly via mobile devices, continue to plague Colombia and law enforcement efforts in this regard have been insignificant.[54] Colombia's San Andresitos markets remain rampant with counterfeit and pirated products, and greater enforcement is needed in order to disrupt such organized distribution of illicit goods.[55]

Colombia's meaningful progress, particularly its enactment in July 2018 of copyright reform legislation to meet CTPA obligations, and Colombia's steps to clarify and resolve concerns about Articles 70 and 72 of the NDP, warrant the change in designation from the Priority Watch List to the Watch List. As noted earlier, in July 2018, Colombia enacted copyright law amendments to extend the term of copyright protection, impose civil liability for circumvention of technological protection

---

[52] See www.marcasregistro.com.ar/marcas/sistema-de-alertas-de-la-aduana/ (accessed March 18, 2021).

[53] See www.ustr.gov/uscolombiatpa/ipr (accessed March 18, 2021).

[54] See https://ustr.gov/sites/default/files/2019_Special_301_Report.pdf (accessed March 18, 2021).

[55] See https://ustr.gov/sites/default/files/2019_Review_of_Notorious_Markets_for_Counterfeiting_and_Piracy.pdf (accessed March 18, 2021).

measures, and strengthen enforcement of copyright and related rights. Colombia is also actively engaging with the United States on implementing notice-and-takedown and safe harbor provisions for Internet service providers, an additional CTPA commitment. With respect to Article 72 of the NDP, Colombia issued Decree 433 in March 2018, as amended by Decree 710 of April 2018, to clarify that Colombia would not condition regulatory approvals on factors other than the safety and efficacy of the underlying compound. With respect to Article 70 of the NDP, Colombia provided clarification to the Organisation for Economic Co-operation and Development Trade Committee that the Minister of Health would not be given any greater deference than other third parties in opposing a patent application, would not have any formal institutional role to oppose or interfere with patent applications that is distinct from those available to third parties, and would not take any other steps to delay a patent application. The United States commends Colombia on these accomplishments but notes that Colombia still needs to make additional progress on remaining intellectual property (IP)-related commitments under the CTPA, particularly provisions regarding copyright liability for ISPs and accession to the 1991 Act of the International Union for the Protection of New Varieties of Plants (UPOV 91). The United States expects Colombia to make substantial progress on a draft bill that will address online piracy through expeditious removal or disabling of access to pirated content by introducing the bill to the Colombian Congress as early as possible. The United States also expects Colombia to make progress toward accession to UPOV 91. The United States urges Colombia to increase its IP enforcement efforts. High levels of digital piracy persist year after year, and Colombia has not curtailed the number of free-to-air devices, community antennas, and unlicensed Internet Protocol Television services that permit otherwise-licensed content to be retransmitted to a large number of non-subscribers. The United States recommends that Colombia increase efforts to address online and mobile piracy, and to focus on disrupting organized trafficking in illicit goods, including at the border and in free trade zones. The United States encourages Colombia to provide key agencies with the requisite authority and resources to investigate and seize counterfeit goods, such as expanding the jurisdiction of the customs police. Finally, the United States continues to engage Colombia on patent-related matters and encourages it to incentivize innovation through strong IP systems."[56]

Trade Treaties in South and Central America

The degree of intellectual property and border enforcement in South and Central America varies among countries. Logically, rights holders need to establish relationships with Customs and other law enforcement agencies where it makes most sense—in countries where counterfeiting has the greatest financial impact on their businesses. Proliferation of multilateral trade agreements has made IPR enforcement more difficult in some cases because countries with weak IPR laws and border enforcement often are used by counterfeiters as a point of entry and provide access to markets in other countries in the trade zone. For example, Paraguay, positioned between Brazil and Argentina, is a weak link of Mercosur;[57] Brazil and Argentina, together with Uruguay, have more advanced IPR enforcement than Paraguay. Although Paraguay has increased the number of raids and seizures of pirated and counterfeit goods, concerns remain because of its porous borders, ineffective prosecution of IPR violators, and insufficient sentences to deter infringement. "[T]he level of enforcement against rampant piracy and counterfeiting, particularly under the criminal laws, in areas such as Ciudad del Este (which has been named to USTR's Notorious Markets List for several years); judicial inefficiency in intellectual property rights (IPR) cases; lack of protection against unfair commercial use of undisclosed test or other data submitted to the government by agrochemical or pharmaceutical companies; and the use of unlicensed software by the government ..." continue to present challenges to market access by foreign firms.[58]

The following is a discussion of the major Latin America trade agreements rights holders should consider when enforcing their IPR in this region.

---

[56] *Id.*

[57] See § 14.06[5][b] *infra.*

[58] See https://ustr.gov/sites/default/files/files/reports/2015/NTE/2015%20 NTE%20Paraguay.pdf (accessed March 18, 2021).

Comunidad Andina

Comunidad Andina is a free trade area including Bolivia, Colombia, Ecuador, and Peru. The trade bloc was called the Andean Pact until 1996 and was established with the signing of the Cartagena Agreement in 1969,[59] an agreement to integrate and cooperate in the economic development of the member countries, including provision of "adequate levels of protection for subregional products."[60] The associated countries include Chile, Argentina, Brazil, Paraguay, and Uruguay.[61]

Mercosur

Mercosur is trade bloc comprising Argentina, Brazil, Paraguay, Uruguay, and Venezuela. It was founded in 1991 and is devoted to promoting free trade and South American economic integration.[62]

Amazon Cooperation Treaty Organization (ACTO)

ACTO is an international organization for the promotion of development in the Amazon region. The member states are: Bolivia, Brazil, Colombia, Ecuador, Guyana, Peru, Suriname, and Venezuela.

ACTO was created in 1995 to strengthen the implementation of the Amazon Cooperation Treaty (ACT), which was signed in July 1978 and amended in 1998. The Permanent Secretariat was later established in Brasilia in 2002.[63]

CARICOM

CARICOM is the Caribbean Community organization of 15 Caribbean nations and dependencies. CARICOM aims to promote economic

---

[59] See https://en.wikipedia.org/wiki/Andean_Community_of_Nations (accessed March 18, 2021).

[60] See www.comunidadandina.org/ (accessed March 18, 2021).

[61] See www.comunidadandina.org/ (accessed March 18, 2021).

[62] See www.mercosur.int/ (accessed March 18, 2021).

[63] See http://otca.pagina-oficial.com/ (accessed March 18, 2021).

integration and cooperation and share the benefits of integration among members. Its objectives include coordination of members' economic policies and development; expansion of trade; operating as a regional single market for its members (CARICOM Single Market); and handling regional trade disputes.[64]

Central American Integration

The Central American Common Market (CACM) was organized to promote, among other things, regional economic development through free trade, a Customs union, and economic integration of Central American states.

Members include Belize, Costa Rica, El Salvador, Guatemala, Honduras, Nicaragua, and Panama. The Dominican Republic is an associated state. Mexico, Chile, and Brazil are regional observers; the Republic of China, Spain, Germany, and Japan are among the extra-regional observers.

El Salvador, Guatemala, Honduras, and Nicaragua have also formed a group called the Central America Four (CA-4) to foster integration and to this end have introduced common internal borders. Belize, Costa Rica, the Dominican Republic, and Panama join the CA-4 in matters of economic integration.[65]

Africa

Africa is considered to be the world's second fastest growing region.[66] African economies are experiencing a steady growth of GDP and rapidly

---

[64] See www.caricom.org/ (accessed March 18, 2021).

[65] See: www.sica.int/index_en.aspx?Idm=2&IdmStyle=2 (accessed March 18, 2021); http://en.wikipedia.org/wiki/Central_American_Integration_System (accessed March 18, 2021).

[66] McKinsey & Co. August 2012. "Africa at Work: Job Creation and Inclusive Growth." Available at www.mckinsey.com/~/media/McKinsey/Featured%20 Insights/Middle%20East%20and%20Africa/Africa%20at%20work/b%20test/ MGI_Africa_at_work_August_2012_Executive_Summary.pdf (accessed March 18, 2021).

growing technology-based industries. This growth, however, presents challenges to intellectual property rights (IPR) protection and enforcement:

"The World Customs Organization now regards African countries as the main concern in Europe's fight against unsafe and counterfeit goods. Most fakes still originate in China, but Africa is now the main transit route to Europe. Brand owners have opportunities to help shape legislation, especially in developing countries, to remove trade barriers that trigger counterfeiting. While doing so, they can create positive publicity and brand awareness. Regional organizations can be instrumental because they wield significant influence over regional governments. No effort is wasted in trying to stop counterfeiting … ."[67]

Kenya

"Kenya is currently the United States' 96th largest goods trading partner with $1.1 billion in total (two way) goods trade during 2019. Goods exports totaled $401 million; goods imports totaled $667 million. The U.S. goods trade deficit with Kenya was $266 million in 2019."[68]

In May 2011, Kenyan Customs officials seized a shipment of more than 140,000 fake Hewlett Packard (HP) packaging components and labels. This is an example of how "Efforts of the International Trade Administration (ITA) and several other U.S. government agencies to curtail the international sale of counterfeit goods achieved a resounding success … . The seized materials, shipped to the Kenyan port of Mombasa from China, represented a potential loss of $1.3 million in sales to HP … ."[69] This enforcement action coincided with a regional IPR protection

---

[67] P. Hlavnicka. March 01, 2010. "Debunking Common Myths About Counterfeits." *Business Week*. Available at www.bloomberg.com/news/articles/2010-03-01/debunking-common-myths-about-counterfeitsbusinessweek-business-news-stock-market-and-financial-advice (accessed March 18, 2021).

[68] See https://ustr.gov/countries-regions/africa/east-africa/kenya (accessed March 18, 2021).

[69] "Kenyan Authorities Confiscate 10,000 counterfeit HP Components." July 29, 2014. Available www.therecycler.com/posts/kenyan-authorities-confiscate-10000-counterfeit-hp-components/ (accessed March 18, 2021).

workshop held in Nairobi, which included a two-day public/private sector portion and presentations from several major U.S. companies.[70]

South Africa

The South African government has formed an interagency counterfeit division including the DTI, the South African Revenue Service, and the South African Police Service to improve coordination of IPR enforcement. The government has also appointed more inspectors, designated more warehouses for securing counterfeit goods, and improved the training of customs, border police, and police officials. Additionally, the DTI is working with universities and other local groups to incorporate IPR awareness into college curricula and training of local business groups. The private sector and law enforcement cooperate extensively to stop the flow of counterfeit goods into the marketplace.

"South Africa is currently our 39th largest goods trading partner with $13.2 billion in total (two way) goods trade during 2019. Goods exports totaled $5.4 billion; goods imports totaled $7.8 billion. The U.S. goods trade deficit with South Africa was $2.4 billion in 2019."[71]

Nigeria

The Nigerian government's lack of institutional capacity to address IPR issues continues to present challenges to enforcement. Relevant Nigerian government institutions lack sufficient resources to enforce IPR, and legislation intended to implement Nigeria's WTO obligations under the Agreement on Trade-Related Aspects of Intellectual Property Rights has yet to be passed by the National Assembly. Piracy remains a problem despite Nigeria's active participation in the World Intellectual Property Organization and other international fora and the growing interest among Nigerians to protect their IPR. Nigerian artists strongly support IPR as a means of protecting and incentivizing the immensely popular film and

---

[70] *Id.*

[71] See https://ustr.gov/countries-regions/africa/southern-africa/south-africa (accessed March 18, 2021).

music sector in Nigeria. Counterfeit automotive parts, pharmaceuticals, business and entertainment software, music and video recordings, and other consumer goods are sold openly. Piracy of software, books, and optical disk products continues to be an ongoing concern. Also, judicial procedures are slow and reportedly compromised by corruption. However, the government has taken steps to improve enforcement. Efforts to combat the sale of counterfeit pharmaceuticals, for example, have yielded some results. The Nigerian Copyright Commission (NCC) continues to carry out raids and seizures of pirated works, but the effectiveness of such enforcement efforts is constrained both by NCC resources and by the number and persistence of producers of pirated works ... ."[72]

---

[72] See https://ustr.gov/sites/default/files/2015%20NTE%20Combined.pdf (accessed March 18, 2021).

About the Authors

Peter Hlavnicka is currently Venture Partner with R3i Ventures Pte Ltd. in Singapore and Founder and CEO of Singapore based company Phi Ventures Pte. Ltd. specializing in IP and commercialization strategy, tech transfer, brand protection, and supply chain security. While cofounding new ventures in healthcare and tech space, he is also an active investor, mentor, and advisor to start-ups and accelerators globally. Previously Mr. Hlavnicka served as Director Brand Protections APAC at Fitbit (Singapore) Pte. Ltd., Director at Blackberry Ltd. in Waterloo Ontario, Director IP Protection and Enforcement at Dolby Laboratories, Inc. in San Francisco, California. Prior to Dolby, he worked at Avaya, Inc. and Nortel Networks, Corp., where he established and led global IP protection and licensing efforts and strategic pricing. During his 20-plus years at these companies, Mr. Hlavnicka's roles also included strategic pricing, contract management, sales and marketing, operations, and supply chain management. He also served as President and Treasurer of AGMA Global, a nonprofit organization comprising leading hi-tech companies focused on IP protection in the technology sector. He has written and spoken on a number of brand protection issues and contributed to numerous publications, including Business Week. Mr. Hlavnicka received his MSc in Computer Science from the Technical University of Kosice, Slovakia, and his MBA from the University of Western Ontario, Richard Ivey School of Business.

Anthony M. Keats is a founding partner of Keats Gatien LLP, a leading intellectual property law firm in Los Angeles, California. Through his legal practice of more than 35 years, he has developed and enforced the IP of rights holders including the world's leading footwear, fashion, luxury goods, electronics, and entertainment entities, as well as professional sports leagues and global sports competitions. Mr. Keats also represents numerous award-winning individual performing artists and producers in the protection of their creative work. Mr. Keats serves as a member of the College of Experts of Union des Fabricants, Paris, France, and has served on the Board of Directors of the International Anti-Counterfeiting Coalition, Washington, DC. Mr. Keats speaks and writes on a wide variety of intellectual property protection issues. His work has appeared in numerous publications, including Forbes, Fortune, the Wall Street Journal, and the National Law Journal. Mr. Keats was a contributor to the book "Trademark Counterfeiting" and coauthored with Peter Hlavnicka the legal treatise "Protecting the Brand: Anti-counterfeiting and Grey Markets" published by Law Journal Press. Mr. Keats received his BA and MA from Brown University and his JD from the University of San Francisco.

Index

OTHER TITLES IN THE BUSINESS LAW AND CORPORATE RISK MANAGEMENT COLLECTION

John Wood, Econautics Sustainability Institute, Editor

- *Business Sustainability* by Zabihollah Rezaee
- *Business Sustainability Factors of Performance, Risk, and Disclosure* by Zabihollah Rezaee
- *The Gig Mafia* by David M. Shapiro
- *Guerrilla Warfare in the Corporate Jungle* by K. F. Dochartaigh
- *A Book About Blockchain* by Rajat Rajbhandari
- *Successful Cybersecurity Professionals* by Steven Brown
- *Artificial Intelligence for Risk Management* by Archie Addo, Srini Centhala, and Muthu Shammugam
- *The Business-Minded CISCO* by Bryan C. Kissinger
- *Artificial Intelligence for Security* by Archie Addo, Murthu Shanmugan, and Srini Centhala
- *Artificial Intelligence Design and Solution for Risk and Security* by Archie Addo, Murthu Shanmugan, and Srini Centhala

Concise and Applied Business Books

The Collection listed above is one of 30 business subject collections that Business Expert Press has grown to make BEP a premiere publisher of print and digital books. Our concise and applied books are for...

- Professionals and Practitioners
- Faculty who adopt our books for courses
- Librarians who know that BEP's Digital Libraries are a unique way to offer students ebooks to download, not restricted with any digital rights management
- Executive Training Course Leaders
- Business Seminar Organizers

Business Expert Press books are for anyone who needs to dig deeper on business ideas, goals, and solutions to everyday problems. Whether one print book, one ebook, or buying a digital library of 110 ebooks, we remain the affordable and smart way to be business smart. For more information, please visit www.businessexpertpress.com, or contact sales@businessexpertpress.com.

CPSIA information can be obtained
at www.ICGtesting.com
Printed in the USA
BVHW040401160422
634312BV00002B/4